Environmental Culture

Environmental Culture: the ecological crisis of reason is a much needed account of what has gone wrong in our relationship with the environment. Written by one of our leading environmental thinkers, it is a compelling exploration of the contemporary ecological crisis, its origins, and the cultural illusions that lie behind it.

Val Plumwood argues that historically-traceable distortions of reason and culture have resulted in dangerous forms of ecological denial. They have had a widespread effect in areas as diverse as economics, politics, science, ethics, and spirituality, and appear in the currently dominant form of globalisation.

Cutting through the 'prudence versus ethics' debate that has stunted environmental philosophy, Plumwood analyses our ethical and spiritual failures as closely linked to our perceptual and prudential failures to situate ourselves as ecological beings. The further and more radically we separate ourselves from nature in order to justify its domination, the more we lose the ability to respond to it in ethical and communicative terms. Plumwood argues that in the process, we also gain a false idea of our own character and location, including an illusory sense of independence from nature. The results can be dangerous, making us insensitive to ecological limits, dependencies and interconnections.

Environmental Culture: the ecological crisis of reason presents a radically new picture of how our culture must change in order to develop an ecologically rational society. Drawing on a range of ideas from feminism, democracy, globalisation and post-colonial thought, it is essential reading for anyone interested in the environment and our place in it.

Val Plumwood is Australian Research Council Fellow at the University of Sydney. She is an environmental activist, bush-walker, crocodile messenger and a pioneer of environmental philosophy. She is the author of one of the founding books of eco-feminism, *Feminism and the Mastery of Nature* (1993), also published by Routledge.

Environmental philosophies series
Edited by Andrew Brennan

Philosophy, in its broadest sense, is an effort to get clear on the problems which puzzle us. Our responsibility for, and attitude to, the environment is one such problem which is now the subject of intense debate. Theorists and policy analysts often discuss environmental issues in the context of a more general understanding of what human beings are and how they are related to each other and to the rest of the world.

This series examines the theories that lie behind the different accounts of our environmental problems and their solutions. It includes accounts of holism, feminism, green political themes and the other structures of ideas in terms of which people have tried to make sense of our environmental predicaments. The emphasis is on clarity, combined with a critical approach to the material under study.

Most of the authors are professional philosophers, and each has written a jargon-free, non-technical account of their topic. The books will interest readers from a variety of backgrounds, including philosophers, geographers, policy makers and all those who care for our planet.

Ecology, Policy and Politics
John O'Neill

The Spirit of the Soil
Agriculture and environmental ethics
Paul B Thomson

Why Posterity Matters
Environmental policies and future generations
Avner de-Shalit

Environmental Pragmatism
Edited by Andrew Light and Eric Katz

Ecological Feminism
Karen Warren

Faking Nature
The ethics of environmental restoration
Robert Elliot

The Struggle for Nature
A critique of radical ecology
Jozef Keulartz

Environmental Culture
The ecological crisis of reason
Val Plumwood

Environmental Culture

The ecological crisis of reason

Val Plumwood

Routledge
Taylor & Francis Group

LONDON AND NEW YORK

First published 2002
by Routledge
2 Park Square, Milton Park, Abingdon, Oxon, OX14 4RN

Simultaneously published in the USA and Canada
by Routledge
270 Madison Ave, New York, NY 10016

Reprinted 2006

Routledge is an imprint of the Taylor & Francis Group

© 2002 Val Plumwood

Typeset in Garamond by Deerpark Publishing Services, Shannon
Printed and bound in Great Britain by TJ International Ltd, Padstow, Cornwall

British Library Cataloguing in Publication Data
A catalogue record for this book is available from the British Library

Library of Congress Cataloging in Publication Data

ISBN 0-415-17878-9 (pbk)
ISBN 0-415-17877-0 (hbk)

Contents

Introduction   1
Environmental culture and the crisis of reason 3
Culture versus techno-optimism: reason to the rescue? 5
Adding ecology: ecohumanities perspectives 8

1   The ecological crisis of reason   13
The penguin's story 13
Modern heirs of rationalism 16
Dualism and economic rationalism 22
Blindspots of rationalism: the fisheries case 25
A gendered agenda: neither rational, ecological or ethical 31

2   Rationalism and the ambiguity of science   38
The double face of science 38
Disengagement as sado-dispassionate practice 41
The subject/object divide and the ambiguity of science 45
Resolving the ambiguity of science: integrating the 'two cultures' 50
Anthropocentrism and anthropomorphism 56

3   The politics of ecological rationality   62
The rationality of the EcoRepublic 62
The politics of rationality 65
Remoteness and decision 71
Remoteness, autarchy and spatial scale 74

4   Inequality and ecological rationality   81
Liberal democracy and ecological rationality 81
Beyond liberal democracy: deliberative modifications 87
Beyond deliberative democracy 90
*The ecological rationality of procedural and participatory
    democracy 93*

5 The blindspots of centrism and human self-enclosure   97

Rationalism and human-centredness 97
The logical structure of centrism 100
A parallel liberation model of anthropocentrism 106
Economic centrism: nature as class and resource 110
The centric parallel as a practical model 111
Otherising as an impediment to justice 115
The prudential blindspots of anthropocentrism 117

6 Philosophy, prudence and anthropocentrism   123

Is challenging anthropocentrism irrelevant and unhelpful? 123
*Is human-centredness inevitable? The dilemma of prudential
    argument 127*
Is human-centredness inevitable? The argument from standpoint 130
Selfishness and cosmic irrelevance 134
Recognition, prudence and survival 138

7 The ethics of commodification   143

Commodification and person/property dualism 143
Minimalist methodologies of closure 147
Animal rights and vegetarian duties 152
Rationalism, factory farming and use/respect dualism 159

8 Towards a dialogical interspecies ethics   167

Decentring human-centred ethics 167
Ranking, dualism and heterogeneity 170
Ranking and interspecies egalitarianism 172
Framework stances and the myth of mindlessness 174
Intentionality and moral value 180
The intentional recognition stance and non-humans 182
Opening up interspecies ethics 184
Communicative interspecies ethics 188

9 Unity, solidarity and deep ecology   196

The basis of solidarity: identity or difference? 196
Solidarity and oppressive concepts of unity 201
Unity and the political theory of deep ecology 207
The ecological enlightenment of the man of property 212
Is there an eco-socialist deep ecology? 214

10 Towards a materialist spirituality of place 218
Is spirituality more fundamental? 218
'Materialism' and spirit/matter dualism 222
Human-centred spiritualities 223
Indigenous critiques 225
Trickster spirituality: the world as agent 227
Place-based spirituality as oppositional practice 229

11 Conclusion 236

Notes 241
Bibliography 269
Index 279

Introduction

The *Titanic* is a story of technological hubris and decision-making disaster in the face of risk which surely derives some of its continuing fascination for us in the parallel it presents to our contemporary ecological situation. In the ecological parallel to the *Titanic* story, we have reached the stage in the narrative where we have received the iceberg warning, and have made the remarkable decision to double the engine speed to Full Speed Ahead and go below to get a good night's rest. A change of course might be bad for business, we might have to slow down, lose time. Nothing, not even the ultimate risk of the death of nature, can be allowed to hold back the triumphant progress of the ship of rational fools.

But then not much about our behaviour in relation to the ecological crisis has been rational, if we are careful and critical about the meaning of that term. The failure of dominant national and international political institutions to meet the situation of ecological crisis could not be more clear, a course likely to ensure our demise even if the world were not overhung by the shadow of continuing warfare. The often-invoked term 'sustainability' tends to obscure the seriousness of the situation; clearly no culture which sets in motion massive processes of biospheric degradation which it has normalised, and which it cannot respond to or correct can hope to survive for very long. We hear of the failure and permanent endangerment of many of the world's oldest and greatest fisheries, the continuing destruction of its tropical forests and the loss of much of its agricultural land and up to half its species within the next thirty years. Although the long-term portent of such processes potentially disruptive to survival as deforestation, global warming and ocean degradation, is not yet fully grasped, and devastating forms of positive-feedback are a real possibility, a low priority is being accorded the attempt to deal with them. This is not a rational course, and if we are told it is, we need to look more carefully at what is meant by 'rational'.

It is a common observation that the necessary social change which might begin to reduce this impact and begin the construction of a society capable of surviving has not been occurring. We are mostly going backwards in the key area of containing energy consumption, and are facing growing pollution of land, air and water, growing problems of the destruction of the forests, the ozone layer, global warming, acid rain, the disposal of toxic wastes, as well as the multiple crises of rationalist agriculture. Our failure to situate dominant forms of human society ecologically is matched by our failure to situate non-humans ethically, as the plight of non-human species continues to worsen. Rationalised intensive agriculture not only inflicts intolerable living conditions on animals, but increasingly requires massive slaughtering events to stem the disease outbreaks its conditions foster. On the wild side too, primate researchers speak of an 'animal holocaust': we hear of the massive displacement of orang-utans, the slaughter of African gorillas, ivory is once again on the world trade menu, and there is a movement to resume the full-scale slaughter of whales. If even the largest and most closely related animal species are not spared extinction in the wild, what ultimate hope is there for the rest of nature?

All metaphors have their limitations, but those limitations can often tell us something. The *Titanic* myth is liberal-democratic, maintaining a story of equality of consequences, of elite heroism and self-sacrifice, of millionaires and other men standing back while women and children were saved. But in the real ecological world on which we are passengers, unlike the *Titanic*, the millionaires don't go down with the ship, and it's certainly not women and children first. So to understand fully the irrationality of the kind of decision-making that guides our collective course, we must look carefully at where the decisions come from and at the class composition of the passenger lists, at who will perish and who will thrive, and at who is in a position to make good decisions. Above all we need to look self-critically at why bad decisions are made, and under what dominant illusions. Such a scrutiny of the structure of current decision-making in relation to the global ecological crisis is far from reassuring.

If, as I argue in Chapters 1 and 2, a hubristic and sado-dispassionate form of economic and scientific reason is in charge that is exclusionary in focus and acts for a narrow range of interests, our ship has set a bad course, and we need to change our concepts and strategies of rationality. If, as I argue in Chapters 3 and 4, the major decision roles in most polities go to those groups who profit most from the destructive processes that are threatening the biosphere, and who are least likely to be aware of and motivated to take corrective action to halt them, the conclusion must be that we have so far failed to find a good captain – to devise ecologically rational forms of polity that are adequate to respond to the crisis and guide us safely home. And if, as I argue in Chapters 5 and 6, rational hubris is part of culture-wide blindspots associated with anthropocentrism that foster illusions of invincibility and hide our real danger, we should become sufficiently sceptical about the dominant directions of travel to oust the mad captain, get out the maps and begin to chart a new course. In doing the latter, we may be helped by some experienced counter-hegemonic piloting, which is the subject of Chapters 7–10, exploring some aspects of a partnership model for healing the dysfunctional ecological and ethical relationships we have created with nature.

Environmental culture and the crisis of reason

The deterioration of the global ecological context of human life demands from our species a clear and adequate response, but we are seemingly immobilised, even though it is clear that at the technological level we already have the means to accomplish the changes needed to live sustainably on and with the earth. So the problem is not primarily about more knowledge or technology; it is about developing an environmental culture that values and fully acknowledges the non-human sphere and our dependency on it, and is able to make good decisions about how we live and impact on the non-human world. For the dominant global cultures of the west, the response to the crisis must either be about democratic cultural change of this kind or it must be about top-down solutions imposed on a supposedly recalcitrant citizenry, as in the extreme example of the Eco-Republic I discuss in Chapter 3.

I use the term 'cultural' here in several ways; first to recognise some multiplicity in standpoints, situations and responses, and second, to mark a contrast with the fantasies of top-down strategies for ecological survival that seem to tempt many scientists and even some citizen environment groups. Since, as I argue in Chapter 3, such eco-authoritarian strategies are doomed over the longer term, (genuinely) democratic cultural change strategies are our best hope. The focus on culture marks a contrast with the kind of reverse ecological analysis, often originating in reductionist population biology, that reads the reductionism it adopts towards non-human species back into the human context and discounts the vital role of cultural difference, and by implication, projects of cultural and social change that can help us acknowledge our ecological embeddedness. It also marks a contrast with economic reductionist or determinist ways of addressing ecological issues, common both to Marxism and neo-liberalism, that focus on explanatory and change strategies exclusively or excessively in the economic field. The distortions that have produced the crisis appear across a wide range of areas in the dominant culture and require correspondingly broad projects of change. I use the term 'culture' as a way to focus on how deep, wide and multi-levelled the cultural challenge must be to the systems that relate us both materially and in terms of attitude and ideology to the ecological world we all-too-unwittingly inhabit. In its fullest meaning, developing environmental culture involves a systematic resolution of the nature/culture and reason/nature dualisms that split mind from body, reason from emotion, across their many domains of cultural influence.

The ecological crisis requires from us a new kind of culture because a major factor in its development has been the rationalist culture and the associated human/nature dualism characteristic of the west. Human/nature dualism, as I argued in *Feminism and the Mastery of Nature*, is a system of ideas that takes a radically separated reason to be the essential characteristic of humans and situates human life outside and above an inferiorised and manipulable nature. Rationalism and human/nature dualism are linked through the narrative which maps the supremacy of reason onto human supremacy via the identification of humanity with active mind and reason and of non-humans with passive, tradeable bodies. We should not mistake rationalism for reason – rather it is a cult of reason that elevates to extreme supremacy a particular narrow form of reason and correspondingly devalues the contrasted and reduced sphere of nature and embodiment. Feminist thinker Elizabeth Gross puts her finger on the basic denial mechanism involved in the irrationality of rationalist forms of reason when she writes that the crisis of reason 'is a consequence of the historical privileging of the purely conceptual or mental over the corporeal; that is, it is a consequence of the inability of western knowledges to conceive their own processes of (material) production, processes that *simultaneously rely on and disavow* the role of the body'.[1] The ecological crisis can be thought of as involving a centric and self-enclosed form of reason that simultaneously relies on and disavows its material base, as 'externality', and a similar failure of the rationalised world it has made to acknowledge and to adapt itself adequately to its larger 'body', the material and ecological support base it draws on in the long-denied counter-sphere of 'nature'.

Rationalism and human/nature dualism have helped create ideals of culture and human identity that promote human distance from, control of and ruthlessness towards the sphere of nature as the Other, while minimising non-human claims to the earth and to elements of mind, reason and ethical consideration. Its monological logic leads to denials of dependency on the Other in the name of an hyperbolised autonomy, and to relationships that cannot be sustained in real world contexts of radical dependency on the Other. That the Other is an independent being on whom one is dependent is the child's first and hardest lesson, even before the lesson that the nurturing Other must in turn be nurtured. It is a lesson that some children never properly learn, and neither do some cultures of denial.

Rationalist culture has distorted many spheres of human life; its remaking is a major but essential cultural enterprise. The old reason-centred culture of the west which has allowed the ecological crisis to deepen to the current dangerous point may at one time have facilitated the dominant culture's comparative advantage over and conquest of other more modest and ecologically-adapted cultures on this planet. This is speculation, but what is not speculation is that in an era when we are reaching the biophysical limits of the planet, this reason-centred culture has become a liability to survival. Its 'success-making' characteristics, including its ruthlessness in dealing with the sphere it counts as 'nature', have allowed it to dominate both non-human nature and other peoples and cultures. But these characteristics, and the resulting successes in commodifying the world (or producing 'cargo'), are only too clearly related to our longer-term ecological and ethical failures. We must change this culture or face extinction.

The ecological crisis we face then is both a crisis of the dominant culture and a crisis of reason, or rather, a crisis of the culture of reason or of what the dominant global culture has made of reason. Some might be tempted to suggest that reason is an experiment on the part of evolution, and that its hubris and inability to acknowledge its own dependency on the ecological order show that reason itself is ultimately a hazard to survival. But we would not need to deliver the sweeping and pessimistic judgement that reason itself is dysfunctional if we recognised reason as plural, and understood its political character as part of its social context. It is not reason itself that is the problem, I believe, but rather arrogant and insensitive forms of it that have evolved in the framework of rationalism and its dominant narrative of reason's mastery of the opposing sphere of nature and disengagement from nature's contaminating elements of emotion, attachment and embodiment. Increasingly these forms of reason treat the material and ecological world as dispensable. The revision of our concepts of rationality to make them more ecologically aware and accountable is one of the main themes of this book. Reason has been made a vehicle for domination and death; it can and must become a vehicle for liberation and life.

Culture versus techno-optimism: reason to the rescue?

The role of the dominant narrative of reason in framing the crisis is rarely able to emerge clearly because it is so pervasive, as much taken for granted as part of the framework of our thought as the air we breathe. Familiar explanations of ecological failure are themselves framed in terms of that same cultural narrative, whose culmination we see in the global economic regimes that threaten the biosphere. Thus current environmental thinking tends to gives us a choice of naturalistic versus rationalistic explanations and nostrums. According to the naturalistic version of the dominant narrative, the blame for our plight should be allocated in the usual place, to the symbolically-female, nature side of the hyperseparated and warring pair, reason versus nature. It is fundamentally nature, perhaps as our 'natural' human selfishness or greed, or as our animality and blind instinct to breed,[2] which has led us astray ecologically. And it is reason intensified that will be our hero and saviour, in the form of more science, new technology, a still more unconstrained market, rational restraints on numbers and consumption, or all of these together. But while we remain trapped within this dominant narrative of heroic reason mastering blind nature there is little hope for us. For the narrative itself and its leading characters are a key part of the problem, leading us to reproduce continually the same elements of failure – including the arrogance and ecological blindness of the dominant culture – even while we seek desperately for solutions within it.

Reason in the form of scientific or technical fix[3] also plays the hero in some alternative rationalistic and techno-optimist scenarios. Science will save us, provided we do not lose our nerve or our faith in techno-reason and our will to continue along our current path, however precarious it may seem. This is the scientific equivalent of saying that all will be well if the edicts of the market are applied with even more severity. It is less than rational because it does not take due account of the possibility of being wrong, as any fully rational position must. In another variation, it is reason in the form of the market economy and technology that will solve the problem itself, perhaps by new discoveries, perhaps by bringing about 'natural capitalism', which is set to save the day through voluntarily 'dematerialising the economy' and producing wonders of technological innovation such as the hypercar.[4] The idea of a more energy efficient economy creating more employment with less materials is highly relevant to any improvement, and to ending overconsumption. But only a certain range of problems are touched by this 'dematerialisation' solution.

The term 'natural' in 'natural capitalism' is meant to indicate both the movement of capitalism to less wasteful technology and its moving in that direction 'naturally', without political effort, which is carefully discounted by proponents of Natural Capitalism. But does it seem likely that global capitalism will take such a direction of its own volition when to date its unhampered movement has taken it in precisely the opposite direction, to shedding labour at the expense of increasing materials and energy throughput? The social forces that could or would make 'natural capitalism' take a benign direction of this kind when it is basically unaccountable remain unexplained; 'natural capitalism' is a *deus ex machina*. Increasing corporate embeddedness and responsibility is certainly not the way the rationality of capitalism is going; to assume that it is, that no political and democratic effort will be required to move it in a different direction, is either politically naive or culpably misleading. To the extent that he is 'rational', the corporate hero of the disembedded market locates his operation on a barge in cyberspace, searching for sufficiently ruthless or desperate localities that will minimise his costs, including allegiance, responsibilities, materials and wages. A prioritised and increasingly disembedded global market is rapidly stripping away any social or ecological embeddedness that has been achieved through centuries of democratic struggle in the national economies, using the relentless engine of global competition. To the extent that it negates the need for systematic action or deeper rethinking, relying on 'natural' capitalism to arrive and save us simply delays addressing the basic problems, which are not primarily technological but social, political and cultural-symbolic.

Capitalism is going green 'naturally', Lovins et al. suggest, because greater efficiency in materials and energy is in its own interests. But capitalism must surely be divided on this score, since such a reduction is not in the interests of materials and energy producers, a big proportion of the corporate cast and some of the most powerful. In *Natural Capitalism*, efficiency in energy and materials is presented as the whole answer when in fact it is only a portion of the answer. If we used a fraction of the resources we currently use to build hyper-efficient solar-powered trawlers or bulldozers that continue to strip what is left in the oceans and forests, the biosphere could still be seriously damaged. More materials-efficient technologies can be used to destroy nature more efficiently, especially where there is no deeper recognition of limits or of our dependency on healthy ecological systems. It can meet human needs with less, it is true, but it is not human *need* the rationalist economy deals with but effective market demand, which can always be increased. Greater materials efficiency, as a technical fix, can stretch ecological limits, but it is not a substitute for the cultural process of recognising those limits, nor will it necessarily contribute to that process. 'Natural capitalism' *will* deliver some useful innovations, but what ratiogenic monsters, Frankenstein species and other negative innovations will also be created through the system's relentless drive to substitute speed and spatial expansion for reproduction time (as Teresa Brennan has so brilliantly explained),[5] and to replace naturally occurring entities by rationally engineered substitutes that are designed as market 'equivalents' but that have non-equivalent ecologically disruptive properties that do not register in the economic system?

In an alternative version of the techno-optimist fantasy more favourable to state intervention, it is administrative reason that will rescue us. A benign covey of neutral policy makers and economic experts will manipulate 'economic instruments' in the interests of our long-term survival, easing capitalism gently into a dematerialisation act through regulations and 'best practice' standards, while a passive, consenting citizenry waits patiently for this rational economic nobility to save the day.[6] Poll results showing strong and continuing public concern about the environment are cited to allay any fears about the potentially undemocratic character of this kind of solution. The same elite culture and developmentalist rationality that led us into the mess, it is assumed, will lead us right out again, without the need for any other substantial change. As in the imaginatively limited kind of science fiction that depicts a depressingly familiar range of social relationships in highly unfamiliar planetary settings, nothing outside technology itself is really envisaged as changing. The assumption that the political will can come out of nowhere to establish ecologically benign technology regimes by administrative fiat fails to consider that technology in the context of its larger culture, or to ask the key question: in what political and social circumstances could such solutions be stable and effective?[7]

Technofix solutions make no attempt to rethink human culture, dominant lifestyles and demands on nature, indeed they tend to assume that these are unchangeable. They aim rather to meet these demands more efficiently through smarter technology, deliberately bracketing political and cultural reflection and admissions of failure[8]. But we did not just stumble by some freak technological accident into the ecological mess we have made, and it will take more than a few bright boys and better toys to get us out of it. Our current debacle is the fruit of a human- and reason-centred culture that is at least a couple of millennia old, whose contrived blindness to ecological relationships is the fundamental condition underlying our destructive and insensitive technology and behaviour. To counter these factors, we need a deep and comprehensive restructuring of culture that rethinks and reworks human locations and relations to nature all the way down. Reason can certainly play a role in this rethinking, but it must be a fully self-critical form of reason that does not flinch from examining its own role in the crisis.

Adding ecology: ecohumanities perspectives

This book addresses two historic tasks that arise from the rationalist hyper-separation of human identity from nature: they can be summed up as the tasks of (re)situating humans in ecological terms and non-humans in ethical terms. The first is apparently the more urgent and self-evident, the task of prudence, the other is presented as optional, as supererogation, the inessential sphere of ethics. But this is a major error; the two tasks are interconnected, and cannot be addressed properly in isolation from each other. To the extent that we hyper-separate ourselves from nature and reduce it conceptually in order to justify domination, we not only lose the ability to empathise and to see the non-human sphere in ethical terms, but also get a false sense of our own character and location that includes an illusory sense of autonomy. The failure to see the non-human domain in the richer terms appropriate to ethics licences supposedly 'purely instrumental' relationships that distort our perceptions and enframings, impoverish our relations and make us insensitive to dependencies and interconnections – which are thus in turn a prudential hazard. When we take account of such standpoint considerations, we can see that our ethical failures and our prudential failures are closely and interactively linked, casting doubt on any attempt to polarise or treat as sharply discontinuous human and non-human interests and ethics.

One of the problems in standard ways of thinking about the crisis is precisely this rationalist divorce between male-coded rational prudence and female-coded ethics, as if they were separate and non-interacting spheres. This is one of the legacies of rationalism that resonates strongly in the contemporary organisation of life under global capitalism, increasingly monological and insulated from corrective feedback. Rationalist distortions appear especially clearly in the global economic system and its identification of rationality with egoism, and in the dualism of reason and emotion in its many variants. The economic rationalist culture of contemporary capitalism draws on many of the classical rationalist narratives and dualisms of the past, such as reason/emotion dualism, nuanced to fit new contexts and institutions such as the commodity form, which requires the splitting of use from respect. Reason/emotion dualism divorces prudence from ethics, codes the former as rational, and sees the opposing sphere of ethical and ecological concern as dispensable, mere subjective sentiment.

The divorce between prudence and ethics (reflecting also a 'pure self' versus 'pure other' split) has been especially strongly stressed for the non-human sphere in the person/property dualism of capitalism and the associated subject/object dualism of its knowledge systems, in science. These normalise instrumental or 'purely prudential' approaches that treat the non-human, with few exceptions, as property, exempt from ethical concern except of most marginal and precarious kinds. Tough monological stances towards nature based on the identification of rationality with disengagement and egoism, as I argue in Chapters 1 and 2, are thus able to draw on historically-established cultures of reason/emotion dualism and the still-powerful traditional male-coding of reason in contrast to emotion in order to masquerade as rational.

Taking account of the role and history of human/nature dualism in dominant culture means then that change is not just a matter of adding to our stock of knowledge a 'new' area of scientific ecology, but is also a matter of changing culture by countering long-standing insensitivities and rationalist distortions in a wide range of areas, including knowledge itself. For reasons deriving from the subject/object knowledge structures I discuss in Chapter 2, science is usually seen as the appropriate place to locate ecological concern and discussion. To supplement scientific studies demonstrating global warming scenarios and scientific models indicating a potential for collapse of basic systems and services, many scientists appeal to methodological and decision-theory considerations of precaution and risk (the so-called 'Precautionary Principle'). These principles have many problems. If, as Haller (2000) argues, such narrowly rational mathematical risk arguments are rather more ambiguous and less conclusive as logical reasons for changing course than they are often taken to be, this does not mean, contra Haller, that we have no other intellectual resources for decision and must rely on such bases for decision as pure emotion, intuition, tradition or simple self-interest. None of these will provide adequate guidance in the future we face, individually or collectively.

The ecological 'humanities' enable us to bring to bear a whole further range of considerations that are hardly 'non-intellectual', including arguments of a more historical, self-reflective and self-critical cast which consider the limitations and failures of correctiveness in dominant forms of rationality and the illusions of anthropocentric culture. These standpoint considerations are the basis for the arguments I advance here, and they are I think the sorts of considerations that inform the better kinds of social and personal decision-making. We should not be persuaded to think of decisions as the dilemmas of stripped-down actors in rational choice scenarios, prisoners of the 'purely rational', abstract constructs assumed to know nothing of the social forces and past trajectory which have produced their problems. Our capacity to gain insight from understanding our social context, to learn from self-critical perspectives on the past and to allow for our own limitations of vision, is still one of our best hopes for creative change and survival. This book investigates some standpoint sources of our ecological blindspots, including, in Chapters 5 and 6, the anthropocentric perspectives and culture that make us insensitive to our ecological place in the world. The centric analyses of anthropocentrism, I argue, unlike the many rationalist-inspired accounts given by philosophers, extend and illuminate the major counter-hegemonic critiques of our time and provide useful guidance for ecological activists.

The analysis of anthropocentrism presented in Chapters 5 and 6 draws on the analysis of centrism suggested by several liberation movements. It has major implications for activism, theory and philosophy, and supports a counter-hegemonic program in philosophical methodology, ethics and the philosophy of mind, which is discussed in Chapters 7 and 8. As outlined in Chapter 9, activists interested in countering human-centredness can also draw usefully on theorisations offered by other liberation movements of the concept of solidarity, for example through the cultivation of the 'traitorous identity'. The Otherisation of nature bears on a key question of justice – the concern with obstacles to justice, especially forms of partiality and self-imposition that prevent us from giving others their due.[9] One important approach to justice suggested by the analysis of anthropocentrism is meth-odological, one of studying up rather than studying down, shifting the onus of proof from inclusion to exclusion and moving the ethical focus from the evaluated item and the dubious question of their 'qualifications' for ethical inclusion and attention (studying down) to the different and largely neglected question of the ethical stance of the human evaluator (studying up) and their own moral status. What requires critical philo-sophical engagement in the context of anthropocentric culture is self rather than other, the limits imposed by the human rather than the nature side of the ethical relationship, the ethical stance of closure rather than the ethical stance of openness.

In thinking about these issues I have drawn on many sources, most strongly on the work of feminist and ecofeminist philosophers and scholars. I found the partnership ethics suggested by Carolyn Merchant to be the model that most consistently matched my intuitions about what has gone wrong and about how we might remedy it. Thus in Chapter 6 I try to cast light on the prudence/ethics split via a dialogue between partners Ann and Bruce (A and B) that models the ideas about relationships many philosophers have thought suitable for humans and nature. I explore in later chapters, especially Chapters 8 and 10, the obvious remedies for Ann and Bruce's dysfunctional partnership: namely, replace monological by dialogical relationships in order to set up the logical and cultural basis for negotiation. This means abandoning the tough hyper-rationalist stances that emphasise human superiority, reason, mastery and manipulation, human-centredness and instrument-alism. We do not have to approach the more-than-human world in these terms, and if there is a choice of frameworks, it would be less than rational to ignore or dismiss others more suitable for our context of ecological crisis. In our current context then, it is rational to try to replace the monological, hierarchical and mechanistic models that have characterised our dysfunctional partnership with nature by more mutual, communicative and responsive ones that could put that partnership on a better basis.

The formal project of adding ecology and nature to the annals and dialogues of western philosophy has only just begun, but is fraught with special difficulty because of its rationalist bias and background. Modern philosophy has tended to sanction the tough stance of minimising recognition of the non-human world that has been identified with science and rationality, (for example this is one way the Principle of Parsimony has been interpreted). That 'sceptical' temperament coincides neatly with the thrust of capitalism to maximise the class of other beings that are available to be treated without ethical constraint as resources or commodities. We philosophise from a time which shows all around us the disastrous effects of the desensitisation to nature that is part of the reductive narrative and the dominant human-centred rationality. Not only is it rationally possible to choose a richer and more generous framework, it is in the present context of ecological destruction essential to do so – in the interests of ethics, prudence AND reason.

1   The ecological crisis of reason

The penguin's story

I lived for a while in the 1990s in a small cabin along the Bass Strait coast of Tasmania. Most mornings, when I went down to the beach to walk a kilometre or two along the shore, I saw the bodies of dead Fairy Penguins lying on the beach. Sometimes I would find as many as 20 bodies over a relatively short distance. This was deeply troubling, not only because these little penguins are for me love-inspiring creatures, but also because they are now rarely encountered on the mainland of Australia, where in my youth they were not uncommon. Mostly their decline is put down to dogs, both domestic and wild, killing penguins as they come ashore nightly to their burrows in the dunes to breed. I found dog footprints near the bodies, and in the little village behind my cabin, every house had a dog or two, many free to roam at night. I seemed to be watching here the same process of extinction as on the mainland.

There was a bigger story hidden here however. One day as I stood by the edge of a gentle surf I saw the waves bringing in a small object. I waited with toes dug into the foamy sand as it washed in towards me on the tide, until finally it arrived at my feet. The tears streamed down my face as I saw that it was another Fairy Penguin, its body fresh and unmarked, as if it had just died. Whatever had happened to this one, I knew it had not been killed by dogs. Weeping, I picked up the small perfect body and carried it home to my cabin, hoping against hope that it would revive. It did not. I gave the dead penguin to a vetinary friend I had met at a duck-shooting protest to do an autopsy. A week later he phoned me. The penguin, he said, had not been killed by predation or pollution – the penguin had starved to death. I rang the relevant government department to discuss the issue, but found no help or interest there. Soon I became too ill with a debilitating, long-term virus to pursue the issue, and had to return home to the mainland to recuperate. But the thought of that penguin still triggers my grief, not only for those lost penguins but for the other accelerating losses in the larger narrative of human rule of the earth.

It was many years later that I was able to piece together a bit more of the penguin's story. Fish farms situated thousands of miles away along the Western Australian coast had a year or so previously received permission to import feed for their farmed salmon made from wild South African fish. Long-established quarantine restrictions were lifted – Australia was in a global market now, and the farms could buy the South African pilchards at a fractionally cheaper price than local pilchards. The imported pilchards spread plagues of disease into local stocks which lacked immunity, much as European invaders had spread disease into the indigenous populations of Australia, North and South America. Waves of death spread along the Southern Ocean coastline, and are still spreading, in which millions upon millions of local pilchards died. Pilchards are an important part of the oceanic food web. Populations in many places were virtually wiped out, and those marine creatures whose diet relied heavily or seasonally on them starved. That was the probable source of death for my penguin, and doubtless for many another.

Small stories like this are nested within medium and large stories. The death of the penguin at the hands of the global free market was a medium-grade episode in a much bigger sleuth story, which detects many more such catastrophes at the hands of killers less often named, seemingly more remote, nebulous and immaterial. These are systems rather than concrete individuals or classes, forms and patterns of thought and organisation, systems for ordering our lives, choices and practices, systems of property formation and distribution – systems of rationality, as we tend to say. The story as I have discerned it so far is this: heavily implicated in both the logic of the global market and the death of the penguin are distorted forms of human rationality whose simple, abstract rules of equivalence and replace-ability do not fit the real, infinitely complex world of flesh and blood, root and web on which they are so ruthlessly imposed. Rationality, or some ways of practicing it, is the villain and not the hero of this detective story, contrary to the way such stories are usually told. In arguing against them however, I am not arguing against the practice of reason but arguing for better forms of reason that will be more, not less rational, in the current state of the world. Reason has been captured by power and made an instrument of oppression; it must be remade as a tool for liberation.

These ratiogenic patterns of thought and organisation – monological, rationalist, hyper-capitalist, colonising and centric – seem at first to be ghosts, shadowy, insubstantial figures, mere phantoms of the real world of political action. But as we scrutinise them more closely we can learn to recognise their very real and material traces intertwined in our lives, and in the lives of penguins. Their fingerprints are to be found in the multiple crises of natural limits that now confront us everywhere; their crimes include the ratiogenic degradation of the atmosphere, the oceans, the forests, human food systems, and agricultural land, the ratiogenic crises of pollution and of human health, and the holocaust of animal life. With the increasing power of their technological and economic weapons, their circles of ratiogenic devastation extend ever more widely, even to the global commons and the great natural cycles and processes governing the planet itself.[1]

The crisis or failure in which we stand is conventionally said to be a crisis of ecology, which suggests a crisis or failing of nature. In reality, the 'ecological' crisis is a crisis or failing of reason and culture, a crisis of monological forms of both that are unable to adapt themselves to the earth and to the limits of other kinds of life. Postmodernists write of a 'crisis of reason', but their over-culturalised sensibilities have trivialised the rational crisis and identified it with a critical crisis. The ecological crisis of reason involves a quite practical, concrete and material set of crises on multiple fronts, and one of its most important expressions is the ecological crisis. The crisis of hegemonic reason, as I shall show, is very much more than a crisis of esteem; maladapted monological systems of reason and mastery are creating a material crisis of life or death, for us and for the larger systems of life on this planet. As I argued in Plumwood 1993, the roots of these systems of mastery lie buried in antiquity, even if their historical projects of subduing and colonising nature have come to full flower only in modernity. The ecological crises they produce result from a certain lack of fit or adaptation of societies structured by hegemonic ration-ality to their ecological and social realities. The ecological crisis is the crisis of a cultural 'mind' that cannot acknowledge and adapt itself properly to its material 'body', the embodied and ecological support base it draws on in the long-denied counter-sphere of 'nature'. Given this lack of fit, hegemo-nic rationality is in conflict with ecological rationality and survival. The denial of embodiment and illusion of individual autonomy that makes up what Teresa Brennan calls the Foundational Fantasy of the west,[2] helps to explain why an economic and social order can continue to be presented as rational when it systematically erodes biospheric systems such as the ozone shield and unbalances the carbon cycles that contribute in crucial ways to the survival of planetary life.

The face of global capitalism shows the lineaments not of ignorance but of denial. As the pilchard disaster illustrates, the ecological relationships its disembedded economic system creates are irresponsible, unaccountable, and especially for those in privileged contexts, invisible. The system gives those eating salmon from the fish farms no idea of the trail of death, disease and suffering their meal leaves behind. We can find out what is available in the market to meet our desires and at what price, but we cannot without great difficulty trace where it came from or what its real costs are, in terms of the earth. Under current rules for global trade, it may soon be illegal to inquire. As Jennifer Price argues in *Flight Maps,* commodity culture actively erases such connections, encouraging us 'to focus on the meanings we make, but not on our complicity in the economic networks through which people convert nature and human labour into the stuff and sustenance of everyday lives'.[3] Remoteness negates responsibility, for consumers, workers and shareholders. In rationalist commodity culture, we are actively prevented from exercising care and living in ecologically-embedded and responsible ways.

In the stampede to apply the abstract, universal formulae of property formation to the particular, living places of the earth, the specific ecological relationships needed to maintain larger processes that support biospheric systems are not factored in and can be risked for little gain. The earth is made up of such local living places, and a way of ordering human life, however highly theorised and mathematised, that does not acknowledge them does not belong to the earth; its real allegiance is to a more abstract planet, a timeless, immaterial realm of numbers that can sustain no life. Yet this rationalistic agency that is in the process of killing its own earthly body sees itself as the ultimate form of reasoning planetary life, and seeks to impose itself universally, prioritising its models and enforcing them maximally across the globe and even beyond. Because the system is self-prioritising and has eliminated or colonised political, scientific and other potentially critical and corrective systems, it has little capacity to reflect on or correct its increasingly life-threatening failures or blindspots. This kind of rationality is irrational, despite its hyper-rational trappings; just *how* it is irrational, both for humans and for penguins, is the main subject of this book.

Modern heirs of rationalism

The hypothesis I am recommending here is that dominant forms of reason – economic, political, scientific and ethical/prudential – are failing us because they are subject to a systematic pattern of distortions and illusions in which they are historically embedded and which they are unable to see or reflect upon. These blindspots especially affect the way we understand our relationships to nature and to one another, and they derive especially from the hegemonic origins of these patterns of thought, which have identified the biospheric Other as passive and without limits, its frontiers an invitation to invasion. It is the special form of failure such monological and hegemonic forms of reason are subject to that they misunderstand their own enabling conditions – the body, ecology and non-human nature for example, often because they have written these down as inferior or constructed them as background in arriving at an illusory and hyperbolised sense of human autonomy. These distorted forms are currently devastating the world under the guise of reason.

Why is reason like this? My answer is: because concepts of rationality have been corrupted by systems of power into hegemonic forms that establish, naturalise and reinforce privilege. Rationalist dualisms especially justify elite forms of power, not only by mapping the drama of the master subject and his Others onto a dualism of reason and nature, but by mapping many other aspects of life onto many other variants of these basic forms. The polarising aspects of dualism involve sorting a field into two homogenised and radically separated classes, typically constructing a false choice between contrasting polarities in a truncated field which can be conceived in much more equal, continuous and overlapping ways. Dualistic reason/nature polarisation naturalises radical inequality between sharply distinct but collaborating groups and justifies the privilege of the winners, as more rational. Its polarities justify and help establish remoteness for privileged classes from any ill-consequences of their property formation processes for the environment and for human health and well-being. Polarisation also cuts sympathy and identification with the losers, and facilitates various forms of remoteness from ill consequences for the privileged groups. Hegemonic definitions of the winners' agency and achievement allow denial and backgrounding of the Other's contribution to the outcome, naturalising appropriation by the hyper-rational 'achiever', as master subject, of what the less powerful are or have done. This includes naturalising the master subject's appropriation of their labour and its product.

Dualism and rationalism function together as a system of ideas that justifies and naturalises domination of people and events by a privileged class identified with reason, who deserve to be in control and to be disproportionately rewarded. In the economic rationalist sphere, these elements yield a recipe for polarising structures of radical inequality based on those who are winners in terms of a mechanism for distribution that can be represented as rational and dispassionate, and for perpetuating this situation via a powerful rationalist system of ideas that is so strongly elaborated and entrenched culturally that it can secure a kind of 'consent' even from the losers.[4] Rich cultural elaborations of the basic reason nature/dualism maximise control and supply confirming structures in as many places as possible. When they are mapped onto powerful basic systems like gender to become intertwined with identity and the fabric of life, they become almost impossible to see, separate and question. Such systems are highly functional for naturalising oppression, but fatally fallible for adapting us to the environments that sustain us.

But thus to indict rationalist influence on the dominant forms of rationality is not to embrace its polar opposite of irrationalism, rejecting reason in all its forms, or to indict the exercise of reason itself as a faculty. Rationalism is not the same as reason, just as scientism is not the same as science,[5] although rationalism has shaped our understanding of both reason and science, in the same way that scientism shapes the understanding, practice and agenda of science. Rather rationalism is a doctrine about reason, its place at the apex of human life, and the practice of oppositional construction in relation to its 'others', especially the body and nature, which are simultaneously relied upon but disavowed or taken for granted. Rationalism constructs dominant forms of rationality in terms of monological ways of organising and exercising reason in the global free market that do not allow the non-human others of the earth enough access to the earth's natural wealth to survive. These dominant rationalist forms of rationality not only doom the non-human world, they will leave humans themselves little chance of survival if they continue on their present course.

Faced with the decline and disruption of the non-human sphere, and its likely spillover into our own species decline, we are entitled to conclude that rationalist rationality is irrational, in the sense that it is maladapted to the environment it depends on. To say this though is not to withdraw hope, because these distorted forms of reason are not the only kind, and an analysis of their failures can help us challenge and change them. If forms of rationality that treat the earth as plunder, previously perhaps part of the conditions for 'successful' western domination of the planet, have become a danger to us and to the rest of the inhabitants of the earth, we need to seek out higher order forms of reason that can reflect critically on these failures and develop new forms. These will be ecologically sensitive forms of rationality that judge what currently passes for reason by the standards of ecological success or failure, among other things. In choosing thus, we would not be acting irrationally; in the light of our fully ecological embodiment as human animals, our critical and corrective behaviour would be more and not less rational.

Rationalism has given us a deeply anti-ecological narrative of reason that has guided much of the development of western culture, with the ecological crisis as its climax. This narrative or ideology tells us that reason, above all else, is supreme in the world, and that reason is associated especially with the dominant class, even defining it. The universe is ordered completely by rational principles, which the representatives of reason can discover and use in re-ordering the world for the benefit of rational beings.

Rationalism sees life as a march of progress, which consists of reason subjugating the supposedly inferior and passive sphere of nature in the body and in non-human life. In hegemonic rationalist constructions of reason, the body and nature are treated as lower, a sphere to distance from and subdue. Dualistic constructions of reason and nature, mind and body, spirit and flesh create polarising metaphors and understandings of these elements which are woven through many kinds of social division in the dominant culture. These constructions erase the agency and contributions of women, the body, materiality and the more-than-human world.

In the historical rationalist imaginary, women and other 'lesser beings' are the Others of reason, which is treated as the province of elite men who are above the base material sphere of daily life and are entitled to transcend it because of their greater share in Reason. It is not only women that have been constructed as oppositional to western rationality, culture and phil-osophy, but also the slave, the animal, and the barbarian, all associated with the body and the whole contrasted sphere of physicality and materiality. It would be naive to assume that these deep-seated conceptions of reason as the province of elite males are merely 'ideas', 'abuses' of a basically neutral concept that have had no effect on its interpretation and construction. Rather they have constructed reason as the leading character in a modern rationalist narrative of domination of the Others. From this narrative we derive the myths – still strongly persisting – of women's more emotional and unstable nature, as well as the contemporary myths of an invincible and heroic male-coded techno-reason that will solve our current problems and wrest a shining future from the jaws of crisis.

The inability to see humans as ecological and embodied beings that permeates western culture is one of the major legacies of this aspect of rationalism. It means that the ecological support base of our societies is relied on but denied in the same way as the sphere of materiality and the body is denied in classical rationalist philosophy. Humans are seen as the only rational species, the only real subjectivities and actors in the world, and nature is a background substratum which is acted upon, in ways we do not usually need to pay careful attention to after we have taken what we want of it. This is the rationality of monologue, termed monological because it recognises the Other only in one-way terms, in a mode where the Others must always hear and adapt to the One, and never the other way around. Monological relationships block mutual adaptation and its corol-laries – negotiation, communication and perception of the Other's limits and agency.

As I argued in *Feminism and the Mastery of Nature*, such a narrative of mastery as rational supremacy can be traced in the dominant culture of the west since the high period of classical civilisation, as an ideology justifying the dominance of a civilised elite and their chief values, identified increasingly with reason. The representatives of reason then were the male elite who did not need to be concerned with the bodily sphere of labour or materiality. They were the supremos at the apex of the great chain of being, the rational hierarchy which awarded disvalue according to decreasing participation in reason and supposedly increasing participation in materiality. Reason, the 'manly' element in the soul, was opposed to the inferior and corrupting 'female' elements, which included the supposedly 'soft' areas of the emotions and the senses. So rationalism inscribes in culture a series of dualistic oppositions between reason, abstraction, spirit and mind on the one hand, and materiality, the body, the emotions, and the senses on the other. Reason in the human was lodged in the higher body and especially the head, not in the base bodily regions below the waist, and in the case of the larger world the seat of reason and value is in a timeless abstract higher realm beyond the lower material domain of earth.

Reason so conceived is radically apart from the 'chaotic' material, bodily, ecological and social order, which is treated as an inessential and inferior constituent of life. In Platonic rationalism, the true objects of proper knowledge, and the underlying reality that deserves our respect, lie not in the world disclosed to us by experience, which is appearance only, but in the objects of the permanent and pure abstract 'rational' ideal world distant from and uncontaminated by the impure world of sensory or bodily experience – the Forms, numbers, and astronomical bodies. These can be known only by the special devotees of reason, not by the common run of humans. Impartial, disengaged reason is not only superior to but basically independent of the bodily, emotional and personal elements of human lives, which have as their end the flourishing of reason, identified with the elite of humans. These dualistic constructs are reflected in contemporary rationalist culture not only in the culture of knowledge and its concepts of purity, universality and impersonality or disengagement, but also in pecuniary culture and its influential dualisms and false dichotomies of prudence and ethics, use and respect, person and property, subject and object.

From its beginning in classical times, this rationalist imaginary has acquired great cultural resonance and flexibility through rich cultural elaborations of the concept of reason which have given it a starring role in a variety of narratives used to bolster the dominant order and justify oppressive practices from slavery to colonialism. It was always one of the advantages of the classical rationalist system that it provided a foolproof way to blame the losers – in terms of their alleged deficiency of reason, demonstrated by their being losers: this is the basis of Aristotle's argument for slavery. By the same stroke it established the hegemony of the privileged, the landed and leisured warrior class of classical civilisation who were supposedly the prime exemplars of ideals of reason, and justified their privilege in terms of the assumption that the rational faculty they instantiated was the highest element in human life to which others were to be subordinated.

Many regimes and many oppressions have since lent their colour to this hegemonic imaginary of reason and nature. In patriarchal thought, men represent reason and rightfully control the world as well as the dangerous emotionality, irrationality and reproductivity of women, who are 'closer to nature'. In the colonising, racial supremacist version, it is inferior and 'barbarian' others who are closer to nature, an earlier and more primitive stage of our own rational civilisation, who receive only benefits when more advanced masters of reason, the colonisers, come to take away their land to put it to proper, rational use. In the story of the coldly scientific Hero of Reason, knowledge is tortured from a passive, inert and feminised nature in order to establish 'the empire of man over (mere) things' and realise human salvation as victors of a subjugated and rationalised earth (rather than as supplicants in a remote and sub-rational heaven). For the liberal-capitalist property formation mythology of western colonisation that bases itself on hyperbolised Lockean concepts of autonomy, property is formed from the rational labours of white European Heroes upon a passive, captive virgin earth called 'nature'. In the old Soviet socialist version of the rationalist imaginary, reason played the part of the techno-bureaucrat, [as] the pre-eminent Hero of Reason who ordered production and conquered nature, resulting in the rule of a ruthless and maximising productivism.

In contemporary forms of rationalism, losers (some suggest this will be more than 80 per cent of us), such as the first world unemployed or third world subsistence farmers, are less rational, and in the rational hierarchy are placed in the position of 'nature', rationally deficient as slaves were in classical times: if they lose under the current market rules, they have failed to make of themselves something rational or efficient, something the supremely rational machinery of the free market can use. They become waste, part of the sphere of externality, collateral economic damage. The fault is in them, not in the machinery or in its rationality, which is neutral, detached, and, beyond all question, supremely rational. Since it places the market in control over so many domains of human existence, economic rationalism has great power to shape culture; its cultural media and ideals can promote identification with the rich and successful 10 per cent who are winning, and reflect their standards and styles of resource over consumption. It can portray poor people and low consumption lifestyles in negative or contemptuous terms.[6]

In the imaginary world of the global capitalist economy, it is the corporate manager who operates in the supremely rational domain of the market who most fully expresses reason, and it is his hyper-rational mathematical mechanisms of scientific commodification which conquer the mindless and passive sphere of nature. In terms of Teresa Brennan's energetic psycho-analytical concepts, this cultural mythology of male-coded reason master-ing female-coded nature is a 'sadodispassionate' drama, where the hero uses the dualism of reason/emotion and associated ideals of detached rationality to deny or cut off empathy or identification with the Other.[7] The sado-dispassionate is the doctor who experiments on his or her fellow creatures, such as the disabled put to death in Nazi institutions. He feels nothing when he should feel empathy, and we recognise this as a grievous moral failing. The sado-dispassionate is the dominant mode of the Rational Heroes in science and capitalism. Given the Hero's current treatment of the global environment, we have reason to suspect that the west's sado-dispassionate cultural drama of reason and nature may unfold to a conclu-sion where the Hero of Reason chokes the life from his planetary partner in his final sadistic act of mastery.

Dualism and economic rationalism

Some have termed the application of the rationalist agenda in the economic sphere 'economic rationalism',[8] but it has also been called 'economism'[9], 'neo-liberalism', 'laissez-faire economics', 'economic funda-mentalism', and more recently 'extreme' or 'turbo-capitalism', an intensi-fied form or new stage of capitalism. But neither it, its dominance or its symbolism is completely new. Modern economic rationalism maps the heroic narrative of the modern economy onto the older heroic narrative of the supremacy of male-coded reason and its radical separation from contaminating female-coded spheres of the body and emotions. Economic rationalism has replaced the classical warrior of earlier rationalism by the corporate warrior of the global economy. It establishes their privilege through the subordination of all other aspects of social life to the form of economic organisation controlled by corporations and loaded in their favour, the rationalist 'free-market'. The market is portrayed as a detached, disengaged, supremely rational mechanism, free from 'irrational' interfer-ence, as the supreme social end and the measure of the worth ('efficiency') of other social ends. But it can only appear in this neutral and dispassionate guise as 'rational machinery' because the historical social relations that have selected its rules and established its cast of players in far from neutral ways have been disappeared from view. Once this abstraction from historical reality has been achieved, the culture of market rationalism can proclaim the supremacy of the market as the ultimately fair and rational way of ordering life.

Employing the same rationalist background logic, economism insists that reason-coded market mechanisms and 'market processes' be privileged over other 'messier' social and political domains and processes. Priority is demanded also for those forms of social organisation associated with the market, which are also seen to be supreme in rationality. Not only must the operations of the rational-coded 'free market' be maximised, in spatial scope as well as intensity, but entrepreneurial methods and models must be applied in universities, in public administration, in welfare agencies – wherever possible, even where they are plainly inadequate and corrupting, as in energy infrastructure and supply. The widest possible application of the methods and mechanisms of the market will create a maximally rational and 'efficient' society. This last form of hegemonic rationalism retains the historic emphasis on the superiority and strong separation of elite reason from sordid or alien material elements of nature which are allowed no real agency, adding an interpretation of rationality as egoism and the maximising of the interests of a disembedded and disembodied self, the self-contained rational actor of free market theory.[10]

Since the contemporary economic rationalist model has significant parallels to older systems of hegemonic rationalism developed in the west, the terminology of rationalism is in these respects illuminating and can help us understand the workings of the modern global market economy as a hegemonic system.[11] It can also help us to understand the source of the irrationalities and blindspots that are pushing us beyond the limits of ecological safety. In conformity with the tenet that reason is the supreme value in the universe, the economic form of rationalism privileges the abstract over the contextual and experiential, imposes the universal formula on the local, and everywhere exhibits the typical rationalist desire for the permanence and purity of abstraction and mathematisation. Many have noticed that the rational mechanism of the market is given in this system not just an overly prioritised but even a godlike role.[12] The god of the free market is manifested in economic forces which should never be questioned or disobeyed. As reason is seen as the ruling element in human life, so the market of the rational economy is worshipped by its acolytes as a kind of abstract potentate, a rational juggernaut more inexorable in ideal conception than any human one: constant market reports celebrate the potentate's changeable moods and read out lists of the day's sacrifices or advancements. The rational god is tended by ministering priesthoods of politicians and economic experts, whose task is to placate the god and to engage in endless rounds of speculation, prediction and opinion as to its state of health.

The economic form of rationalism seeks to order the world rationally by bringing it into compliance with its own uniquely rational doctrines and universal 'laws', prioritising pure theory over impure reality regardless of the consequences.[13] Regarding the world as imperfect if it fails to conform to its own perfect and self-evident theories and prescriptions, economic rationalism interprets the disasters it inflicts on others not as indicating faults in its framework but as indicating that a 'correction' is taking place, or in the few cases where it does concede failure, as an indication that its disciplinary regime was not applied with sufficient severity. This approach encourages fatalism among its adherents about the adverse impacts of its applications. Such a system has very poor correctiveness, and is ill-equipped to come to terms with its failures or to rethink its approaches in the light of them.

The global free market is a monological, rationalist system whose extreme dominance over social life is the chief mark of neo-liberalism. The chief idea of neo-liberalism or economic rationalism, that it is rational to maximally entrust our social lives to the rule of a godlike economic mechanism and its ministering covey of expert economists, has appeared before in history, but what is different this time is its intensity, duration and global reach. The last two centuries of economic management in the west have varied in the degree to which they have been prepared to place social life under the control of the allegedly self-regulating market. Extreme forms of economic rationalism like the ones we encounter today also appeared in the industrial revolution,[14] the British enclosure movement, and in the economic liberalism that refused assistance to famine-stricken Ireland. They make up a historical archipelago of privilege and inhumanity marked by the insistence that supremely rational market forces must rule unimpeded, no matter what the human and ecological cost to marginal others, and that compassion and care for others is less than rational, a 'luxury' ranked below the welfare of the rational god.

Beyond all its other follies, the global free market shows its rationalist origins and its irrational course in its ecological disembedment, its disregard for the enabling ecological preconditions of human and non-human life. That is really what the term 'free market' means – a disembedded market whose rules are freed from any social responsibility or any recognition of our embedment in a constraining ecological order. In such a disembedded market society, the ecological support base can be systematically presupposed but at the same time systematically denied or demoted in importance and deprived of the resources it needs to renew itself, in the same way that the sphere of materiality and the body is presupposed but denied in rationalist philosophy.[15] In this denial, which is one expression of the ultimate irrationality of economic rationalism, it is the heir of the Platonic rationalist doctrine that heroic reason is sufficient unto itself in the universe, all else being inferior, replaceable and ultimately inessential.

Rationalist hubris gives no value to preserving the original resources of nature, such as the wild fish stocks of the oceans and natural genetic stocks. It finds them inessential and wanting, and proposes the construction of superior rational substitutes – bio-engineered organisms and systems with shorter reproduction times tailored to fit more exactly rational purposes and market slots, lacking untidy, inconvenient and superfluous qualities not required to fulfil market demand. It aims to remake the earth into a more rational form. To the extent that it exhibits these kinds of qualities, the economic system which is being impressed upon the globe via the creation of a global rationalist free-market is a true system of rationalism in the image of the classical form, and exhibits a similar range of blindspots to that form, especially the rationalist failure to make contact with the earth and to situate human life in ecologically embodied and embedded ways.

Blindspots of rationalism: the fisheries case

I will illustrate and motivate this theoretical account of how dominant forms of economic reason have come to such startling misunderstandings of their own importance and vulnerability by some examples. The contemporary processes of ecological destruction of the forests and oceans, for example, seem to give clear warning of these blindspots in our economic rationalist course. Nothing brings home the extent of ratiogenic (reason-generated) damage to the earth more sharply than the crisis of the oceans: fish is the world's most traded international foodstuff, and in historical, evolutionary and health terms one of the most important human foods. A recent FAO study shows the massive effects of global markets and fishing technology on the world's fish stocks: 75 per cent of the world's fish stocks are acknowledged to be either over-exploited or approaching over-exploitation, leaving only 25 per cent that are not threatened.[16] The global fishing economy is unsustainable, although the global market system, by moving from one overfished species to another species not quite yet at that point, is failing to communicate this in ways that might give warning of or avert impending ecological collapse.

The crisis of the oceans and the decline of world fisheries demonstrate that the most serious kinds of contemporary ecological failure emerge from the character of our dominant systems of rationality and their overconfidence, and not from failure to apply or extend systems of rational management far enough, as is usually suggested. Most world fisheries have been under rational and scientific management for the better part of the twentieth century, but still nearly all these managed fisheries have been exploited past ecologically sustainable limits, or will shortly be if present trends continue.[17] In most of these cases, even where there has been good advance warning of ecological disaster, ecologically damaging harvesting systems and technologies developed in accordance with maximising forms of economic rationality have still not been withdrawn or successfully resisted. Usually it was not so much that biological limits were theoretically recognised but factually underestimated; such limits were simply not recognised or investigated. As Rogers (1995: 10) notes of the now failed Atlantic cod fishery, the political objective was the maximisation of present values and this took virtually no account of the biological properties of the stock. Nor was science able to speak unambiguously for limiting the catch; marine science continually overestimated the resilience of stocks, and from different kinds of scientific advice that were available, those voices that suited the desire to continue fishing at high levels were selected and heard.[18]

Rather than withdrawing or scaling down, the economic rationalist imaginary reconceives the critical wild ocean resource base in reassuring terms as inessential and replaceable,[19] for example through the new technologies of fish farming, which are claimed to have the potential to both replace and to supplement overfished wild fisheries and allow them to recover. Closer scrutiny of these claims reveals however that known technologies of fish farming presented as superior reason-created substitutes are relatively inefficient and less sustainable in energy terms. Their tendency to spread disease and pollution to wild fish and their continued over-use of wild fish populations as food for farmed fish actually worsens the situation of the critical wild stocks even further, since it takes 4 kg of wild fish to bring 1 kg of farmed fish to market.[20] This is just one example of the many failures of ecological rationality delivered on a systematic basis by hubristic forms of rationalist economics and their concepts of substitutability.[21] It seems that we are dealing here, in the inherent inability of economic rationalism to acknowledge limits, constraints and forms of dependency on what lies outside itself, with a systematic form of rationalist delusion, that rationality is independent of and able to rationally re-create the world by itself.[22]

What are the conceptual mechanisms by which such a rationalist delusion could come about? The failure to recognise the limits arising from other living beings and systems is the product of a monological and deeply human-centred view of humans and of nature. According to the monological story written into property formation and value rules, nature is a passive field for human endeavour, a malleable order that has no agency or autonomy of its own and imposes no real constraints on us. It is not only totally available for its owners' remaking as they see fit into a more rational and marketable form, but better so remade, 'improved'. In the free market, nature is to be rationally ordered through a system in which it is a commodity or potential commodity, a set of replaceable, interchangeable units answering to human demand and lacking limits which might inhibit that demand. Rationalist economics then maps the world and everything it can reach within it in the reductive terms of trade flows, economic resources and profit potential.

Our own species appears in this system as 'outside nature', as essentially intellectual beings, 'rational choosers' calculating maximum satisfaction and not essentially reliant on the earth, beings whose basic ecological demands have no more legitimacy than any other desire, however trivial. Other species appear, when they appear at all, through a reductive and human-centred framework, in a rationalised and commodified form; as commodities, they are food for the insatiable appetites of the free market, exchangeable and tradeable 'things' that can create no restraint or impose no limits, but are simply available for human use, a use divorced from respect. This is a system which hyperseparates respect and use, 'persons' and 'property' as a division between the traders, who can (if they have enough resources) lay claim to subject status and rights, and the traded, who are available to be treated as 'objects' that can be maximally exploited. This radical separation and the cultural constructions of person/property, respect/use and subject/object dualism associated with it are major ethical and epistemic structures that make the commodity form and the free market possible. I address them throughout this book. They are expressed perhaps most clearly in rationalised agriculture's treatment of animals in the factory farm. (See Chapter 7).

This form of rationality is built on the myth of autonomous reason and autonomous man, inheriting the rationalist failure to situate the human in ecologically embodied and socially embedded ways. It misunderstands both the human and the ecological relationships that underlie human life, just as it misunderstood the relationships in the pilchard disaster, hiding from us our dependency on the ecosphere and on each other. Feminist thought has mapped the basic conceptual systems involved in contemporary hegemonic constructions of agency. These are the other side of hyperbolised conceptions of autonomy 'conjoined with individualistic conceptions of subjectivity and agency'.[23] The self-made man is for the most part a hyper-separated autonomous self whose illusion of self-containment is built on denying or backgrounding the contributions of subordinated others and re-presenting the joint product in terms of a hyperbolised individualistic agency who is to be treated as the only or primary 'achiever'.[24] The other's contributions are thus relied upon but at the same time disappeared or denied. The 'misunderstanding' involved here is functional for the purposes of appropriation, but can be very dangerous in other contexts. We are in just such other contexts in our ecologically embedded lives.

The rules of capitalist economics have beatified a contractual, privileged and rationally 'autonomous' master subject, recently identified as Business Man, and have also universalised certain related exclusions. Business Man looks at costs and benefits from a very limited angle, considering only his own firm and what can be monetised, leaving out the rest of society and leaving out the 'externalities'. The hegemonic economic equipment that universalises such a rationality is wildly unsuited to the range of conditions it is now generalised to cover. The hegemonic concept of property based on this formula has built into it the denial and appropriation of certain back-grounded kinds of prior contribution or labour, and the representation of this contribution as inessential. This gives rise to a common pattern or 'logic' of oppression or exploitation which includes a hegemonic concep-tion of agency that denies or backgrounds the contributions of subordi-nated others and re-presents the joint product in terms of the agency of the master subject. The category of Others whose collaborative agency is assumed but denied or backgrounded in this master conception of property include women, whose labour in the household is assumed but denied by the 'autonomous subject' as household head in his appropriation to himself of the social and economic rewards it makes possible.[25] They also include the non-propertied citizens, both the workers and the wider group once termed 'the rabble', whose background contribution to production, and to the society and the infrastructure which made this production and property possible, is assumed but denied in the appropriation of the product by the master subject. And these Others include the colonised, whose prior lands and assets and prior or continuing labour are assumed but denied and appropriated in the formation and accumulation of the colonisers' prop-erty.[26]

Primary among the Others whose contribution is assumed but denied is nature, the sphere of the non-human, including animals, plants and the biospheric cycles and processes of which they are part. The relation of the colonising master subject to the sphere of nature is one of centre to periph-ery. The centre sees the peripheral other or external sector as a place outside itself ('elsewhere') that can be used for dumping negative externalities (pollution, excess goods) and for collecting positive externalities. Ships arrive in the colonies laden with convicts and younger sons of the elite, and return to the European centre (the 'home' country) laden with seal or whale oil. To be such an externality is the role of nature in the economic rationalist imaginary. One of the major conceptual means by which this simultaneous reliance on but disavowal of nature is accomplished is through the hegemonic construction of autonomy and agency. A centric

or colonising system typically differentiates very strongly between a privileged, hegemonic group awarded full agency status who are placed at the
centre and excluded peripheral groups who are denied agency and whose
contribution is discounted, neglected, denied, or rendered invisible. The
contemporary form of globalisation is a centric colonising system which
does just this with the contribution of non-humans. In economic rationalism, the ecological support base of our societies is systematically relied on
but systematically denied in the same way as the sphere of materiality and
the body is denied in rationalist philosophy.

One of the consequences of this denial and treatment of the ecosphere as
externality is that its continued performance in supporting 'civilisation' is
assumed, but restraint is not exercised or resources made available to enable
it to reproduce or to continue to function without decline in that role. This
kind of denial of ecological embeddedness appears throughout cultures in
the grip of hegemonic reason, which develop dysfunctional blindspots
where culture and nature interface, (for example the centric delusion
that humans live in culture and non-humans in nature).

Centric global economic systems of property formation are shaped in
terms of the rationality of the master subject as such an autonomous,
separative self. They erase the agency of both social others and of nature,
both as land and as pre-existing, enabling annexation of ecological systems
and their products, just as they erase or downgrade the agency involved in
'women's work'.[27] This is a centrist monological structure and it has the
irrationalities and blindspots of a centrist system. But at the same time it is
less powerful than it knows, and partly because its dynamic of colonisation
denies it certain kinds of knowledge – especially self-knowledge, knowledge of its own limits, and certain knowledges of the other. It can easily
come to believe its own propaganda; eventually it really comes to think it
can do without the others, that it has succeeded in making them dispensable.

These conceptual blindspots are features of frameworks of rationalist
dualisms which have been used for millennia to naturalise power, including
the one that informs the 'empire of men over things', the human domination of nature. When the colonising party comes to believe that they are
radically different and superior to the subordinated party, who is coded as
nature, they can come to believe too that they are beyond ecology and
unlike other animals, especially in urban contexts. They are likely to devalue or deny the Other's agency and their own dependency on this devalued Other, treating it as either inessential and substitutable or as the
unimportant background to their foreground. Thus women's reproductive
labour in house labour and childraising are treated as inessential, as the
background services that make 'real' work (the work of the male) and

achievement possible, rather than as work or achievement themselves. The conceptual means by which this simultaneous reliance on and disavowal is accomplished is through the hegemonic construction of agency. In highly androcentric frameworks like that of Aristotle, women's reproductive agency was backgrounded as an adjunct to or mere condition for real agency, which was claimed for the male reproductive role, the woman being substitutable, merely 'the nurse' for the male seed. Aristotle's age erased women as social and political agents, enabling Aristotle to disappear women's reproductive agency in his award of the reproductive ownership of the child to the father. Aristotle saw the father as contributing the rational element of form as compared to the mother's contribution of mere matter. In this hegemonic construction the father emerged as the only active agent in a reproductive situation which we now conceive as normally involving joint and mutual agency. In terms of its recognition of nature's agency and contribution to our lives, modern economic rationalist society remains at the same level as Aristotle's theory of reproduction.

The increasing gulf in global capitalism between winners and losers, between consumption and production, and the growing remoteness and irresponsibility of chains of production and distribution are one of the products of hegemonic conceptions and relations of agency institutionalised in global property formation systems. I discuss this remoteness further in Chapter 3. We can see the same mechanism as that employed by Aristotle at work in current moves to place patented natural organisms under the aegis of intellectual property rights as the creations of reason, (assumed to be the identifying property of the centre). This is a process in which the contributions of other non-human systems and agencies are disappeared in the same way as the being and labour of the mother in Aristotle's schema. When the other's agency is treated as background or denied, we give the other less credit than is due to them. We easily come to take for granted what they provide for us, and to starve them of the resources they need to survive. This is of course the main point of hegemonic construals of agency and labour – they provide the basis for appropriation of the Other's contribution by the One or centre. The 'profound forgetting' of nature which ensues from the hegemonic construction of agency, the failure to see externalised nature as a collaborative partner or to understand relations of dependency on it, is the basis of the now global economic system of self-maximising economic rationality in which the maximum is extracted and not enough is left to sustain the life of the external others on which the rational system, unknown to itself, depends. The more Business Man can disembed himself by hyperbolising his autonomy and denying the collaborative agencies on which his wealth relies, the more he can appropriate for himself, and the less likely he is to have to share with others whatever wealth is generated. By his lights, this is rational; from a more embedded perspective, it is the opposite of rational.

A gendered agenda – neither rational, ecological or ethical

The dominant economic system of economic rationalism and the plausibility of its goals rely heavily on the prestige accorded reason and rationalism in the west as part of the rationalist cultural inheritance I have been outlining, as well as its typical set of dualistic oppositions. These include the dualisms of reason versus the body and nature, and especially that of reason versus emotion, which has many variants in contemporary culture. The economic rationalist imaginary draws on typical rationalist metaphors and oppositions which are highly gendered: reason requires the rule of a pure, detached and impartial rational calculus, 'soft' emotions such as sympathy and ethical concepts of social care are opposed to its own 'hard' discipline of economic mathematisation and quantification. Rational decisions must be made 'by the head and not by the heart', and to describe someone's statements or positions as 'emotional' becomes a form of abuse. Economic rationalism posits as supreme and universal a system of rationality interpreted in the gendered terms of rational egoism, whose paradigm abstract subject, Rational Economic Man, establishes the blueprint for 'rational' human activity by maximising his own interests and gains at the expense of others. In the economic rationalist imaginary of the machine, rational efficiency means a mean, lean, tough machine, shorn of compassion and of anything not instrumental to a self-maximising end, the victory of well-oiled economic clockwork in ordering the chaotic, messy sphere of social need and human desire.

Largely because of this ability to play on the gendered and dualistic symbolism of the historic rationalist imaginary, we have been persuaded to accept as the ultimate expression of rationality a neo-liberal system which is neither rational nor ethical and which is destroying the ecological basis of human life. When we look harder, we can see that there is nothing rational about governing life through the free market. To the extent that it is disembedded, it provides a poor guide to what people need and even to what they want. To the extent that it ignores its effects on nature, it is irrational. It has been counted as rational mainly because of its claims to disengagement, to be apart from the 'messy' sphere of emotionality and attachment. Because of its distancing from these supposedly irrational elements, it has been able to pose as neutral and disengaged even while enriching the few and immiserating the many. But there is nothing rational about trampling on emotion and marginalising ethics, any more than there is in disregarding ecology. We are emotional and ethical beings, as well as ecological ones.

Neo-liberalism has succeeded in passing itself off as rational largely because it plays a tough rationalistic gender game. The implicitly andro-centric structuring of the rationalist economy appears in the fundamental motivating form of rationality it assumes, the rational egoism of the self-contained and self-maximising individual or separative self, as pursued by its rational master subject.[28] Rational Economic Man has in an extreme form features conventionally associated with masculinity, such as egoism, rational and calculative capacities. This rational egoist master subject hails from a more abstract planet than our own; he does not need to take the concrete, locatable earthian form of a particular individual or class of individuals, such as the top-hatted, cigar-smoking millionaire of popular past insurgent imagination. Much of the development of modernity has involved encoding the rationality and properties of this master subject into apparently impersonal, bureaucratic mechanisms and institutions expres-sive of the general machinery of hegemonic, and especially economic, rationality. That's why they can so easily appear neutral and impartial, and thus 'rational'. Androcentrism has been merged into the rules of the game, and the processes for selecting those who can play. Androcentrism is written into the roles of master subjects of the property formation and corporate systems, the Man of Property and Business Man. That's why women own so little of the earth. Many of the same rules that exclude women are used to exclude non-humans, ensuring that they don't get their fair share of the earth either, and that the system is anthropocentric in the same way that it is androcentric.

Among the characteristic gendered dualisms economic rationalist culture relies on to naturalise its exclusions as rational are those of private versus public. The defining features of an economic rationalist order created via the naturalisation and universalisation of the model of rational egoism are a 'double dualism' of public and private which radically sepa-rates the economic (public) sphere from the sphere of the household on the one hand and the economic (private) from the (public) sphere of politics on the other.[29] In these contrasts, concepts of public and private play a dual role. The 'productive' and 'public' economic sphere is defined against the 'private' or domestic sphere of the household as the domain of reproduc-tivity, 'provisioning', care for the ecologically-situated body, and also, most importantly, the sphere of emotional attachment, altruism and ethics. Prudential-egoist strategies and modes are sharply distinguished from supposedly 'ethical' and altruist ones, coding the former as rational in contrast to the second as irrational, and naturalising the disengaged separa-tive self as the ultimate rational actor. This means that it is not only women's reproductive and caring work that is excluded from 'public' and economic rationality, but also much of the area of the ethical and the ecological, taken to be represented by and confined to the 'private-domestic'. On the other side, the economic ('private') is defined, in a double disembedment, against the political ('public'), taken to be a sphere of dialogue and negotiation with those who make up the political community. Whether ethics is conceived as purely individual and private, handed over to women and the household as guardians of ethics as in the Victorian period, or located wholly or partially as part of the public/political sphere, the outcome of these divisions is the concept of 'the economy' or 'business' as a male sphere of rational competition completely unconstrained by ethics and excluding sentiments of compassion or sympathy.

This means that rationality is held to be primarily economic, egoist, and atomistic. Supplementing this double dualistic construction is a narrow definition of rationality in terms of a calculus of maximising self-interest. This urges us to privilege the domain in which self-interest operates over other domains of human life, as ultimately the most rational form and arbiter of other forms. Prudential-egoist virtues and goals are sharply opposed to 'ethical' altruist ones and only the former conform to these concepts and ideals of rationality. Before long these ideals of rationality spill over into other parts of life; egoist maximisations of monetary values become the normal model, even in regions where they are irrational, destructive of trust or go against important cooperative or altruist traditions, such as in social infrastructure provision, medical practice and the helping professions.

Those self-maximising and *monological* forms of rationality built on the model of the self as an isolated, atomistic self-contained individual, the separative self, are not only unethical but also irrational and prudentially hazardous. They are especially hazardous and self-destructive when applied in what are really contexts of interdependency and of self-in-relationship – the normal real-life context. Here they encourage inappropriate strategies of maximisation and competition that harm the self (or One) because they do not take account of its connections to the Other. In these contexts of interrelationship, not monological but different *dialogical* strategies aimed not at self-maximisation but at negotiation and mutual flourishing are rational. But a dialogical model requires a basic level of mutuality and equality, give and take, response and feedback, that is not available in monological systems. Dialogical logics assist conflict resolution, conversation, and fair exchange. It is significant that these dialogical systems are not the kind of formal reasoning systems the intellectual life of the west has made pre-eminent, but rather monological logics that impose a centrically-conceived One upon a passive Other.[30]

A strategy can seem rational when applied in a hypothetical context of hyperseparation but be completely irrational when applied in a real-world context of interrelationship. The monological denials of dependency and interconnectedness are major sources of the irrationality of rational egoism and the rationalist economics based on it in the context of real, ecologically embodied life. The hyperbolised autonomy assumed in economic theory lies behind some of the current world order's ugliest and most destructive acts as well as its most irrational ones, since it universalises competitive and self-maximising economic behaviour. Rationality as maximising the separative self is interpreted as driving the hardest bargain against the Other, squeezing the most out of the Other that is the 'resource', licensing ruthlessness. It maximises 'efficiency', 'competition' and the corporate bottom line, dictating that the battery chicken cannot have an extra inch of cage space, or that fish-catching technology be designed to take the biggest catch, whatever the cost to non-target species. Its economic rationality proposes the superior wisdom of feeding diseased animal carcases to confined herbivores, discounting predictable risks in crossing species barriers, as well as potentials for creating new diseases and moving them through the food chain. It proposed the same sort of thing for fish meal and fish farms, and now it is proposing it again for genetic engineering.[31] The proposition that such monological strategies are rational can only seem plausible to people remote from their operations and concrete effects, because the illusion that they are rational cannot easily be maintained in the local and immediate worlds where concrete relationships of embodiment and interconnectedness are harder to discount and ignore.

Gendered forms and metaphors are used to support person/property and related respect/use and subject/object dualisms that provide the ethical foundations for these denials and for the commodification of nature. These metaphors reinforce monological and mechanistic symbolism depicting the non-human sphere as a 'mindless body', passive, manipulable, and wanting in rational agency, at the same time as they promote the privileging of their own hyper-rational masculinist forms. Hegemonic conceptions of human agency that deny all these others, women, the colonised, the 'hired hands', and nature, are linked to denials of dependency, which are in turn linked to the application of inappropriate strategies and forms of rationality that aim to maximise the share of the 'isolated' self and neglect the need to promote mutual flourishing. Thus supposedly rational economic subjects are able to assume the contribution of nature in the form of a continuing support base for production, accumulation and renewal, but also to deny it in failing to recognise and allow for nature's reproduction and continuation.[32]

Such systems conspire to conceal from us our dependency on nature, to overestimate our autonomy and manipulative ability, to claim invincibility so we believe we know no limits, and so devise Promethean projects like growing indefinitely on earth, taming space and terraforming Mars. According to its story, nature has no agency or autonomy of its own and imposes no real limits on us. Ideally, nature is to be rationally ordered through a system in which it is property, for sale to the highest human bidders. Hegemonic constructions of agency that justify appropriation are especially encouraged in the culture/nature dualism typical of western thinking because its systems of appropriation are based on the idea of the separative self applying labour to 'pure' nature, as in Locke's argument. The process opens the way for enrichment, but its other side is that the blinkered vision involved is a problem for prudence as well as for justice in the case where the One is in fact dependent on this Other, for the One can gain an illusory and over-comfortable sense of their own ontological independence and ecological autonomy. It is just such a sense that seems to pervade the dominant culture's contemporary disastrous misperceptions of its economic and ecological relationships. Countering this denial requires recognition, but 'recognition' here must mean much more than just 'remember' (as in the case of Mother's Day) – recognition means, at least, incorporating that knowledge of their agency into economic institutions and distribution of social resources and rewards.

As we have seen, among the main sources of irrationality in the rationalist economy are hyperbolised concepts of individual 'autonomy' and hegemonic constructions of agency that legitimate unjust appropriation and denials of dependency on others, including nature, and forms of reason/emotion and public/private dualism that present disengagement and egoism as rationality and marginalise ethics and emotionality, including care for human others and for nature. Many feminists have critiqued these, emphasising as alternatives care perspectives that stress emotional and dispositional forms of care for nature, as a more-than-instrumental basis of concern. As feminist theorists of care have pointed out, in the service of the opposition rationalism presupposes between emotion and reason, between ethics and economics, women have been denigrated as only half-ethical beings, while our civilisation is driven by conceptions of both reason and ethics which exclude or denigrate what women have been taken to stand for.[33] In a rationalist economy which defines its hardness in opposition to the symbolic woman, as Other, and which increasingly invades every corner of our lives, we should not be surprised to find that care and compassion for others are increasingly inexpressible in the public 'rational context', a context that is defined against the domestic sphere in which care has been confined. Ethics has long been individualised, etherealised and disempowered by confinement to the sphere of women and the household and its exclusion from state-political and economic life.[34] The global economic rationalist economy intensifies that split to catastrophic levels.

The double ethical disembedment of the global market economy means that it is stripped of both the ethics of the public sphere, that of public probity and collective good, and also the ethics of the private sphere, of care, compassion and personal relationship. Its status as an ethics-free zone, one that cannot even be imagined as caring and compassionate, testifies to its essentially sado-dispassionate character. An ethics-free market, as I will presently show, is as much a hazard as a rudderless engine, and especially dangerous when it is permitted to control so many spheres of life. As the ethics-free rationality of the economic sphere colonises other spheres of life, the rationalist machinery of the sado-dispassionate economy is coming for us too – it has already constructed our work and much of our own lives in the same oppressive terms that demand that we leave emotional expression, self-direction and creativity, along with love and communication, in the carefully limited and shrinking zone marked 'personal'. It has long discarded care for both human and non-human others as inefficient in the relentless drive for economic competition. Emotional experiences can still be shared with household members, but the public and economic spheres are increasingly occupied by a narrow egoism and by work structures that are more insecure, less expressive and creative and more and more like those of factory-farmed animals.

Recipes for escaping our situation are explored in the rest of the book, and include the development of critical forms of rationality that are able to undertake the critique of maladapted forms. We must replace sado-dispassionate stances of rationality with caring and life-affirming ones that can work to realise a harmonious and joyful co-existence with our planetary partners. Among our objectives should be the development of a culture that can create alternative strategies and concepts to the oppressive rationalist and dualistic structures that make oppression pervasive in everyday life under globalisation. At the level of economy, an integrative struggle against the systemic excision of ethics and ecology from our economic lives would aim beyond the dualisms of the rationalist imaginary for 'a cultural reconnection of home, workplace and polity that recognises the reproductive, productive and political aspects of most human activities'.[35] The growing exclusion of justice, care and ecological responsibility from the economic sphere in the interests of global competition affects all of us in different ways, but these different ways can still bring us together into the larger struggle for ecological and ethical forms of rationality as they affect both human and non-human spheres. This defines the project for a new re-embedment of economic life within ethical, social and ecological life as a struggle to defeat the global rationalist machinery that is making nearly all of us into Others to ourselves, into less than we could be.

2 Rationalism and the ambiguity of science

The double face of science

Science is often identified as the ally and saviour of the environment, especially since scientists have spoken out on climate change and have added the authority of reason to environmental concern in many areas. This face is real enough: science has played an important and often crucial role in exposing environmental damage and aiding opposition to it. But modern technoscience also has an uglier but less remarked face: technoscience has contributed to producing the environmental crisis at least as much as to curing it, applying to highly complex situations and systems specialised and highly instrumentally-directed forms of knowledge whose aim is to maximise outputs, often with devastating results. Four out of five scientists now work for corporations which bring precisely such an orientation to bear: thus we can link overfishing to fisheries science and fishing technology, land salinisation and degradation to irrigation and agricultural technology, the disasters of intensive agriculture and genetic engineering to biological, agricultural and forestry science, exotic species introductions of agricultural science aimed at 'controlling pests' or maximising production to chains of indigenous extinctions, and transportation, combustion and refrigeration technology to global warming and the ozone hole. In fact to a large extent the environmental crisis *is* ratiogenic damage, the creation of technoscience aimed at increasing production without due regard for effects on larger self-regulating systems containing many unknowns.

Some would give the bad part of this technoscience complex the name 'technology' and call the good part 'science'. 'Science' then becomes a protean concept whose size and boundaries change in different contexts in a similar way to a basking reptile, expanding its form to take full credit for all the benefits of its applications when aiming to maximise its access to the sun of public funding, but retreating to a 'pure' form with minimised extension when confronted with the chilly task of taking responsibility for any damage or harm. One of the aims of such strategic boundary shifts in terminology is to maintain the ideology that 'science proper' can do no wrong by displacing attention and responsibility for any ill-effects onto externalised activities or onto parties identified as 'outside' science proper, for example, onto 'technology', or 'society' and its 'use' of science[1]. This strategy protects technoscience from critical appraisal but by the same token fails to encourage the development of self-critical thinking within technoscience. Evasive strategems of this kind cannot take the place of the responsible and ethical thinking technoscience needs and has yet to evolve.

To prioritise the kind face of technoscience over the ruthless one would be to ignore the fact that economic rationalism and productivism ensure that the research directions of technoscience are increasingly dominated by the narrowly instrumental and productivist goals of corporations, rather than by broader and more integrated knowledge agendas. If an ecosocially disembedded rational economy hand-in-hand with a sado-dispassionate productivist science were to become the twin forces shaping human history, the future would look very grim indeed. What relationship between these two can we discern here, and what forms of science might help us? Both capitalism and the state/military complex depend on technoscience to keep military and production forces ahead in competition. We might regard technoscience as involving a separable form of rationality that is influenced in various ways by the rationalist economy, or we might see closeness here as approaching identity, and view the rationalist engine of commodification that now dominates history as a hybrid form consisting of scientific reason developed and put in the service of the market under capitalism. The framework of the global order is not I think a singular, monolithic form of economic rationality which somehow selects or determines all the rest, but an oligarchy of collaborative rationalities that combine to produce outcomes that benefit associated elites, such as the ecological crisis. They work together (and sometimes against one another) as a system of interlinked rationalities in which each has some potential for independence and is not simply reducible to the economic form. But the present political context of neo-liberalism has encouraged the economic form to dominate over the others, which develop corresponding rationalist distortions.

For example scientific, political, ethical and administrative rationality failures have all played a role in producing the fishing overkill of the last two decades. This is borne out in the case of the Canadian Atlantic cod fishery, where scientific, administrative and political rationality all failed to stop over-fishing.[2] However we spell out the scenario of mutual selection, there can be no doubt that the love affair or at least excessive intimacy between technoscience and capitalism is strongly implicated in the fishery collapse scenario. Some of the effects of the capture of technoscience are illustrated in the way technology design and the research orientation of science in the fisheries case is dominated by the productivist goals of the rationalist market. Fisheries science in Canada during the period leading up to the collapse of the once-great Atlantic cod fishery in the 1990s exemplified what Rogers calls 'a production model view of nature', a reductionist conception which treats appropriate knowledge in the instrumental terms of development and production. The relationships so developed are monological because they are responsive to and pay attention to the needs of just one party to the relationship.

Such approaches are prudentially dangerous for a number of reasons. Monological approaches to nature are dangerous in the context where we press limits, especially limits we have not gauged. Another is that they are very narrow, focussing on just those aspects of the other that can be exploited rather than aiming at a more rounded form of knowledge. According to a Canadian analysis of the cod fishery collapse, 'In Canada, which exports $3 billion worth of seafood a year, research until recently focussed almost exclusively on ways to find, count, and catch more fish'.[3] Marine science here was an adjunct to maximising production goals and helped to legitimate excessive exploitation by claiming to establish safe levels that were not and could not in fact be established.[4] More basic research was neglected in favour of crudely instrumental and productivist goals – increasingly the kind of science corporations and economic rationalist bureaucrats are willing and able to fund. 'In doing that' acknowledges marine researcher Richard Beamish 'we ... sacrificed the opportunity to understand the mechanisms in the ecosystem better'.[5] The neglect of non-production goals that aim to 'know the object in its fullness' feeds the mechanist illusions that nature is passive and open for the taking, and that that taking can be analysed down to some subset of self-contained technological problems that can always be solved. What is neglected in such instrumental, productivist science is hardly insignificant. Another ocean researcher states 'We think that photosynthesis and the carbon system have been affected [by overexploitation] in the eastern one-third of the Pacific, but we can't say for sure because we don't have the measurements'.[6] Narrowly instrumental, human-centred goals and methodologies aimed narrowly at prediction and control have been an established part of modern science since its inception, and can't just be written off as 'bad science'.[7]

The dominance of the economic sphere over other spheres means that scientific research and warning systems that have a potentially corrective role in the ecological crisis have themselves been largely compromised, both by this kind of crudely instrumental research direction and more directly by fear of offending privatised funding sources.[8] The outcome is that these different spheres of rationality tend to display complicity and convergence instead of correctiveness. It is a major compounding of the ecological irrationality of the rationalist economy that it is permitted to compromise potentially independent and corrective forms and sources.[9] The capture of an increasingly large part of science by the rationalist economy is part of a larger program of cooption of other systems of rationality, which I will discuss in subsequent chapters. In the case of science, mechanisms of capture range from the direct corporate sponsorship of science and employment of scientists to more indirect mechanisms of funding and political influence.

Disengagement as sado-dispassionate practice

This kind of overt influence, although widespread and increasingly institutionalised, is the tip of the iceberg however;[10] the deeper conceptual structures that predispose science to such collaboration and capture are my concern here. They include basic conceptual frameworks like subject/ object dualism and the demand for disengagement. In these, rationalism is again implicated, especially in the historical development of reductionist and nature-devaluing forms of scientific epistemology that make possible both the commodity form and the subservience of knowledge to it. Modern scientific knowledge prepares itself to be shaped as a servant of the corporation and the rationalist economy through endorsing sado-dispassionate rationalist models of personal objectivity as emotional neutrality and ethico-political disengagement. Such a science is aptly characterised in Brennan's terms as 'sado-dispassionate'; as we have seen, emotional neutrality or the absence of emotion in certain contexts (most obviously that of harmful experimentation) is not an admirable trait but an indication of a deep moral failing.[11] Disengagement and neutrality are as mythological in science as in the market, but the insistence on these ideals creates a commitment vacuum in science, reduces the ability to resist cooption by economic forces, and works systematically against a science committed to socially responsibility. In support of capitalist structures, modern science has invested strongly in subject/object dualism, the epistemic analogue of person/property dualism, which is basic to the commodification of nature. Methodologies of disengagement licence ratiogenic domination and damage to the other that is studied, an ethically-minimising stance with respect to that other, and neglect of the need for responsible and self-critical methodologies. Alternative forms of science are both possible and necessary for survival.

The concept of scientific disengagement is a powerful constituting and normative mythology for science, and perhaps, given the strong and continued gendering of reason/emotion dualism in dominant global culture, the one that most strongly marks science out as a masculinist activity. The rationalist construction of disengagement as objectivity demands the exclusion of considerations which have to be left out or put aside as corrupting in order to achieve a properly objective judgement. Objectivity is usually seen as excluding the emotional, the bodily, the particular, the personal, and of course especially the 'political'. Rationalist influences devaluing the body and emotionality and identifying them as feminine are clearly influential here. Although there is now a great deal of work which shows that the ideology accords poorly with actual scientific practice and scientific discovery,[12] the ideology of objectivity has its uses, one of them being the facilitation of control by privileged social groups, and this ideology shows no sign of weakening.

Interpretations of objectivity as oppositional to the body and the emotions (both thought of as forms of nature) have a long pedigree in rationalist thought. In Platonic rationalism, knowledge is gained in spite of the body, which is interpreted as a hindrance to knowledge. In later Cartesian rationalism, the ideal of knowledge as freedom from doubt and as objectivity is also interpreted as freedom from the body and its deceptions, weaknesses and hindrances, its personal and emotional ties.[13] Knowledge, interpreted oppositionally as pure thought, involves setting aside 'all distractions and passions which obscure thinking'.[14] Obstacles to knowledge according to such a rationalist interpretation include not only animality and the body itself, (both coded as female), but also material reality, practical activity, change, the emotions, sympathy, and subjectivity.

As Evelyn Fox Keller points out, the insistence on such a concept of impartiality or disengagement imposes a rigid barrier between subject and object which excludes relationships of care, sympathy and engagement with the fate of what is known, constructing connection as a source of error and the object known as alien to the knower. Such knowledges involve monological relationships: they imply the closure of the knower to the known, for the knower is construed as one who can change the other to make it conform to desire but who cannot be themselves changed by this other. The other can be known completely, and in the absence of consent – knowledge can be wrung from it, as a form of power over it. The withholding of recognition and respect (as forms of engagement), and the adoption of an ethically exclusionary or amoral knowledge stance towards the world, leaves the field for mechanism and for instrumentalism towards the object of study. The ruling out of care and respect as foundations for the knowledge relationship dictates an instrumentalising politics in which what is known becomes a means to the knower's ends, whether through direct manipulation or through simply figuring in the knower's schemes as a 'case', an experimental or observational means to intellectual or academic gratification or advancement. Apologists for rationalist science such as Hayward[15] picture the role of Enlightenment science in terms of the Hero of Reason overcoming human-centredness; however, such disengaged forms of science not only cannot challenge, but are actually major supports for human-nature dualism and human-centred worldviews.

In the absence of care and respect for what is studied and of responsibility to those who will be affected by it, it is inevitable that the knowledge relation is constructed as one in which the known is merely a means to the knower's ends or to the ends of power which they, in the absence of respect and care, will come to serve. The presence of a politics is particularly clear when the item known is itself threatened, and especially when it is threatened for ratiogenic reasons, as a direct result of what has been learnt about it. The politics of the emotionally-neutral anthropologist who does not care whether the indigenous people he or she studies are harmed or not through their knowledge-gathering illustrates this clearly, as does the politics of the natural scientist whose work opens the way for destructive exploitation of what is studied. Power is what rushes into the vacuum of disengagement; the fully 'impartial' knower can easily be one whose skills are for sale to the highest bidder, who will bend their administrative, research and pedagogical energies to wherever the power, prestige and funding is. Disengagement then carries a politics, although it is a paradoxical politics in which an appearance of neutrality conceals capitulation to power.

The objective knower must not only deny all relationship to and care for what they know, but also deny any elements which would 'locate' them or their perspective to present themselves and their knowledge as absolute and transcending location. The limits and social shaping of knowledge imposed by the knower's identity and their cultural or personal 'slant' or 'set' are disappeared in the presentation of such a knowledge as emerging from a universal perspective, or as transcending perspective, as 'the view from nowhere'.[16] One does not have to be an extreme epistemological relativist to reject these sorts of accounts of knowledge which disappear the knower. All viable and current epistemological theories have had to concede that the knower is active not only in seeking and selecting observational input but in constructing knowledge, that knowledge is a social activity, not the passive and 'neutral' reception of raw, 'pure' observational data by presocial individuals. The impossibility of fully unlocated and disengaged knowledge means that the demand for objectivity as disengagement in practice translates as the demand that there be no visible engagement.

This framework of disengagement is hegemonic, cloaking privileged perspectives as universal and impartial, and marking marginalised perspectives as 'emotional', 'biased' and 'political'. The 'value-free' stance will normally be taken to involve accepting the effects of power, since the powerful have the advantage of inertia, whereas the oppressed must act to disrupt the *status quo* from a passion for change. The demand for disengagement thus tends to favour the perspectives of the powerful, who have only to announce the realities created by power and to employ the well-practiced conceptual and emotional distancing mechanisms which legitimate the exploitation of the objectified and oppressed. The rationalist interpretation of objectivity as it stands is a mystifying notion that is useful in enabling dominant groups to pass their interests off as universal.[17] A less hegemonic form of scientific rationality and interpretation of objectivity could give us a more accountable and less dangerous science.[18]

My ethico-epistemological proposition is that knowledges that involve injustice to those who are known do not provide accurate or ethically acceptable forms of knowledge. Additionally, that the sado-dispassionate mode is prudentially irrational, especially as an ecological mode. We need, both for prudential and ethical reasons, for our own sakes and that of earth others, to develop communicative and caring rational and social forms and to cast off monological and sado-dispassionate forms – especially sado-dispassionate science, in favour of ones that affirm and nurture the earth. As Sandra Harding has pointed out, a 'purely rational' science that could somehow stand apart from all values could not be ethically or socially responsible or counter centric frameworks and values that reduce prospects for scientific accuracy. It could not distance itself from projects which are conceived in racist and sexist terms, such as those of Nazi science.[19] It is a very serious drawback of the presentation of knowledge as absolute and transcending location that it hinders self-critical forms of engagement which can acknowledge the limitations of particular knowledge locations and place the subject of knowledge on the same critical, causal plane as the objects of knowledge.[20] In the context of the ratiogenic complicity of science in over-exploitation, self-critical forms are surely what we need. As Harding argues, there are much more effective dialogical ways to counter partial and distorted beliefs that do not demand a generalised emotional detachment – for example in the form of dialogical contexts in which those most likely to be affected by and able to detect forms of bias (for example, women and other Others) are able to contest centric and undemocratic constructions of science. A more dialogical and less hyper-separated interpretation of the subject/object relationship together with a dialogical interpretation of objectivity would give us a better, more democratic and communicative form of scientific rationality, and one less open to capture by those economic forces that increasingly rule our world.

This kind of analysis points towards a complex, connected set of rationality failures linked to rationalism as the main factors in the fisheries collapse. In the background, high levels of human-centredness (as I will argue in Chapter 5, a prudential hazard) create blindspots, general lack of awareness in the dominant culture of ecological embeddedness, nature's agency and limits, and human dependency on the non-human sphere. Maximising economic rationalism is insensitive to or discounts ecological ill-effects, is inflexible and requires the constant 'throughput' of nature. There are other potentially corrective warning and control systems which might act as a check, (for example techno-bureaucratic and scientific rationality). But they either have their own reasons for seeking an economic maximisation,[21] or they are dominated and corrupted by economic forces and actors. All these players, including economic rationality, encourage and select for monological forms of scientific rationality which are strongly human-centred and consider non-human lives to be replaceable and sacrificeable. They reinforce narrow scientific goals of prediction and control, an orientation to instrumentalism and domination, an ethically-minimising stance for nature, and a minimally self-reflective science. We are dealing here with a set of systematic, self-reinforcing distortions to which the distortions of economic rationality are central, especially at present, but which are not simply reducible to a single factor or 'driver', and which combine and collaborate to produce the ecological crisis.

The subject/object divide and the ambiguity of science

We have noticed that these economic forms go hand-in-hand with and select in favour of monological forms of science. Not only the history of science, but most of its theory and conceptual methodology, being based ultimately in rationalism, collude in endorsing monological forms. The radical separation of the subject of knowledge from its object is an epistemological foundation stone of monological science, of the commodification of nature, and of capitalism, one cemented in place by rationalist readings of surrounding concepts that devalue nature and treat it as replaceable. In this form of monological and dualistic thinking,[22] subjects set themselves radically apart from objects of knowledge in a way that refuses objects elements of commonality, mind or intentionality. The 'object' is an intentional nullity, never itself a reciprocal knower or active in disclosing knowledge, never itself the subject of a narrative we can hear. In the subject/object division the 'object' is treated as passive, the one acted upon, and the knower is the active party who forces knowledge from the reluctant or mute object. This passification of the objectified is a prelude to their instrumentalisation; since as a vacuum of agency, will and purpose, they are empty vessels to be filled with another's purpose and will. As a corollary to this passification, the subject/object division backgrounds or denies the agency of the one studied and any limits respect for this might impose on the knower. This kind of relationship fits very well with the treatment of knowledge as power over the one conceived as object; it is a monological account of the knowledge relationship because it is never envisaged as potentially reciprocal and because qualities of mind, activity and agency are assumed to fall onto one side, the side of the knower. In subject/object dualism we can recognise the distinctively 'modern' mechanistic view of nature as a purely material world empty of agency, mind and purpose, a 'clockwork' background to the master narrative of human consciousness and endeavour.

Evelyn Fox Keller has briefly outlined an account of the gendered development of this arrogant and monological approach to knowledge.[23] I will interpret and elaborate on this a little differently to bring out its rationalist origins and influences. The classical rationalist tradition, as we have seen, holds reason to be the supreme good in and the supreme force driving the universe, and sees human reason or intellect as the only proper basis of human knowledge and human culture. Reason, coded as male, maintains itself in a precarious and hostile relationship with the corrupted world of 'nature', thought of as the domain of emotionality, the senses, and the sphere of biological changes, of 'coming to be and passing away'. In this form nature, the body and the biological 'world of changes' were associated with women and other lower groups such as slaves and 'barbarians' or non-Greeks, in contrast to a strongly separate, higher realm of reason, ideas and 'spirit' associated with elite, Greek men. In this schema, the corrupted sensory and material world must be too unworthy to provide real knowledge, just as it cannot provide real love.

Knowledge is the product of reason, not of the senses or the body. Platonic rationalism held the proper locus of knowledge to be the semi-divine rational laws, the abstract and eternal mathematical and celestial bodies. These lent their rational prestige to knowledge and could be known by human reason as (male) like to (male) like. The rational, celestial realm is seen as active in disclosing knowledge, which is symbolically depicted as an erotic relationship of mutuality between male subjects of equal status.[24] True knowledge is knowledge of this higher realm, and the proper attitude of the knower to the known is respect, awe and wonder.[25] Plato thus delineates a highly respectful form of knowledge that can be interpreted as a subject–subject relationship but with a highly restricted cast of high prestige rational 'subjects' in what is now the 'object of knowledge' position. These are treated as other subjects rather than as objects, and are seen as active rather than as passive in the creation of knowledge. However despite this feature, it is essential not to universalise or romanticise the Platonic account: this true form of knowledge can be gained only when reason is maximally separated from the lower realm of the body and the senses, and is not available at all for the lower, material and sensory world of nature (coded female). And its male-to-male erotic imagery is 'respectful' in a highly exclusionary and non-extendable way, in contrast to the debased eroticism of sex with women, who, like the sensory world, are unworthy.

Rationalist interpretations of knowledge as a matter of the authority of rational tradition, of theory and principle rather than of observation and sense perception remain dominant until the great empiricist transition of the Enlightenment, uneasily so in their latter period. In the key movement which makes modernity and manipulative technoscience possible, Enlightenment empiricism shifts the locus of knowledge to the lowly material objects which the older Platonic rationalism held to be incapable of providing knowledge and to be unworthy of proper rational study. But although empiricism challenges this facet of the rationalist knowledge model, what it fails to challenge is the lowly status rationalism accorded the material and sensory realm, summed up in its symbolic status as female. It leaves this feature of its parent tradition unaltered, and instead recasts and regenders the knowledge relationship itself as a subject/object type of relationship between superior and inferior, between a rational active subject of knowledge, both typically and symbolically coded as male, and a mindless passive object of knowledge coded as female.

Empiricist philosophers and scientists re-present knowledge in terms of a new model which retains the nature-devaluing features of the old but which unlike the old now validates the pursuit of empirical knowledge. In this new model, knowledge of the inferior material and sensory sphere is not to be sought for its own sake, as in the rationalist model, but is strongly associated with power and manipulation. Male knowers are seen as wringing empirical knowledge from a nature pictured as a debased and passive female slave tortured to yield up her secrets. Because this model retains so many key features of rationalism there is a case for viewing it as a 'rationalist-empiricist' tradition rather than as an independently empiricist one.[26] In general terms, the Enlightenment transition that constitutes the empirical turn moves from a respectful model of knowledge directed towards a very restricted range of collaborating abstract subjects coded male to a disrespectful model directed towards an unrestricted range of passified objects in nature, coded female.

This puts a different light on the remarkable rash of metaphors presenting knowledge as sexual violence that emanated from early modern scientists in the newly enlightened empiricist mould, in which nature is depicted as a pliant female from whom knowledge is to be wrung by force. Through 'inquisition' and 'interrogation' Nature 'with all her children' is to be conquered and subdued, bound to service and made a slave.[27] In her classic 1980 book *The Death of Nature*, Carolyn Merchant contrasts the mechanistic account of nature arising with the Enlightenment with earlier respectful and organic models of nature as a living, maternal being. We can however see the articulation of these images of sexual violence as expressing *both* the shift from the organic model (present in both peasant and pre-urban European and indigenous non-European contexts) to the modern mechanistic model and *also* the shift from the rationalist to the rationalist-empiricist model of knowledge more influential among intellectual groups. What they indicate especially is the movement away from a respectful model to a power perspective.[28] This revolution opens the way for our modern view of nature as a purely material world empty of agency, mind and purpose, the 'object' or 'clockwork' background to the master element of human consciousness and endeavour. This arrogant model of knowledge as forced or tricked from a mindless and passive nature by a superior exclusively active and rational human mind replaces earlier rationalist models in which human reason meets its match in an actively disclosing, rational celestial world which evokes awe, wonder and a sense of human limitation from the knower. The new model in contrast evokes from the knower a sense of human superiority to nature and of freedom from its limits. The empirical object of knowledge remains unworthy, as in the older rationalist tradition, but its investigation can be justified in instrumental terms, as enabling the rationalisation of the world in ways beneficial to human knowers.

The modern rationalist-empiricist model is explicitly about power, instrumentalism, individualism, and human-centredness. The 'empire of man over things' (now 'mere things') becomes the explicit aim of the new subject/object science.[29] As we have seen, knowledge, instead of being a collaborative effort between knower and known, in part the creation of a nature conceived as rationally knowable, is reconceived as entirely the creation of a rational (male) knower who monopolises agency and reason. Since the knowledge forced from a passive nature by human effort is seen as generated exclusively by the work of the human knower, it can in effect be owned by that knower and be used for ends that are of benefit exclusively to that owner. Knowledge is simultaneously instrumentalised and privatised, open to be harnessed to private economic power.[30]

Most of all, the Enlightenment model, despite its orientation to external nature, makes the knowledge relationship monological and strongly anthropocentric, appropriating not only knowledge itself but its fruits and ends exclusively for the human. The ambition to 'establish and extend the power and dominion of the human race itself over the universe' is lauded as wholesome and noble, more so than any mere national or clan-based ambition.[31] In the monological modernist version of arrogant and anthropocentric knowledge, the hyper-separation between the subject and object positions in the knowledge relation, between human reasoner and non-human 'object', is now strongly marked. Not only are knowers as a group more strongly equated with the category of the human (since nothing now is willingly 'given' by nature), but both slave and machine models express the denial to nature of any uniqueness, agency and power. Both power and agency in the knowledge relation are exclusive to the scientific knower, the subject whose knowledge is construed as a means to power over another defined as object. As subject the knower is unique, agentic and has intrinsic value, but as an object of knowledge nature is passive, replaceable and has only instrumental value. A nature represented in mechanistic terms as inferior, passive and mindless, whose only value and meaning is derived from the imposition of human ends, is simply replaceable by anything else which can serve those ends equally well – it can be reduced and regimented, the more so as those ends are defined in monological and minimally interactive terms. As you wipe out one species of fish, it can be replaced with another, in theory without limit.

In the new Cartesian fantasy of mastery, the new human task becomes that of remoulding nature to conform to the dictates of this form of reason and achieving salvation on earth rather than in heaven, since man now becomes his own god. It is now through science rather than religion that man will achieve salvation, in the form of freedom from death and bodily limitation.[32] This doctrine is not just an abstract past concept but an active present ideology which touches all our lives. Arrogant monological knowledge is an effective tool for colonising programs which organise the world in favour of dominant elites; it can draw on older traditions in which knowledge is the most valuable thing in the universe, as well as on older rationalist assumptions concerning the primitive nature of women, indigenous and non-white peoples, to help shape the arrogant knowledge agendas of establishing gender and racial supremacy which were so influential in nineteenth century colonial science.[33] But it can also contribute to and draw on newer forms of domination. Its vision of mastery and salvation remains the underlying project of research into space colonisation and into genetic engineering, cloning and other life-extending technologies that seem set to further entrench a privileged 10 per cent at the eventual expense of immense ratiogenic harm to both human social groups and the earth's environment. Modernist science seems to lack any alternative imaginary that would allow it to forsake the rationalist-empiricist vision of the Enlightenment, even as its sinister aspects become more apparent.

Resolving the ambiguity of science: integrating the 'two cultures'

What seems particularly useful in this understanding of the rationalist-empiricist transition of the Enlightenment is that, in addition to allowing us to put culturally dominant traditions of rationalism back into the explanatory picture, it clearly signposts an alternative road not taken, which appears as an uncompleted task for modernist science and its understanding of the subject-object division. The obvious question this kind of historical account throws up is: instead of accepting the original rationalist devaluation of non-human nature as too unworthy to provide knowledge, and recasting the empirical knowledge relationship towards nature in terms of superior/inferior and subject/object, as rationalist-empiricism does, why not take the other option, to challenge and recast the nature-devaluing aspect of rationalism and retain something like the mutualistic subject/subject relationship of the later Plato's vision – but now with a broader focus on the natural world rather than the ideal/abstract world? This alternative[34] then would aim for a form of subject/subject relationship more like that of Platonic rationalism – but without its restriction to rational objects of knowledge. It would be able to recast knowledge as a relationship of awe and wonder and nature as something to be known for its own sake, not just as a means to power over it or for the benefit of human beings.

Now this project is not a minor piece of conceptual technofix, rather it involves a major cultural project with ramifications through many areas beyond science and epistemology. To begin with, in making a respectful extension to include the world of nature it is essential to rework the Platonic male-to-male gender coding of the Platonic knowledge relationship. Since this coding makes knowledge an exclusionary relationship in which the respect due to the ideal male-coded realm gains its prestige and meaning in contrast to the disrespect extended to its contrast class in the female-coded material realm, we cannot simply extend the prestige of the hard form to the soft by adding in this latter class.[35] The implications for a larger cultural project of communicative and non-exclusionary ethical forms of relationship are explored in later chapters. For knowledge, the possibility of developing the alternative road not taken that would lead to a respectful orientation towards nature rather than the dominant manipulative one suggests a major epistemic and cultural program. In this project, a subject/subject knowledge orientation would legitimate and be expressed in different methodologies of reciprocity, generosity and communication, in place of the monological methodologies of reduction and human-centredness that abound in contemporary subject/object science. These reductionist projects include the minimisation of nature's mindfulness and agency (Ockemism)[36] and the maximisation of human empire and control at the expense of the rest of creation. They include also the assumption that the 'object' of knowledge lies outside the bounds of ethics, which is concerned exclusively with the human. This program too is pursued in later chapters of this book.

When we try to explore this alternative subject/subject road however, we soon discover that it is blocked off by a series of knowledge structures that owe their origins to the very same problem. These structures enforce a rationalist-influenced division, this time in the form of the 'two cultures' disciplinary divisions that frame the very foundations of western knowledges and which are based themselves on the very subject/object division we are trying to think our way around.[37] Development of the socially responsible and reflexive forms of knowledge that are so essential for democratic and ethical outcomes is impeded by the great split in the western episteme between the two cultures, corresponding to the split between nature (science) on the one hand and culture (philosophy and the humanities, cultural studies) on the other. It is not that the existence of multiple cultures of knowledge is itself problematic – multiple knowledge cultures can legitimately reflect different kinds of experiences and life orientations – but rather that the way the field is partitioned dualistically into the particular gender- and nature-coded forms I have identified hides from us certain hybrid possibilities and inhibits the development of certain mixed forms that are crucial for an ethically integrated science and an ecologically-integrated humanities knowledge field.

The idea that we humans are completely immersed in a self-enclosed sphere of our own we can call 'culture' while non-humans are part of a non-ethical sphere of 'nature' is the leading assumption that corresponds to and structures these disciplinary exclusions.[38] Indeed the problem can be taken to lie just as much in this concept of culture as in the concept of nature. The idea that human life takes place in a self-enclosed, completely humanised space that is somehow independent of an inessential sphere of nature which exists in a remote space 'somewhere else' is of course a major expression of culture/nature dualism. Its variant, human/nature dualism, has told us that there are totally separate narratives here with totally different casts of characters. The ecological crisis is forcing us to see that our apparent human immunity from the Heraclitean ecological narrative of nature is an illusion – that we too are positioned equally and along with the whole cast of non-humans in the drama of the ecological world of populations, species, and the flows of the food chain. The crumbling of human/nature dualism is also making us aware of our relationships with non-humans as subject to ethics as much as ecology. Both kinds of narratives must now be seen as applying to both groups; all our lives are situated in both culture and nature. We can no longer retain the comfortable human-centred illusion of separate casts of characters in separate dramas. Our disciplinary structures must reflect that knowledge.

Hyper-separation is also maintained by the same rationalist-empiricist collaboration we have analysed as lying behind the subject/object division, which has given us a corresponding hyper-separated division between the sciences and humanities. We find in the 'humanities' a form of knowledge that is subject/subject in orientation, which treats the other studied as a mindful, intentional or 'subjective' being who is the subject of a life narrative, and with whom we can experience solidarity and sympathy. This form of knowledge, however, conventionally sees its subject matter as confined to the human, and as extending to the non-human only in indirect and derivative ways. The non-human is supposed to be the sphere of the 'objective', of 'hard science' where subject/object constructions reign supreme. The ground of the 'eco-humanities' and the subject-subject sciences we wish to reclaim has been artfully disappeared by these disciplinary divisions. Thus dualistic construction frames in hyper-separated terms the familiar distinction between subjective and objective realms, the first term identifying the 'soft' areas of 'cultural studies' and the humanities, the second the allegedly 'hard' areas of the natural sciences.[39] The first is conceived as a female-coded, self-reflective, positional form of knowledge oriented to the study of the human sphere, emphasising interpretation and relativity of construction, and leaning professionally towards a culture and philosophy of idealism as opposed to realism. Its focus on social construction and humanistic knowledge appears to exclude more than a passing and indirect concern with or for non-human nature, which tends to be identified as an extension of the human or social (it can be covered in terms 'nature writing' for example, a human study). The second identifies itself as a male-coded, superior 'hard' form, devoid of emotional or positional impurities and able to give detached consideration to external objects of knowledge. The non-human as subject misses out both ways, since it can appear only indirectly in the subjectively-oriented forms and only as object in the objectively-oriented ones.

In fact in this dominant conception, these dualised epistemic forms are not only hyper-separated (as we have seen, there is in fact far more continuity between these 'hard' and 'soft' realms of knowledge than dominant modes of conceiving them admit) but distorted in other reciprocal and complementary ways, in the same way as gender codes of the masculine and feminine self are hyper-separated and reciprocally distorted in multiple ways. If the 'soft' form, coded as feminine, is supposedly locked inside subjectivity and confined to internal forms of human self-knowledge that effectively exclude a concern with non-human nature, the canons of the second form that orient it exclusively to a hard external nature ensure that it is poorly able to reflect critically on itself and its positional aspects, since it has built its contrasting identity on 'objectivity', interpreted as the irrelevance of the subject's positionality and total exclusion of emotional and caring involvement.[40]

What we have is a science that is monological, instrumental, that has been encouraged not to question its ends, and these features make it a good servant of power. What we *need* for a viable future is an integrated democratic science that is dialogical, non-reductionist and self–reflective – a science that can bring itself and its ends under critical and democratic scrutiny. We need above all an *ethical* science: sado-dispassionate science has used the ideology of disengagement to wall itself off from ethics just as effectively as capitalism has done through the ideology of the private sphere. Both 'hard' and 'soft' forms are inadequate for the purpose of integrating ethics with the attempt to gain knowledge of non-human nature. The technoscientific form is prevented from attaining self-reflective and ethically integrated knowledges, to the extent that interrogation of the knower's own affiliations or limitations of perspective is inadmissible, along with ways to address 'soft' questions of ethics and responsibility. The softer 'feminine' literary paradigm which is often counter-asserted in post-modernism is only rarely able to break out of the limitations of enclosure within a human-centred epistemic idealism and use/mention confusion which makes everything thinkable into a human construction.[41] Since each form of knowledge operates by different canons and tends to define itself against the other, integration to create an ethically responsible form of technoscience and a form of the humanities not dedicated to human-self enclosure is especially difficult. The emphasis in hard, tough and cynical forms of science on ensuring that nature does not 'fool' us leads to a stress on manipulative experimental design and the control of nature, but relatively little effort goes into considering the equally important issue of whether and how we, the knowers, might be fooling ourselves, how our knowledge frameworks and perspectives may be limited or distorted by our sado-dispassionate ethical and epistemic positioning.

As an alternative to these dominant projects of domination, we can glimpse further, as yet only partially formally articulated, care models of knowledge that open up new possibilities for responsible forms of science and that empower rather than disempower ethical and socially engaged perspectives. Breaking the hold of the subject/object division is a big help;

to begin with, we can turn to certain kinds of imaginative literature which write nature as agent, re-subjectivising and re-intentionalising the non-human as an ethical and intentional subject of narrative. This need not always be as radically intentionalising as Aldo Leopold's encounters with thinking mountains or Thoreau's with heraldry among the lichens, but it can still speak arrestingly of agency, learning, creativity and design among such 'spectacular beings'as winged dinosaurs, as in the scientific writing of Eric Rolls or the nature writing of Annie Dillard.[42] Although these blended genres do not as yet have the prestige of 'tough' science, they can help us retell the mechanistic narratives told by reductionist science in more memorable, more generous and more helpful ways. As well as imaginative science, we need corresponding narratives that can situate humans ecologically, as in the new discipline of environmental history and in the ecological humanities more generally.

We can also turn for help in envisaging a non-reductionist science and a compassionate and democratic rationality to disciplinary practices of care for the other that is studied. Anthropology is a discipline that sits astride the divide between subject/object and subject/subject orientation, and which has been challenged greatly in recent years to reconsider the subject/object model. Its highly articulate indigenous 'objects of study' have placed it under notice to move towards a subject/subject model in which knowledge is based on the consenting and cooperative disclosure of other active subjects, and which carries an ethic of care for, attention and accountability to those who are studied. In this case, those in the 'object' position speak of how and under what conditions they would wish to be studied as subjects, and in this they can be taken to speak also for others in the 'object' position and to define the conditions for an ethical and dialogical subject–subject knowledge relationship. The discipline of anthropology and its new-found ideals of respect, solidarity with and advocacy for an actively disclosing other to whom the student attends could provide a counter-framework to models of disengagement, disrespect, over-manipulation and reductionism that remain characteristic of the monological nature-oriented tradition of 'hard science' we have been tracing. The role of anthropologists employing rationalist subject-object models in the abuse of the Yanomami people of the Amazon detailed in Patrick Tierney's *Darkness in El Dorado* has been taken as a case of science illegitimately using methodologies for human subjects it should keep confined to non-human animals. Rather than being interpreted as a reason to further hyper-separate the treatment of humans from the treatment of non-humans, such cases provide an occasion to rethink the whole subject-object mode of knowledge, for both human and non-human subjects.

Realising the potential for an ethically-integrated science of care and responsibility means moving beyond the knowledge dualisms to an integrated form of knowledge which is able to escape the dualisms of subject/object, hard/soft and reason/nature. Caring rationalities are among the forms of ethical engagement made visible by a framework of scientific rationality that is socially engaged and accountable, but the term can also serve to identify an alternative model that resists the dominant sado-dispassionate rationalities. Caring rationality sees ethics and social responsibility as a crucial part of science and of the scientist's task, to be integrated at all levels, including especially that of the individual researcher. Some individual scientists may already operate wholly or partially within dialogical and care models rather than in the theoretically dominant frameworks demanding ethical and emotional disengagement and objectification, finding in the nature they study the basis for awe and environmental commitment rather than instrumentalism and an inflated sense of self.[43] Nevertheless the powerful monological models I have outlined above represent ideologies the dialogical model will have to displace in both practical and theoretical terms if it is to be re-born as a general institutional practice of science rather than remain as the unrecognised and largely disempowered personal ethical ideal of some individual knowers.

The subject/object doctrines of the disengagement of the knower and the passivity of the known not only help create the two cultures split that impedes the development of an ethical science, but are also leading assumptions behind the over-reliance on manipulative strategies for knowledge-gathering that helps to create the problem of ratiogenic damage in experimentation. Over-reliance on experimental manipulation is often supported by the contemporary institutional context in which knowledge is produced, which gives rise to unreflective adherence to legitimating formulae and professional intellectual schedules. This context for knowledge replaces the breadth of observation and experience of nature that could inspire the ideas of a Darwin and a Humboldt. In the knowledge factory situation, an emphasis on manipulative scientific study which rearranges nature according to rigid, set formulae sanctified as 'methodology' can make observation almost indistinguishable from the control of nature.

There is a strong convergence between contemporary manipulative models and the Baconian model in which nature is tricked or forced into disclosing information that is wrung from her with the destruction and travail of rearrangement. The manipulative model thus in effect assumes a passive nature and closes itself to the possibility that nature itself discloses and can be a partner in the production of knowledge.[44] In contrast, there are dialogical models of scientific discovery which treat nature as active in the production of knowledge, and articulate ethical and social engagement with respect for what is studied. When Darwin speaks of the Galapagos as 'the great laboratory of evolution', or when Humboldt speaks of rocks and pumice as speaking the history of the earth, we are encountering a practice of treating nature as active in the production of knowledge, as inviting the attentive observer to receive her disclosures.[45] The dialogical paradigm stresses instead communicative methodologies of sensitive listening and attentive observation, and of an open stance that has not already closed itself off by stereotyping the other that is studied in reductionist terms as mindless and voiceless.

Anthropocentrism and anthropomorphism

But is it not anthropomorphic and irrational, hopelessly romantic and unscientific, to talk of nature in this way, in terms of agency, communication and so on? A time-tested strategy for projects of mastery is the normalisation and enforcement of impoverishing, passifying and deadening vocabularies for what is to be reduced and ruthlessly consumed[46]. This seems to be the main contemporary function of the concept of anthropomorphism, especially to the extent that it aims to delegitimate intentional description of non-human others. As I argued in *Feminism and the Mastery of Nature*, there is no good logical reason why we should not speak of the non-human sphere in intentional and mentalistic terms, as we do constantly in everyday parlance, and would hardly be able to avoid. I will argue here that there is no good basis for the general claim that speech is invalidated by anthropomorphism merely on the ground that it attributes intentionality, subjectivity or communicativity to non-humans. And we do not have to make any major adjustment or 'stretching' of the concept of agency to count earth others and nature as agents if, for example, we understand by an agentic being 'an independent centre of value, and an originator of projects that demand my respect'.[47] So what is the problem in these ways of speaking according to the anthropomorphism charge?

We need to distinguish various senses of anthropomorphism, including general and specific senses. The general concept and charge of anthropomorphism, as Mary Midgley has argued,[48] is in its usual sense and definition thoroughly confused. It is ambiguous as between attributing to non-humans characteristics humans have, and attributing to non-humans characteristics only humans have. Both senses are problematic, in slightly different ways, when used to support the claim that the attribution of characteristics such as subjectivity to animals must be anthropomorphic. The first sense, that something is anthropomorphic if it attributes to non-humans characteristics humans have, presupposes that there is no overlap of characteristics between humans and non-humans. That is, it assumes a hyper-separation of human and animal natures and attempts to enforce upon legitimate representations of non-humans such a radical discontinuity. This sense should clearly be rejected, not only because it is based on a demonstrably false assumption of radical discontinuity, but because it can be used to delegitimate virtually any depiction of non-human subjectivity that made sense to us. The second sense of anthropomorphism – attributing to non-humans characteristics only humans have – is not open to this objection, but is open to the further objection that its use to delegitimate the attribution of subjectivity and other contested characteristics to non-humans is simply question-begging. It assumes just what is at issue, what opponents of mechanistic models contest, that non-humans do not have characteristics such as subjectivity and intentionality humans also possess.

As Midgley notes, the focus of this sense of the concept tends to be otiose and human-centred. If something is to be faulted for attributing to non-humans characteristics they do not have, it is sufficient to point out that this is an inaccurate way of representing them, and the inaccuracy itself provides (in a suitably veridical context) sufficient independent ground for rejecting such an attribution. Unless there is a good reason for addressing the question of similarity to humans, it is simply anthropocentric to go on to bring every source of comparison and focus of assessment back to humans and to the question non-human similarity or difference from them, as the concept of anthropomorphism tends to do. Beyond the confused senses of anthropomorphism I have discussed above, the features being problematised under that description can often be better characterised in terms of anthropocentrism rather than anthropomorphism (see Chapter 5). But in the same way, the charge of anthropocentrism cannot be used in a general way to delegitimate representations of non-humans as communicative subjects; charges of anthropomorphism require much more work to situate and establish as damaging than is usually accorded them.

The critic of representing animals in intentional or communicative terms often draws on another sense of anthropomorphism, which we might call weak anthropomorphism,[49] that makes it very hard or impossible for representations of non-humans to avoid being assigned the label anthropomorphism. In this weak sense the fault of anthropomorphism is located in the presentation of non-human communication 'in human terms', from a human conceptual location. Any representation of speech-content for a human audience will have to be an interpretation in terms of human concepts, and in that weak sense, a background level of anthropomorphism is always likely to be present. What is much more difficult to demonstrate is that anthropomorphism of this background kind, in the weak sense of employing a human conceptual apparatus or conceptual location, is necessarily harmful or invalidating, or that there are no practices which can counter it. The question is not whether or not some degree of humanisation of perspective is present in any particular human representation of non-human agency or communication, for it always will be at the background level, but how damaging it is, what is its meaning, and what practices could be used to counter it if and where it needs to be countered?

Where the charge of anthropomorphism can lead to the application of more stringent standards to the representation of non-human communication than are used to judge the success of comparable human representation, it is itself liable to the counter-charge that it is anthropocentric. Arguments of this kind are often advanced to show that any representation of non-human communication is rendered illegitimately anthropomorphic because of problems of translation and indeterminacy, although similar problems are familiar in the representation of human cultural difference. There are parallel difficulties for both cross-cultural and cross-species representation: a weak cross-cultural analogue to background anthropomorphism is involved in virtually any translation project, for example, and in any attempt to 'bring over' one culture's forms into another's. To avoid delegitimating all such attempts, we would need to distinguish the impact of weaker and stronger forms of anthropomorphism, just as we need to distinguish weak and usually harmless forms of anthropocentrism from strong and damaging forms (see Chapters 5–6). Weak forms are unavoidable but not necessarily harmful, while strong forms may be damaging but are by no means inevitable. As with anthropocentrism, the confusion between the two forms gives rise to the illusion that damaging forms are inevitable.

A further problem with this translation argument is that, although it looks as if this sense appeals to a concept of anthropomorphism different from the objectionable general one, it is in danger of degenerating into a similarly weak and general form. To bring this out, we need to ask, what is the contrast class? What mode of representing, animal subjectivity or communication, beyond its bare recording without any attempt to convey a meaning or place in, say, an animal's life (as in commentary-free films of wolves howling or whales making sounds), would not be subject to this kind of objection? Any representation for a human audience will have to be, in some sense, an interpretation in human terms, just as any representation of a non-European culture's speech for a European audience would have to be in European terms, in the sense that it will have to try to locate the meaning of the speech in terms of the closest equivalent forms of life. The problem we run into here is the problem familiar from the case of representing human cultural difference, of translation and indeterminacy.[50] There are many well-known traps and difficulties in such representation and in establishing or assuming equivalence in forms of life. There can be real problems in representing other species' communicative powers or subjectivities in terms of human speech, but they do not rule out such representation in any automatic way.

A commonplace motivation for raising the charge of anthropomorphism is a rationalist-Cartesian policing of human–animal discontinuity, to maintain the human observer's distance from and indifference to the animal observed. Biologist Marian Stamp Dawkins[51] argues, against the reductionist view that there is no way humans can come to know non-human experience, that we can use the same method for non-human experience that we use in the human case, namely entering into the 'same-but-different' world of another similar but differently-situated individual. In general though, what is required here, as for the case of crossing anthropocentric boundaries I discuss in Chapter 5, is a double movement that seeks to understand both similarity and difference 'in dynamic tension'[52]. Although there is in response to the dominant Cartesian-rationalist stress on discontinuity often a need to provide a counterstress on continuity between the human and animal, there may still be a point in more specific and limited senses and charges of anthropomorphism. The question of anthropomorphism can often be raised with some greater validity in the context of the denial of difference which is a key part of structures of subordination and colonisation to which animals are subject. The charge of anthropomorphism may then legitimately draw our attention to a loss of sensitivity to and respect for animal difference in humanising representation.

A more valid concept of anthropomorphism we might appeal to here would treat it as analogous to, say, certain ways of criticising eurocentrism which would object to representing the non-European other in terms of a European norm. This sense would enable an argument that the mode of representation adopted in particular, specific cases denied or did not respect the difference of animals and represented them in terms of a human model. This is certainly possible, and indeed often happens. When a monkey is dressed in human clothes, made to ride a circus bicycle and ridiculed as a degenerate form of the human, when in the same representation the animal's own differences and excellences are denied or neglected, we clearly have a highly objectionable form of anthropomorphism, which is also likely a form of anthropocentrism. Notice though that this kind of patronising and difference-denying anthropomorphism is by no means inevitable in the representation of non-humans in intentional terms, and that it expresses a colonising dynamic. The concern about lack of respect for non-human difference can validly extend to cover even well-meaning animal rights attempts to assimilate animals within the model of the person, in contexts where there has been no associated attempt to deconstruct the person/property dualism formative of liberalism.

As in the case of the human other, so in the animal case such representations must always raise questions about simplifying and assimilating the other. However there can be no general argument that such cross-cultural perspectives presenting another's viewpoint are deceptive or illegitimate. Cross-species representation, like cross-cultural representation, is not automatically colonising or self-imposing, and may express motives and meanings of sympathy, support and admiration. Rather, specific cases have to be argued on their merits, not just in terms of the alleged intrusion of non-indigenous or human impurities, but in terms of the kinds of insights they present or prevent and the moral quality of their representation. We need to put into place here practices which can counter colonising tendencies in these contexts. For example, representation should keep in mind the distinction between claiming to *be* the other rather than to represent an other's perspective, to see or speak *as* the other rather than to see or speak *with* or in support of the other.[53] In the case of translation and indeterminacy, counter-practices could require an effort to note non-equivalences in forms of life and to treat difficulties about translation as sources of uncertainty and tentativeness. Using the problems of such an approach as a model, we might expect an appropriate methodology for dealing with cross-species conceptual difference and translation indeterminacy to be one which stressed corrigibility and open expectations. Dealing with both human and non-human cases of translation indeterminacy requires openness to the other and careful, sensitive, and self-critical observation which actively seeks to uncover perspectival and centric biases.

A related argument would be that, although non-humans do have intentionality, subjectivity and communication, the representation of that communication in the terms of human speech is always invalidly anthropomorphic, depicted in excessively human terms. This however seems to demand perfection and to be over-general, and we could appeal to the parallel phenomenon of cross-cultural translation to argue that not all translation efforts are doomed. Miscommunication and assimilationism is not the inevitable outcome, although there are as in the human case better and worse translation attempts. There are weaker and stronger senses here again: an unwarrantedly eurocentric depiction of another culture's customs and speech would fail to note these difficulties as sources of uncertainty or tentativeness. An appropriate and modest way to deal with indeterminacy in non-human as well as human cultural contexts would be to note uncertainties and present alternative interpretations of problematic cases. The problems of representing another culture's or another species communication however pale before the enormity of failing to represent them at all, or of representing them as non-communicative and non-intentional beings. This is an incomparably greater failing.

Beyond these specific contexts, the charge of anthropomorphism is a pseudo-scientific, rationalist convention which tries to reinforce human/ nature dualism through an enforced conformity to hyper-separated vocabularies. This dualism of speech complements the dualism of nature and culture in hegemonic concepts of autonomy, rationality, and property. If our dominant concepts of technoscience and economic rationality are ones that treat nature as a nullity, it is small wonder that the outcome of their enormous growth and progress as a force for remaking the earth is a progressive nullification and decline of nature. It is well past time we abandoned the sado-dispassionate scepticism about animal minds and the anthropocentric Cartesian double standards that insist that the mindfulness we can airily assume for humans must be rigorously 'proved' for non-humans (a task that can easily be made impossible to succeed in by a variety of strategems of exclusion).There is no reason to identify this kind of scepticism with rationality. A more generous methodology or stance that is fully within our rational powers opens the space for fuller kinds of recognition and possibilities for relationship with the more-than-human world which sceptics dismiss as impossible or irrational. In the present context of ecological destruction, where we desperately need ways to increase our sensitivity to and communicativity with the others of the earth, should we insist on retaining monological methodologies and sophistries like the myth of anthropomorphism that were designed to facilitate exploitation? Should we, in the context where we have the possibility of developing a more generous narrative and dialogical form of rationality that allows more sensitivity to the other, bend and strain our reasoning faculties to keep our options confined to the old reductive models? If this sado-dispassionate stance is rationality, it is a form not well adapted to its own or to our survival.

3   The politics of ecological rationality

The rationality of the EcoRepublic

Let us imagine a future ecological and global version of Plato's great rationalist utopia, the EcoRepublic. A global scientist military leader, notable for his rationality and brilliant scientific knowledge, establishes an order of EcoGuardians in order to generate a global bureaucratic-military class or caste of dispassionate, hyper-rational scientific decision-makers. Their skills in ecological decision-making, like those of Roman consuls, are employed in the various national provinces, coordinating across world society to deal with the massive ecological problems a global capitalist economy has fathered on an injured and captive nature. The revolutionary leader chooses the initial group of EcoGuardians, who go on to clone themselves and train their replacements from infancy in every field of relevant knowledge, to become finally members of their order of Reason and representatives of the Empire, that of the Men of Reason over mere things.[1] The corporation they represent becomes supreme in the business of the planet. The EcoGuardians avoid mixing with the rest of the population, so as not to let attachment compromise their judgement, which often has to be harsh and punitive. They take a pledge to lead austere and Spartan lives, and always to put species survival and planetary health before every human desire.

We can further imagine that the EcoRepublic has come into existence because a working party of corporate scientists and economists in 2099, faced with a severe global ecological crisis, has identified the conditions of *compliance* and *flexibility* as the two major political requirements needed to enable the human race to make the necessary sacrifices to survive into the next millennium. Scientific reason must now be left to save the earth, since market democracy has failed, and in the EcoRepublic scientific reason is in charge – perfect, objective, uncontaminated by ridiculous prejudices and emotions, and constantly improving itself. Rational rulers demand a compliant world community, and lots of flexibility for dealing with environmental problems. They will require maximum freedom and speed, without cumbersome constituency or time-consuming debate. A top-down, military style decision-making chain will be maximally flexible, allowing lightning changes in policy and direction to be sent down from the hyper-rational Scientist Commander and his team. In the perfectly ecorationalist society this thinking gives rise to, the EcoGuardians, a quasimilitary as well as scientific order, acquire total power to force compliance from the global population with the rules and quotas the EcoGuardians specify for every human community on earth.

An improvement in the world's ecological problems is duly reported, but the basis for the report is mainly the area around the order's headquarters where most EcoGuardians live when they are not on provincial tours of duty. The improvements come at a horrendous price in human lives (by now very little non-human life remains). Many people hate the order for its policies of random hostage taking and extermination of citizens from nations which do not meet their standards, the number executed being in exact rational proportion to their nation's degree of offence. Initially, the EcoGuardians stick to their mission of global coordination and enforcing the global population's compliance with their leader's ecorational edicts. But over time, ecological and human problems proliferate in what remains of the global market economy, and the badly degraded places increasingly join up to make large decaying patches on the face of the planet occupied by diseased, forgotten people. The EcoGuardians increasingly turn inwards and confine themselves to their own scientifically protected planetary places. They themselves are well taken care of, and they lead such remote lives they don't seem to know or care about what is happening outside their Biospheres, the elite enclaves they have designed where they spend their time working on aging research.

Back in the badlands, most people know things have gone badly wrong, but are too disabled by their situation, their material, educative and spiritual deprivation, and by the demands of the EcoGuardians, to do anything about the situation. Nevertheless, badlanders have some ideas about what might be done. Decision-making and its competences has been monopolised by the remote elite of EcoGuardians, who have sorted things out so that 'Complaining' carries a long prison term, and questioning an Ecoguardian's orders is punishable by death. Despite this, a few badlanders try to get their knowledges and ideas through to the decision-makers. If their society's formal structures are so monological and authoritarian that the arteries of communication and change from below are thoroughly blocked, they will have little chance of survival, unless they can oust the oligarchy and become their own decision-makers.

The scientific oligarchy of the EcoRepublic is an extreme and imaginary case, but the poor correctiveness and failure of ecological reflexivity and responsiveness to ecological deterioration it displays are something it increasingly shares with actual contemporary forms of global capitalist society. Indonesian environmental analyst George Aditjondro relates some of the effects of an 'intra-ASEAN oligarchy' on his region's environment.[2] In South-East Asia and especially Indonesia, forest fires destroy huge and growing areas of rainforest and agricultural land in Sumatra and Kalimantan on an almost annual basis, with enormous environmental impacts. Fires together with logging destroy habitat for the critically endangered Orang-utan and devastate forests which are among the richest in the world for species diversity. From the fires alone, the smoke and haze, which last for up to 3 months, cause acute human ailments, and the majority of those who suffer are rural poor. In addition there is loss of forest-derived food and income, accelerated soil erosion, sedimentation of waterways, and major contributions to ozone, acid rain, and greenhouse gases. Every year the smoke and haze disrupt tourism, transport and business not only in Indonesia itself but in Singapore and the Malaysian Peninsula. The economic losses from the fires within Indonesia are very great, estimated to be equivalent to 2 per cent of annual GDP. Yet burnt land is released by the Indonesian government for palm oil plantations, and there is a low level of governmental action and concern about them in the region. Why? According to Aditjondro, 'The answer to the question lies in the fact that the most dominant driving force in the recurrent fires is the palm oil industry in Indonesia, which involves the main business conglomerates in Indonesia partly or wholly owned by members of the Suharto family, with a growing number of Malaysian joint venture partners. ... These vested interests in the two neighbouring countries are further reinforced by various region-wide joint ventures and investment houses'.[3]

We can see several features in common between the imaginary eco-authoritarian and the real Indonesian case, although one represents scientific-administrative and the other 'unfettered' market rationality. Both systems are monological, having very poor feedback at key points and very poor correctiveness from other social spheres, which they have weakened to the point of silence, hence very few self-reflective and self-critical resources. Because it gives scientists a free hand, the initial Eco-Republic scenario represents a social structure not unlike that proposed by ecological oligarchs such as Garret Hardin and William Ophuls, and secretly dreamed of by many scientists.[4] The EcoRepublic's privileging of groups seen as pre-eminent in rationality may be a dream of rationalism, but we can nevertheless imagine this society dying of a kind of rationalist arteriosclerosis.[5] Institutions that encourage and express self-critical rationality are poorly developed in the EcoRepublic, which could reflect its generation from the least self-critical forms of current knowledge, dominant economics and establishment science. As Beck, Giddens and Lash (1994) suggest, self-critical rationality, institutions and dispositions of knowledge are necessary conditions for dealing with ecological crises. Much is required in the way of critical feedback, including institutions which encourage speech from below and deep forms of democracy where communicativeness and redistributive equality are found across a range of social spheres.

The EcoRepublic illustrates what can happen when crucial reflexive and communicative feedback is undeveloped, disabled, or discounted. In a highly centralised society like the EcoRepublic it would be relatively easy to lose ecological correctiveness, since this is not linked across social spheres to other forms of social correctiveness, for example to justice. Failure could be the consequence of the isolation of a ruling elite together with the silencing and disabling of other human groups who have key roles in providing ecological communication. It could result from communicative failure, or from the failure of decision-makers' motivation, even in the presence of good information networks, to use their power to maintain ecological relationships. We may imagine that, for the EcoRepublic, privilege and remoteness progressively erode the political and scientific elite's capacity to hear and to care about what is happening to degraded natural communities or their human inhabitants. In the forest fires case too, other potentially corrective and communicative systems, such as democracy and administrative rationality, have been co-opted, disabled, suppressed, or left undeveloped. The poor, who suffer the main ill-effects from the fires, have virtually no voice, while those who benefit from them and are remote from their ill-effects, cushioned by their privilege, have great influence. Another potentially critical and corrective system, complaints from a neighbouring state that was badly affected by smoke haze, has been cleverly disabled by drawing its political elite into the small but powerful and privileged group of corporate beneficiaries.

The politics of rationality

The forest fire case is one of those tragic but entrenched and seemingly unstoppable processes we see so often around us, which justify fears for the future of the planet. In this case, oligarchical economic rationality walks all over the other social spheres, which are far too weak to even articulate any opposition.[6] Can we identify a prime mover in this case? This question calls up a large area of ideological contest. Economic liberals or rationalists might say that the rationality of the global market has not penetrated deeply enough as the dominant discipline for this society. Marxists would say the driver is the economic system of capitalism, anarchists basically blame the state and its coercive forces, and some radical feminists would invoke patriarchy. Each of these postures is developed along competing reductionist lines, so that either the state or the economy or masculinity is the fundamental source that explains all. As a reduction, each angle is limiting; the economic reductionist approach, in addition to aping the dominant mentality of economic rationalism that puts the economy always first, obscures not only relative independence but also collaborations and conflicts between different spheres of rationality, in which rationalist distortions are expressed in diverse ways that create a complex and reinforcing structure. We have already seen collaboration between such distinct rationalities in the different strategies for excluding ethics by economic rationality (through the private sphere) and science (through the ideology of disengagement).

Other reductions are afoot however; thus Alan Carter gives us a 'State Primacy' thesis, as a counter-reductionism to that of Marxism. He seems to have a point in the forest fire case, since the dominant economic players rose to their positions of market power through their command of authoritarian military hierarchies which eliminated competition and suppressed potentially corrective social forces. They remain highly influential after losing state power through their continuing command of market power. It is not only economic forces and corporations that have an interest in prioritising the economic and maximising economic outputs, as Carter points out, but also state, military and techno-bureaucratic forces.[7] But this argument really only supports some measure of relative independence, that the state is a 'major player', not a thesis of primacy of the state. A refutation of economic reductionism does not show that some other form of reductionism should take its place. However, states should be recognised as both relatively independent and internally diverse, and as capable of generating through their own productivist maximisations and dynamics of power similar decision-making distortions to those I discuss below.

Economic rationality in liberalism is, notoriously, identified with individual self-interest, and further identified in economic rationalism with maximising outcomes for market players. Yet these are extremely limited kinds of rationality that are immensely problematic if applied in wider contexts, and often even in their own contexts. For example, if we consider the forest fires case, it seems plain that the interests of a very few are served, and that of vastly more (and more worthy) others are attacked. Should we, because the few have market power and the many do not, dignify the conflagration of values the fires represent with the exalted name of 'rationality'? Surely not. Similarly, it is in the interests of techno-bureaucratic forms of interest and power to find and employ the most efficient means to a specified set of ends. This is 'instrumental rationality' in the sense of Weber, but it does not in the least follow, as Marcuse pointed out, that these ends themselves are rational. They may be insane.

I believe we should reject the current usage that invariably relativises the term 'rationality' and gives it over to the maximising of self-interest, and especially to the pursuit of a crude and narrow interpretation of it as maximising monetary values. To designate the forces that set the forest fires as 'rational' has first, the effect of endorsing and naturalising the limitation of the interests to be considered to those who possess market power – surely an indefensible and highly politically charged limitation of vision. Second, it endorses limiting the interests to be considered to a supposedly isolable individual set in a world of interconnection and relationship where no such isolability can be found. Both political systems I have described, the imagined and the real, have the numerical and expert trappings of rationality, yet neither produces rational outcomes from the perspective of all those affected by them, nor by the standards of more defensible concepts and projects of rationality that situate us as embedded and embodied beings.

Such a more defensible concept gives rationality the meaning of living as a coherent and minimally conflicted being, with desires enough in harmony with what can be hoped and wished for, and a life in which action can satisfy enough of them, having regard to the kind of beings we are. Rationality can thus be a satisficing rather than a maximising concept,[8] and one that has regard to the wholeness, cohesion and survival projects of an organism. This quasi-Aristotelean concept makes rationality a matter of balance, harmony, or reconcilability among an organism's identities, faculties and ends, a harmony that has regard to the kind of being it is. Since we are embodied and ecological beings, our life rationality must involve some kind of compatibility with the biological systems that support our lives. By these standards of organismic or life rationality the sort of system that can encourage the forest fires is a travesty of rationality.

Several writers, especially John Dryzek (1987) have elaborated a useful related concept of ecological rationality, initially defined as 'the capacity of a system to maintain or increase the life supporting capability of ecosystems consistently'.[9] In the context of the sorts of capacities for ecological damage now available to most human cultures, self-reflective and organised social capacities to correct human-induced ecological deterioration are required for human ecological survival. For modernist societies capable of very major and rapid ecological impacts, to lack adequate ecological correctiveness is like having a vehicle which is capable of going very fast but has a faulty or poorly developed brake and steering system. In the case of an organism, we could expect a similar imbalance between functions to lead to rapid death or extinction. For these high-impact contexts, it is tempting to define ecological rationality in more active terms than Bartlett's, as the capacity to correct tendencies to damage or reduce life-support systems. An ecologically rational society would be sustainable to the extent that its corrective capacities enable it to make consistently good ecological decisions that maintain viable ecological relationships and coordinate them with its social organisation.

Ecological rationality under this conception draws on both organismic rationality and critical rationality. It has a use for critical rationality operating across a range of human spheres to critically relate social and individual goals to the ecological communities in which human societies are embedded. The EcoRepublic demonstrates a failure of ecological rationality through the more general failure of critical rationality in the social and epistemological spheres. The EcoGuardians believe that their rational knowledge must save the world, and pour resources into knowledge, but resist adequate development of its self-critical functions. One reason for this failure might be that the EcoGuardians are unable to recognise their own knowledge as politically situated knowledge, hence fail to recognise the need to make it socially inclusive, sensitive to its limitations, and actively engaged with its boundaries and exclusions.[10] Relying on claims to objectivity to create a hegemonic 'we' whose truth claims dominion over all others, the EcoGuardians construct a form of knowledge that it is insensitive in the very area in which the main ecological threats tend to present themselves, the area given news of by marginal voices, in speech from below.

How does ecological rationality relate to rationalism and to other forms of rationality? As there are different forms of rationality, so there are different failures of rationality. Ecological rationality includes that higher-order form of critical, prudential,[11] self-critical reason which scrutinises the match or fit between an agent's choices, actions and effects and that agent's overall desires, interests and objectives as they require certain ecological conditions for their fulfilment. Initially such an inquiry might aim at developing a balance between ecologically destructive capacities and corrective capacities, although a more sensible and ambitious objective would aim at phasing out destructive capacities and evolving a sympathetic partnership or communicative relationship with nature. A civilisation which lacks or underdevelops ecological rationality, which sets in motion massive processes of biospheric and ecological degradation which it cannot respond to or correct, does not match its actions to the survival aims it may be assumed to have. Unless it has for good reasons chosen a path of self-extinction, its actions display a rationality failure in the ecological area in the same way that the actions of someone in the grip of a terminal addiction may be thought of as displaying a rationality failure, as contrary to their overall wishes and well-being.

Among the questions raised here under the rubric of rationality are those of the match between means and ends, the organisation and consistency of ends, whether some ends presuppose others, and whether subsidiary ends are overwhelming major ones, for example. In these terms there is a strong case for conceding a certain kind of priority (which I shall call basic priority) to ecological rationality; ecological rationality is a higher court, which sits in judgement on the behaviour of lower courts. This is because a certain level of ecological health, like individual health, is ultimately an essential precondition for most other projects. But also like individual health, ecological rationality does not have to be expressed in a single specific form, but can be realised in relation to various projects and in terms of many different possible healthily-organised lives. Conceding this kind of priority to ecological rationality is not however to assume any form of ecological reductionism, nor is it to assume a Malthusian approach giving automatic privilege to ecological factors in explanation and discounting or occluding social ones. Indeed I shall be arguing in the next chapter for a strong link between ecological rationality and social equality.

We had better not try to understand ecological rationality or, as I shall show, any of its main supporting concepts, in a rationalist way that links it to the doctrine of the separateness and supremacy of reason in human life. As the example of the EcoRepublic illustrates, ecological rationality is in opposition to the elevation of reason to Promethean status[12] and its election as the ultimate value. A concept of ecological rationality can resist rationalist leanings, for example by rejecting dualistic understandings of humanity and nature, and rejecting any assumption that rationality has some monopoly of the capacities we need to mobilise for survival. Ecological rationality critiques those rationalist and dualistic forms of reason that deny the social and ecological ground which supports our lives, and are unable to acknowledge their own insufficiency or the material and ecological conditions of their own production or continuation. If, as I have argued in *Feminism and the Mastery of Nature*, these over-elevated and dependency-denying forms of rationality can be traced to the historical alignment of dominant forms of reason with elite social formations, ecological reason as a new and more fully self-critical form of reason must forge different political alliances.[13] Ecological rationality brings into question ordinary forms of rationality.

In these terms we can see the ecological crises of limits pressing us on multiple fronts – the oceans, the atmosphere, the forests, biodiversity loss, pollution and human health – as indicators of rationality failures that bring up for question our dominant systems of knowledge and decision-making. The situation of the forests and fisheries raises many questions about ecological rationality. Questions of ecological rationality emerge when, despite what we think of as sophisticated systems of ecology, information, and observation, few ecological limits are anticipated sufficiently far in advance to avoid damage from human over-exploitation. The ecological rationality of knowledge development is at issue when despite major existing levels of damage, more resources are poured into developing further exploitative capacities while corrective capacities remain seriously underdeveloped or are curtailed. Ecological rationality raises questions about scientific rationality in the situation where dominant forms of science have tended systematically to underestimate the seriousness and imminence of limit problems, and to overestimate the resilience of the ecological systems in which we are embedded. In the sphere of global politics, the failures of the Earth Summits and climate change conventions raise disturbing questions about the ecological rationality of our present systems of national and global governance and their ability to stem escalating processes of ecological injury or to match constraining to destructive capacities.

As a resting point for explanation, the concept of ecological rationality would have dubious strategic value. The tensions the concept flags rather invite further questions, especially about what kinds of societies would consistently make good ecological decisions.[14] As we increasingly press ecological limits, these are perhaps the most important questions of our time. As John Dryzek's work shows, criteria of ecological rationality provide much political discriminatory power, which can help us critique the ecological irrationality of the EcoRepublic and the system that produces the forest fires. It is clear that authoritarian political systems, especially the military systems organised around protecting privilege which still control so much of the planet, provide very few means or motivations for correctiveness and ecological feedback, especially those important kinds which come from below and register advanced ecological and social damage. This remains so where such systems are combined with the global market, which also provides a poor mechanism for registering such damage. Both political argument[15] and general observation make a case for ruling out military and oligarchical systems as possible routes to solving environmental problems, contrary to the arguments of the authoritarian school of environmental thinkers who pin their hopes on ecological and scientific oligarchy. But as we will see, the concept also has much to tell us about the 'normal' democratic systems of the developed, rationalised world and about alternative small-scale ideals.

Remoteness and decision

If the oligarchical structure of the EcoRepublic is said to be flexible, clearly care is needed in defining flexibility here: in the EcoRepublic, as increasingly in contemporary concepts of work flexibility[16], the concept of flexibility is misleadingly one-way, going down but not up.[17] And even if we grant regimes of ecological oligarchy possession of both flexibility and powerful *means* to enforce compliance with environmental regulation[18], what is unexplained is how they can develop or maintain the political conditions for knowledge[19] or communication of this damage or for guaranteeing the rulers' *motivation* to use these powerful means for the purpose of protecting nature or ecological relationships. A major reason why the EcoGuardian structure is unsatisfactory for ecological decision-making is that their position as a privileged elite can give them a high level of remoteness from the consequences of their decisions, since the EcoGuardians themselves may be able to use their privilege to ensure they can escape many of the effects of ecological damage, and they have poor communicative and other motivating links to others who are affected. We can see the same remoteness at work in the forest fires case and in many other cases where remote corporate or governmental elites make decisions they do not have to live with. In centric oligarchical and authoritarian regimes especially there is a fatal lack of ecological correctiveness in part because the quality of decision-making suffers from forms of remoteness which dissociate decision-makers very strongly from consequent ecological damage and which can distort decision-makers' knowledge of and motivation to correct that damage.

Remoteness allows a high level of dissociation between costs and benefits, between elite consumption benefits and ecological damage. For example, those who benefits from consumer items from the forests can make themselves remote from the soil erosion, loss of life opportunities and increases in malarial disease and adverse health impacts of forest burning that afflict local forest dwellers and resource suppliers, often treated almost as badly as the 'resource' itself. Because it allows such high levels of dissociation between production and consumption, remoteness can greatly distort decision chains. If the beneficiaries are consumers in the global market, politically powerful in comparison to the local suppliers who bear most of the negative consequences, the ecological and social costs of production may not register at all in comparison to the benefits, in any significant political or economic measure. At a minimum and in contrast to the extraordinary dissociation of the global marketplace, an ecologically rational economic system would create careful links and networks between production and consumption that would enable meaningful processes of learning and responsibility to take place. Anything less is ecologically irrational, indeed suicidal.

Dryzek (1987, 1996) argues that an ecologically rational polity should meet various conditions which he believes point towards discursive democracy. It should be robust (capable of performing in different conditions), flexible (capable of adjusting to new situations), resilient (capable of correcting severe disequilibrium), and allow negative feedback ('react against human-induced shortfalls in life support capability'), coordinate responses and actions across different circumstances and boundaries, and match the scale of decision-making systems to the scale of ecological problems. The EcoRepublic may fail on all these counts, but it fails perhaps most significantly in another important axis with major implications for democratic and ecological polities – remoteness. Remoteness reduction is a good decision-making principle, because remoteness disturbs feedback and disrupts connections and balances between decisions and their consequences that are important for learning and for maintaining motivation, responsibility and correctiveness. I will argue that Dryzek's conditions can usefully be supplemented by a further range of considerations about the effect of remoteness on the correctiveness of ecological decision-making and explore some of their implications for liberal democracy. A remoteness principle of ecological rationality is that, other things being equal, an ecologically rational form of agency would minimise the remoteness of agents from the ecological consequences of their decisions (actions).[20] The principle aims to provide agents with the maximum motivation to reach responsible ecological decisions, to correct bad ecological decisions, and to minimise the possibilities for ecojustice violations which systematically redistribute rather than eliminate adverse ecological consequences.

The most obvious way of avoiding the ecological consequences of your decisions is living somewhere remote from the places and people they affect, *spatial remoteness*. But the sort of conditions that can distance a decision-maker from consequences is much more than just spatial remoteness, which is just one of the distortions that can make decision chains ecologically irresponsible and irrational. If we generalise bioregionalists' insights about decision-makers bearing consequences, we can see other relevant kinds of remoteness. They include *consequential remoteness* (where the consequences fall systematically on some other person or group leaving the originator unaffected), *communicative* and *epistemic remoteness* (where there is poor or blocked communication with those affected which weakens knowledge and motivation about ecological relationships), and *temporal remoteness* (being remote from the effect of decisions on the future). The air conditioner is a prize piece of *technological remoteness*, generating thermal well-being in places of prominence and privilege by generating thermal and other ills it takes no responsibility for in remote or disregarded 'waste' places conceived as 'externality', including the biosphere.

An understanding of the effect of remoteness may hold the key to making ecological rationality compatible with democracy and avoiding authoritarian or highly centralised approaches to securing sustainability. There is a convergence between minimising remoteness in a decision-making system and maximising democracy in Mill and Dewey's sense that those who bear consequences in a democratic system must have a proportionate share in the relevant decision-making.[21] The close connection between remoteness and bad decision-making means that the sharing of consequences and risks, especially in the ecological case, is an important criterion for determining political and decision procedures, communities and boundaries. The concept of remoteness also provides a way to focus on the kinds of political patterns that make some places better at the price of making other more distant places ecologically worse. Remoteness covers not only those direct consequential forms in which those who make decisions are enabled to avoid their adverse ecological consequences, but also communicative and epistemological forms of remoteness, in which they are remote from news or knowledge of these consequences. This kind of remoteness can involve communicative barriers or compartmentalisation both between decision-makers and damage to non-human nature, and also between decision-makers and those human beings associated with damaged nature. Remoteness principles thus confirm what the ecological behaviour of stratified and authoritarian systems also suggests, that an ecologically rational society cannot be found where the kinds of political structures and culture necessary for human justice and communicativeness are also lacking. The same point applies to nature itself. As Hayward observes 'only in a culture where humans are accustomed to listen to one another will there be any real prospect of heeding nature's protestations too'.[22]

The link between a society's incapacity to heed speech –warning or distress signals –from below in human society and ecological warning signals from non-human nature is especially significant in those cultural nodes of global capitalism whose culture is rationalist in flavour, drawn by a deep and strong-flowing historical current associating devalued humans and devalued forms or spheres of non-human nature. Global market-based distributive systems augment these cultural systems in making a close association between vulnerable and abused places and vulnerable and abused people. Remoteness is a decision-making feature which links ecojustice and ecological rationality, prudence and ethics. The concepts of ecojustice and remoteness point to cyclical, positive feedback processes which enable the transfer of inequalities and harms from the social to the ecological sphere and back again, in much the same way that inegalitarian societies foster the transfer of harms across social spheres.[23] When the remoteness from ecological harms of privileged groups most influential in decision-making systems meets a parallel silencing in the same decision-making systems of those most vulnerable to ecological harms, the social stage is set for major failures of ecological rationality. Remoteness has major implications for ecologically rational social structure. I will argue that remoteness is a rationality feature preventing contemporary liberal-capitalist societies, apparently the most promising candidates for ecologically rational societies, from dealing effectively with ecological problems. But first, I will look at the identification of remoteness with spatial remoteness characteristics of bioregionalism.

Remoteness, autarchy and spatial scale

It is the bioregionalists principally who have argued that small-scale communities that are designed specifically around recognition of their ecological relationships can best counter the adverse contemporary effects of remoteness on correctiveness and ecological decision-making.[24] In these types of communities, bioregionalists think, ecological relationships will be more clearly visible. People who are less epistemically remote from these relationships will be more sensitive both to signals from nature and to the ecological harm done by their consumption and production decisions. Second, in bioregional communities, decision-makers will not be remote from decisions made about distant places and other peoples' lives, as centralised decision-making must be. Instead, when participatory decisions are made in a local community, decision-makers have to live with the ecological consequences of their decisions, including the ecological effects on themselves, their community, neighbours and direct descendents. And third, because democracy can only be truly participatory at the level of the small, face-to-face community, people will be in a position to have the knowledge and motivation as well as the democratic and communicative means to make good ecological decisions, decisions that reflect their own extended long-term and familiar interests as well as those of their local ecologically-defined communities. Indeed under such conditions these apparently divergent interests can be thought of as convergent and harmonious, if not identical. The democratic participation that societies on a human scale supposedly make possible would guarantee maximum feedback and correctiveness, exactly what is missing in the EcoRepublic and its real-life market counterpart.

Although the appeal of bioregionalism is often put down to nostalgia for the past, the remoteness conditions suggested by bioregionalism indicate a search for ways to maximise relevant ecological feedback and obtain the best conditions for ecologically benign decisions. The conditions that decision-makers should live in ways that make transparent the relevance to their own lives of the ecological relationships of their communities, and that they are minimally consequentially and epistemically remote from the ecological consequences of their consumption and production decisions, conduce to decision-making based on maximum relevant knowledge and motivation. Decision-makers who have little or no opportunity for remoteness from the ecological consequences of their decisions should, other things being equal, be well motivated to make decisions that are ecologically benign. 'An obvious way of preventing pollution of rivers from riverside factories would be to force the management of the factory to drink downstream water', writes Johan Galtung .... [Let] those who have made the beds have an obligation to lie on them' (Galtung 1986: 101).

Thus bioregionalists have succeeded in identifying an important dimension of ecological rationality that is concerned with different kinds of remoteness. The ill-effects of remoteness on decision-making suggests decision-making communities should be defined to a major extent by shared consequences and risks, especially shared ecological consequences. In the first instance, this clearly indicates an enhanced role for local communities. Local and regional communities have been disempowered and marginalised, especially as economic communities, first by centralising processes of nation state formation and subsequently by globalisation, and beyond that again by the high status rationalism has accorded the abstract, universal, urban and disembodied sphere it identifies with reason over the immediate, embodied, and sensory aspects of life associated with local and particular knowledges and ways of working. Work by Stephen Marglin and Frederique Apfel Marglin has shown how such rationalist mind/body, mental/manual, local/universal, theoretical/practical, knowledge/labour splits in the west have encouraged consequential remoteness by disconnecting theory and practice. These splits given us correspondingly fragmented lives, but ones that are more easily controlled by rationalist forms of power.[25] Spiritual remoteness that reinforces these splits has been a major feature of rationalist religions, as I discuss in Chapter 10. Relationships to places of belonging are an important part of a good ecologically-situated life. The cultural, including the economic, recovery of the local dimension is an essential part of recovering the more rounded and integrated sense both of self and of place that must go into good ecological decision-making.

Nevertheless it is a mistake to identify the problem too closely with spatial rather than consequential remoteness, and to identify the remedies too closely with autarchy and smallness of scale.[26] The problem of remoteness is grasped too narrowly if we think of it only as a matter of 'power-out-of-place, having roots in no place nor allegiance to any people' (Plant 1992: 4). The contemporary rootless, unplaced form of global power is highly damaging, but its 'placed' predecessor, the colonial form of power which makes all the earth's places subsidiaries to and resources for a few 'civilised' central places, is damaging too. True, having hypothetically got people 'back in place', the autarchic bioregionalist usually proposes a participatory political structure which will empower people from that place, who are assumed then to bear their own consequences,[27] a structure that at least does not silence and disempower the consequence bearers. The addition of political power is supposed to connect absence of spatial to absence of consequential remoteness. It is essential to add some extra ingredient like this to any simple autarchy formula since it is crystal clear from everyday observation that spatial smallness of a community operating within existing economic structures is not sufficient to prevent serious ecological damage. It is important to consider the full range of options relating to size because there is a huge gap between the ideal ecological consciousness attributed by bioregionalists to autarchic communities and the actual consciousness and behaviour of the small-scale communities we can see around us. Those communities that do not meet their consumption from their own production – the normal ones we encounter these days – may even be more than usually desperate, uncritical and vulnerable to unfavourable terms of exchange and to various kinds of corporate blackmail to get 'jobs for the town'. Although small-scale communities can reduce epistemic and responsive remoteness, and in some areas such as energy use can greatly reduce consequential remoteness,[28] they can often also offer people fewer alternatives to damaging forms of economic activity, so that benefits from reducing remoteness can be offset or cancelled out.

It is however one thing for bioregionalists to draw attention to the importance of remoteness and to stress links to place, and quite another to assume complete autarchy or small-scale self-sufficiency. This may actually increase other kinds of remoteness and obscure certain kinds of non-local relationships, including ecological relationships. There are several problematic aspects to autarchic forms of bioregionalism.[29] A closer look suggests that the conditions of small-scale self-sufficiency assumed to be the leading feature of ecological communities are neither necessary nor sufficient to guarantee that other important forms of remoteness are avoided. Observable small-scale communities (like the one I live in) suggest that proximity to local nature does little to guarantee the first condition of the bioregionalist, the transparency to inhabitants of ecological relationships and dependencies. The need to respect and maintain these relationships can still be obscured or overridden by other cultural factors, for example by the distorting and backgrounding force of anthropocentric cultural traditions, by the conditions of both general and ecological education, or by the intractability of local economic and social relationships. Even with goodwill, many ecological impacts may neither be containable nor evident at the level of the local community, for example, the contribution of local animal waste to the global store of biospheric methane. Familiarity with the wildlife of a particular community might tell you that a certain animal is common locally, but it will not tell you that it is very uncommon or extinct everywhere else, information that may be crucial to encouraging enough restraint to allow the animal to survive the intensified local demands of a small-scale self-sufficient economy. Here autarchy could actually hinder the transparency of ecological relationships and the development of a critical sense of place that can situate local relationships and communities in relation to wider communities.

This kind of problem would arise in intensified form for small communities that are self-sufficient, to the extent that they tend to be epistemically as well as economically self-enclosed. 'Living close to the land' may under the right conditions help generate knowledge of and concern for ecological effects of production and consumption within a local community, but neither this closeness nor the local ecological literacy it might help generate is sufficient to guarantee knowledge of ecological effects and relationships in the larger global community or even a larger regional one. This requires a larger network, whose formation seems unlikely to be assisted by economic autarchy. To the extent that contemporary ecological effects are rarely likely to be contained within a single political community, autarchy is in general in conflict with the participatory principle that those most affected by decisions should have a proportionate share in making them. Similarly, small-scale communities, including self-sufficient ones, may have difficulty in meeting John Dryzek's conditions of coordination across boundaries, flexibility, and matching scale to ecological impacts.[30] One of the attractions of the ideal autarchic community, supposedly, is that we keep the externalities, positive and negative, entirely for ourselves by producing what we consume and consuming what we produce.[31] Such self-containment may be harder to achieve than to theorise, and it is doubtful that our species has ever been able to achieve it. But unless consequences can be locally contained in this way, autarchy is not likely to be the best way of matching the scale of decision-making with the scale of ecological impacts to take responsibility for those wider ecological effects that are inevitably generated even by small-scale autarchic communities.

Nor does smallness of scale guarantee the absence of politically-based kinds of remoteness. Even face-to-face autarchic communities can make themselves epistemically and consequentially remote from ecological consequences through opportunities to redirect ecological harms from privileged to marginalised citizens, onto the future, and onto other less powerful communities. The extent to which this is possible within any given small-scale community depends on its political organisation, among other things, and especially on what sorts of opportunities for redistribution of ecological consequences these structures offer them. This would also be true of an economically self-sufficient community, unless we again make the question-begging and highly improbable assumption that it could be self-sufficient in its ecological impacts. The match between small scale and remoteness reduction is not as good as autarchy advocates have thought both because remoteness is more plural than they allow and because both human-scale and autarchy as such are much too politically and structurally underdetermined. This means that only under special conditions of political and cultural structure that are usually left unspecified would such face-to-face communities be likely meet optimum overall conditions for remoteness reduction.[32]

At this point autarchists, especially those of doctrinaire anarchist bent, usually wheel out the concept of federation or cooperation with other similar autarchies to explain how these sorts of difficulties can be met in their system. Autarchic communities will come to voluntary agreements with other autarchic communities and cooperate with them to reduce external ecological impacts. But federation here looks like a *deus ex machina*, a bare possibility assumed to save the day but insufficient to offset the circumstance that for a self-sufficient community, other communities appear as externalities. To posit self-sufficiency is to invite the hegemonic construction of agency and autonomy which has been such a powerful theme in the dominant culture. In the absence of wider community and economic relations, it is hard to see how federation among autarchies can provide a guaranteed or even likely prospect of the formation of the larger confederated communities the solution of larger-scale ecological problems in effect requires. The fact is that autarchy simply reproduces at the community level what liberalism assumes at the individual level, the atomistic, autonomous, self-contained self with no essential ties to others and no imaginable motive for cooperating with other atoms. For this cooperation we require a relational self[33], not an atomistic or self-enclosed one, and a matching economic vision of interdependence.

The basic appeal of autarchy is the idea of eliminating the gap between production and consumption and thereby eliminating remoteness. But this could at best work for some forms of immediate spatial remoteness, and not perfectly even for them, and a very large price is paid for this solution in terms of economic interaction. Fortunately, the extreme dissociation between production and consumption that is reaching such catastrophic proportions under global capitalism can be remedied without bringing production and consumption into a relation of unity or identity. For example, an alternative might be to create links and networks of meaning between production, consumption, and reproduction. As we have seen, these 'cables of meaning' would need to be sufficiently dense to enable meaningful connections of learning and responsibility to travel between producers and consumers, as they must for ethically and ecologically responsive and responsible relations of production and reproduction. Where appropriate cables are laid between producer and consumer communities that allow learning and feedback, sustainable and responsible resource management might begin to be possible.

In place of the extreme autarchic solution of eliminating exchange in order to eliminate remoteness, there is thus the option of restructuring exchange so that it maintains equivalent levels of remoteness. An economic structure which seems to evade this false dichotomy and is a good candidate for overcoming build-ups of remoteness through systems of exchange is Galtung's concept of self-reliance.[34] Self-reliance, as an economic organising principle for local communities, nations and regions, encourages the empowerment of local communities and potential self-sufficiency in the area of basic needs, to provide economic security and reduce a community's vulnerability to exploitation. But it also encourages exchange under strong conditions of equivalence that make it as fair and equal as possible. In place of centrist forms of exchange that export negative externalities from the centre and import positive ones from the periphery, fair exchange aims for a balanced distribution of broadly conceived costs and benefits so that they fall equally on both sides. Galtung's exchange principles,[35] allowing exchange at the same level of externality, processing and environmental regulation but not at different levels, curtail possibilities for consequential remoteness via systems of exchange; because the principle requires ecological regulation and adverse ecological consequences to be maintained at equivalent levels, it would not be possible for privileged communities to avoid them via unfair or centrist forms of exchange, or for underprivileged and underregulated ones to be selected via 'comparative advantage'.[36] These principles allow international and planetary interdependence and interaction to take a 'horizontal rather than vertical' form that can defeat both remoteness and centrism. Such a form of interdependence would replace free trade by fair trade, globalisation[37] by planetary organisation, mobilising interdependence from the periphery rather than from the centre, its present direction of growth and development.

What we discover from this investigation of remoteness then is that an ecologically rational economy that minimises remoteness will also be an ethical economy, one that opposes the centrisms of domination and embraces principles of fairness, justice and equality in exchange. In the light of examples like the Indonesian forest fires, where terrible injustice and ecological damage go so closely together, this conclusion should not be totally unexpected. To validate an ecologically rational and ethical economy that minimises remoteness, we need to defeat the rationalist hyper-separations between reason and emotion, prudence and ethics that are inscribed in the dominant global economy and its surrounding culture. Associated with these rationalist splits is the portrayal of egoism (equated with prudence) and 'disengagement' as rationality[38] as we have discussed in previous chapters. These rationalist splits disempower ethics, leaving it as a private afterthought to public rationalism, constructing the economy as impervious to considerations of justice, while disengagement, egoism and the absence of care masquerade as rationality. The exclusion of ethical concern in the economy validated by rationalist methodology is problematic for many reasons, prudential as well as ethical; for example the myths of self-containment they foster and the incentive they provide to disregard the welfare of externalities such as trading partners has long been a source of instability and insecurity in the dominant economy. I will further discuss this rationalist split, the hyper-separation between prudence and ethics, in Chapter 6.

Remoteness principles are consistently, blatantly and perhaps maximally violated by the dominant global order, but this is due to its centrist political and economic organisation rather than to its global spatial scale. Since laissez-faire market forms permit extreme levels of consequential, communicative and epistemic remoteness, and neoliberalism is increasingly successful in maximising the social areas where this kind of market is used for decision-making, global neoliberalism must be close to maximising consequential ecological remoteness. The present form of the global market economy creates unprecedentedly high levels of dissociation between consumption acts and production acts and between them and their ecological consequences, actually encouraging remoteness as a form of comparative advantage. Thus global capitalism scores at a very high level of ecological irrationality. The EcoRepublic might keep the lamp of human reason sputtering for another century or two before the flame finally dies from want of rational correctiveness. The continuation of the regime of global capitalism may well see that lamp extinguished much sooner than that.

4   Inequality and ecological rationality

Liberal democracy and ecological rationality

If remoteness has political as well as spatial conditions and expressions, this allows us to consider other crucial areas and ways to reduce remoteness other than minimising the spatial scale of communities, ways that might bear on improving the ecological rationality of larger-scale societies (for example, by making ecological relationships more transparent in their economic and cultural systems). This suggests that we should investigate remoteness reduction as a political and not only a spatial organising principle for ecological rationality. This chapter draws out some implications of dominant forms of globalisation for an ecologically irrational distributive politics which permits those most influential in decision systems high levels of remoteness from ecological consequences and gives them a corresponding capacity to distribute ecoharms onto others who are silenced and disempowered.

Inequality, whether inside the nation or out of it, is a major sponsor of ecological irrationality and remoteness, especially where it creates systematic opportunities and motivations to shift ecological ills onto others rather than to prevent their generation in the first place. Inequality combines with geographical remoteness to generate excellent conditions for epistemic remoteness, creating major barriers to knowledge and offering massive opportunities for redistributing ecoharms onto others in ways that elude the knowledge and responsibility of consumers and producers along with concern for ecological consequences. Under conditions which allow both remoteness and rational egoism to flourish, such actions even emerge as mandatory for the rational self-maximiser, since the logic of the global market treats the least privileged as the most expendable, defining them as having 'the least to lose' in terms of the low value of their health, land and assets, and, by implication, of their lives.[1] This logic helps ensure that the least privileged are likely to feel the first and worst impacts of environmental degradation, as in the case of much global deforestation, pollution, waste dumping in poor and coloured communities (such as Warren County), and environmentally hazardous working and living conditions for the poor. As it comes increasingly to dominate over other spheres, the global market systematically violates complex equality, enabling 'one good or one set of goods [to be] dominant and determinative of value in all the spheres of distribution'[2], facilitating the positive feedback patterns adding ecological ills to social ills which are the mark of ecojustice violations.

Theoretically, it seems, a democracy where all have input into decisions should have a low level of remoteness and a maximum of ecological rationality. It should have a high level of correctiveness because it should maximise the informational base relevant to environmental degradation. It should enable all affected citizens to be heard and to have their issues addressed by responsive decision-makers.[3] But in actually-existing liberal democracy, it doesn't seem to work quite like that, and it is commonly observed that liberal democracies are not performing well either in remedying ecological crises or in listening to disadvantaged citizens.[4] Shallow forms of democratic politics provide only weak forms of ecological rationality, not well correlated with correctiveness on ecological or social matters, and their inequalities allow privileged groups many opportunities for remoteness. But from this observation we can draw few conclusions adverse to the ecological rationality of the deeper forms of democracy that are better placed to enable systematic reductions in remoteness.

Identifying the structural features that account for these rationality failures of liberal democracy is more difficult than noting the failures. Dryzek (1992) argues persuasively that the political and administrative spheres of liberal capitalism are unable to respond adequately to the complexity of the ecological problems generated by its imprisoning capitalist production systems. The interest group interpretation of liberal democracy is another feature which is highly problematic from the perspective of ecological rationality. It is increasingly apparent that the form of 'interest group' politics that flourishes in liberal democracy is unable to create stable measures for the protection of nature, or to recognise basic ecological priority,[5] that ecological well-being is not just another interest group concern but ultimately a condition for most other interests. This failure is an aspect of its denial and neglect of collective life. The conception of democracy and decision-making in terms of a central state mediating a multiplicity of competing (private) interest groups takes egoism, inequality and domination for granted, provides poorly for collective goods, and allows systematic redistribution of ecological ills to weaker groups. It places many key environmental values in a disempowered private realm beyond the reach of politics.

The liberal individualist model, as is well known, stresses a view of politics as the aggregation of self-interested individual preferences increasingly market-weighted individual preferences. As Nancy Fraser notes, this means that 'political discourse consists of registering individual preferences and bargaining, looking for formulas that satisfy as many private interests as possible. It is assumed that there is no such thing as the common good over and above the sum of all the various individual goods, and so private interests are the legitimate stuff of political discourse'.[6] The upshot of treating environmental interests this way is, at best, the process of progressive compromise between environmentalist interest groups and exploitative interests, and in this process, as it is easy to show in the case of forests and biodiversity, it is very difficult to maintain environmental values over the long haul.

For other ecological issues too, the liberal interest group model is highly problematic. Collective goods, which cover a major range of environmental cases, are not well treated. For many generalisable interests, the liberal interest group model faces the collective action problem in which an unquantifiable, highly diffused, generalisable and perhaps not easily detectable ecological harm is pitted in a political contest against a quantifiable economic benefit accruing to a small (often very small) but highly concentrated and influential group. Interest group models tend to give poor results in this situation, while generating much community polarisation around environmental issues. (Both fisheries and forest issues exemplify this pattern.) Models stressing compromise between interest groups have a poor track record on many environmental problems, rarely stopping ecologically destructive activities as opposed to introducing ameliorative modifications which allow major damage to persist while also 'giving something' to ecological action groups.[7] These modifications sometimes represent worthwhile ecological gains in limited areas but rarely halt the overall progress of ecological damage.

However, a further major set of reasons for liberal capitalism's failures of ecological rationality derive from the structural features that generate both inequality and remoteness in systematic, large-scale and connected ways. One of the ways in which the rationalist heritage is expressed in liberal political terms is through the liberal equation of equality with formal equality in the legal and democratic spheres and the neglect of equality as economic democracy and distributive equality. Liberal democracy as an interest group model produces, not as a matter of accident, radical economic inequality, often in association with ethnic, gender and other kinds of marginality and cultural subordination, which feed liberal capitalism's structural potential and need for the differential distribution of ecoharms, and generate failures of environmental justice. Environmental theory has mostly tended to assume that ecoharms are generalisable, affecting all people within an abstract national community more or less equally, and that ecological rationality should be approached therefore through a politics of the 'common good'. The appeal to many environmentalists of the small-scale communitarian ideal also tends to support the framing of ecological rationality issues in terms of the politics of the common good. While adherents of this approach are right to note that liberal democracy deals poorly with the politics of the common good, these perspectives also collude with the powermasking tendencies of liberal politics to create a widespread perception of ecoharms as innocent and accidental distributions of damage affecting everyone more or less equally. As a result many green theorists have been reluctant to take seriously questions of distribution of ecoharms.

Thus according to Ulrich Beck (1995), the politics of class conflict is mainly concerned with the distribution of social rewards, which is inequitable in class-differentiated societies. In contrast, he claims, in risk society ecological ills tend to be distributed more evenly, cutting across boundaries of class and power. This view is summed up in his aphorism: 'Poverty is hierarchical, while smog is democratic.' (Beck 1995: 60), a memorable and widely quoted statement. But unfortunately for Beck's theory, many ecological harms, including smog, are distributed just as unevenly as most commodities. A smog map of Sydney, for example, correlates the heaviest air pollution areas very closely with low socio-economic status. The veil of uncertainty Beck tries to throw over ecological harms is already thoroughly rent, by class, race and gender as well as other forms of inequality.

The assumption of equality and generalisability in ecoharms holds good only for a certain range of ecoharms – those forms of degradation which have highly diffused or unpredictable effects not amenable to redistribution – and it holds even for many of those only very partially. It is hard to think of anything more likely to be generalisable than global warming, with its predictable outcome of increasingly extreme climatic events from which we all suffer in unpredictable ways. Events like the 1995 Chicago heatwave, where the 500 or more who died were mainly poor elderly people unable to afford air-conditioners, show that even these generalisable kinds of ecoharms tend to affect disproportionately those who already suffer from a social distribution deficit. So even in such apparently generalisable cases, what may mean discomfort for someone higher up the social scale may mean death to someone more marginal. For those kinds of degradation that are more localised and particularised in their impacts, such as exposure to toxins through residential and occupational area, much the same kind of politics of distribution of invulnerability can be played out as in the case of other societal goods.

For a range of environmental ills resulting from the institutions of accumulation, then, some considerable degree of redistribution and remoteness from consequences is possible along lines of social privilege. This is the basis of the ecojustice phenomenon known as 'environmental racism' (which should often be termed, in my view, 'environmental classism'). The socially privileged groups in a society can most readily make themselves remote from these easily perceived and particularised forms of environmental degradation; if their suburb, region or territory becomes degraded or polluted, they can buy a place in a more salubrious one. When local resources become depleted, they will be best placed to make themselves remote from local scarcities by taking advantage of wider supply sources and markets that continue to deplete distant communities in ways that elude knowledge and responsibility. They can buy expert help and remedies for environmental health and for other problems, and they are better able to mobilise in the public sphere for action on the ecological and other problems which concern them. Their working life is likely to involve a minimum of environmental pollution and disease compared to marginalised groups – for example compared to the US farm workers whose immediate life-expectancy is estimated to be 20 years below the national average.[8] At the same time, privileged groups are those who consume (both directly for their own use and indirectly for income generation) the greatest proportion of resources, and who have the strongest economic stake in the sort of accumulation which generates environmental harms. That is, the most socially privileged groups can make themselves relatively spatially, consequentially and epistemically remote from redistributable ecoharms. They will usually have the most to gain and the least to lose from the processes that produce ecoharms, and their interests will often be better satisfied if ecoharms are redistributed rather than prevented. Some parallel conclusions can be drawn for ecological goods.

The situation is not much better for generalisable harms and damage to collective goods. Because socially privileged groups can most easily purchase alternative private resources, (clean water for example) they have the least interest in maintaining in generally good condition collective goods and services of the sort typically provided by undamaged nature. In terms of their own experience, privileged groups are also likely to be more epistemically remote and distanced from awareness of both their own and nature's vulnerability and limits. For some very general forms of environmental degradation (such as nuclear radiation or biospheric degradation),[9] the ability of privileged groups to buy relief from vulnerability to environmental ills is ultimately an illusion. But for the key groups who are active in political decision-making it may still be the master illusion, fostered by their remoteness in other areas, sustained by their social privilege, and influential in their choices and attitudes. The socially privileged also have a political opportunity to redistribute collective goods in their favour, via privatisation, which guarantees them superior access, and insulates them from many kinds of limits and scarcity. In short, the inequalities which thrive in liberal democracy provide systematic opportunities for consequential and epistemic remoteness in the case of both non-collective and collective goods.[10] Liberal capitalism thus provides a set of impersonal NIMBY mechanisms which guarantee that an important range of ecoharms, from both redistributable and collective sources, are redistributed to marginalised groups.

In a polity like this where the socially privileged have the main or central role in social decision-making, decisions are likely to reflect their relatively high level of consequential, epistemic and communicative remoteness from ecological harms. From the perspective of ecological rationality then, these are among the worst groups to be allocated the role of decision-making. Yet in liberal democracies they are precisely the ones who have that role. The finding that it is socially privileged groups who are selected as politically active and effective in the liberal political structure is so well supported by empirical studies that Carole Pateman describes it as 'one of the best attested findings in political science'.[11] That there is a complementary silencing of those marginalised citizens on whom most ecoharm falls is attested by the unresponsiveness of liberal systems to their redistributive deprivation and cultural subordination. Several indirect sources are available to provide information about the ecoharms of the marginalised and about prevalent ecological ills, including, in liberalism, the discourse of the public sphere and the market. If the market, considered as an information system about needs, registers information not equally but according to 'market power' (income), information about the needs of those without 'market power' registers very little. Bad news from below is not registered well by any of liberal democracy's information systems, hardly at all by the market, and often poorly by liberal democratic, electoral and administrative systems. Yet it is precisely this bad news from below that has to be heard if many crucial forms of ecological damage are to be socially registered and opened to political action.[12]

The epistemic remoteness of privileged groups from the kinds of ecoharms that fall on marginal others impacts strongly on information and on the public sphere to the extent that privileged experience is hegemonic. This can create a general level of silence and epistemic distancing from these submerged kinds of ecoharms which can affect even those who suffer most from them. The consequential and epistemic remoteness of privileged groups from certain kinds of harm is reflected in what counts as ecological issues in the dominant public spheres.[13] The occupational health hazards of minority workers, the systematic poisoning of millions of migrant agricultural workers and the dumping of toxic wastes on poor communities can pass unremarked while environmental attention is focussed on consumer issues which impact on more privileged groups[14] or on issues concerning 'good nature'. Again, socially privileged groups often aim to set themselves apart from otherised groups (in the process of hyper-separation discussed in earlier chapters and in Plumwood 1993a) through overconsumption, and develop a culture celebrating consumption. If these consumerist values come to dominate in the public sphere, the cultural hegemony of social privilege can contribute to ecological damage as much as its economic domination.

There is clearly a serious problem about the ecological rationality of any system that allows those who have most access to political voice and decision-making power to be also those most relatively remote from the ecological degradation it fosters, and those who tend to be least remote from ecological degradation and who bear the worst ecological consequences to have the least access to voice and decision power. My argument implies not only that the inegalitarian power structure of liberalism is ecologically irrational, but also that the political and communicative empowerment of those least remote from ecological harms must form an important part of strategies for ecological rationality. There are many specific contextual forms this empowerment might take, such as access for community action groups to resources like public funding, but its general conditions surely require institutions which encourage speech and action from below and deep forms of democracy where communicative and redistributive equality flourish across a range of social spheres.

Beyond liberal democracy: deliberative modifications

The discussion above has suggested principles about who must be able to speak and participate effectively in the political process if the sorts of ecoharms suffered to a disproportionate degree by marginalised groups are to be subject to effective political action. As advocates of deliberative democracy note, the liberal interest group model which treats people as private political consumers provides little encouragement for the development of any public ecological morality, for collective responsibility or problem solving, or for people to transform their conception of their interests, their convictions or sympathies in response to social dialogue with affected groups.[15] To resolve conflicts over ecological harms through such means of reducing remoteness, we may need to create contexts in which both harming and harmed parties can communicate,[16] in which the harmed group is not disadvantaged as communicators and the harming group is neither remote (consequentially or epistemically), nor privileged in some other way in the decision-making process.[17] We can extend these conditions for equal dialogue and consensus to other matters. Ideally, to enable such transformation of interests to occur more readily, those who depend on producing the harms to earn a living should have a sufficient degree of confidence and social responsibility, overall access to economic flexibility, to social support and work reconstruction to be able make occupational and technological changes without incurring significant life penalties. This means that such penalties would need to be as far as possible collectively borne. None of these conditions can be well-realised in liberal forms of democracy; rather they point towards deliberative, participatory or radical forms of democracy.

To some however the problems I have outlined suggest not that any major or general transformation of liberalism is required but rather that the problems can be resolved by adding minor and highly localised deliberative modifications to liberal democracy, such as stakeholder panels designed to address specifically ecological issues. Thus Denis Collins and John Barkdull (1995) assert that classical liberalism is the most ecologically rational system (although they consider only one source of comparison, the Soviet bloc), and that a solution to the kinds of ecological difficulties of liberal capitalism I have outlined can be found in the form of stakeholder panels that can operate within it to create dispute resolution dialogue between harming and harmed groups. Not only does this not involve any major repudiation of liberal thought, they argue, but this kind of intervention has a respectable pedigree in the thought of that father of liberal capitalist theory, Adam Smith.

As in the case of bioregionalism, the extent to which stakeholder panels can provide a solution depends upon many factors which are not specified in the model, which is radically underdetermined and ambiguous. It seems likely that the outcome will be partly dependent on how stakeholders are selected and how judicial functionaries are chosen, for example. But there is also a radical ambiguity in stakeholder panels as Barkdull and Collins describe them as between a judicial model (with an impartial judge), a voluntary interest group bargaining model, and a deliberative model attempting to arrive at a consensus about the common good. The first two return us to the liberal problems I have discussed above. To the extent that the third deliberative interpretation is intended, stakeholder panels may really represent a major modification and suspension of the interest group model, but they also provide an implicit admission that the classical liberal model Collins and Barkdull have set themselves the task of defending is inadequate for ecological rationality. My own experience of stakeholder panels suggests that, while there can be useful elements of social deliberation and consensus seeking in the negotiation phase of the discussions, the interest group model which is so problematic for environmental issues tends to remain the basis upon which final political decisions are made. On such an interpretation, stakeholder panels will not only inherit the problems of liberal interest group bargaining, but will also inherit its difficulties in the ecojustice area and in representing adequately collective goods and public interests. Negotiation between harmed and harming parties must include advocates for and ways of representing more-than-human nature and also for the 'public interest' or collective good. Both of these are among the potentially harmed parties, but they are omitted in many versions of the stakeholder panel and in Collins' and Barkdull's discussion.

Collins and Barkdull concede that business is responsible for most ecoharms and that the poor or racially marginalised are the recipients of most ecoharms. But first, we are entitled to be puzzled as to why, if judicial panel-bargaining is so easily able to solve the kinds of ecological injuries Collins and Barkdull concede to be closely connected to social privilege, they are unable to solve the originating problems of social inequality they implicitly identify at the source of the problem. Second, Collins and Barkdull do not explain how, in the situation of major, systematically produced, and strongly embedded inequalities they concede between the parties to the negotiation, stakeholder panels that bring them together to negotiate will overcome the problem that the harmed parties will often be in the same unequal position as they are in these other kinds of negotiations and contracts, such as the labour contract, and other kinds of speech contexts such as the liberal public sphere and the courts. The appearance of a solution here depends upon the liberal-rationalist assumption that such panels will successfully *bracket* or set aside as irrelevant social inequality. Third, they leave unexplained how the negotiation model will overcome the acute problems for the marginalised of silencing and political participation many theorists have identified as the failure of the liberal public sphere.[18] Unless stakeholder panels can somehow overcome pervasive social inequality to provide more than formal and assumed equality of voice, there is a danger that the panels would function in hegemonic ways to secure the appearance of consent from affected parties to solutions which may not truly represent their voice or interest in stopping the injury. In the context of what Carole Pateman has called 'the wider failure in liberal democratic theory to distinguish free commitment and agreement from domination, subordination and inequality' (Pateman 1989: 83), it seems more likely that the panels would function to manufacture consent, by generating the hegemonic 'we' which subsumes the marginal 'I'. In short, it is hard to see how stakeholder panels can meet the conditions for transformation of interests and deliberative process I have suggested above without a larger context of equality between the negotiating parties.

The same point holds for attempts to introduce veils of uncertainty. We might try to reinterpret Beck's thesis of risk society as a higher-order normative rather than a descriptive thesis, prescribing that effective political action to stem ecological harms is most likely if ecological risks are equally born and no group can be confident of escaping them. Beck's thesis is certainly more plausible in this form, which suggests a veil of uncertainty approach to involving those groups most influential in decision-making in reducing ecological harms.[19] There is some apparent convergence between this strategy and the strategy of empowering the least remote, to the extent that a more equal society will distribute ecological risks more equally and have a thicker veil of uncertainty. But the converse does not hold, a veil of uncertainty strategy does not necessarily imply greater equality, since veils of uncertainty as limited devices for specific institutional uses are quite compatible with highly unequal and unjust social arrangements in the larger society. We can imagine the EcoRepublic simulating the greater uncertainty produced by equality by introducing some kind of stochastic ecological ordeal for decision-makers, for example assignment by lot to a highly polluted area, as a device to counter some of the dangers of remoteness. Yet it is hard to see what could motivate or maintain such measures in the context of the EcoRepublic. Similarly it is hard to see how such indirect strategies emphasising uncertainty could be made thorough or effective as general ways to deal with ecological damage without a larger context of substantive equality which cannot be provided without major transformations of liberal capitalism.

Beyond deliberative democracy

We have seen that the radical inequality generated in liberal capitalism is a major remoteness factor that hinders the ability to respond both to collective forms of ecological degradation and also to those forms which impact differentially in terms mediated by privilege (ecojustice issues). Radical inequality acts as an incentive to redistribute rather than eliminate ecological harms, and to substitute private ecological goods for collective ecological goods. Inequality creates barriers to communication about ecoharms, both in the form of information and feedback on ecological degradation and its human impacts, and to responsiveness to this information as articulated need, as well as distorting information flows, public sphere knowledge and culture. Inequality is both itself a hindrance to ecological rationality and an indicator of other hindrances. The kind of society whose democratic forms open communication and spread decision-making processes as equally as possible should, other things being equal, offer the best chance of effective action on these significant kinds of ecoharms. Thus systems which are able to articulate and respond to the needs of the least privileged should be better than less democratic systems which reserve effective participation in decision-making for privileged groups.

In an ecologically rational society, ecoharms to marginalised groups as well as to other groups would be able to emerge as important issues in the public sphere, and those most subject to (potential) ecological harms would have an understanding of them and an effective political and public sphere voice. A strong and diverse public sphere not dominated by privileged groups and able to hear the bad news from below is essential to remoteness reduction. If the ability of all those who are injured and as with nature to have their needs considered is linked to their ability to participate in the political structure,[20] this suggests again that the elements of an ecologically rational and responsive democracy will have to be sought within the tradition which interprets democracy as widespread popular participation, choice and involvement in decision-making, or which draws on communicative or deliberative concepts of democracy that emphasise the public sphere.

Many of those dissatisfied with shallow interest group democracy have turned to the idea of a deliberative or communicative process to obtain a stronger account of democracy. In this model, democracy is envisaged variously as a process of participation, of deliberation, or of communication: the last two, it should be noted, somewhat narrowing the concept of participation in a potentially rationalist and inegalitarian direction. In my view, remoteness reduction requires us to go beyond these conceptions to a deep form of democracy that involves a justice dimension as redistributive equality[21], equality and plurality of communicative process[22], and complex equality.[23] It requires not only a strong public sphere but perhaps more: communicative and participatory ideals and institutions that not only permit but actively solicit the voice from below. A strong case can also be made, I think, for solidarity and social citizenship, as well as robust collective life, as likely to reduce remoteness and increase ecological awareness and responsibility.[24] And as I argue in later chapters, it is also crucial to develop a democratic and non-anthropocentric culture which displaces reason/nature dualism in its various contemporary expressions, as a condition not only of greater human equality, but as the basis of more ecologically sensitive and communicative relationships with the natural world.

The notion that an ecologically rational society would need to take a participatory form derives some of its appeal from the idea that ecological harms are generalisable, so that, once these harms are recognised, general participation should be able to solve the problem of correcting them through consensus formation. If all are equally affected, and all are equally decision-makers in a participatory Rousseauan exercise of the general will, participatory democracy should be the obvious choice for a political framework to satisfy remoteness principles. But as we have seen, many ecological harms in modern large-scale societies have strong redistributive aspects based on various kinds of privilege, and this is even clearer in many third world social contexts, such as the forest fires example. Political structures and ecological strategies premised on a 'common good' framework will be insufficient to deal with them, since major parties are left out. As Iris Young notes 'where some groups have greater symbolic or material privilege than others, appeals to a 'common good' are likely to perpetuate such privilege'.[25] Participatory projects that aim to form a 'general will' through face-to-face decision-making are open to the objection that they assume simplistic, mystifying or oppressive projects of unity.[26] Thus communitarian and civic republican frameworks which posit a common good but lack any orientation towards recognising either difference or social equality will be correspondingly lacking in conceptual resources for tackling these redistributive features and will not foster ecological rationality in this area.

There are several more plausible recent refinements of the participation concept which replace the instrumental liberal concept of interest group bargaining by the concept of a participatory, communicative or deliberative procedure which is not valued only instrumentally, in terms of the results it produces, but itself carries intrinsic value as democratic process: John Dryzek's discursive democracy and Iris Young's 'communicative democracy' are two such refinements (both of Habermas original communicative process idea). Dryzek describes discursive democracy as an attempt to 'rescue communicative rationality from Habermas' (Dryzek 1990: 20). According to Habermas the liberal public sphere approximates the ideal speech situation of communicative rationality, constituting 'a warning system with sensors that, though unspecialised, are sensitive to the entire gamut of society'.[27] That is, the liberal public sphere is taken to represent a deliberative arena where everyone, despite other inequalities, has an equal opportunity to speak. And this is just what I have been suggesting we need for ecological rationality.

The ecological rationality of procedural and participatory democracy

Could such a strong public sphere come to the rescue and sufficiently counter the effects of remoteness elsewhere in a system? Not, I shall suggest, without larger transformative changes that are necessary to give a more adequate representation of the bad news from below. Once the formation of the public sphere in ways which reflect the cultural hegemony of privileged groups is recognised, its rescue potential appears much more contingent. Iris Young (1990, 1995) points up the exclusions produced by a model of critical deliberation which fails to recognise cultural specificity and other hegemonic baggage in the assumption of disengaged reason as the basis of deliberative process in the public sphere. Young's discussion shows how rationalist conceptions of speech distort and narrow both what is counted as legitimate speech and who is thought of as qualified to be a speaker. Since western deliberative norms, Young argues, are hegemonic and agonistic, different 'voices' and styles of communication need to be recognised and accorded equal legitimacy in any discussion-based process which aims to be open to all. Gendered and class or race-based norms of assertiveness and gendered speaking styles are signs and expressions of social privilege which exclude and silence. Dominant western norms of deliberation follow the strongly entrenched cultural pattern of reason/ nature dualism, privileging speech which is dispassionate and disembodied.

Young's analysis of cultural hegemony provides some illuminating philosophical confirmation for the empirical work confirming the domination of the public sphere by privileged groups (Pateman 1989). A communicative arrangement which aims to be non-exclusionary must be one which 'attends to social difference, to the way power sometimes enters speech itself'. But although Young's communicative democracy represents perhaps the most inclusive process account to date in terms of allowing for a multiplicity of voices, there are several remaining problems in her approach to communicative inequality as difference and the exclusive orientation to process. Young's account of silencing is based on a multicultural or ethnic recognition paradigm which aims at the expression of difference: '…communicative democracy' she writes, 'is better conceived as speaking across differences of culture, social position and need, *which are preserved in the process*' (p. 143, my emphasis). There are several problems here. First, this model is not appropriate for certain kinds of differences. If some differences are *injuries*, ways of incapacitating speech or expression even in the most favourable cultural paradigm, should our orientation be so exclusively to representing, expressing and preserving difference, or do these kinds of differences demand also an orientation to healing action, to actively working for their elimination?[28] Should class differences and other disabling differences directly attributable to subordination be 'preserved in the process' and viewed simply as a positive resource to be affirmed or represented? Those who are disabled by or in their difference cannot be empowered by affirming or preserving such differences. In the absence of distinctions between kinds of differences,[29] this formula disappears class differences and discounts the role of redistributive inequality in closing the public sphere to certain kinds of voices.

The hidden rationalist assumption here that social or redistributive inequality is irrelevant to political equality (a liberal version of mind/body dualism) and has no bearing on the ability to participate in the public sphere has been justly criticised by Carole Pateman and Nancy Fraser, among others. As Fraser (1997) states, to declare social inequalities, hierarchies and status differentials bracketed or irrelevant to deliberation is not to make it so. If participatory or discursive democracy proliferates formal structures for participation and deliberation without considering and creating the material conditions necessary for equal participation, the result can only be what Carole Pateman calls 'miniliberalism'. One source of the neglect of redistributive equality in liberal concepts of political equality are concepts of justice and equality defined in terms of reason and the state.[30] These definitions inherit the distortions of rationalist conceptions of reason which deny the conditions of reason's own production. To guarantee genuine equality of speech, discursive democracy has to attend to the conditions of social and cultural equality which will make equal participation in the public sphere more than a formal possibility. A discursive form of democracy which permits the silencing of those groups most likely to bear ecological harms and continues to select privileged groups as major participants in the same way as liberal forms will have no obviously better claim to reduce remoteness or to be ecologically rational.

The second problem is related to the first but is more general, and turns on difficulties of adopting an exclusively procedural approach to hearing the bad news from below (whether the procedure is based on Habermas or Rawls). The idea that equality of access to social goods is entirely a matter of getting the right process for political communication has come to be widely accepted in the last 20 years. But an exclusive orientation to process neglects the other half of the process/product relationship, the redistributive *outcome* of the communicative process, and the relations of reciprocal corrigibility that must hold between process and product. For many activities, we may need to decide if a process is working well by seeing if it is turning out the right sort of product; the quality of a product can act as a test for the adequacy of the process, as the quality of the process can for the product in the democratic context. We can recognise this reciprocity of process and product even where the process is conceived as valuable in itself. A process of artistic expression, for example, may have value in its own right as an expressive process, but both we and the artist will still often want to assess that process, at least in part, in terms of the kinds of products it turns out. Although an artistic process, unlike an instrumental one, is not judged entirely in relation to its product, an artist will often attempt to keep a balance between attention to the process and attention to the product, modifying each in the light of the other. Where process and product are reciprocally corrigible, a choice between a concept of democracy driven exclusively by process and a concept which treats process in exclusively instrumental terms, as purely a means to some predetermined outcome, is a false one. If communicative processes are themselves, as Young suggests, imbued with power, communicative processes and democratic products must be among this 'reciprocal' group, and we must seek ways to check and modify allegedly equal communicative processes, for example in terms of the kinds of distributive product which emerges from them.

The convergence of communicative and substantial inequality has important implications for democracy in contexts of radical inequality. Voices from below damaged or excluded by a flawed communicative process cannot effectively proclaim or contest their own exclusion within the framework it offers – since to do so would be a version of the Liar Paradox. Thus an illusion of adequacy and completeness of the communicative process may be produced, especially for dominant groups, which cannot be corrected on a purely procedural level. To that extent also, external checks of fairness, such as that provided by the product, are essential. Where the process of equal communication is revealed as politically problematic, as subject to all kinds of hegemonic modification, inflection and interference, (as Young's arguments do so reveal it), checking and modifying the communicative process by reference to the distributive outcome is clearly essential. If a process of political communication is working well, if it is inclusive and open in a real and not just formal way to all, it should be articulating the needs of all communicants and thus producing a certain kind of distributive product. *That product is substantive social and distributive equality.* Can we imagine a situation where a process whereby everyone has a genuine and equal opportunity to communicate needs and goals will result in a distributive outcome of serious social deprivation for some, and of substantial over-affluence for others? I believe that we would be entitled to conclude from the distributive product that such a process is seriously flawed as a process of equal communication, and that the process has not yielded an adequate form of communicative democracy. The identification of equality with formal and communicative equality to the neglect of material equality represents a etherealisation of democracy which suggests an underlying allegiance to that same abstract planet from which Plato came (and to which he has no doubt retired).

I want to draw out several points in conclusion. Ecologically rational societies would attend to various kinds of remoteness, including especially those consequential kinds based on social inequality. A society which aimed to reduce consequential remoteness and open ecojustice issues to effective political action would need, among other things, to be participatory and communicative, and it would need to be a society of substantial equality and democratic culture. Where we have good reason to believe that a hegemonic 'we' has subsumed an excluded 'I', and that existing inequalities will skew processes of communication and public sphere activity for a long time to come, we can't just hope that sufficient redistributive equality will emerge in the course of an apparently open communication process. A political structure that aimed to hear the bad news from below could not just rely on hoping to *represent* 'below' in apparently fair communicative processes, even where they *are* open to wide expressions of cultural difference. (This is especially so where it is privileged groups who determine when a process is 'fair', which they are most likely to do). Rather such a structure would need to *eliminate* class as a position of silence and radical marginality, and would need to adopt substantial social equality as a major redistributive and transformative objective.[31] My argument has suggested that an ecologically rational society would need to be more ambitious in this direction than any society we now know, but that this may ultimately be the condition of our ecological survival.

5 The blindspots of centrism and human self-enclosure

Rationalism and human-centredness

'The world of culture and nature, which is actual,' writes Gary Snyder 'is almost a shadow world now, and the insubstantial world of political jurisdictions and rarefied economies is what passes for reality.'[1] For Platonic rationalism too, the world of the body, the senses and nature, the world of coming-to-be and passing away, was unreal, a shadow world. It was the timeless immaterial world of abstractions and numbers, which Plato called the ideas or Forms, that was the true and real world, perfect, gleaming and immaculate to those who saw it in the brilliant light of reason. Snyder's image of the inverted priorities and understandings of the dominant culture in which abstract political and economic relationships subordinate and erase immediate ecological and sensory ones rings true. On top of the background rationalist heritage in the dominant culture, our time is witnessing a great resurgence of rationalism, fuelled both by the dominance of the control and quantification-obsessed global economy and by cyber-rationalism. This is exemplified in the recent hype about the 'weightless' economy, which comes very close to denying the necessity of the material world.

A weakened sense of the reality of our embeddedness in nature is seen in the cultural phenomenon of ecological denial which refuses to admit the reality and seriousness of the ecological crisis. This Illusion of Disembeddedness is an index of how far we have come in what Jennifer Price calls 'losing track of nature' – and in the process, losing track of ourselves as ecologically constrained beings. 'Ecological denial' is one of its children – the response to the crisis in which the bulk of the social effort and energy is not put into dealing with crises such as greenhouse gases but rather into denying that a problem exists or into giving it an extremely low priority. Dominant policies of ecological denial add to the evidence that the ecological crisis is not just or even primarily a crisis of technology, but is rather a crisis of rationality, morality, and imagination. Ecological denial is a highly dysfunctional response to the crisis which can only deepen it. It is a very likely outcome however when democratic structures that can address inequality and change social frameworks are not working and these are seen as unchangeable. It will be a pity for the human species if this kind of (un)consciousness is still dominant at the time when the ecological crunch comes for our food and energy production systems, which will not be long off.

Rationalist culture has fostered a version of human-self enclosure and human-centredness: to the extent that rationality is taken to be the exclusive, identifying feature of the human, (or as Aristotle tells us in the Nichomachean Ethics 'reason more than anything else *is* man') and that the rational is identified with what is worthwhile, reason-centredness implies human-centredness and its correlate, human self-enclosure.[2] The weakening of the sense of ecological reality Snyder refers to, with attendant low levels of consciousness of the ecological embeddedness of human life, is just one of the damaging effects of human-centredness (or anthropocentrism).[3] The concept of anthropocentrism is often rejected because it is not appreciated that not all the ill-effects fall on the 'nature' side of monological and centric relationships. Human-centredness promotes various damaging forms of epistemic remoteness, for by walling ourselves off from nature in order to exploit it, we also lose certain abilities to situate ourselves as part of it.

Centrism is often represented as if its distortions affected only the weaker party to the relationship, 'the victim', but this idea is widely rejected by oppression theorists as illusory and as an example of 'studying down'. Both dominating and subordinated parties are deformed by centric constructions, not only the obvious sufferer, the one exploited in the relationship. Modern western masculinity is constructed for example through its identification with a rationalist concept of reason whose opposition to emotion estranges men from many aspects of their emotional lives.[4] Rationalist influence makes philosophers treat centrism as if it were a matter of cognition, beliefs about superiority and inferiority. But it is much more a matter of moral epistemology, of frameworks for noticing, perception, attention and focus, and for self-perception, in framing concepts of autonomy for example. Centrism is tested by behaviour rather than avowal. The distortions of centrism in the character of the dominant party are obscured because centric standpoints universalise a master perspective, in which these distortions, appearing as laudable or as inevitable, become part of the framework of cultural reality. Studying these distortions ('studying up') can help establish the limitations and irrationalities not only of master subjects but of the world they make, the dominant order. Because the master perspective lacks certain kinds of self-knowledge, such a study can reveal various kinds of culture-wide rationality failures. From that master perspective what is being done is rational, but there is much that the master perspective does not, cannot see because certain things are unavailable or obscured in the dominant framework. Master perspectives are hegemonic and shape cultural locations in direct proportion to their distance from the control of the centre.

The overall effect of hegemonic centric structure at the level of ideas is not only to justify oppression by making it seem natural but also to make it invisible, by creating a false universalism in culture in which the experiences of the dominant 'centre' are represented as universal, and the experiences of those subordinated in the structure are rendered as secondary or 'irrational'. Alternatives to these structures are no longer visible at all once the master standpoint has become part of the very framework of thought. In the case of androcentrism, identity and experience is represented in masculinist terms as that of elite males. In the case of ethnocentrism and eurocentrism (racism), identity and experience is represented in the world-views of a dominant race or ethnically privileged group and other experiences are suppressed or backgrounded. In the case of the Illusion of Disembeddedness, backgrounding has gone to a further stage: the activity of nature is denied or disappeared – we 'lose track of it', in a world of growing remoteness, often in culture-wide ways, even when it is performing essential services for us. The epistemic and ethical failures involved in 'losing track' in turn support human-centred and reason-centred illusions of human identity as outside and incidental to the natural world. These assume a great prudential and ethical gulf between the welfare of 'persons' who can own and operate in the market and those lesser beings, especially those conceived as 'property', who can be owned and traded. These latter are assumed to have no agency or limits of their own that need be factored in and that could inhibit property-formation. This framework of assumptions provides the ethical underpinnings for capitalism and the commodification of nature.

The epistemic and moral limitations and dualisms associated with human-centredness are, I shall argue, harmful and limiting, even in their subtler and weaker forms. People under their influence, such as those from the western cultural traditions in which anthropocentrism is deeply rooted, develop conceptions of themselves as belonging to a superior sphere apart, a rational sphere of exclusively 'human' ethics, technology and culture dissociated from nature and ecology. This self-enclosed outlook has helped us to lose touch with ourselves as creatures who are not only cultural beings but also natural beings, just as dependent on a healthy biosphere as other forms of life. Through seeing ourselves in terms of mastery as primarily rational, non-animal beings who are 'outside nature', we are subject to illusions of autonomy, service and control, taking the functioning of the 'lower' sphere, the ecological systems which support us, entirely for granted, needing some grudging support and attention only when they fail to perform as expected. Rationalist constructions of human-centredness and their associated ethical and epistemic exclusions and illusions have in the modern age helped western culture and the economic rationality of capitalism achieve its position of dominance, by maximising the class of other beings that are available as 'resources' for exploitation without constraint. An analysis of human/nature dualism and some of the larger formation of human centredness will show us why they are now, in the age of ecological limits, ecologically irrational − a danger to all planetary life.

As the human-centred culture of our modern form of rationalism grows steadily more remote and self-enclosed, it loses the capacity to imagine or detect its danger. But if this form of reason judges that nature is now inessential to its life, ecological catastrophe will deliver the verdict of a higher court that reason has failed to recognise its ground in nature. Human-centred culture springs from an impoverished and inadequate conceptual and rational world; it is helping to create in its image a real world that is not only ecologically, biologically, and aesthetically damaged, but is also rationally damaged. That is, human- and reason-centred culture may be rationalistic in its exclusionary stress on rationality, but human-centredness is not ecologically rational. To demonstrate this, I will make use of parallels from liberation politics that critique eurocentrism and androcentrism to develop an appropriation model of anthropocentrism or human-centredness, and then use standpoint theory to show that such a framework of beliefs leads to dangerous perceptual and conceptual distortion and blindspots such as the Illusion of Disembeddedness.

The logical structure of centrism

The model of anthropocentrism I now sketch would construct, as a first approximation, a 'human-centred' parallel to the concepts of hegemonic centrism which have been the focus of the critiques of liberation movements, and their critical concepts of androcentrism, eurocentrism, and ethnocentrism. I outline below the chief structural features of hegemonic centrism, drawing on features of such centrism suggested by feminists Simone de Beauvoir, Nancy Hartsock, Marilyn Frye, and critics of eurocentrism such as Edward Said and Albert Memmi. These colonisation models of eurocentrism are especially appropriate, I suggest, if we are attracted to thinking of earth others as *other nations* 'caught with ourselves in the net of life and time', as Henry Beston writes so powerfully. Human-centredness is inflected by its social context, and the model I shall outline is drawn from critiques of appropriative colonisation developed especially by Edward Said, as a model for the capitalist/scientific appropriation of nature. I illustrate the structure with examples drawn from counter-centric theorists and from the colonisation of indigenous peoples, especially the case of Australian Aboriginal people, whose oppression combines elements of ethnocentrism and eurocentrism.

A hegemonic centrism is a primary-secondary pattern of attribution that sets up one term (the One) as primary or as centre and defines marginal Others as secondary or derivative in relation to it, for example, as deficient in relation to the centre.[5] Nancy Hartsock conjectures that this kind of structure is common to the different forms of centrism which underlie racism, sexism and colonialism, which therefore support and confirm one another.[6] The shared logical characteristics of the centric structure enable us to think of such centrism as a determinable with the specific varieties as determinates, in which there is much room for political inflection and cultural variation.[7] Dominant western culture is androcentric, eurocentric and ethnocentric, as well as anthropocentric. In historical terms, it is reason-centred, where reason is treated, as in the rationalist tradition, as the characteristic which sums up and is common to the privileged side of all these contrasts and whose absence characterises the Other.[8]

A hegemonic centrist conceptual structure is normally erected on the foundation of a dualism, (which is quite distinct from a simple dichotomy or exclusive and exhaustive division).[9] Dualism is an emphatic and distancing form of separation (hyper-separation or dissociation) which creates a sharp, ontological break or radical discontinuity between the group identified as the privileged 'centre' and those subordinated. There are several further features that distinguish dualisms and hegemonic centrisms from dichotomies and distinctions. First, the representations involved, being those of power, often have the power to create their own realities. 'The vision and the material reality propped each other up, kept each other going' writes Edward Said of Orientalism, a self-reinforcing expression of eurocentrism in the field of knowledge (Said 1978: 44). The Other is '*contained* and *represented* by dominating frameworks' (Said 1978: 40). And second, dualistic construction results in polarisation and therefore *false* dichotomy. Full-scale dualisms have the following logical characteristics of radical exclusion and stereotyping that set up polarised classes:

Radical exclusion

Radical exclusion marks the Otherised group out as both inferior and radically separate.[10] The woman is set apart as having a different nature, is seen as part of a different, lower order of being lesser or lacking in reason. This kind of hyper-separation involves not just difference, but defining the dominant identity against or in opposition to the subordinated identity, by exclusion of their real or supposed qualities. Hyper-separation is a form of differentiation that is used to justify domination and conquest. Thus 'macho' identities emphatically deny continuity and minimise qualities shared with women. Colonisers exaggerate differences (for example marking themselves off from the Others in terms of exaggerated cleanliness, 'civilised' or 'refined manners', body covering, and alleged physiological differences between what are defined as separate races). They may ignore or deny relationship, conceiving the colonised as less than human, without souls. The colonised are described as 'stone-age', 'primitive', as 'beasts of the forest', and contrasted with the civilisation and reason attributed to the coloniser. Exclusionary motives often generate absurdly fine distinctions in order to maximise separation and maintain images of discontinuity, such as the 'half-caste', 'quarter-caste' and even finer orders of distinction found in Australia and in the US 'one drop' rule.[11]

One of the functions of this hyper-separation is to mark out the Other for separate and inferior treatment. Separate 'natures' explain, justify and naturalise widely different privileges and fates between men and women, coloniser and colonised, justify assigning the Other inferior access to cultural goods, and block identification, sympathy, and tendencies to question inequalities. A sharp boundary and maximum separation of identity enable the beneficiaries of these arrangements to both justify and reassure themselves. Sharp boundaries and discontinuity in the case of the colonised are often maintained in terms of theories of racial purity and supremacy. Typically supremacist classifications reconstruct a highly diverse field in which there may be many forms of continuity in terms of two polarised and internally homogenised 'superior' and 'inferior' racialised or genderised classes.

Homogenisation/stereotyping

Homogenisation/stereotyping occurs when differences within an Otherised group are disregarded.[12] The Other is not an individual but a member of a class stereotyped as interchangeable, replaceable, all alike, homogeneous. Thus essential female nature is uniform and unalterable. The colonised are stereotyped as 'all the same' in their deficiency, and their social, cultural, religious and personal diversity is discounted as they 'drown in an anonymous collectivity'.[13] 'Orientals were almost everywhere nearly the same', writes Said, discussing Lord Cromer's views.[14] Their nature is essentially simple and knowable (unless they are devious and deceptive), not outrunning the homogenising stereotype. 'Orientals' notes Said, 'for all practical purposes were a Platonic essence which any Orientalist (or ruler of Orientals) might examine, understand and expose' (Said 1978: 38). Homogenisation is a striking feature of pejorative slang, for example in talk of 'slits', 'gooks', and 'boongs' in the racist case and in similar terms for women.

Both dominant and subordinated identities of a dualism tend to be treated in somewhat homogenised terms as exemplifying certain fixed natures, and some homogenisation is applied to both sides to create the necessary polarisation. But homogenisation and stereotyping apply especially to subordinated identities because they lack the power to require recognition of their diversity. Notice how these features result from power and work together: thus, to the One, sensitivity to differences among the Others is of little importance, unless they affect his own welfare, because power or force can take the place of sensitivity, whereas sensitivity to differences among the masters is likely to be very important for the survival of the subordinated. Diversity which is surplus to the centre's desire and need does not require respect or recognition. Thus knowability and lack of diversity is likely to be strongly stressed for the subordinated group.

Radical exclusion and homogenisation/stereotyping function jointly to set up the typical *polarised structure* characteristic of dualism, described by Marilyn Frye as follows: 'To make domination seem natural, it will help if it seems to all concerned that the two groups are very different from each other and...that within each group, the members are very like one another. The appearance of the naturalness of dominance of men and subordination of women is supported by the appearance that...men are very like other men and very unlike women, and women are very like other women and very unlike men'[15]. The Other is stereotyped as the homogeneous and complementary polarity to the One: Said writes 'The Oriental is irrational, depraved (fallen), childlike, 'different'; thus the European is rational, virtuous, mature, 'normal'.'[16] Men are stereotyped as active, intellectual, inexpressive, strong, dominant and so on, while women are represented in terms of the complementary polarity as passive, intuitive, emotional, weak, and submissive. To counter polarisation it is necessary to acknowledge and reclaim continuity and overlap between the polarised groups as well as internal diversity within them. Men can be emotional and do childcare, women can be rational, gay or straight.

This polarised structure itself is often thought of as being dualism, but dualism is usually symptomatic of a wider hegemonic centrism, and involves a further dynamic of colonising interaction in the features set out below. This is a dynamic of denial, backgrounding and reduction which frames and justifies the processes of colonisation and appropriation applied to the radically separated and subordinated party in the logic of the One and the Other.

Denial, backgrounding

Denial, backgrounding: Once the Other is marked in these ways as part of a radically separate and inferior group, there is a strong motivation to represent them as inessential. Thus the centre's dependency on the Other cannot be acknowledged, since to acknowledge dependence on an Other who is seen as unworthy would threaten the One's sense of superiority and apartness.[17] In an androcentric context, the contribution of women to any collective undertaking is denied, treated as inessential or as not worth noticing. 'Women's tasks' will be background to the aspects of life considered important or significant, often classified as natural in involving no special skill or care. This feature enables exploitation of the denied class via expropriation of what they help to produce, but carries the usual problems and contradictions of denial: 'Women's existence is both absolutely necessary and irresolubly problematic for phallocratic reality' (Frye 1983). Denial is often accomplished via a perceptual politics of what is worth noticing, of what can be acknowledged, foregrounded and rewarded as 'achievement' and what is relegated to the background. Women's traditional tasks in house labour and childraising are treated as inessential, as the background services that make 'real' work and achievement possible, rather than as achievement or as work themselves. Similarly, the colonised are denied as the unconsidered background to 'civilisation', the Other whose prior ownership of the land and whose dispossession and murder is never spoken or admitted. Their trace in the land is denied, and they are represented as *inessential* as their land and their labour embodied in it is taken over as 'nature'. Australian Aboriginal people, for example, were not seen as ecological agents, and their land was taken over as unoccupied, 'terra nullius' (no-one's land), while the heroic agency of white pioneers in 'discovering', clearing and transforming the land was strongly stressed.

Incorporation

Incorporation[18], assimilation: In androcentric culture, the woman is defined in relation to the man as central, often conceived as a lack in relation to him, sometimes crudely as in Aristotle's account of reproduction, sometimes more subtly. In Simone de Beauvoir's classic statement *'humanity is male and man defines woman not in herself but as relative to him; she is not regarded as an autonomous being...she is defined and differentiated with reference to man and not he with reference to her; she is the incidental, the inessential as opposed to the essential. He is the Subject, he is the Absolute, she is the Other'* (de Beauvoir 1965: 8). If his features are set up as culturally universal, she becomes the exception, negation or lack of the virtue of the One. The Other is marked as deviation from the centrality of the One, as colour is a deviation from the 'normal' condition of whiteness. Her difference, thus represented as lack, represented as deficiency rather than diversity, becomes the basis of hierarchy and exclusion. The Other's deficiency invites the One ' to control, contain, and otherwise govern (through superior knowledge and accommodating power) the Other' (Said 1978: 48).

The colonised too is judged not as an independent being or culture but as an 'illegitimate and refractory foil' to the coloniser (Parry 1995: 42), as *lack* in relation to the coloniser, as negativity,[19], devalued as an absence of the coloniser's chief qualities, ('backward, lack of civilisation'), usually represented in the west as *reason*. Differences are judged as deficiencies, grounds of inferiority. The order which the colonised possesses is represented as disorder or unreason. The colonised and their 'disorderly' space is available for use, without limit, and the assimilating project of the coloniser is to remake the colonised and their space in the image of the coloniser's own self-space, own culture or land, which is represented as the paradigm of reason, beauty and order. The speech, voice, projects and religion of the colonised are acknowledged and recognised as valuable only to the extent that they are assimilated to that of the coloniser.

Instrumentalism

Instrumentalism appears as a special case of incorporation in relation to agency and value.[20] The Other's independent agency and value is downgraded or denied. Traditionally, the woman is conceived as 'passive' and her agency is subsumed within the agency of the male who is her 'protector'. She lacks independent ethical weight, being valued as a means to others' ends in the family rather than accorded value in her own right, deriving her social worth instrumentally, from service to others, as the producer of sons, carer for parents, etc. 'Woman's nature' and woman's virtue are defined instrumentally, as being a good wife or mother, classically as 'silence and good weaving', romantically as being there to please. Where she is conceived as lacking any independent value or agency, she does not present any limit to intrusion (unless this limit originates in her relationship to another male) – thus her boundaries permit or invite invasion.

Similarly, the colonised Other is reduced to a means to the coloniser's ends, their blood and treasure, as Said notes, available to the coloniser and used as a means to increase central power. The coloniser, as the origin and source of 'civilised values', denies the Other's agency, social organisation and independence of ends, and subsumes them under his own. The Other is not the agent of their own cultural meanings, but receives these from the home culture through the knowledgeable manipulations of the One (Said 1978: 40). The extent to which indigenous people were ecological agents who actively managed the land, for example, is denied, and they are presented as largely passive in the face of nature. In the coloniser's history, their agency is usually disappeared: they do not present any resistance to colonisation, and do not fight or win any battles. Since the Other is conceived in terms of inferiority and their own agency and creation of value is denied, it is appropriate that the coloniser impose his own value, agency and meaning, and that the colonised be made to serve the coloniser as a means to his ends, (for example, as servants, as 'boys'). The colonised, so conceived, cannot present any moral or prudential limit to appropriation.

The sharing of this logic of Othering between different kinds of centric oppression helps to explain the ready transfer of metaphors between them, and the reinforcement of the ideologies of 'nature' which support one kind of centric oppression by drawing on the Othering logic for another.[21] Thus racial and ethnic inferiorisation drew strongly on assimilating racially subordinated groups to women, or to animals and children. The rationalist ideology of reason as an elite characteristic in opposition to Otherised characteristics such as emotion, animality and the body played a major role too in replicating the logic of Othering through different spheres of oppression.[22] Conversely, the sharing of the basic logic of Othering helps explain the way liberation perspectives and insights have historically supported one another and transferred from one area of oppression to another, for example in the nineteenth century between women's oppression and slavery, and in the mid-twentieth century from movements against racism to feminist movements. And as we shall see, the historical development in our time of a critical environmental approach to the human-nature relationship has exhibited this pattern of political transfer of insights from other liberation perspectives in an especially striking way.

A parallel liberation model of anthropocentrism

We can now spell out a parallel concept of 'human-centrism', and characterise as anthropocentric those patterns of belief and treatment of the human/nature relationship which exhibit this same kind of hegemonic structure. By extension we can categorise as anthropocentric certain cultures and formations of identity which typically host such patterns. In anthropocentric culture, nature and animals are constructed according to the same logic of the One and the Other, with nature as Other in relation to the human in much the same way that women are constructed as Other in relation to men, and those regarded as 'coloured' are constructed as Other in relation to those considered 'without colour', as 'white'.

Radical exclusion

An anthropocentric viewpoint treats nature as radically other, and humans as emphatically separated from nature and from animals. It sees nature as a hyper-separate lower order lacking continuity with the human, and stresses those features which make humans different from nature and animals, rather than those they share with them, as constitutive of a truly human identity. Anthropocentric culture endorses a view of the human as outside of and apart from a plastic, passive and 'dead' nature which is conceived in mechanical terms as completely lacking in qualities such as mind and agency that are seen as exclusive to the human. A strong ethical discontinuity is felt at the human species boundary. An anthropocentric culture will tend to adopt concepts of what makes a good human being which reinforce this discontinuity by devaluing those qualities of human selves and human cultures it associates with nature and animality in the human self, and thus also to associate with nature inferiorised social groups and their characteristic activities, real or supposed. Thus women are historically linked to 'nature' as reproductive bodies, and through their supposedly greater emotionality, and the colonisers' indigenous people are seen as a primitive, 'earlier stage' of humanity. At the same time, dominant groups associate themselves with the overcoming or mastery of nature, both internal and external, and the management of colonised groups. For all those classed as nature, as Other, identification and sympathy are blocked by these structures of Othering.

Homogenisation/stereotyping

Nature and animals tend to be seen as all alike in their lack of consciousness, which is assumed to be exclusive to the human, and the range and diversity of mindlike qualities found in nature and animals is ignored. The model promotes insensitivity to the marvellous diversity of nature, since differences in nature are attended to only if they are likely to contribute in some obvious way to human welfare. The difference of nature is a ground of inferiority, not just of difference. Nature is conceived in terms of interchangeable and replaceable units, (as 'resources', or standing reserve) rather than as infinitely diverse and always in excess of knowledge and classification. Homogenisation leads to a serious underestimation of the complexity of nature, and is implicated in mechanism. These two features of human/nature dualism work together to produce a polarised understanding in which there are two quite different substances or orders of being in the world, a spiritual and a mechanistic one, consciousness and clockwork.

The famous presidential remark 'You've seen one redwood, you've seen them all,' invokes a parallel homogenisation of nature. An anthropocentric culture rarely sees animals and plants as individual centres of striving and need, doing their best for themselves and their children in their conditions of life. Instead nature is conceived in terms of interchangeable and replaceable units, (as 'resources') rather than as infinitely diverse and always in excess of knowledge and classification. Anthropocentric culture and science conceive nature and animals as inferiors stereotyped as alike in their lack of reason, mind and consciousness, which is withheld from the non-human sphere through the enforcement of a hyper-separated 'rational' vocabulary. Once they are viewed as machines or automata, minds are closed to the range and diversity of their individual and collective mindlike qualities. Recognition of the respects in which non-humans are superior to humans is suppressed. Assimilative and instrumental models promote insensitivity to the marvellous diversity of nature, attending to differences in nature only if they are likely to contribute in some obvious way to human interests, conceived as hyper-separate from those of natural species and systems. As we saw in the fisheries case, epistemic and ethical frameworks of commodification lead to a serious underestimation of the complexity and irreplaceability of nature. Thus scientists assume their own genetically engineered replacements for natural species and varieties are always superior, although they have not been tested for survival over a range of conditions nearly as rigorously as naturally evolved varieties.

These two features of human/nature dualism, radical exclusion and homogenisation, work together to produce in anthropocentric culture a polarised understanding in which the human and non-human spheres correspond to two quite different substances or orders of being in the world. In the mechanistic model, these orders are thought of as minds and machines.

Backgrounding, denial

Nature is represented as inessential and massively denied as the unconsidered background to technological society. Since anthropocentric culture sees non-human nature as a basically inessential constituent of the universe, nature's needs are systematically omitted from account and consideration in decision-making. Dependency on nature is denied, systematically, so that nature's order, resistance and survival requirements are not perceived as imposing a limit on human goals or enterprises. For example, crucial biospheric and other services provided by nature and the limits they might impose on human projects are not considered in accounting or decision-making. We only pay attention to them after disaster occurs, and then only to restore the status quo, to fix things up. Where we cannot quite forget how dependent on nature we really are, dependency appears as a source of anxiety and threat, or as a further technological problem to be overcome.

As we have seen in Chapter 1, hegemonic accounts of human agency that background nature as a collaborative co-agency feed hyperbolised concepts of human autonomy and independence of nature.

Incorporation (Assimilation)

Rather than according nature the dignity of an independent other or presence, anthropocentric culture treats nature as Other as merely a refractory foil to the human. Defined in relation to the human or as an absence of the human, nature has a conceptual status that leaves it entirely dependent for its meaning on the 'primary' human term.

Thus nature and animals are judged as 'lack' in relation to the human-coloniser, and devalued as an absence of qualities said to be essential for the human, such as rationality. We consider non-human animals inferior because they lack, we think, human capacities for abstract thought, but we do not consider those positive capacities many animals have that we lack, such as remarkable navigational capacities and ultraviolet perception. Differences are judged as grounds of inferiority, not as welcome and intriguing signs of diversity. The intricate order of nature is perceived as disorder, as unreason, to be replaced where possible by human order in development, an assimilating project of colonisation. Where the preservation of any order there might be in nature is not perceived as representing a limit, nature is available for use without restriction.

Instrumentalism

In anthropocentric culture, nature's agency and independence of ends are denied, subsumed in or remade to coincide with human interests, which are thought to be the source of all value in the world. Mechanistic worldviews especially deny nature any form of agency of its own. Since the non-human sphere is thought to have no agency of its own and to be empty of purpose, it is thought appropriate that the human coloniser impose his own purposes. Human-centred ethics views nature as possessing meaning and value only when it is made to serve the human/coloniser as a means to his or her ends. Thus we get the split characteristic of modernity in which ethical considerations apply to the human sphere but not to the non-human sphere. Since nature itself is thought to be outside the ethical sphere and to impose no moral limits on human action, we can deal with nature as an instrumental sphere, provided we do not injure other humans in doing so. Instrumental outlooks distort our sensitivity to and knowledge of nature, blocking humility, wonder and openness in approaching the more-than-human, and producing narrow types of understanding and classification that reduce nature to raw materials for human projects.

Economic centrism: nature as class and resource

Nature as resource, as labour, and as externality is also the subordinated Other in systems of oligarchical economic centrism, where there is radical economic inequality and hyper-separation between classes, those of 'persons' who are owners (increasingly corporations and their personnel) and those who are counted as property or as externality. This hyper-separation is reinforced in the division between high and low culture as well as in cultural practices such as excess or conspicuous consumption. Radical class differentiation is reinforced through a division of labour which is often framed in terms of reason/body dualism in which rational managers control hired 'hands', while inequality is justified as a matter of desert through a culture of rational meritocracy rewarding 'rationality' and 'individualism', that is, hyperbolised autonomy. Many tasks of decision-making and management which can beneficially be amalgamated with the practical or manual aspect of work are reserved for managers, with the purpose of setting them apart as a distanced and controlling elite.[23]

Splitting or hyper-separation and backgrounding or denial work together to produce typical hegemonic constructions of agency. This is well illustrated in the Marglins' study of dominating forms of knowledge.[24] Knowledge which in some cultures remains integrated and fully embodied is in western cultures often split into a superior abstract 'rational' form versus an inferiorised 'practical', experiential and embodied form, usually reflecting the different status of the different groups possessing it. The split opens the way for the dominance of abstract 'rational management' over those reduced to serviceable bodies that carry out the tasks management plans and dictates, and also allows appropriation of agency and rewards on behalf of those counted as rational managers. The dominant party can afford to 'forget' the other, provided they continue to function in serviceable ways or are replaceable (substitutable). If their level of distancing and denial goes deep enough, managers may be inclined to do so even where the other is not replaceable.

Both backgrounding and splitting are hazardous for those in this category of 'nature'. 'Forgetting' may mean that connections and feedback crucial to continuing the service can be blocked, and 'splitting' and remoteness means that abstract decision-makers may never be brought to face the failure of their rational edicts on the ground, because that has become externality, 'someone else's department'. In private enterprise and private property culture, the 'forgetting' of nature's agency and contribution is often paralleled by the forgetting of the importance of social infrastructure, which under economic rationalism and centrism is similarly either privatised (often with disastrous consequences) or starved of resources to the point of breakdown. Dramatic system failures usually have to occur before the situation is rectified. In the case of nature, rectification might not be possible.

In the system of property formation, the Other that is not to be made part of the self through incorporation is conceived as externality, that place remote from the self or home for which no responsibility is accepted and from which resources can be taken or waste deposited. The inferiorised groups are classified as either waste or as resource, but centrist society need not be without mobility: it is possible for those in the 'waste' category (for example as the unemployed) to make the transition to the 'resource category, for example as workers paid below-subsistence wages, (or in a previous colonial age, as foot soldiers). As Lovins *et al.* (2000) point out, things can move from being in the waste product category to being resources for more production. This transition from the category of waste to that of resource can be speeded up and enlarged in scope, but this will not necessarily remedy or address the basic mindset, or the basic problem. Whichever category you are in, it is bad news to find yourself on the wrong side of the nature/culture and person/property boundaries, for you will either be discarded or instrumentalised, thrown away or eaten.

The centric parallel as a practical model

Liberation movements have not provided a significant source of wisdom for the forms of philosophy that have critiqued anthropocentrism, such as deep ecology, which has preferred to draw instead on various sources which promise to provide an uplifting alternative religion of cosmic character. In contrast, the appropriation model of human-centredness, like the other liberation models focussing on behavioural criteria for centrism rather than on discursive claims and avowals, has considerable practical and political force. The model can suggest ways in which this human-centred structure can be countered through appropriate social change and what amounts to good ecological education. Countering anthropocentrism is not only feasible, it is actually what good ecological activism is geared to accomplish. The general counter-hegemonic strategy suggested by the analysis may be summed up as the replacement of monological relationships with nature by dialogical ones that are responsive to the other on their own terms.

Ecological thinkers and activists can try to counter radical exclusion (the first feature of anthropocentrism on the Othering model) by emphasising human continuity with non-human nature and animals. The main theme of ecological thinkers like David Suzuki is that we have somehow lost sight of the fact that humans are animals, and have the same dependency on a healthy biosphere as other forms of life. By bringing about a better understanding of human embeddedness in nature, we contest dualised conceptions of humanity which treat humans as 'outside nature' and above the ecological fate which has overtaken other species. We aim to challenge or disrupt conceptions of human identity and virtue based on the exclusion or devaluation of characteristics shared with non-humans, such as emotionality and embodiment. We stress instead human relatedness to and care for the natural world. We should remember also that terms like 'nature' lump seals and elephants along with mountains and clouds in the one sphere of alleged mindlessness. This is a kind of internal homogenisation, which we contest by promoting an understanding of nature's amazing diversity.[25]

To counter the features of backgrounding and denial, ecological thinkers and green activists try to puncture the Illusion of Disembeddedness, by raising people's consciousness of how much we all depend on nature, and of how anthropocentric culture's denial of this dependency on nature is expressed in local, regional or global problems. There are many ways to do this. One important way, for those with a theoretical bent, is to criticise institutions and forms of rationality which fail to acknowledge and take account of this dependency on nature, such as conventional economics. Through local education, activists can stress the importance and value of nature in practical daily life, enabling people to keep track of the way they use and impinge on nature. They can create understandings of the fragility of ecological systems and relationships. Those prepared for long-term struggles can work to change systems of distribution, accounting, perception, and planning so that these systems reduce remoteness, acknowledge our embeddedness and allow for nature's needs and limits. Bringing about such systematic changes is what political action for ecological sustainability is all about.

There are also many ways to counter incorporation. We can work in many cultural fields to displace the deeply rooted traditional view of non-human difference as 'lack' and the devaluation of non-humans as inferior versions of the human species. We can aim to replace it with an affirmation of non-human difference as an expression of the richness of earthian life, and a view of non-humans as presences to be encountered on their own terms as well as on ours. In terms of biological education, activists work to counter incorporation when they create an understanding of nature's own complex ecological order, and of the developmental story of species and of the earth. Activists of all kinds work to counter incorporation when they engage critically with the systems and institutions which imperil the precious non-human presences around us, such as growth-maximising economic systems, or when they oppose destructive development in areas which carry their own complement of more-than-human life. In opposition to destructive incorporation into the human sphere, they may join a streamwatch group or a group to protect or restore local wildlife, for example.

Instrumentalism involves the assumption that all other species are available for unrestricted human use, although it is unlikely that many of those steeped in the ideology of human supremacy will see humans as mutually and reciprocally available for non-human use (for example, as food). Instrumentalism in this form is a clear expression of anthropocentrism and of an arrogant attitude to the other which sees it in the guise of a servant of the self. One of the most important things to aim to establish in any strategy for countering instrumentalism then is some degree of human humility and sensitivity to nature's own creativity and agency. Another very important strategy here is the cultivation or recovery of ways of seeing beings in nature in mind-inhabited ways as other centres of needs and striving, to replace the reductionist view of them as mere mechanical resources for the use of the centre that is the self. All the above forms of activism may be mobilised in these tasks. But it is often also important to demonstrate the imprudence of anthropocentrism, for example by showing the extent of uncertainty and the limits of our knowledge. This strategy may be especially important where anthropocentrism takes the form, as it often does, of arrogance wrapped in the garments of science. Narrowly anthropocentric cognitive and aesthetic relations to nature can be countered in a variety of ways: for example, promoting alternative caring and attentiveness towards the land, learning about non-anthropocentric models other cultures may be using, and generating local earth narratives which can place local relationships with nature in a deeper, more storied and less narrowly productivist framework of attachment.

The analysis has major implications in theory and philosophy, for example in the approach to methodology, ethics and the philosophy of mind, which I discuss in Chapters 7 and 8. As I outline in Chapter 9, activists in countering human-centredness can draw usefully on the theorisations offered by other liberation movements of solidarity through the cultivation of a 'traitorous identity', since a self-critical approach both to the self and to the larger culture is an important part of the agenda. But the exercise is far from being mainly about theory and personal change, although these have an important role to play. As we can see, countering anthropocentrism is a program with major practical and activist implications, and the agenda it generates coincides strikingly with the ecological education and sustainability agendas of the environment movement. To someone looking for cosmic transformation, much of it may seem disappointingly ordinary. In fact however, it is precisely this ordinariness that gives it its practical power. In short then, a non-rationalist liberation model of anthropocentrism can draw together, deepen and help explain the basis for activist practice, as well as providing a good foundation for self-reflexive activism. Many ecological activists are already doing the sorts of things that are necessary to counter the historical legacy of human-centredness.

This is not to deny that there can be more and less thorough forms of environmental understanding, nor to claim that every form of environmental activism engages fully with anthropocentrism. There can of course, as in all other areas of social change, be more and less thorough forms of understanding, deeper forms which look at longer term solutions and shallower forms of content with quick-fixes that address a restricted range of interests, as well as solution orientations focussed mainly on maintaining the power systems that are the underlying problem. But the relationship between theory and practice is misdescribed in terms of a choice between a shallow ecology movement concerned with practical activism versus a deep movement concerned with philosophical and spiritual growth, which does the real job of challenging human-centredness. Rather an anti-anthropocentric or 'deep' movement is an implicit but integral part of the politics of ecological activism and of ecological education *once these are understood in sufficiently thorough ways.*[26] Personal spiritual practices cultivating awareness of connection to nature and others are central to some ways of working against human-centredness, but as we have seen, we must also take prudent account of the way our insensitivity to nature impacts adversely on our own welfare. There are many ways we can challenge anthropocentric culture, and all of them are urgent. In all the areas of counter-work I have discussed, the environmental movement of the last half-century has had amazing success, considering the short time involved. But that success is far less than the huge scope of ecological and survival challenges that a deeply anthropocentric culture now requires.

Otherising as an impediment to justice

The Otherisation of the non-human is first and foremost a question of justice. Its modes of distancing from and reducing the Other bear on a key question of justice – the concern with obstacles to justice, especially forms of partiality and self-imposition that prevent us giving others their due.[27] Although in the universalist/impersonalist tradition justice is interpreted in terms of distance from attachment and particular relationships, it is, as Marilyn Friedman argues, better interpreted as the absence of the kinds of biases exhibited in Otherisation and similarly oppressive forms of conceptualisation or treatment. If, as Friedman suggests, giving others their due is the most basic sense of justice, we must see the treatment of non-humans in reductive and Otherising frameworks as radically less than they are as an important kind of injustice. When we treat nature and animals in polarised terms as part of a radically separate, simpler order, we do them an injustice, as we do also when we see them as less evolved, inferior beings.

The injustice of Othering the non-human is perhaps clearest in the case of the reductive treatment of animals. There is also injustice in the traditional stances of the dominant culture that would deny any application of ethics to non-humans, treating humans, and only humans, as ethically significant in the universe, and deriving those limited ethical constraints they admit on the way we can use nature and animals entirely indirectly, from harms to other humans. These are fairly obvious and easy to recognise as forms of anthropocentrism. But just as other forms of supremacism and centrism, for example those based on race and gender, appear in various forms and guises, so there are weaker and stronger, more upfront and more subtle forms of human-centredness. Despite our contemporary context of accelerating human destruction of the non-human world, traditions of general and direct ethical exclusion for non-humans are strongly defended by many philosophers and some environmentalists. Some philosophers, most notably Kant, have advocated admitting the others of the earth indirectly to ethical status, because we can learn from cruelty to animals 'bad habits' that affect our behaviour towards those who really count, human beings. Such indirect positions are heavily human-centred because non-humans are admitted to value only in a secondary way, entirely as a function of their relationship to humans. Other philosophers are critical of these strong forms of human centredness, but nevertheless cling to subtler forms which remain anthropocentric and are overly restrictive in their ethical recognition of non-humans. Recent environmental ethics has produced many examples of more subtle anthropocentric forms, for example, assimilationist positions which allocate moral consideration or value to non-human beings entirely on the basis of their similarity to the human. Such claims are unjust for non-humans in the same way that assimilationist frameworks that allocate worth to individuals of another culture, for example an aboriginal culture, just on the basis of their similarity to the dominant (white) colonising culture are unjust.

As we have seen, our insensitivity and injustice towards nature is a prudential hazard to us and should be rejected on that ground alone; but we must still place the recognition of injustice first, rather than continuing to prioritise our own interests as suggested in the concept of enlightened self-interest. Enlightened self-interest is only as good as the assurance that the actor will remain enlightened, and there is a major question about what can guarantee that regularly in the absence of a dispositional ethical base of a non-egoist kind such as care or respect. The concept of enlightened self-interest is an unsatisfactory way to theorise the situation, both because self-interest cannot provide such an assurance, and because the concept hovers uneasily between an unclear ethical recognition of the claims of the other and an attempted reduction to some form of rational egoism. Part of its appeal is this ambiguity between an instrumentally-based concern for others and tighter connections based on forms of relational selfhood. As an indecisive way of acknowledging that interests can be relational, it must still face a choice between the centric-instrumental mode that reduces the reasons for acting differently to the interests of the self, and a counter-centric mode that accepts outcomes for the other as reasons. The first position, that refuses to concede injustice for the other, leads to contradiction, since at the bottom it retains the centric-instrumental or rational-egoist mode which creates the prudential hazard in the first place, hoping only to turn aside its ill-effects for self. The second position that does concede injustice escapes this, but can be seen as a way of addressing the connections between our interests and our injustice to earth others which tries to stay within the framework of rational egoism by assuming some kind of purely contingent and temporary convergence between our fully-considered interests and those of the other.

The logic shows though that environmental concern can't just be a recognition of prudence which does not *also* involve recognition of injustice. In the sense in which this is what people mean by talking about 'enlightened self-interest', environmental concern therefore cannot just be a matter of enlightened self-interest. Changes to the One have to go deeper and wider than that in the dominant culture, and a recognition of prudence that does not extend to a recognition of injustice tries to minimise self-change. The strategy of acting only out of concern for effects on self in this case might be compared to the strategy of a dominant One, say an individual or social group, who assents to a process of social reconciliation with a subordinated Other not out of any real recognition of injustice to them but as the minimum concession they can make, and just in the hope of getting or keeping a quiet life. One thing to be said about this is that it simply will not work; the One has to concede injustice in order to effect a sufficient change to provide any guarantee that the same approach will not immediately be repeated somewhere else where it may be equally damaging – that is, evidence of dispositional change. That's why it's so important to be able to say 'Sorry'.

Reductive and Othering modes of conception herald other forms of injustice, such as distributive injustice, preventing the conception of non-human others in ethical terms, distorting our distributive relationships with them, and legitimating insensitive commodity and instrumental approaches. We must take much more seriously concepts of distributive justice for non-humans, as not inferior or lower in priority to human justice issues. Interspecies distributive justice principles should stress the need to share the earth with other species (including difficult and inconvenient ones like snakes, crocodiles and bears – animals that are predators of humans or of animals under human protection) and provide adequate habitat for species life and reproduction. Distributive injustices to non-humans fostered by the Othering framework include the use of so much of the earth for exclusively human purposes that non-humans cannot survive or reproduce their kind. They include also rationalistic farming systems that reduce the share of resources allowed to earth others to the minimum required for productive survival, such as veal crate or battery egg systems. Just remedies for these oppressive and unjust distributions involve measures for a fairer sharing of the earth with other species. Assigning more land to earth others, whether in the form of areas exclusively for their use (as in some wilderness areas and national parks), prioritising their welfare in many multiple use areas and requiring human behaviour to adjust, and encouraging more non-human use of exclusively human areas like cities and suburbs are examples. These are all matters of inter-species justice that are jeopardised by human-centredness.

The prudential blindspots of anthropocentrism

A very important feature of the Othering model of human-centredness is that it validates the ecological insight that a human-centred framework is a serious problem not only for non-humans *but for human beings themselves.* The logic of Othering in the case of nature need not be completely parallel to that of human oppression (which includes features associated with reciprocal consciousnesses that are not mirrored here) for us to be able to draw some useful and perhaps even startling conclusions from it. The blindspots of this logic of Othering as applied to nature support my thesis that reason in its current form is a danger to our survival. We have been considering the hypothesis that the reason the rationalist culture of the west has been able to expand and conquer other cultures as well as nature was that it has long lacked their respect-based constraints on the use of nature – a thought that puts the 'success' of the west in a rather different and more dangerous light. This would make the west's superior ability to generate 'cargo' not a technological accident, as suggested by Jared Diamond, and not, as we have traditionally assumed, a badge of superiority, but rather subject to a version of the paradox of power, in which the conditions that produced our initial success can be extrapolated to predict our eventual failure. The anthropocentric logic I have been analysing has been mistaken for rationality since the Enlightenment, as conceptual machinery for getting the most out of the Other which is nature. But an analysis of centric blindspots shows that it is actually the opposite of reason. Following that anthropocentric logic will be destructive for us to the extent that we are encouraged to be unaware of the way other organisms support our lives, and that we are enmeshed in ideologies of self-containment, self-enclosure and autonomy that are illusory and hegemonic.

The centric structure provides a form of rationality, a framework for beliefs, which naturalises and justifies a certain sort of self-centredness, self-imposition and dispossession, which is what eurocentric and ethnocentric colonisation frameworks as well as androcentric frameworks involve. The centric structure accomplishes this by promoting insensitivity to the Other's needs, agency and prior claims as well as a belief in the coloniser's apartness, superiority and right to conquer or master the Other. This promotion of insensitivity is in a sense its function. Thus it provides a very distorted framework for perception of the Other, and the project of mastery it gives rise to involves dangerous forms of denial, perception and belief which can put the centric perceiver *out of touch* with reality about the Other. The framework of centrism does not provide a basis for sensitive, sympathetic or reliable understanding and observation of either the Other or of the self; centrism is (it would be nice to say 'was') a framework of moral and cultural blindness.

Think, for example of what a eurocentric framework led colonisers such as Australians in the past to believe about indigenous people: that they were semi-animals, without worthwhile knowledge, agriculture, culture, or technology, that they were wandering nomads with no ties to the land, and were without religion. Colonisers believed, despite the existence of over 300 indigenous languages, in a simple, uniform indigenous character. They failed completely to understand the relationship between Aboriginal people and the land they took, or to recognise indigenous management practices. The eurocentric framework told those intent on settlement that the Aboriginal presence imposed no limits on their actions, that the land was *terra nullius,* simply 'available for settlement'. Thus, it created a belief system which was the very opposite of the truth, and evidence to the contrary was simply not observed, was discounted or denied. As a number of feminist thinkers have noted in the case of scientific observation, a framework of perception and reason designed for subjugating and denying the other is not a good framework for attentive observation and careful understanding of that other, and even less is it one for evolving life strategies of mutual benefit or mutual need satisfaction.

If human-centredness similarly structures our beliefs and perceptions about the other which is nature, it is a framework for generating ecological denial and ecological blindness in just the same way that euro- and ethnocentrism is a framework for generating moral blindness. The upshot of such a structure in the case of nature is a perceptual framework and form of rationality which fosters insensitivity to the intricate patterns and workings of nature, encouraging those who hold it to see only a disorderly other in need of the imposition of rational order via development. In this framework, the Other is conceived monologically as a form of the self, and cannot be truly encountered. The human-centred framework is insensitive to the Other's needs and ignores the limits they impose, aggressively pursuing self-maximisation. Just how aggressive this can be and how little space it leaves for the other can be seen from the way animals are treated in the name of rational agriculture, with chickens and calves held in conditions so cramped that in a comparable human case they would clearly be considered torture. Its logic of the One and the Other tends through incorporation and instrumentalism to represent the Other of nature entirely in the monological terms of human needs, as involving replaceable and interchangeable units answering to these needs, and hence to treat nature as an infinitely manipulable and inexhaustible resource.[28] We saw the effects of this in the fisheries case.

Is a centric structure always a dangerous one for the oppressor? In one sense it seems the answer must be no, or there would not be so much oppression in the world. But the illusory framework of centrism often seems much more immoveable and stable than it actually is, especially to those near the centre. It is often rather more convincing for those who are doing well from it and who approximate to or identify closely with the centre than for those who are excluded. How dangerous the standpoint of the One is depends much on the context and on objective relationships of dependency. In the case where the One has no dependency on the Other at all, the One can no doubt afford to behave like the Agha Mohammed Khan, who ordered the entire population of the city of Kerman murdered or blinded. (That was in the days before people were a resource.) If the One is radically dependent on the Other, the weakening and killing of the Other will of course be fatal for the One. Where the sense of apartness from and power over the Other is accurate, oppression may be maintained for a time, although rarely indefinitely because such a worldview generates continuing dependencies on Others that are denied or 'forgotten', and some of these will eventually be fatal.

The problem is that this sense of power and autonomy is often illusory, and because of the logic of centrism the powerful (who are in charge of the dominant order) are not in a good position to know when it is or is not. The logic of centrism is a way of hiding certain things, of making contingent and changeable relations of domination appear to be matters of natural inferiority and superiority, but in the process some crucial information can become unavailable. The framework of centrism is like a one way glass, for its logic makes it much more likely to be discerned as problematic by the oppressed – who can come to experience a 'disjunction', a sense of 'lack of fit' between the framework and their own experience.[29] *The logic of centrism naturalises an illusory order in which the centre appears to itself to be disembedded, and this is especially dangerous in contexts where there is real and radical dependency on an Other who is simultaneously weakened by the application of that logic.* To the extent that the Other is effectively subdued and their ability to thrive is accordingly affected, they are able to contribute less and less to the welfare of the One. It is my belief that the situation with humans and planetary nature is one of radical dependency, and that this is fatally hidden from those who currently hold power in the world – hidden by the very pervasiveness of that power.

All the features of the logic of centrism then support the illusions that are naturalised in the master perspective of the One, such as the Illusion of Disembeddedness, the sense of being radically apart from a separate inferior order which is passive and malleable, and which impinges only in minor (and often annoying) ways. To the extent that we distance ourselves radically from nature in conception and action, we are unable and unwilling to situate ourselves back in nature and frame our lives ecologically as embodied beings. We are unable to understand our ecological relationships except in the most abstract terms, the province of the specialist. The standpoint of the Centre generates, through the radical exclusion of mind-like qualities appropriated for the human, a mechanistic 'supply-side' conception of the world which is unable to see in nature other centres of striving and needs for earth resources, generates unreflective and instrumental forms of knowledge that frame the world in arrogant and self-maximising terms that do not adequately allow for what is not known and perhaps cannot be known. We dissociate ourselves from nature in order to manipulate it, but then cannot empathise with it or relate to it dialogically.

The feature that makes this human-centred framework of rationality especially dangerous in the case of nature is that it encourages a massive denial of dependency, fostering the illusion of nature as inessential and leaving out of account its irreplaceability, non-exchangeability and limits.

As part of its historic denial, the human-centred framework backgrounds and fails to understand the complexity or importance of the biospheric services provided by global ecosystem processes, at the same time as it overestimates its own knowledge and capacity to control them in a situation of limits.[30] We can see the signs of this overestimation in various recent events, ranging from the collapse of fisheries across the world to the failure of Biosphere 2.[31] The denial of dependency combines with the western master story of human hyper-separation to promote the illusion of the authentically human as outside nature, invulnerable to its woes. A framework which is unable to recognise in biospheric nature a unique, non-tradeable, and irreplaceable sustaining other on which all life on the planet depends is deeply anti-ecological. It is because it challenges the Illusion of Disembeddedness that the development of ecological world-views has been so profoundly revolutionary.

Now, let us put this distorting framework of ecological denial beside the reality of our total dependency on the biosphere and the reality of the present human level of resource use, in which human activity consumes as much as 40 per cent of the net photosynthetic product of the earth, in a pattern which has been doubling every 25–30 years. This figure shows that our species is reaching for the goal of diverting most of this planetary energy for its own immediate purposes, increasingly requisitioning for itself the biospheric resources others need to survive. It gives us an indication of the extent to which the intentional structure of those processes which maintain the planetary biospheric systems we take for granted is being rapidly and indiscriminately overridden by the very different structures of human society. Foremost among these in the present global political context is the exchange-value-maximising structure of the market.

The juxtaposition of these two features, the dominant rational framework which locates humanity outside nature and denies or backgrounds dependency on biospheric services, alongside the reality of our ever-increasing encroachment on the natural systems on which we depend, is alarming. As we move into an historical epoch of our relationship with nature in which we impact in unprecedentedly powerful ways on natural systems, our sensitivity to these systems and to our own vulnerability is dulled and our vision obscured by the distorting lenses of the centric framework that aided our expansion in a different era. The human-centred framework may once have been functional for the dominance and expansion of Western civilisation, removing constraints of respect for nature that might otherwise have held back its triumphs and conquests. But in the age of ecological limits we have now reached, it is highly dysfunctional, and the insensitivity to the other it promotes is a grave threat to our own as well as to other species' survival. The old anthropocentric model that binds our relationships with nature within the logic of the One and the Other prevents us from moving on to the new mutualistic and communicative models we now so urgently need to develop for both our own and nature's survival in an age of ecological limits.

6 Philosophy, prudence and anthropocentrism

Is challenging anthropocentrism irrelevant and unhelpful?

The arguments against human-centredness I have advanced in the previous chapter include a strongly prudential one for the human species – that anthropocentrism leads to denials and epistemic distortions that are especially dangerous in our present global context. The use of arguments from prudence in relation to anthropocentrism is, however, philosophically controversial, as is anthropocentrism itself. The concept of anthropocentrism has not been well dealt with by philosophy, which has contested much but failed to establish any constructive theory. Some ecophilosophers have interpreted anthropocentrism as present when there is any concern at all with human prudence or with the human species, seeing concerns relating to human welfare as inevitably 'shallow' and human-centred. Other philosophers have accepted the same assumptions about human-centredness and, contraposing, seen this absence of concern relating to human interests as a reason why the concept of anthropocentrism can have little relevance to policy and little to offer either the theorist or the activist. Still others have reached the same conclusion about the irrelevance of the concept through the argument that human-centredness is inevitable for humans and therefore can offer no useful guidance or discriminatory power.

My argument challenges all these assumptions and objections. Most philosophical critics of the core distinctions have considered only very thin and unsympathetic accounts of human-centredness, and many have mistakenly identified the issue of human-centredness with the question of instrumental/intrinsic value. The key issue of situating humans ecologically, the part of the framework of human-centredness and human/nature dualism that has the most direct bearing on the environmental crisis, is neglected when human-centredness is identified with instrumentalism and with the issue of applying ethical concepts to non-humans. This goes some way towards explaining why some have seen little value in the concept. I shall show too that there is nothing inevitable about adopting the stances and assumptions characteristic of human-centredness. Arguments about the nature and ethics of human-centredness do enable us to draw conclusions about what it is prudent for us to do, and about the general nature of prudential rationality and its mistaken rationalist identification with egoism. The objections to deep thinking are based on a false dichotomy assumed on both sides; we do not have to choose between basing our resistance on human concerns *or* basing them on non-human ones. Counter-centric ethics enables us to advance both arguments based on our own species welfare and on that of the other, taking account of prudence but also giving the good of our planetary partners[1] meaning and weight as reasons for acting differently. It can also help us understand how our own danger is connected to our domination of earth others, how this dynamic develops and is expressed. The assumption that a counter-hegemonic inter-species ethics and human prudence cannot overlap is wrong, as is the identification of human-centredness with instrumentalism which often supports it. In this chapter I show just *how* and why these common objections about human-centredness and prudence are wrong. They rest on rationalist hyper-separations of prudence and ethics, and on rationalist-inspired misinterpretations of 'anthropocentrism' to accord with the universalist/impersonalist philosophical tradition of rationalism.[2]

Anthropocentrism, properly interpreted, is a very useful concept for both the activist and the theorist and should be a major conceptual focus of environmental critique. The project of countering and subverting the human/nature dualism that is part of human-centredness and resituating humans in ecological terms is perhaps the one most characteristic of the environment movement. And as we have seen, concepts of 'centrism' have been at the heart of modern liberation politics and theory. Feminism has focussed on androcentrism, phallocentrism, and phallogocentrism as theoretical refinements of its central concept of sexism, as well as on the connection between these forms of centrism and other forms of centrism. Anti-racist theory critiques ethnocentrism, movements against European colonisation have critiqued eurocentrism, gay activists critique heterocentrism, and so on. The environment movement's flagship in this critical armada has been the notion of human-centredness. It is remarkable then that philosophers have so rarely thought to consult these other movements and concepts for clues about how to theorise anthropocentrism; this failure may well reflect the conservative, largely privileged white male face of contemporary philosophy and its general failure to engage with the relevant social change movements and theories.

A number of recent critics[3] however have rejected the concept of human-centredness on the grounds that it is unnecessary, divisive, and

unhelpful as a practical and theoretical tool. Some of this critique is directed against the way the concept has been used by some deep ecologists to
divide environmentalists rigidly into 'deep' and 'shallow' varieties. Thus
Norton argues that 'the theory that environmentalists should be sorted into
two camps according to commitment, or lack thereof, to the principle that
nature has independent value... [leads] us to no important differences
between environmentalists and their critics among deep ecologists' (p.
236); consideration for future generations and the interests of 'the
human species as a whole', both of which Norton assumes to be anthropocentric, will, he claims, give identical results to the critique of anthropocentrism. We do not need a challenge to the framework of human-
centredness, which is in any case politically awkward and embarrassingly
non-mainstream. Norton calls for a unified approach, but his attempted
reconciliation between 'anthropocentric environmentalists' and those who
would challenge anthropocentrism is not a compromise but depends on
finding ways to subsume or dismiss as unimportant just those environmental values (for example in Leopold's thought) that challenge human-
centredness.

Norton claims to do the same job as the critique of anthropocentrism
with a principle of 'enlightened self-interest' – an overriding Principle of
Convergence between human and non-human interests, that 'policies
serving the interests of the human species as a whole, and in the long
run, will serve also the 'interests' of nature, and vice versa' (p. 240). But
can we *always* demonstrate that the human species' interest will suffer if
earth others are not spared, and that humans will lose more than they may
gain? It seems to be a problem for this position that the human species has
not died out with loss of the Thylacine and the Passenger Pigeon; (some)
humans may have lost something here, but surely not nearly as much as
those they have driven to extinction. To pose the argument only in terms of
the human losses is to weaken, not strengthen it. Certainly, humans
depend on non-human nature and thus have convergent interests, but
they depend on some parts of it much more than others. Suppose the
species in question is a predator of or troublemaker for humans? The
principle appears to provide no means to deal with such conflicts of interest, which it simply assumes will not occur, and it is disturbingly vague.
What is 'the interests of the human species as a whole' and who and what
can establish it? There is a fatal looseness in the concept of convergence
which leaves it open how convergence is obtained, and which is therefore
consistent with obtaining it by means which always prioritise the interests
of one of the parties. This will presumably be the human party, since the
non-human one is not permitted to carry any independent ethical weight,
on pain of reversion to a normal environmental ethic. When we inquire

into these issues more closely, we can see that the principle may be fine as rhetoric, but in practice is unlikely to provide a general or workable framework for the conservation argument.

In fact the plausibility of the Convergence Principle depends on an oscillation between empirical/contingent and necessary/a priori status. If the principle is contingent, and asks us to establish the case for non-human survival always and only in terms of human interests, we risk providing no opposition to development in cases where humans have a lot to gain from non-human extinctions – and these are the key conservation cases. There are plenty of cases where humans have gained by taking over land other species occupied, and where eviction has meant death for non-human individuals and communities: most human farmland has been obtained in this way. With such a restricted type of argument, not only will the tally not always come out on the non-human side, but the whole argument mode that is opened up will tend to place non-human interests in the balance to weigh against human ones. On the other hand, if the principle is treated as a priori or normative, it must be a disguised or de facto version of an anti-anthropocentric ethics, but one that is inferior to an openly stated ethical principle because by basing itself on an assumed identity of interests it does not enable us to theorise conflict cases. But again, these are the most common cases the movement particularly needs to argue well.

Where they are not simply disguised versions of anti-anthropocentric environmental ethics, Norton's supposedly 'unifying' substitutes are not equivalents as he claims. Rather they represent a significant weakening of anti-anthropocentric conceptions of environmental ethics, because they do not allow us to consider or present outcomes for species other than the human species as reasons (unless derivatively).[4] If only arguments based on outcomes for humans are allowed, the principle involves a weakening which narrows the green critique and cuts its important connections with the human-based liberation movements which helped inspire it in the first place, as well as with the closely related movement for animal liberation. By only allowing reasons about human outcomes to count as reasons, the principle greatly contracts our potential argumentation base – which could otherwise appeal to both kinds of reasons – without giving us any clear argumentation gains in return. The underlying reason why Norton wants to insist on this restriction is the assumption that we have to make a choice between arguments based on human interests and arguments based on non-human interests, because considering human interests (and future human interests) is anthropocentric. As this chapter will show, these assumptions are mistaken.

Dobson and Norton both express concern over the unnecessary divisiveness they think the critique of anthropocentrism engenders. There are some valid points in their critique of the deep/shallow division and especially the 'failure of ecophilosophy to make itself practical' which I take up below. However, division among environmentalists is not necessarily as destructive or undesirable as Norton assumes. Some (if not all) of what is involved in the worry about the division between the deep and shallow approaches is an authentic, if sometimes unfortunate and debilitating, problem about framework challenges which is by no means peculiar to the environment movement. Any movement (feminism is a good example) involved in forms of social change which try to challenge major, entrenched cultural norms finds itself in a conflict of choice between, on the one hand, moderate strategies aiming for 'success' in terms of immediately achievable political changes within the framework and on the other, radical strategies of mounting more difficult, long-term and extensive forms of cultural challenge to framework norms. To insist on unity is to support the status quo and defeat the dynamic of change and challenge.

While the level of conflict between framework and non-framework challenges ('shallow' and 'deep') can often be augmented or reduced by various theoretical and practical strategies, it cannot simply be wished away by reconceiving the difference in terms of 'two tasks', different but in no way conflicting.[5] The conflict is real to the extent that a framework challenge is needed, and to the extent that conventional political work for change in a given society demands conformity to the problematic framework. Although serious splits and Othering hinder the interchange process, the search for 'unity' among environmentalists on terms which deny either side of this dilemma is seriously misguided. The conflict certainly cannot be adequately resolved by abandoning the more strenuous and challenging forms of framework critique and the conceptual tools associated with them, on the grounds that they prevent unity and make moderates uncomfortable, especially in the corridors of power. As many social movements have shown, movement vigour and long-term effectiveness depend not so much on unity as on an appropriate tension and dynamic interchange between moderate and radical elements to enable mutual goal maintenance and redefinition; loss of either vigour or vision results when either party vanquishes the other, or when productive interchange ceases. And framework challenges and conflicts are the very place where philosophy most clearly show its practical value.

Is human-centredness inevitable? The dilemma of prudential argument

It is sometimes argued, against any concern with human-centredness, that an ethic based on human interests is not only all that is needed for the conservation of nature but all that is *conceivable*.[6] We are humans; we cannot avoid thinking in terms of our own interests. In fact, if somehow we actually could put our own interests completely aside, we would be left with a totally useless ethics. No one would find it compelling. An ethics that considered only effects on nature and ignored humans would be irrelevant to the practical politics of environmental activism and would cut itself off from real policy debates.[7] This objection certainly has to be taken seriously. We do need, as humans, to take good care of ourselves, not leaving ourselves unsafe, unprotected or unprovided for, in short, to be prudent. 'Prudential' argument in this context then would be argument for avoiding certain environmental practices which considers the effect of those practices on the safety, survival and welfare of human beings. Ozone depletion and pollution harm human health, overfishing destroys resources for future humans, global warming could unleash potentially catastrophic climatic change and extremes, and so on. If the core theoretical distinctions of environmental philosophy indeed must tell us that it is human-centred to take good care of human interests, if they force us to condemn as human-centred all such prudential criticisms of our treatment of nature that refer to the damage its degradation does to human beings, then they would make the ideal of escaping human-centredness quite impractical. And if, as some critics go on to argue, the ideal of avoiding human-centredness also provides only vague alternative reasons for avoiding environmentally-degrading actions, it is a real liability for practical action.

But are we in fact forced to condemn as human-centred all prudential types of environmental argument? I think this is a misinterpretation of human-centredness as well as a misinterpretation of prudence. Consider for a moment the parallel case of egocentrism. We would usually say that someone was egocentric if, among other things, that person consulted only their own outcomes, welfare or interests in deciding what courses of action to follow, and ignored outcomes for others or failed to consider them as presenting reasons for or against the action being considered (this is the extreme case – often we would say someone was egocentric when they just gave other people's interests excessively low weight). But the definition of prudence as taking care of and protecting yourself does not imply that you cannot *also* take care of others, any more than your taking care of orange trees means that you cannot also take care of lemon trees. Considering your own interests does not imply that you cannot also consider others' interests as well as, or as related to, your own. Prudence does not consist of counting *only* one's own interests as reasons for acting or not acting, as in this case, but in taking one's own interests into account in a consistent way, and counting injury to them as among your reasons for avoiding an action. The idea of prudence says nothing about consulting your own interests *to the exclusion of others*. That is not prudence any more than it is rationality – it is selfishness, or egocentrism.

Similarly, the ideal of avoiding human-centredness does not imply at all that humans should not be prudent, or that we cannot consider the effect of environmental damage on our own human interests along with the effect of our actions on other species and on nature generally. The critics' objection rests on identifying prudence with something much stronger – with a kind of species selfishness that treats other beings *solely* as means to our own, human ends. Kant tells us that humans are to be conceived as ends-in-themselves and cannot be treated as merely means to our ends, and though Kant himself restricted this kind of standing to humans, environmental philosophy typically proposes to generalise it. But the crucial phrase here is '*no more than*'. We must inevitably treat the natural world to some degree as a means, for example, as a means to food, shelter and other materials we need in order to survive, just as we must treat other people to some degree as means. In the circus, the performers may make use of one another by standing on one anothers' shoulders, for example, as a means of reaching the trapeze, but our obligation to avoid using others solely as means (or *instrumentalising* them, as philosophers term it) does not imply banning the circus. What is prohibited is unconstrained or total use of others as no more than means, *reducing* others to means – tying some of the performers up permanently, for example, to use as steps.[8]

In short, then, prudential reasons and non-prudential reasons for action are not mutually exclusive; prudential and non-prudential reasons can combine and reinforce one another, and may not always be sharply separate, since any normal situation of choice always involves a mixture. The problem lies rather in the refusal to go beyond questions of human well-being and the exclusion of non-humans from morality and value as no more than tools, unworthy of any moral consideration in their own right. Only by identifying prudence with this radical kind of species selfishness can critics discover a malaise in environmental ethics. There is a difference between prudence and egocentrism, between a sensible concern which considers our own interests, perhaps together with the interests of others, and a selfish and exclusive preoccupation with our own interests which fails to consult the interests of others at all. (One can see why the dominant global order might have wanted us to confuse them, and in whose interests it would be to do so). To be prudent in our dealings with nature is both essential and benign from the perspective both of nature and of ourselves; while to be governed by egocentrism or by instrumentalism in our dealings with nature is damaging but far from inevitable.

Is human-centredness inevitable? The argument from standpoint

The argument just considered concludes that anthropocentrism is unavoidable because some degree of prudence is unavoidable. A related argument reaches the same conclusion by arguing that some kind of human *standpoint* is unavoidable. This standpoint argument for inevitability has appeared frequently over the years of debate in environmental ethics, but I will look at the most recent and perhaps also the most uncompromising rejection of the ideal of non-anthropocentrism, an argument recently proposed by William Grey.[9] William Grey rejects any need for notions of anthropocentrism, declaring robustly that the search for a non-anthropocentric ethic is a hopeless quest and that anthropocentric perspectives are benign, natural, inevitable, and quite adequate for an environmental ethic. Grey asserts without any qualification the even stronger thesis that nature itself is not something which can intelligibly be valued independently of human interests[10], or what he evidently takes to be the same (but which is actually quite different), that *constraints on human conduct can take into consideration only human interests, that only humans can be morally considerable.*[11]

In Grey's 'cosmic' sense of anthropocentrism, a judgement can be claimed to be anthropocentric if it can be made to reveal any evidence of dependency on a human *location* in the cosmos, on human scale or 'human values, interests and preferences'.[12] Grey motivates his cosmic reading of this key concept of environmental philosophy by analogy to the shift from a geocentric (earth-centred) to a heliocentric (sun-centred) view of the universe. Prior to the Copernican revolution, the sun was assumed to revolve around the earth, but Copernicus defeated this geocentrism by taking a more impartial and modern view of the universe which showed the earth to revolve around the sun. The universalist/impartialist tradition and ideals of knowledge as disengagement and as distancing from particularity and the body, emotionality and attachment (values) are obvious influences in arriving at such a concept of anthropocentrism. Thus to avoid anthropocentrism, Grey writes, 'we [must] eschew all human values, interests and preferences'.[13] In fact many philosophers have been influenced by the impersonalist reading to argue that anthropocentrism is inevitable and harmless. Thus Mannison (1980: 54) writes of an anti-anthropocentric ethic as one 'divorced and detached from the needs and interests of human evaluators', Thompson (1990: 158) writes of the supposed invalidity of 'a covert reference to the human point of view, to our interests and concerns', while Hayward (1998: 45) objects that 'anyone's view of the world is shaped and limited by their position and way of being within it'.

In the same way that Copernicus overcame 'parochialism' by moving to a less limited, less earth-centred viewpoint, so overcoming anthropocentrism, these philosophers assume, requires a move away from human locality and human perspective to a view of the world *'sub specie aeternitatis'*, through cosmic rather than human spectacles. Thus to defeat anthropocentrism we must distribute our preferences with perfect detachment and perfect impartiality of concern across humans and non-humans, to achieve at last a view-from-nowhere which abandons all specifically human viewpoint on or preference about the world. It is no surprise that this turns out to be impossible, and Grey, like these other philosophers, then proceeds to the conclusion that anthropocentrism is vindicated and environmental philosophy in general shown to be misguided.

The real problem is that liberal/rationalist moral theories and deep ecology have between them offered us a choice between two unviable interpretations of anthropocentrism, in terms of 'intrinsic value' and rationalist impersonalism on the one hand versus an analogue of rationalist thinking based in concepts of unity and detachment on the other. These two accounts have converged on the problematic 'cosmic' concept of anthropocentrism which has no political oomph and does nothing to make clear the central dynamic of domination of nature that makes our current situation dangerous. That's why the critique appears to have nothing to offer. Despite their confident dismissals of the anthropocentrism issue, these philosophers have made no case for adopting the cosmic-rationalist reading of anthropocentrism they examine, as opposed to other readings, and do not consider an adequate range of alternative meanings, including those that model centrism in terms parallel to the thinking of contemporary social movements.[14] Is this not to ignore, in the critique of centrism, the most relevant and critical movements of our times as sources of interpretation? As we have seen, this relevance can be captured by modelling logics of centrism across areas of application, and we can add to our depth of knowledge of oppression in the process.

This means that the arguments of these critics have a rather serious methodological flaw. Of course, as with any other concept, we can find some readings of the concept of anthropocentrism which bring it out as useless and irrelevant. Cosmic anthropocentrism is one of these. But to be able to dismiss the entire critique of anthropocentrism as useless and irrelevant, one has to establish considerably more than this. It has to be shown that there is no (obvious) reading in which it is useful and relevant, that no more favourable and well-established reading has been ignored. This the critics have not done, and cannot do, since, as I argued in Chapter 5, there is such a reading, one with a firm basis in critical culture and activism. The identification of the problem with intrinsic value or cosmic anthropocentrism will do nothing to explain to us why our current course is dangerous because for that we need the connection between the polarising class-forming dynamic and the hegemonic dynamic to understand how illusions of disembeddedness develop.

In the standpoint argument for the inevitability of cosmic anthropocentrism, the basic steps are these:

Premise 1: To avoid anthropocentrism, we must avoid any reliance on human location or 'bearings' in the world, any taint of 'human interest, perception, values or preferences', 'human standards of appropriateness', 'human concerns', and such tell-tale signs of human origin as 'recognisably human scale'.

Premise 2: But this task is impossible, as demonstrated by various examples of absurd results, the discovery of obvious human reference in normal judgements, and by general argument. For example, Grey argues that we cannot adopt a completely impartial time scale without losing 'recognisably human scale', and that when we lose this, there is no ground for preferring any one state of the universe over any other.

Conclusion 3: Therefore anthropocentrism is unavoidable, and the demand for its avoidance is conceptually confused.[15]

I think it can be conceded that it is impossible for humans to avoid a certain kind of human epistemic locatedness. Human knowledge is inevitably rooted in human experience of the world, and humans experience the world differently from other species. Nevertheless, this kind of human epistemic locatedness is not the same as anthropocentrism, adequately understood. Grey's argument runs together two very different things: *ethical interest* and *epistemological locatedness*. In order to treat another person or being with sensitivity, sympathy and consideration for their welfare, we may often need a process of ethical reflection; this means, according to Iris Young, that we may have to take some distance from our own immediate impulses, desires and interests in order to consider their relation to the demands of others, their consequences if acted upon, and so on. But as Young notes, this process of standing back a little from the self does not require that we adopt a 'cosmic' point of view emptied of *all* particularity and all trace of our own location, that is somehow universal or the same for everyone, and it is hard to see how such a 'view from nowhere' could lead to any useful action at all.[16] Many ethical theories have seen moral reasoning as requiring some version of empathy, putting ourselves in the other's place, seeing the world to some degree from the perspective of an other with needs and experiences both similar to and different from our own. This may be said to involve some form of enlargement of or going beyond our own location and interests, but it does not require us to *eliminate* either our own interest or our own locatedness, rooting out any trace of our own experience and any concern for our own needs. If it did require this, the practice of moral consideration for others *would* be just as impossible as the avoidance of anthropocentrism is claimed by Grey to be. If we eliminated all knowledge of our own experience of suffering, for example, not only would we be unable to consider ourselves properly, but we would have no basis for sympathy with another's suffering.

The confusion involved in Grey's argument comes from a similar confusion between overcoming a narrow restriction of ethical concern to the self and eliminating all epistemic trace of self – between selfishness on the one hand and having a particular standpoint or epistemic location (locatedness) on the other. We can see from everyday experience that ethical concern should not be identified with mere location, for the fact that we are located, partially at least, in our own experience or that of our cultural group does not mean that we cannot and should not be considerate of people other than ourselves or of people outside that group. Indeed, the same kind of argument as Grey advances would show that we must all inevitably be selfish, since we are all 'located' in terms of a perspective that arises in part from our own personal experience. Once we make this distinction between ethical concern and mere location, we can begin to see why anthropocentrism is incorrectly identified in these impersonalist terms as a necessary feature of locatedness and particularity. As we shall see, it is far better identified as a moral and political failing closely allied to selfishness or egocentrism.

There is another interesting and revealing fault in Grey's argument. Grey also 'essentialises' or 'reifies' the category of the human, privileging it over all other possible descriptions of ourselves we might adopt. After all, we need not have described ourselves by the term 'human', since being human is only one of the things we are, and the category human is also included in many other categories. We are not only humans, but also primates and vertebrates, for example. If we use any of these other more inclusive descriptions of ourselves, we will not be able to reach Grey's conclusions that we cannot consider ethically non-human others who are primates or vertebrates. If we use any less inclusive ones, such as 'Greek', 'male' or 'white', Grey's reasoning will oblige us to leave some categories of the human outside ethical consideration and enable us to reach some obviously objectionable conclusions, such as that male humans cannot ethically consider female humans, for example. So Grey's argument has to take the description 'human' and its defining contrast against the nonhuman world to be in some sense more *fundamental* than any of these other possible descriptions. But there is no obvious logical case for doing this, and doing so seems to reveal a certain kind of bias already in favour of the human – an anthropocentric bias, it would seem. So Grey's line of argument reifying and essentialising the human begs the question – it already assumes precisely what is at issue, the privileging of the category 'human' and thus the validity of anthropocentrism.

There is also what we could call an 'interest' version as well as a standpoint version of this same cosmic argument. The interest version argues that we must be anthropocentric because we cannot totally eliminate our own human interests. But we can respond in much the same as before: why should we need to? The equivalent of Grey's assumption in the human case would be to assume that unless we can totally eliminate all concern for ourselves or our own interests, we have no alternative but to behave selfishly towards others. But we know that it is possible to consider both our own interests and the interests of others. Why should we have different standards for the non-human case? To aim for the total elimination of our own interest in ethical action is unrealistic and unwise, presenting us with a false choice between self-abnegation or egocentrism – either totally neglecting or being totally enclosed in our own interests. And thus, once more, 'cosmic' anthropocentrism is unmasked as the product of a family of arguments which rely on shifts and ambiguities like these to demonstrate some version of philosophical egocentrism, where the crucial equivocations between locatedness and restriction of ethical concern to the self often lie buried in the concept of 'selfish interest'. In fact, it is no more necessary for humans to be human-centred that it is for males to be male-centred, or for whites to be eurocentric or racist in their outlook. Human-centredness is no more inescapable than any other form of centrism.

Selfishness and cosmic irrelevance

The argument for cosmic anthropocentrism presented by Grey is also an argument for human selfishness, with a structure that parallels that of similar arguments for individual selfishness. It is a species version of the perennially appealing, but long-refuted doctrine of philosophical egocentrism. But as Bishop Joseph Butler demonstrated so clearly in the eighteenth century,[17] and as we all know from our own experience, egocentrism is no more inevitable than any other kind of centrism, including anthropocentrism.

We can grasp the parallel between anthropocentrism and egocentrism more easily by looking at an example. I shall model the debate between those who reject and those who defend anthropocentrism in terms of the following dialogue, in which Ann accuses Bruce, not of being 'human-centred', but of being *self-centred*, of giving insufficient weight to her needs. Bruce responds in the same way as Grey, the cosmic anthropo-centrist.

Ann: 'I think you ought to do a bit more of the housework around here. I'd like a chance to write some philosophy too. I think you're really self-centred, you only think about your own interests, you never think about my needs at all'.

Bruce: 'I see you're being emotional and confused again, darling. Don't you know *everybody's* self-centred. There's absolutely *no* way to avoid it. We *all* give weight just to our own interest. That's what you're doing too. We're all located in space and time, none of us can eliminate our bearings in the world or distribute our concern equally over everything. We all see the world from that perspective of the self. Inevitably our own experiences, interests, values and preferences, stan-dards of appropriateness must colour and shape our universe, underlie everything we think and do...'

The dialogue is interrupted as Ann throws the dish mop at Bruce, and adds some remarks suggesting he is rationalising his own self-centredness.

'What's all that rubbish got to do with it! Ann says. 'I'm asking you to take over some more of the housework!'

'But I *can't* says Bruce 'That's what I'm trying to explain to you! I can't because I can only really consider *my own* interests. Yours don't count at all, unless I *choose* to give them some weight. I might do that if it was *in my interest*, but you'll have to show me how it is – how you might try to *please* me better if I did, for example. But you haven't done that yet, have you? You've just got angry, and...'

The dialogue closes with some more frustrated remarks from Ann, which I won't repeat in detail, but which are to the effect that Bruce is a narcissistic idiot unable to consider others. Divorce follows shortly after. It was plainly inevitable: Ann and Bruce are not on the same wavelength at all. Ann asks for more weight to be given to her interests. Bruce responds with an epistemological locatedness argument that self-centredness is inevi-table, so he can't do what she asks. Bruce's ultimate hint of a concession indicates he will agree to Ann's request, if he ever does, only in expectation of something she shouldn't be required to give, that is, for the wrong sorts of reasons, out of concern for *his* interests, not out of respect and consideration for hers. This will tell on their relationship in the long run, even if they reach a temporary compromise now.

Bruce's response is totally *inappropriate* to Ann's request. Ann asks for fairness and consideration, Bruce meets her with philosophical cant about locatedness and philosophical egoism. His and Ann's positions appear to meet, but actually they do not. That is why Ann, in the same position as the critic of human-centredness, believes she has been fobbed off. Her respondent has not caught the sense of her claim, has the wrong kind of self-centredness in mind, perhaps because he has been badly educated, or perhaps because he is in bad faith. There is certainly some reason to suspect the latter, since he is using his argument to refuse to do something we all know perfectly well he could do, give more weight to Ann's needs.

Now in just the same way, it seems to me, the response of the cosmic anthropocentrist completely misses the point of the case against anthropocentrism, and misrepresents the sorts of demands that are being made in terms of it. Interpreting the green critic of anthropocentrism as asking for a better deal for the non-human world – a larger share, more concern, more weight, more awareness, attentiveness – gives a rather better reading of the basic thrust of environmental activism than the cosmic idea of viewing the world *sub-specie aeternitatis*. Not that it is never helpful to try to take the cosmic perspective, to think about our humanity in the context of the immensity of the universe, for example. In some circumstances, such a perspective may have much to offer us. My point is rather that it does not connect appropriately with the kind of ecological politics or activism we are concerned with here. Certainly the cosmic perspective is not the only perspective an anti-anthropocentrist could take.

Thus it seems that the defender of cosmic anthropocentrism responds in the same perverse way as Bruce. The defender makes an epistemologically-grounded point about the inevitability of human locatedness, ultimately using it to justify a human species version of the self-centredness and philosophical egocentrism Bruce defends. The cosmic anthropocentrist is, for the purposes of the debate over how to reconstruct the culture in more ecologically-sensitive terms, operating with a similarly perverse understanding of anthropocentrism. Of course that concept is out of kilter with ecological politics and ecological activism. Fortunately, as we have seen in Chapter 5, it is by no means the only plausible candidate for an account of anthropocentrism. The liberation model I outlined there can readily meet the objections of impossibility and impracticality directed against the cosmic account of anthropocentrism. The liberation model does not demand that we humans perform the impossible feat of abandoning a human epistemological location, but it does demand that we abandon the human ethical and political equivalent of self-centredness.

The philosophical egocentrism Bruce appeals to is a remarkably persistent, widespread, and socially-fostered fallacy; nevertheless, if the persistence of the argument from cosmic anthropocentrism was only due to the logical confusions and equivocations of philosophical egoism, it is unlikely that the defenders of anthropocentrism would have raised the perverse cosmic argument so persistently. What complicates the issue further is that this perverse cosmic sense of anthrocentrism is not entirely a straw man, but has been given sustenance by accounts of anthropocentrism found in some deep ecologists, as well as by opponents of environmental ethics. The reasons for its appeal lie in its rationalist roots plus the prospect it holds out of an easy victory over the critic of anthropocentrism. Its use by ecophilosophers is harder to understand, but can be explained in terms of a failure to distinguish between two crucially different models of anthropocentrism which are based on different contrasts, comparisons and extensions. These are first, cosmic anthropocentrism based on the rationalist model of detachment from all human concern, and second, the liberation sense of anthropocentrism I developed in Chapter 5. Many ecophilosophers appeal to both senses as suits their argument – inconsistently, since the models are incompatible. For example deep ecologists such as Arne Naess and Warwick Fox both call on the liberation sense from time to time,[18] but the model which is developed in detail and relied on primarily in deep ecology is the cosmic model or transpersonal reading which treats overcoming anthrocentrism in terms of the overcoming of personal attachment.[19] Feminist thinkers have pointed out that this understanding of the key concepts involves a masculinist and rationalist demand for absence of emotional attachment and discarding of particular ties.[20]

Cosmic non-anthropocentrism, as we have seen, is based on the model of detachment from all human concern and the achievement of a cosmic perspective. We can model the perversity of this concept too in terms of parallels to other liberation concepts of centrism. In terms of the concept of ethnocentrism, the equivalent of Grey's position on anthropocentrism would be that in order to overcome ethnocentrism we would have to abandon all cultural location or centredness. An historically important and much discussed special case of ethnocentrism is eurocentrism, which treats Europeans[21] or their culture as the dominant colonial centre or norm in terms of which others are deviant, peripheral or inferior. For this case, recent anti-racist and post-colonial scholarship argues, quite contrary to Grey, that what is actually required in overcoming eurocentrism is not abandonment of all location but the affirmation of certain epistemic locations, especially of those cultural locations or identities that are suppressed under eurocentrism, to allow the development of a 'polycentric' or an 'acentred' world.[22]

Similarly, a close look at male-centredness (androcentrism) shows us why we can't interpret escape from centrism as the escape from epistemic location in the way the cosmic model tries to do, as requiring epistemological detachment or elimination of bearings. The equivalent of Grey's argument in the case of androcentrism would imply that to counter the male-centredness of culture we would need to abandon all gender location or perspective (both male and female), to achieve the gender equivalent of a view-from-nowhere. But many feminists have argued[23] that 'gender-blindness' or neutrality will in the context of male-dominated culture tend to be no more than appearance and will hide rather than displace the operations of the masculine model as the cultural norm. Part of countering the model of the dominant centre is a positive and multiple kind of epistemic 'centering'. Thus feminists celebrate women's alternative ethical and knowledge styles, and attempt self-recovery and positive identity through women's history and women-oriented projects. In the context of the oppression deriving from this kind of centrism, the claim to centredness, to one's own centre as epistemic and cultural location or identity, takes on especial importance as a way of regaining self-definition in the face of the tendency of the single dominant centre to incorporate and assimilate elements treated as periphery or as 'Other'. Again, this liberation project need not mean replacing one form of hegemonic centrism (androcentrism) by another (gynocentrism).

Recognition, prudence and survival

But by providing reasons for considering nature based on human prudence, are we not perpetuating the very human-centredness and instrumentalism we should seek to combat, considering nature only in relation to our own needs and as means to meet those needs? This issue reveals another major area of difference between the cosmic model implying elimination of human bearings and the liberation model of human-centredness of the sort I have given. Only in the confused account of anthropocentrism as cosmic anthropocentrism is it essential to avoid anything which smacks of human bearings and preferences in the interests of pursuing superhuman detachment. On the liberation account of human-centredness, there is no problem or inconsistency in introducing some prudential considerations to motivate change, or to show why, for example, human-centredness is not benign and must lead to damaging consequences for humankind. To gain a better understanding of the role of prudence in the kinds of changes that might be required, let us return to the marital example of Bruce and Ann.

Let us suppose that instead of leaving right away, Ann persuades Bruce to try a visit to a marriage counsellor to see if Bruce can change enough to save their relationship. (We will have to assume that Bruce has some redeeming features I have not described here to explain why Ann considers it worthwhile going to all this trouble). After listening to their stories, the counsellor diagnoses Bruce as a textbook case of egocentrism, an individual version of the centredness structure set out above. Bruce seems to view his interests as somehow radically separate from Ann's, so that he is prepared to act on her request for more consideration only if she can show he will get more pleasure if he does so, that is, for instrumental reasons which appeal to a self-contained conception of his interests. He seems to see Ann in instrumental terms not as an independent person but as someone defined in terms of his own needs, and claims it is her problem if she is dissatisfied or miserable. Bruce sees Ann as there to service his needs, lacks sensitivity to her needs and does not respect her independence or agency.[24] Bruce, let us suppose, also devalues the importance of the relationship, denies his real dependency on Ann, backgrounds her services and contribution to his life, and seems to be completely unaware of the extent to which he might suffer when the relationship he is abusing breaks down. Bruce, despite Ann's warnings, does not imagine that it will, and is sure that it will all blow over: after a few tears and tantrums Ann will come to her senses, as she has always done before, according to Bruce.

Now the counsellor, June, takes on the task of pointing out to Bruce that his continued self-centredness and instrumental treatment of Ann is likely to lead in short order to the breakdown and loss of his relationship. The counsellor tries to show Bruce that he has underestimated both Ann's determination to leave unless there is change, as well as the sustaining character of the relationship. June points out that he may, like many similar people the counsellor has seen, suffer much more severe emotional stress than he realises when Ann leaves, as she surely will unless Bruce changes. Notice that June's initial appeal to Bruce is a prudential one; June tries to point out to Bruce that he has misconceived the relationship and to make him understand where his real interests lie. *There is no inconsistency here; the counsellor can point out these damaging consequences of instrumental relationship for Bruce without in any way using, endorsing or encouraging instrumental relationships.*

In the same way, the critic of human-centredness can say with perfect consistency, to a society trapped in the centric logic of the One and the Other in relation to nature, that unless it is willing to give enough consideration to nature's needs, it too could lose a relationship whose importance it has failed to understand, has systematically devalued and denied – with, perhaps, more serious consequences for survival than in Bruce's case. The account of human-centredness I have given, then, unlike the cosmic account demanding self-transcendence and self-detachment, does not prohibit the use of certain forms of prudential ecological argument, although it does suggest certain contexts and qualifications for their use.

In the case of Ann and Bruce, June the counsellor might particularly advance these prudential reasons as the main reasons for treating Ann with more care and respect at the initial stages of the task of convincing Bruce of the need for change. Prudential arguments need not just concern the danger of losing the relationship. June may also try to show Bruce how the structure of egocentrism distorts and limits his character and cuts him off from the main benefits of a caring relationship, such as the sense of the limitations of the self and its perspectives obtained by an intimate encounter with someone else's needs and reality. Prudential arguments of all kinds for respect are the kinds of arguments that are especially useful in an initial context of denial, while there is still no realisation of that there is a serious problem, and resistance to the idea of undertaking work for change. In the same way, the appeal to prudential considerations of ecological damage to humans is especially appropriate in the initial context of ecological denial, where there is still no systematic acknowledgement of human attitudes as a problem, and resistance to the idea of undertaking substantial social change. *Although reasons of advantage or disadvantage to the self cannot be the only kinds of considerations in a framework which exhibits genuine respect for the other*, the needs of the self do not have to be excluded at any stage from this process, as the fallacious view of prudence as always instrumental and egocentric suggests.

But once June's prudential argument has broken Bruce's initial resistance to considering change, June can and should go on to supplement these prudential arguments for considering Ann, framed in terms of disadvantages for Bruce from failing to do so, with further kinds of considerations *which treat outcomes for Ann as presenting moral reasons in their own right*. Only when he does so can Bruce fully encounter Ann as another person, an equal moral centre, and only then will he really begin to realise the full benefits of the relationship, for the full rewards of personal relationships of care only come when we have ceased to be primarily focussed on the benefits we ourselves may gain from them, and are focussed upon the other. These further considerations June introduces then are not primarily oriented to outcomes for Bruce, that is, *they are not instrumental*. These larger reasons why Bruce should consider Ann that June introduces later in her counselling sessions can open up the couple's exploration of the strategies for respecting, negotiating and balancing the needs of self and other they need to develop. These will probably have to emphasise improved communication, about mutual emotions, needs, desires and limits. They may involve, especially for Bruce, a more mutualistic reconception of self and self's needs as a self-in-relationship, formed in a balance of mutual transformation. But although reasons of advantage or disadvantage to Bruce cannot be the only kinds of considerations June introduces to Bruce if she is aiming to help Ann re-negotiate the relationship in a framework that is respectful of Ann, June does not have to exclude these questions or Bruce's needs from consideration at any stage from this process of re-negotiation, as the fallacious view of prudence as always instrumental and egocentric suggests.

For example, it would be prudent for Ann to want to be assured that consideration of her needs will be a settled feature of Bruce's behaviour towards her, to ask for some dispositional security that he is likely to continue considering her needs. So Ann will probably want to be sure Bruce is now acting out of the right underlying reasons of care which support counterfactual and dispositional consideration of her needs, rather than the sorts of narrowly instrumental and ephemeral ones Bruce puts up to her in their earlier dialogues. This is a prudential aspect of care, but a counterfactually extended one. Although there is a basic opposition between the exclusively instrumental mode which reduces the other to a means to the self's ends, and the respect/care mode which acknowledges the other as a different centre of agency and value, prudential reasons can quite properly supplement and balance a care perspective, and care itself must have prudential aspects (Hampton 1993).[25]

The case of Ann and Bruce is meant to illustrate the role of prudence in maintaining durable ethical relationships, as well as to provide some guidance as to what we might do to improve our currently failing 'partnership' with nature. But of course the sorts of prudential reasons for considering nature I outlined earlier which invoke the threat or danger from the ecological blindspots induced by anthropocentrism are by no means the only kinds of reasons the liberation model suggests for regarding anthropocentrism as a prudential liability. Another very important set of reasons why human-centredness is a problem derives not directly from its ill effects on the colonised, on animals and nature themselves, but more indirectly from its distorting effect on the colonisers, on human identity and human society. The structure of human-centredness distorts and limits the possibilities for what we can become as humans in much the same way that the structures of racism and sexism do for coloniser identities and for masculinist identities, and the structure of egocentrism does for Bruce. The logic of human-centredness which conceives nature, external and internal, as the 'lower', denied aspect of self and society, also constructs dominant human identity and virtue by exclusion as the identity and virtue of the master, built on the exclusion of a lower order of alterity and externality both within and without.

This kind of structure precludes the formation of properly integrated selves and of certain beneficial and satisfying kinds of relationships with others and with nature. Again, just as we do not realise the benefits of personal relationships of care until we have ceased to be primarily motivated by or focussed on the benefits we gain from them, so we can realise fully the rewards of experiencing the other of nature as another centre only when our primary focus is not our own gain or even safety. And to the extent that anthropocentric frameworks prevent us from experiencing the others of nature in their fullness, we not only help to imperil ourselves through loss of sensitivity but also deprive ourselves of the unique kinds of richness and joy the encounter with the more-than-human presences of nature can provide. To realise this potential, we will need a reconception of the human self in more mutualistic terms as a self-in-relationship with nature, formed not in the drive for mastery and control of the other but in a balance of mutual transformation and negotiation.

Ultimately, a durable relationship between we humans and our planetary partners must be built on the kinds of perceptual, epistemic and emotional sensitivities which are best founded on respect, care and love. So if we aim to make our relationship with nature a durable one, as we must do for survival, we can learn something from the plight of Ann and Bruce. Environmental critics of the far-from-durable present must similarly aim, through ecological education and institutional change, to develop in the culture the right sorts of prudential and care-based, non-ephemeral reasons for considering nature's interests, supporting counterfactual and dispositional bases for concern of the sort care can provide. We must aim to establish better communicative relationships with nature in all its aspects, as a preliminary to learning to balance human needs with nature's needs and limits. In this way we can begin to replace the old instrumental and mechanistic models which guided the development of the west during the centuries of conquest, and meet the challenge of our time to realise the new models of communication and care which are now struggling to emerge.

7 The ethics of commodification

Commodification and person/property dualism

In his 1996 book *Kinds of Minds*, distinguished philosopher of mind Daniel Dennett suggests that we have to be careful not to be over-generous in letting non-humans into the category of morally considerability because it could mean there is less in the way of resources available to help under-privileged humans. As we saw in the last chapter, few contemporary philosophers can fairly be accused of such over-generosity, (although there are good methodological reasons for generosity) even if Dennett's argument structure and trade-off assumptions here are acceptable, which, I shall argue, they are not.

A strategy of minimising the group admitted to the class of 'persons' is one aspect of a currently popular position in environmental ethics which revises and updates Cartesianism: Descartes got it wrong to the extent that he excluded higher animals from consciousness, but otherwise got it pretty much right. This neo-Cartesian rationalist position insists on a strong, indeed dualistic boundary between 'persons' and the rest, and as in Cartesianism usually draws on concepts of reason or closely related conscious-ness concepts to justify its inclusions and exclusions. Some versions would extend the boundaries of the person category, on the basis of similarity to the human, to exclude from commodification some 'conscious' higher animals. Neo-Cartesianists of various stripes include animal defence theor-ists Tom Regan and Peter Singer, whose approaches I discuss below. The basic strategy of neo-Cartesianism as employed in animal defence is to attempt to extend the privileged category of the human in human/nature dualism rather than to try to break human/nature dualism down. Neo-Cartesian animal defence theory is an exercise in boundary extension which otherwise retains the basic conceptual framework of Cartesian-rationalist monological relationships in which a rational-conscious mind confronts a mindless and morally meaningless universe.[1] The appeal of neo-Cartesianism is that of the 'minimum-change-from-the-status quo' position, and it is sometimes even advocated on that ground. But the human extensionist approach is limiting and brings many problems and exclusions in its train, such as the difficulty of matching its theory with an ecological ethic.

Neo-Cartesian animal defence theorists have successfully put some issues about animals on the philosophical and social agenda, but have no larger conceptual resources to critique the rationalist framework of commodification that makes so many animal lives a living hell by reducing them to living meat or egg production units. Neo-Cartesianism, like Cartesianism, forms part of the dominant ethical framework which corresponds to the commodification of nature. Some leading features of the ethics of commodification are that it assumes a moral dualism between the group taken to be morally considerable ('persons') and the rest – which are 'things' (and, potentially at least, property), and are assumed not to matter or count ethically at all, hence to be open to rational instrumental use. The position goes on to minimise the extent of the category of the morally considerable, and to strongly dissociate respect or moral considerability on the one hand from use or consumption on the other. Neo-Cartesian moral dualism makes an emphatic division of the world into two sharply contrasting orders, consisting of those privileged beings considered subject to strong forms of ethical concern as 'humans' or 'persons', and the remainder, considered beneath any ethical consideration at all and as belonging to an instrumental realm of resources (or, in the prevailing political context, of 'property') available to the privileged group. This philosophy leaves the maximum amount of the world available for the privileged group of honorary humans to put to the most reductive forms of use, with the minimum identification, sympathy and consideration needed for those in the 'thing' group. Typically, moral dualism organises moral concepts so that they apply in hyper-separated, all-or-nothing ways: for example, a being either has a full-blown right to treatment considered equal to human treatment, or it is not to be subject to any form of ethical consideration at all. The hyper-separation of use from respect and moral considerability has many consequences for everyday life with animals and nature, as I discuss in the last section on the division between pet animals and economic animals.

As I show below, there are good ethical and methodological reasons to reject neo-Cartesianism and associated moral dualism. We have many opportunities to organise the ethical field differently, and many reasons to do so. Extensionist ethical strategies do not fit with an ecological awareness of the kinship and continuity of planetary life. Qualities such as mind, communication, consciousness and sensitivity to others that are used by neo-Cartesianists to support their dualisation of the world are organised in multiple and diverse ways across life forms, ways that do not correspond to the all-or-nothing scenarios of 'consciousness' assumed by moral dualism.[2] A sharp cut-off or boundary for moral consideration is neither necessary nor desirable, and the forms of life that correspond to the dualism between use and respect are unjust and diminishing both for 'persons' and for the great multiplicity of beings that make up planetary life. Finding respectful and reverential ways to use the earth to meet our life needs is a better way to protect nature than a rigid division between spheres of use and spheres of respect or reverence. Neo-Cartesianism may improve our sensitivity to a small range of beings that resemble humans, but it blunts our sensitivities to the much larger class of excluded beings. In the present context of ecological destruction, it would be wise for us to adopt dialogical philosophical strategies and methodologies that maximise our sensitivity to other members of our ecological communities and openness to them as ethically considerable beings, rather than ones that minimise ethical recognition or that adopt a dualistic stance of ethical closure that insists on sharp moral boundaries and denies the continuity of planetary life.

Dennett's trade-off arguments are typical of the politics of conflict that is played out around moral consideration and person/property dualism, in which the moral exclusion of the class defined as 'resource' is represented as nothing less than a matter of justice to less fortunate members of the 'person' class. The rejection of this moral dualism and its duty to exclude non-humans is represented as depriving persons of property or resources that are rightfully theirs. Just as poor whites were seen to be further deprived by the liberation of slaves, and working-class men by the liberation of women, so our duty to underprivileged humanity is seen to require the continued treatment of animals as mere resources, and of trees as mere fodder for timber mills. Although moral dualism constructs concern for non-human nature in this conflictual way, as a deficit of attention or concern for some less privileged human group, the remorseless conflict scenario this assumes can usually be reconceived in complementary rather than competitive ways.[3] If concepts of justice are applicable also on the non-human side, we are, even in the worst case scenario represented by Dennett's trade-off, faced here with an interspecies justice conflict. As in the case of intraspecies conflicts within the sphere of human justice, we have an overriding, higher-order obligation to try to circumvent or eliminate such justice conflicts where possible, and to avoid multiplying and reinforcing them. This translates into a methodological obligation to seek out and favour complementary over competitive constructions of justice spheres, other things being equal. Dennett's approach is unacceptable on these methodological grounds.

As a counter to such unnecessarily conflictual constructions, we need to attend to the ways in which the human and non-human spheres of ethics and justice, although hardly free of some limited and sometimes manufactured conflicts of this kind, can be constructed not as competitive but as complementary approaches which need and strengthen each other. Thus we should note that moral dualism is also a moral boomerang which too often returns to strike down the less privileged sectors of humanity itself when these allegedly 'lower' orders of humans are assimilated to nature and to animals, as they have been systematically throughout western history. Conversely, many forms of ethical practice and sensitivity to others are not only not especially sensitive to whether these others are human or non-human, but can actually be strengthened and deepened generally when we refuse the arbitrary exclusion of non-human others and the self-impoverishment and blunting of sensibilities exclusion involves. That is one reason why opening to and caring for earth others can be a general ethical learning, healing and development practice for both children and adults, (especially for wounded individuals). When we act to reject moral dualism, we can open up ways to reflect critically and sympathetically on the ethical status of the act of exclusion itself, on our own identities, and on ethical practices of boundary-breaking; these meta-lessons are among the most important for human and non-human spheres of ethics alike.

Neo-Cartesian moral dualism is strongly entrenched, as an ethical expression of a corresponding form of life that is entrenched under global capitalism, the dualistic division between persons and property. The economic rationality of capitalism, whose major defining features are the identification of rationality with egoism and competition and the related concern to maximise property formation and economic growth , supports strategies that minimise ethical recognition of the other-than-human world. A closed ethical stance that minimises the class of beings subject to ethical treatment at the same time maximises the class of other beings that are available to be treated with maximum ruthlessness as resources or commodities. The prudential inappropriateness of these strategies and their destructive ecological effects are increasingly evident. A number of polarities and dualistic exclusions cluster around this point, converging to create a conceptual foundation and support network for the Lockean model of property ownership, and more generally, for the person/property dualism that underpins the commodification of nature. This marks a broad and deep gulf between those who can own and those who can be owned and exchanged as property, a division of the world into human and non-human, subject and object, consciousness and mechanism, intrinsic and instrumental value, respect and use, those to whom the protection of justice can be accorded and those from whom it is withheld. Conventional environmental ethics has allowed some pluralism and contest over exactly where the boundary falls between the privileged and the excluded classes, but contesting the larger dualistic division between the traders and the traded has rarely been part of its concern.

Minimalist methodologies of closure

If recognising moral considerability for non-humans opens the door to an interspecies ethic, neo-Cartesian Minimalism, the first position I will consider here, jams the door at the point where it is open just a crack. Minimalism makes a minimal extension of ethical recognition, and thinks about it in anthropocentric terms as just that – an extension of dominant human ethics. The most human-like 'higher animals', who are claimed to be the only possessors among the non-humans of the supposedly defining human characteristic and sentience or awareness[4] may be admitted to the ethical sphere, but the door is firmly closed against all others. Minimalism has as its goal the enlargement of the human sphere of ethics rather than an ethical integration of human and non-human spheres, thus adopting a strategy which, as I argue below, must result in minimal admissions to the privileged class. This ethical stance minimally challenges or reinforces anthropocentric ranking regimes that base the worth of a being on their degree of conformity to human norms or resemblance to an idealised 'rational' or 'conscious' subject; and it often aims explicitly at minimal deviations from the prevailing political assumptions and dominant human-centred ethic they are tied into. It aims to minimise recognition of diversity, focussing on ethically relevant qualities like mind, consciousness and communication only in forms resembling the human and failing to recognise that they can be expressed in many different, often incommensurable ways in an ethically and ecologically rich and diverse world.[5]

A major project for a non-anthropocentric form of culture would be that of developing ethical and epistemic frameworks that can give non-humans a non-derivative, non-secondary or instrumental place. This ethical project cannot be carried out in terms of the neo-Cartesian Minimalist program outlined by Peter Singer and is not well expressed in terms of the concept of rights developed by Tom Regan I discuss in the next section below. These two philosophers have led a commendable and active opposition to the dominant humanistic assumption that ethics is effectively confined to the human sphere, contesting through vigorous argument the historic exclusion of non-humans from western ethics. I think that a strong case can be made for extending some kinds of ethical treatment appropriate to persons to our nearest evolutionary relatives in the primate family, and that it is imperative to extend many elements of human-style ethics to other sentient beings.[6] But I do not see that the possibility of such an extension provides any good reason why we should maintain the stance of closure towards other non-humans. An effective challenge to moral dualism entails recognising the continuity of all life forms and contesting the full framework of human/nature dualism, involving the ethical exclusion not only of animals but of nature itself.

Singer (1998) explicitly advocates Minimalism: a minimal extension of recognition to a few animals most like we humans, and a Minimalist methodology urging minimal departures from the status quo of humanism. Both Regan's rights approach and Singer's utilitarianism are strongly associated with a sentience-reduction position that would make a minimal extension of human-style ethics and liberal rights to a few species of animals who can qualify as 'persons'. Every being outside the 'person' category remains potential 'property', the dualistic contrast class which is capable of being owned and treated instrumentally. Minimalism claims to be anti-speciesist but is not genuinely so in selecting for exclusive ethical attention those animals who closely resemble the human, any more than a culture which values women just in terms of their resemblance to men is genuinely non-androcentric. Minimalism continues to see consciousness in singular and cut-off terms, and discounts the great variety of forms of sentience and mind – hence Singer's conviction that trees have no form of sentient or aware life, (which runs counter both to what is disclosed by any reasonably attentive observation and to scientific evidence). Minimalism is not able to recognise consciousness as just one among many relevant differences between species, differences which are largely incommensurable as to value rather than hierarchically ordered along the lines of resemblance to the human.[7] Rather Minimalism makes consciousness the basis for an absolute ethical positioning of all species within a hierarchy based on human norms. Minimalism does not really dispel speciesism, it just extends and disguises it.

Philosophically too, neo-Cartesian Minimalism attempts a minimal deviation from rationalism and Cartesianism – where rationalism has as its central tenet the doctrine that the rational (usually identified with elite humans) is the only thing that fundamentally counts in the universe. The Cartesian division of the world which was based on the assumption that the criterion of consciousness (which Descartes managed to equate, through various equivocations on the concept of 'thought', with calculative reason) picked out just the class of the human. Animals were automata entirely lacking consciousness.[8] The sentience-reduction position minimally corrects Descartes' error of identifying consciousness with the human, but it retains the exclusion of the original rationalist doctrine that reason is all that matters in the universe, and retains the same logic of exclusion. It shifts the boundary to a new point but still leaves far too much outside, and has the same intense emphasis on the need for a boundary between what counts and what does not.[9] Thus the ethical closure characteristic of Minimalism accepts the Cartesian obsession with consciousness (which derives from the Cartesian interpretation of rationality as the self-transparency of the rational subject), and declares with a similar exclusiveness of focus that 'consciousness in all its forms is what fundamentally counts in the universe'.[10] This claim is objectionable on many counts, one of which is its identification of a *single* end or source for all value (a defect it shares with utilitarianism). A moral dualist approach, it gives some higher animals access to moral consideration on a par with humans, but leaves the great majority still outside in the cold, subject to continued backgrounding and instrumentalisation as the 'ground and home of conscious life'.

Although, as Singer notes, the lauding of reason has traditionally been used to exclude slaves (and of course many other subordinated humans such as women, along with animals) from the category of the fully human, and to interpret this 'human' category in elitist ways, Singer is content with a very minimal dislocation of these rationalist assumptions which leaves most of non-human nature just where it was before, in a sphere of ethical exclusion.[11] Singer defends his exclusion of allegedly non-conscious vegetable life with the claim that 'if a tree is not sentient, it makes no difference to the tree whether we chop it down or not' (Singer 1997). But if a tree is a striving (teleological) and adaptive being, it must select some states to strive for (for example continued life, best development) and others to avoid (death). There is an important sense therefore in which death does 'matter' or 'make a difference' to a tree, and to any living being; since it clearly does strive to avoid death (for example by persistently sending out shoots around obstacles placed to block off its light) it is not the case that all states are indifferent to it. Singer's claim incorrectly and unnecessarily ties the concept of 'making a difference' to consciousness rather than to teleology and intentionality, thus producing an unnecessarily dualised account of the field. Elsewhere he states of plants: 'Such a life is a complete blank; I would not in the least regret shortening this subjectively barren form of existence.'[12] Singer claims to acknowledge continuity, but as these statements make clear, Singer's methodology organises the diverse and continuous field of mind and ethics into a polarised, simple on-off form – that of consciousness or nothing (a 'complete blank', 'no conscious experience at all'), in just the same way as Descartes.

But we do not have to choose such a dualistic framework. We can adopt towards plants, for example, the more graduated and diversity-sensitive Intentional Stance I discuss in the next chapter, recognising them as organised intentional and goal-directed beings which value their own lives and strive to preserve them in a variety of challenging circumstances, and opening to the many possibilities for intentional construction and explanation they can present to us. Even if we accept their non-consciousness (in the terms of Singer's narrow and singular concept of awareness), this does not exclude an ethical approach to plant life. If reasons are not restricted to pain avoidance, we can certainly find plenty of good reasons for relating ethically to trees. We can and should, I think, have great respect and reverence for trees and be grateful to them for the many ways in which they support our lives. This means, among other things, that we must never count their lives for nothing, or treat their deaths or destruction lightly or casually as of no consequence or significance.[13] We can honour them both individually, and in species and ecological community terms as great time-travellers and teachers, and be open to and grateful for the wisdom they have to give us. We do them injustice when we treat them as less than they are, destroy them without compunction, see them as nothing more than potential lumber, woodchips or fuel for our needs, (a form of incorporation), fail to attend adequately to them, radically dissociate from them and deny their organisation as intentional (and perhaps communicative) beings, or adopt the stance of ethical closure or dismissal.

Singer's Minimalism is also a political position urging minimal departure from prevailing liberal, humanistic and Enlightenment assumptions and from the present system of economic rationality.[14] But surely an ecological society will require more than minimal departures from these systems, none of which have been innocent bystanders in the development of the rational machinery which is bringing the stripping of the planet for the benefit of a small elite of humans to a high point of rational refinement. Singer's Utilitarianism reproduces many elements of rationalism, including the adoption of universal, abstract mathematically-expressible formulae for decision, in the best universalist/impersonalist tradition. Also in the rationalist tradition is the content of the Utilitarian formula, with its maximisations (always damaging), illusory precision, its intellectualist reduction of ethics to a matter of rational calculation and quantification, and its corresponding reduction of the important dimensions of decision to aspects of life supposedly susceptible to these rational manipulations. And as we have seen, awareness, the chief ground of ethical consideration, is one, but only one, possible variation on reason or mind, although one that modernism can tie to preferences and hence to agency and property ownership. The most serious objection to my mind however is that any ecological or animal ethics based on Singer's Utilitarianism is committed to a massive program of ranking, quantification and comparison between beings and species – a program which, as I argue in the next chapter, is unworkable, ethically repugnant, and built on a problematic reading of equality. Theoretically, ranking comparisons and tradeoffs between beings are insisted upon by Utilitarianism at virtually every level. This emphasis on ranking does not encourage the kind of thinking that aims for mutual, negotiated outcomes, but rather ones that sanction a sacrificial order determined on the basis of greater approximations to the human.

Politically, the gesture of Minimalism reproduces the polarising Cartesian double gesture characteristic of moral dualism. Descartes replaced the more graduated (although blatantly reason-centred and hierarchical) framework inherited from Aristotelean rationalism with a more humanistic and apparently 'democratic' one that re-organised the field in terms of greater equality amongst the privileged class of humans, extending it to include all humans equally and freeing it from the classical rationalist hierarchy that positioned women as less rational than men and placed slaves alongside domestic animals as minimally rational and considerable beings. However, the Cartesian double gesture at the same time offset this first revolutionary gesture of progressive humanism by a second gesture that intensified the moral dualism between humans and their homogenised contrast category of nature. Singer retains this double gesture of equality and exclusion which opens the door to some at the price of renewed exclusion and homogenisation of others; his moral dualism extends the privileged class slightly to include some animals as persons, but otherwise leaves the Cartesian framework minimally disturbed.

The Minimalist double gesture is a complex and familiar political gesture combining inclusion and exclusion.[15] Some animals are to be included in the category of persons in recognition of their newly-emphasised resemblance to the human and discontinuity from other animals. Such moves to limit and withhold recognition can encounter the same kinds of problems as comparable strategies in other liberation movements that aim to have some privileged group from among the class of the excluded join the master group. We can recognise here the same double gesture some elite feminists made in arguing that women should be admitted to the privileged class of political rights-holders by virtue of their discontinuity with allegedly 'lower groups' such as Negro slaves, and their similarity to the master group, elite white men. The strategy of extending the category of persons without recasting the person/property dualism in terms of which the person category is constructed is bound to fail as an attempt to elevate animals, for exactly the same reasons that similar liberal feminist strategies were and are bound to fail. Such forms of polarising recognition via assimilation to the elite group are of necessity greatly limited in the class to which they can be extended. To the extent that they do not challenge or loosen up the dualistic criteria for inclusion in the privileged group, but only squeeze more items into it, their ultimate effect must be an enlargement of the elite, and a retention or intensification of conceptual strategies of erasure and denial for excluded groups, instead of the recognition of the kinship of all living things in ethical consideration and biological exchange we need for a truly ecological ethic.

As many feminists have urged, we need to learn some new political gestures, including some non-polarising and unambiguously inclusionary ones that affirm non-hierarchical difference and acknowledge solidarity through both diversity and continuity.[16] Many animal rights thinkers advocate that animals should no longer be considered property, a position I thoroughly endorse. But will this opposition to commodifying animals take the closed form of the Cartesian double gesture, as yet another attempt to extend slightly the category of human privilege at the price of retaining and even intensifying the objectification and reduction of the excluded group? Or will it take a more open form that will allow us to question in a more thoroughgoing way the larger ethical framework of anthropo-centrism and commodification of the earth?

Animal rights and vegetarian duties

To the person on the street, the concept of animal rights is synonymous with a challenge to the idea that animals don't count ethically, but for philosophers the concept of rights has been made to carry a lot of additional and more complex baggage. Even environmental philosophers who have been clear about wanting to challenge human supremacism have been sharply divided about rights:[17] although some, especially Tom Regan, have mounted their challenge in terms of the rights framework, many others have found the extension of the rights framework to the non-human world problematic. I am inclined to join them in doubting that the concept of rights offers the best way to challenge the framework I have been discussing and to include non-humans in the ethical picture. The rights framework is useful in a certain range of contexts and is sometimes important for its rhetorical appeal, but even for the case of animals has many limitations, both as a way of theorising non-human ethics and as an activist concept that is capable of focusing and generalising the widespread popular support for animal justice. The fact that the rights concept is difficult to apply to non-humans beyond the case of certain animals that resemble humans means that it tends to support neo-Cartesian moral dualism.

Serious problems which result for animal rights theory include its tendencies to excessive individualism, cultural universalism, and moral dualism. These faults are not only philosophical but political weaknesses. They limit its application for an ecological ethic, limit its effectiveness for animal justice activism, and also for evolving theory that is able to integrate animal justice concerns with those of environmental and human justice movements. Rights theory, like Minimalism, tends to support a closed rather than an open ethical stance: on the rights and 'subject of a life' criteria, most non-human animals – and certainly all of nature – are just as strongly excluded from ethical consideration and just as open to exploitation as they were under the Cartesian dispensation. More crucially, unless supplemented, rights theory involves a moral extensionist approach that supports moral dualism and use/respect dualism, crucial parts of the ethical framework of commodification. Like other forms of neo-Cartesianism, it shifts the boundary of ethical consideration slightly to enlarge the class of persons, but leaves the basic logic of non-human exclusion and hyper-separation unchallenged beyond the new boundary.

The individualistic tendencies of rights theory emerge from the way it takes a complex set of social and political conditions and congeals them into a singular and apparently simple and stereotypical quality of an individual whose rights are violated by another individual who is responsible for their violation. As Benton notes,[18] rights theory proceeds as if 'the moral status of animals were a function of the kinds of beings they are, independently of the diverse relationships in which they stand to human moral agents and their social practices'. It is not the focus on the integrity and autonomy of the individual right-holder which is itself problematic here so much as the stress it gives to discriminating ethically in terms of species rankings and the disincentive this framework provides for any more complex and structural social thinking about the larger social sources of abuse. This is one reason why the rights approach has been able to turn attention away from the structural origins of the atrocities daily committed against animals in the factory farm and commodity framework to the question of the virtue of individual consumers who make a choice of eating animal food, no matter how obtained. It is also one reason why the rights focus, as Benton also notes, tends to be practically not very effective in the many contexts where activism cannot just focus on attacking consumers but requires larger political alliances and actions.[19]

The factory farm/flesh factory is a very important area for political alliances that often receives less attention than it deserves from animal activists in part because of less than ideal connections between the animals movement and other eco-social justice movements. Recent Australian and European legislation banning the production and sale of battery cage eggs shows some of the priorities and possibilities here for harnessing widespread opposition to current forms of economic rationality and their abuse of animal lives in coalitions against factory farming, which represents the worst and largest scale systematic practice of abuse of animals and nature.

A movement that can focus on such areas of broad agreement has the potential for a really amazing and world-shaking coalition, which could include:

- the possibility of coalitions with workers (on wages, conditions and the widespread use of prison and indentured labour in growing and especially slaughtering facilities);
- the potential for alliances with consumers on health issues – for example the use of antibiotics and the prevalence of disease in intensive practices, highlighted by recent findings on very widespread salmonella and the potentially fatal organism *Camphylobacter* in poultry products, and of course BSE in British intensive agriculture and possibly more widely;
- alliances with the local environment movement (on the massive water pollution and other unacceptable ecological and neighbourhood consequences from intensive farms for example);
- alliances with small farmers and local growers on rationalist agriculture's destruction of the small producer and contribution to the vulnerability of local communities;
- alliances with activists on the issues of neoliberalism (economic rationalism) and global trade who look to establishing a beachhead for injecting some compassion, ethics and community empowerment into our economic lives — for both humans and non-humans.

An over-emphasis on personal conversion and vegetarian action resulting from neo-Cartesianism and rights theory means that other forms of popular political action, for example alliance politics, remain relatively under-developed and undertheorised. Rights theory leads to the adoption of poorly contextualised and culturally hegemonic vegetarian strategies which condemn all eating of animals in indiscriminate terms, and do not encourage us to prioritise opposing the most extreme examples of distortion and instrumentalisation of animal lives – the intensive farming practices that treat animals as no more than living meat or egg production units.[20] Recovering a liberatory direction means contextualising the ethics of eating (in a way incompatible with the universalism of rights theory) and adopting a stronger focus on the responsibility of systems of economic rationality for the atrocities daily committed against domestic animals, especially in the factory-farming framework.

The difference between moral extensionist theorisations aimed at extending the privileges of humans and theorisations that aim to break down human/nature dualism is reflected in different types of vegetarianism, in particular, between a moral extensionist, exclusionary form and a critical, contextual and ecological form of vegetarianism that is more inclusionary.[21] Rights theory leads to the adoption of an absolutist, uncontextualised and closed form of vegetarianism as the principal animal defence movement strategy, one in which a culturally universalised focus on the carnivorousness of the individual consumer (sometimes it seems as a form of original sin) takes the place of a stronger critical focus on the responsibility of cultural, political and economic systems. An alternative critical and contextualised position also would require us to avoid complicity in contexts where contemporary food practices abuse animals, but would not place the emphasis on personal purity, would resist the idea that predation is inevitably fallen, and refuse to create an absolutist moral boundary between animals and plants, as a dualism of conscious and non-conscious life in which only the former deserves moral consideration. In principle it seems possible for a position allowing rights to animals to supplement its animal rights morality by some other account of the basis of moral considerability for non-conscious forms of life, and thus to avoid the worst effects of moral dualism. In practice this does not happen because, especially where rights theorists make a close connection to vegetarianism, they are tied to an exclusionary imperative.[22]

This exclusionary imperative derives from the reliance of rights-based forms of vegetarianism on the (unstated) assumption that only those beings not admitted to the class of rights-holders can ever ethically become food. Given this exclusionary imperative, arguments for vegetarianism can, it seems, be based on a simple demonstration that certain animals should be treated as rights-holders, and the vegetarian conclusion immediately follows.[23] But any position which has thus equated availability as food with moral exclusion is thereby committed to moral dualism and to an exclusionary imperative, since it is forced to insist on a substantial outclass of living beings that are morally excluded in order to locate any viable form of eating which allows an ethical basis for human survival. Mostly this exclusionary imperative takes the form of insisting on the complete exclusion of plants and other allegedly non-conscious forms of life from moral status, that is, a position similar to Singer's. The entailment of the exclusionary imperative is a special case of the general problem that the attempt to extend the privileges of human/nature dualism to a wider class of beings results in the continuing ethical exclusion of most of the non-human world, and the intensification of the use/respect boundary around dualised forms of moral privileging that deny the ethical continuity of planetary life.

The other options that are opened up by rejecting the equation of availability as food with moral exclusion, namely some form of ethical eating of beings from within a non-exclusionary morally considerable class, remain unconsidered in moral extensionist positions, but are open to contextual ecological positions to explore. The main strategy of this line of thought would be to question the dualism of use and respect, along with the associated assumption that lies behind the exclusionary imperative, that food or consumption must inevitably be reductive categories. These assumptions are major bulwarks of the commodity form and commodity culture, assumed explicitly by some extensionist theorists, and implicitly by the rest. This alternative line of thought would make potentially ethically available forms of use that respect animals as both individuals and as community members, in terms of respect or reverence for species life, and would aim to rethink farming as a non-commodity and species-egalitarian form, rather than to completely reject farming and embrace an exclusively plant-based form of existence that is doubtfully viable and alien to our own human species life.

The extensionist strategy which gives rise to the alienated project of absolutist ontological veganism thus has as one of its sources incomplete and badly thought out extensionist strategies for deconstructing human–animal dualism. One of the chief assumptions the extensionist strategy supports is the Use Exclusion Assumption, that because food is inevitably a site of domination, degradation, and exclusion, ethical food practice must consist of ensuring that nothing that is morally considerable can ever become our food or be ontologised as edible. As we will see, this key Use Exclusion Assumption, which at first glance may seem plausible, forces a variety of unacceptable conclusions and alienated projects. One of its worst consequences is that the refusal to allow anything morally considerable to be ontologised as edible or useful results in a deep rejection of ecological embodiment for those beings, since all ecologically-embodied beings are food for some other beings. However, just as use need not be a reductionist category, concepts of food need not take the reductionist and ethically excluded form they take in commodity culture, and the Use Exclusion Assumption is an exercise in cultural universalism.

The invisibility of the Use Exclusion Assumption in this context shows how commoditisation is built into our basic concepts for grasping the world. An inquiry into the concept of meat provides a useful route into understanding how 'taxonomy' connects ontology with ethics – how certain strategies of conceptualisation normalise oppression by narrowing ethically relevant perception, erasing key ethical dimensions of situations, and making the Other complicit in their own oppression through the formation of identity. As Carol Adams has argued[24], the concept of meat justifies oppression by hiding responsibility for death and the causal connection between the production of meat and the animal's death. The backgrounding or erasure of these connections in the abstractly quantitative and commodified concept of meat Adams terms 'absent referent'.

'Absent referent' renders unavailable not only the act of killing which makes meat available as a commodity[25], but any recognition of the connection between the meat and the communicative being it once was. The concept of meat enables a radical dissociation between the processes set in motion by our human subjectivity, as the subjectivity of socially connected, purposive and communicative beings, and the process outcome in the production of commodified, quantitatively-specifiable flesh. Such a commodified concept of meat involves a strong, fetishistic form of instrumental reductionism, in which the other is defined in narrow ways that identify them with what is only a part of their being, the part that is of use to us as flesh, and do not recognise that all living beings are much more than that.

There is injustice in all these modes of conception. There is injustice for a communicative and ethical being in being conceived systematically in ways that refuse recognition of their capacity for mindfulness and communication, both within and between species.[26] There is injustice for any striving and intentional being in being constructed[27] in reductive terms as an ethical nullity, or as 'mere' body or mechanism in the fashion of intensive farming, first because such conception singles its referent out for treatment as radically less than it is, and second because instrumental conception defines the Other in terms that assume the right of a 'higher' group to treat them as a resource for their ends. Animals so conceived are subject to both radical exclusion (as having a radically different nature discontinuous from that of the human meat consumer) and homogenisation – they 'drown in the anonymous collectivity' of meat. The radical exclusion of the meat concept generates a conceptual distance or boundary between humanity and its 'meat' which blocks sympathy and reduces the risk of identification. The reductiveness of the meat concept involves a conceptual strategy designed to block recognition of these injustices.

The overarching influence behind all these specific modes of and motives for reduction is the Cartesian-mechanistic reduction of the non-human animal to its body, and the refusal of recognition of animal kinship as beings of mind, intention and communication. Mary Midgley (1983) and Barbara Noske (1989, 1997) are two philosophers who have pointed out that the moral failings implicit in the modern, commodified concept of meat owe their philosophical genesis to Cartesian rationalism and the mechanistic model. But from the injustice of the modern western reductive institution of meat and the moral cowardice and denial of its conceptual strategies, we cannot conclude that there might not be other, less ethically problematic ways to conceive non-humans both as communicative others and as food. The indigenous recognition that one of the central philosophical problems of human life is that 'all our food is souls' points towards non-reductive understandings of food that could help resolve the moral failings of 'bad faith, moral supremacy, [and] self-deception'[28] implicit in the meat concept. However, these understandings form part of a different 'form of life', in Wittgenstein's sense,[29] and are neither practically nor conceptually available within the context of contemporary commodified food relationships.[30]

The conceptual means by which reductionist concepts of meat are culturally universalised and more respectful and less alienated forms of use are occluded in Adams' work are worth examining in detail. Adams fails to distinguish between the concept of 'meat' – a culturally specific construction which, as she shows, involves high levels of commodification, homogenisation, reduction, denial of kinship and hyper-separation – and other possible constructions of animals as edible food that do not have these features. The term 'meat' is used equivocally, and is ambiguous, being used on the one hand as a term for the condition of being animal food (edible) that is conceived in this culturally specific way as meat, and on the other as a cultural generic term for any kind of animal food.[31] Since the term 'meat' in Adams' work functions ambiguously between the culturally specific (determinate) concept of meat and the culturally generic (determinable) category of animal food, the latter can be treated as if it were invariably a reductionist-commodity practice, and so the attitudes associated with reduction and commodification are made to appear as invariable concomitants of any form of animal food. The ambiguity allows the absolutist vegetarian to generalise the animal food construction of a specific abusive culture to the constructions of any possible culture. To the extent that the ruthless, reductionistic and hyper-separated treatments of animals as replaceable and tradeable items of property characteristic of the commodity form and of capitalist economic rationality come to appear as inevitable aspects of animal food and of human predation or consumption – which, of course, they are not – total abstention from animal food can be made to appear the only possible course.

Adams' parallel treatment of use and instrumentalism extends vegetarianism, prohibiting animal use as food, to veganism, prohibiting any kind of use. Human/nature dualism constructs a polarised set of alternatives in which the idea that humans are excluded from any form of use is complemented at the opposite extreme by idea that non-humans are totally instrumentalisable, forming a contrast based on radical exclusion. Ontological veganism again strives to extend the dualised human status to the non-human area in the name of equality, re-envisaging non-humans also as beyond any form of use. Thus Carol Adams argues against any use of the animal other (for food or anything else) as involving instrumentalising them, stating that 'the ontologising of animals as edible bodies creates them as instruments of human beings' (Adams 1994: 103). Instrumentalism is widely recognised (although often unclearly conceptualised) as a feature of oppressive conceptual frameworks, but instrumentalism is misdefined by Adams as involving any making use of the other, rather than the treatment of the other as *no more than* something of use, as merely a means to an end.[32] We must inevitably treat the natural world to some degree as a means, for example, to food, shelter and other materials we need in order to survive, just as we must treat other people to some degree as means. What is prohibited is unconstrained or total use of others as means, reducing others to means. We cannot give up using one another, but we can give up use/respect dualism, which means working towards ethical, respectful and highly constrained forms of use.

Rationalism, factory farming and use/respect dualism

Neo-Cartesianism is bad politics and bad methodology. It is bad politics because its half-hearted and a historical analysis stops short of enabling us to grasp the important connections between forms of oppression that could provide the basis for a common framework of opposition and coalition, or to grasp the connection between ethics and commodification. The gulf neo-Cartesianism retains between those privileged biospheric groups admitted to the ethical sphere, as right-holders or as 'conscious' beings, and the many who remain instrumentalised as Other, as mere resources for the first group, corresponds in the dominant economic framework to the gulf discerned between the few that can own and those many who can ethically be owned, traded and commodified. Neo-Cartesianism is bad methodology because at the level of intellectual analysis at least, we should determine our stance here not by a mind-shackling principle of minimal departure from the status quo, but in terms of the potential for multiplication of alliances and for articulating a common struggle. This must be a struggle especially against the machinery of rational egoism and self-maximisation which, in the form of a maximising economic rationality of global reach, is now disrupting so catastrophically the fabric of human and non-human life.

The ethical dualism neo-Cartesianism insists we must retain is then a key element in supporting the rationalist economic regime which is commodifying the world, which neo-Cartesianism would also vary only minimally. The regimes of factory farming are the product of this self-maximising calculus, of the rationalist economy stripped of all ridiculous and corrupting human emotion and compassion. These regimes aim always to extract the most from the other who is the resource, relegated in this ethical dualism to the role of the pre-ethical condition for the privileged ethical life. The rationalist economic calculus which divorces 'rational' and 'efficient' political and economic life from care, compassion, social and ecological responsibility is the ultimate modern expression of the west's ancient rationalist opposition between reason and emotion, male and female, culture and nature, use and respect, in which it has now ensnared the entire globe and all its species.

The dissociation of use and respect or moral considerability underlies the uncomfortable division in contemporary culture between the pet animal and the economic animal. Reason/emotion, public/private, person/property and use/respect dualisms construct the contrast between the private pets – with whom so many of us share intense subjective lives – and the reductively conceived and atrociously instrumentalised 'factory-farmed' animals. The hyper-separation between emotion and reason, respect and use is reflected in the contrast between the only partially commodified 'pet' animal and the fully commodified 'economic' animal. 'Pet' and 'meat' animals are defined in dualistic terms as hyper-separated and complementary animal categories, with the hyper-subjectivised and emotionally-invested 'pet' privileged over the undersubjectivised and emotionally-devested 'meat'.

These hyper-separations are well illustrated in the movie *Babe*, which introduces us to the meat as a speaking subject, a position which immediately disrupts the reductionist commodity form of 'meat'. 'Babe' is the name of an innocent, an original, Christ-like pure soul, the young pig rescued from the horrifying animal gulag to whom the first news of the dirty secret of meat is eventually revealed in the family farm outhouse by the revolutionary duck Ferdie – where the meat comes from, where 'Babe' ('babies') himself comes from, in an act of disillusionment which neatly parallels that of the human child newly discovering reproductive and sexual relationships. ('Not the Boss'! breathes the incredulous Babe, in parallel with the child's shocked 'Not my parents !') It is from the malevolent farm cat though that Babe finally learns the full hurt of the dreadful secret the factory farm and the sinister farm meathouse hold. The unspeakable is finally spoken: pigs are meat, pigs are subjects, and pigs suffer the reductive violence which denies, distances from and hides their subjectivity. Babe is only called 'pig' while he is alive, but 'they use a different word, 'pork or bacon'', after you are dead', explains the satisfied cat, revelling in her privileged, protected status. As Babe's innocence is stripped away bit by bit, we see the gradual unveiling of various levels and kinds of animal injustices – the baring of the 'world of wounds' we all somehow learn to come to terms with as part of our loss of innocence and 'adult' accommodation to an oppressive world.

What I found particularly illuminating in the film was the exposure of the levels of hierarchy among animals created by human colonisation in the small human empire of the farm, an empire which makes concrete human desire and human will in its social relations and its rational design of the earth and of the animals themselves. The film displays the key role of these boundaries of exclusion and levels of hierarchy among animals in maintaining the practices of meat and the non-subject status of the meat animal. The dogs, in the canine equivalent of human chauvinism and rational meritocracy, attribute their privilege with some complacency to their greater intelligence, but that facile fabrication is disrupted for us nicely by Babe's pig intelligence in some of the film's earliest scenes. Thus Babe's demonstration of intelligence and communicative ability disrupts the dog Fly's comfortable assurances to her puppies that 'only stupid animals' are eaten. What is exposed as unstable, duplicitous and oppressive here is the conventional boundary and contract on which the relatively privileged status of the pet and 'house' animal is based, which bears on the privileged status of dogs and cats in western society.

Because it reveals the conventionality and instability of the considerability hierarchy among animals, the film provides us with the materials to reconstruct the Contract or political origin story for the privileged group of 'pets' or personal companion animals. In early times, hunting, farming and shepherding man ('the Boss') in certain societies made a contract with certain wolves: the contract was that they would be given a respected role and position very different from that of other animals, that *they would never be meat*, in return for help with a critical task. That task was their active help in the oppression and imprisonment of other animals, whom they would, using their more-than-human sensory or physical skills, help confine and construct as meat. *In return for their help in constructing other animals as meat, not only would they themselves never be meat, they would be 'looked after', given a share of the meat themselves.* Their subjectivity would be recognised, and the reductive Cartesian conception would never apply to them. The working animal might often be a 'familiar', like the sheepdogs in *Babe*, the subject of a deeply personal relationship, but also accorded the dignity of a co-worker and acknowledged for their skilful contribution to economic life. In the same sense that various human mythic Contracts or founding political stories are about dividing the spoils, this was a Contract not only about cooperation in economic life but about mutual benefit in meat. But as the disruptions of 'Babe' neatly demonstrate, inclusion in the contract class has nothing to do with 'intelligence', and everything to do with complicity.

This Old Contract, originally a cooperative work contract according privilege in return for complicity in the practice of meat and the domination or elimination of the non-contract animals, is later under the Modern Contract extended to *the privileged companion animals* – the pets – with whom so many of us continue to share our lives, but extended in a new form. As production moves out of the household at the beginning of the modern era, the role of farm-household animals is transformed in the new separation of public/private in much the same way as the role of women. Both the working farm wife and the working farm animal now become subject to the modernist polarity that construes 'rational' economic relationships in alienated, masculinist and narrowly instrumental terms as hyper-separated from moral and affective familiar relationships, and affective relationships as occurring in a highly circumscribed 'private' sphere of altruism supposedly untainted by economic considerations. The 'familiar' working animal of the contract class is replaced by the bourgeois 'pet' who, like the bourgeois wife, leads a sheltered life in a protected private household.[33]

The hyper-separation between the 'pet' animal and the 'meat' animal is intensified as the meat animal becomes subject to the rationally instrumentalised mass-production regime of the factory farm or laboratory. The 'familiar' animal disappears, and the complementary polarity of the subjectivised and underemployed 'pet' animal and the reduced and instrumentalised 'meat' animal takes its place. As 'Babe' reminds us, the 'familiar' working animal could integrate reason and emotion, economic and affective, public and private elements, and exemplify animal skill, difference and mystery.[34] In the Old Contract relationship (at its best), 'familiars' were skilful and respected co-workers, whose economic role was based on their difference from the human and their consequent ability to extend human senses and human powers; in the Modern Contract relationship (at its worst), the pet is a servile toy or dependent lacking both autonomy and mystery, often conceived in humanised terms as a childlike or inferior self, and for such structural reasons increasingly marginal to human lives.[35] These are of course the extremes of a possible continuum, but one that in practice tends to be configured in response to the political forces underlying the Old and Modern contracts. If the pet and the meat tend now to monopolise the roles these forces have left open, what has disappeared is the possibility of the animal 'familiars' 'Babe' reimagines for us – *the same animals integrated into our economic as into our affective lives* – and at the same time the possibility of a less alienated form of economic life which integrates not only the real but the symbolic animal in the form of affective creativity.

For urban dwellers, which is, increasingly, most of us, animals of the Modern Contract class of pets usually now represent our main contact with the animal world. This is unfortunate, because the Modern Contract defines the pet in opposition to the meat animal and reflects and repeats many of the duplicities, denials and exclusions involved in the surrounding western institution of meat. The exclusionary form of the original contract of complicity in meat is retained and intensified in the Modern Contract with the pet, usually a carnivore whom the owner continues to feed on the flesh of other 'meat' animals. The malevolent cat in *Babe* is seen thus profiting from the death of the Christmas duck Rosanna; in real life, non-privileged animals assigned to the 'meat' side of this dualistic hierarchy die to make meat for the pets of people who think of themselves unproblematically as animal lovers – kangaroos, dolphins, penguins, anonymous and rare marine animals in yearly billions are slaughtered at some remove to feed the cats and dogs whose own deaths as meat would be unthinkable to their owners.

If the 'pet' is defined in terms of the same Modern Contract that defines the 'meat' animal, we can understand as complementary constructions the strongly dualistic boundaries of the 'pet' and 'meat' animal; the pet animal is a communicative and ethical subject, ideally subject to consideration and fit for human companionship, the meat animal is denied all these things. If the pet and the meat are complementary polarised aspects of the same contract, it is this tainted and hidden relationship that enables our simultaneous claim to love some animals and to have a right to ruthlessly exploit other animals who are not very different, to simultaneously admit pet subjectivity and ignore or deny meat-animal subjectivity. The Old Contract dignified the role of contract animals, but presupposed an instrumental relationship to other animals, and this division becomes a pet/meat dualism in the contract of the modern era. This genealogy does much to explain the extraordinary contradictions involved in our contemporary treatment of animals and our claims to love and respect animals. For example, it is these dualistic contracts that 'animal lovers' honour when they, perhaps even sometimes as vegetarians or vegans themselves, bring into existence and even breed carnivorous pet animals whom they feed on the 'meat' of other animals; or whom pet lovers irresponsibly introduce to inappropriate environments where they are permitted to make other animals meat and to disrupt balanced and negotiated communities of free-living animals.[36]

The moral dualism of both the Old and the Modern Contract helps construct the taboo against recognising the subjectivity of the meat animal, as well as the general failure to recognise animal subjectivity, and produces the moral evasions of meat, especially factory-farmed meat. Most people have had some positive experiences with animals such as dogs or cats, have at some time allowed themselves to experience them as narrative and communicative subjects rather than as Cartesian 'machine-animals' or as mindless bodies. But the ethical dualism and impermeability of this contract boundary prevents them transferring this awareness to other animals considered 'meat animals' or to wild animals, reflected in the contradiction of the animal lover's horror taboo against eating dogs and contrasting indifference or complacency about the horrific treatment of the 'meat animal'. The recognition drama of *Babe* takes us some distance then towards pushing over this key barrier to a better consciousness of the moral and ecological status of all animals, showing us how Babe is excluded from contract status as meat, and how both Babe and the sheep are oppressed by the contract and by the privilege of the dogs and cats.

But in another crucial way the film fails to resolve some key ambiguities surrounding the contract. For we can also read Babe's liberation in the end of the film as his joining or displacing the dogs in the contract, recasting him in the role of non-violent communicator with the rest of the farm animals. Is Babe's liberation then to be set within the Old Contract's complicity in the oppression of non-contract animals, and the Modern Contract's dualism of the meat and the pet? Is it merely the correction of a mistaken individual placement in the hierarchical species order of rational meritocracy the contracts preserve? Or does it open up a new possibility: that Babe's liberation can somehow be extended to all other animals? To the extent that it is an exclusionary contract, in which some make a living by complicity in instrumentalising, imprisoning and oppressing others, the contract cannot be extended to provide liberation for all. The attempt to use such a contract as a basis for liberation reproduces the pattern of re-erecting the barrier of moral dualism in a new place, slightly extending the class of persons while leaving the person/property dualism unquestioned.

Here we come up against the limits imposed by the liberal understanding of liberation as individual salvation and by its occlusion of its key underlying dualistic constructions, which applied to the animal sphere generates the same problems that various human liberation movements encounter within liberalism. If Babe is to be saved within the limits of privilege the contracts define, or because he is included in the category of persons in recognition of his newly-discovered resemblance to the human and discontinuity from other animals, we can recognise this as the double gesture of neo-Cartesianism, of extending the privileged class but intensifying or further entrenching the exclusion of an outclass open to unconstrained use. The door opens to admit a few, but closes to keep the rest outside where they were. One boundary of moral dualism is momentarily penetrated, but the rest remain in place or new ones are constructed. So the film apparently displays Babe's liberation, but leaves us with the big questions about whether Babe will be admitted alone, with all other pigs, with some other pigs, with all other animals, or with everything we might consider food?

An anti-anthropocentric rethinking of human–animal associations and the farming relationship would need to reject the Old Contract the movie Babe shows us, in which 'the Boss' undertakes to allow familiars the meat of other animals that are treated as beneath moral consideration. Moving beyond these contracts[37] does not imply though that we have to forgo all systematic association with animals, but rather that we have to be prepared to consider carefully the politics of human/animal relationships and test them against the criterion of realisation in a society where none are morally excluded and made available for the horrors of the gulag. But if the concept of the 'pet' is tainted by the same contract and public/private duality that defines the 'meat', where do we start? I think that the attempt to negotiate a new communicative model of relationship with animals could start from the concept of the 'familiar' *Babe* makes visible again, because the 'familiar' relationship escapes some of the rigidity of the pet/meat dualism; thus the relationship with the working animal was often strongly communicative, built on a respect for animal difference, and unified rather than split the rational-economic and emotional connection with the animal.

A familiar could be an animal with whom we can form some kind of communicative bond, friendship, protective relationship, companionship, or acquaintance. The familiar may, if you are very lucky, be a wild free-living animal in your local surroundings you can see sufficiently often to come to know individually. (A contradiction between human friendship and the 'wildness' of an animal is only a problem if we define 'wild' in terms of the absence of the human, rather than as 'free-living'.)[38] Relationships with local lizards, birds, and occasionally friendly mammals like wombats, are some examples of familiar relationships. Or familiars may be domesticated or semi-domesticated animals with whom we have economic as well as affective relations not dependent on the moral exclusion of other animals. These possibilities start to become available to us once we begin to see beyond the dualisms that underpin the contracts.

An attempt to rework the 'familiar' relationship for a new time must clearly reject the familiar's traditionally oppressive roles in relation to other animals. But many of the domestic animals who suffered so greatly under the contracts, hens, ducks and geese for example, could thrive as human familiars since they can associate with humans in ways that enable the formation of communicative relationships, mutual enjoyment, and exploration – without requiring a further class of excluded animals who must exist instrumentally to provide them with meat.[39] We have to ensure that we take responsibility for any harm our familiars may do to ecological communities or to communities of free-living animals, whose welfare I believe should, in the event of conflict, take priority over human desires for animal companions. Combining this new/old kind of 'familiar' personal and moral relationship with animals with a new kind of economic relationship, as *Babe* imagines, must lead towards a major revisioning and restructuring of economic life.[40] But the potential rewards are great, since such a strategy indicates routes towards breaking down those key contemporary versions of reason/emotion and public/private dualism that help construct the linked forms of alienation involved in the human workplace and the animal gulag. To the extent that *Babe* helps us reimagine the animal as potential familiar rather than as pet or as meat, it offers us a glimpse of an overgrown but still discernible path which could begin our journey towards a non-oppressive form of the mixed community and a liveable future respectfully shared with animals.

8 Towards a dialogical interspecies ethics

Decentring human-centred ethics

The logic of Othering suggests that it is not the primitiveness and unworthiness of the Other but our own species' arrogance that is the main barrier to forming ethical and responsive relationships with earth others. To defeat this logic, we must adopt a counter-hegemonic program to restore planetary balance and establish dialogical and carefully nego-tiated relationships with our planetary partners of the sort that could enable us to survive in the long-term. As the decline of the Other we are beginning to induce gathers momentum, this project becomes more urgent. One implication is a re-orientation of focus and methodology in and around interspecies ethics, but a counter-hegemonic program also has implications for focus and methodology in a number of other disciplinary areas and in science. An important corollary for knowledge gathering orientation is that the rationality of Othering our planetary partners must be countered by an alternative self-critical rationality of 'studying up' to find the source of our problems and difficulties with nature.

Environmental philosophy has produced many examples of anthropo-centric and hegemonic forms: they include especially the extensionist posi-tions we have already met which allocate moral consideration to non-human beings entirely on the basis of their similarity to the human. Such claims are hegemonic for non-humans in the same way that assim-ilationist frameworks that allocate worth to individuals of another culture, for example an indigenous culture, just on the basis of their similarity to the dominant (white) colonising culture are hegemonic. Such a schema based on sameness to the human treats earth others as of value just to the extent that they resemble the human as hegemonic centre, rather than as an independent centre with potential needs, excellences and claims to flourish of their own.[1] Similarly centric is the demand that assessments of the other's worth be based exclusively on either similarity or difference to the human; this is a sure sign of a centric treatment of otherness, in which all comparisons and judgements turn on deviation from the centre. In a less hegemonic scenario for judgements of moral worth, both continuity and difference from self would be in play, and criteria independent of both considerations would be regularly invoked. Many projects in environmental philosophy are anthropocentric in this way, either explicitly stating similarity to the human as the basis for moral worth, or implicitly appealing to this through selecting 'independent' criteria normally taken to define or characterise the human, such as rationality, mentality, or consciousness, and then evaluating non-human beings along this single axis to arrive at a species meritocracy with humans (by no means accidentally) emerging at the top.

The account of human/nature dualism and anthropocentrism presented in Chapter 5 provides a basis for an alternative strategy to such human extensionism as a guide for environmental ethics. This involves adopting a counter-hegemonic methodology and program in ethics that aims to decentre the human and break down human/nature dualism on the ethical front, rather than to expand the category of privilege to take in a few of the more human-like non-humans. Applying such a counter-hegemonic program would not only reject entrenched human-centred ways of framing environmental ethics but would revolutionise its entire conception. Human-centred conceptions of environmental ethics interpret it in terms of 'studying down', as a quest to discover which parts of nature are sufficiently 'well qualified', usually by being proved to be enough like we humans, to deserve some sort of extension (the leftovers) of our own ample feast of self-regard. On an alternative approach that frames the problem in terms of 'studying up', it is not so much a question of whether earth others are good enough for ethically rich relationships, but of whether we (western) humans are.[2] A crucial part of environmental ethics is scrutinising the anthropocentric prejudices and otherising stances we hold that are obstacles to interspecies justice and which prevent us from relating to earth others as fully and ethically as we might otherwise do. We need to adopt specific programs to counter these. I have already discussed moral dualism, but some of its further elements might include:

- Denaturalising and making available for critical reflection and choice framework and methodological assumptions that Otherise the non-human.
- Dealing with ethical hyper-separation, the highly influential legacy of hierarchical, exclusionist and rationalist modes of thinking in accounts of ethics, mind and communication, for example concepts of human

superiority in a Great Chain of Being and the myth of non-human mindlessness.

- Avoiding unnecessary species-ranking, otherising behaviours and reductive stances and establishing the framework for an interspecies egalitarian ethic.

- Dealing with obstacles to interspecies justice in our ways of framing the other, and adopting methodologies and stances of openness rather than methodologies of closure. This is an important preliminary to interspecies justice and communication.

- Opening up ethics, for example by making the human/other species distinction less central to our ethical thinking, and decentering the human and the human-like in vocabularies and conceptions of ethics.

- Developing conceptions of the human self and human virtue that can prioritise caring for the planet.

When we do these things, I suggest, we find a rich variety of contextually specific ethics that are applicable to interspecies relationships. These include many of the context-specific ethical frameworks we apply to other humans, plus a further range that are specifically concerned with issues of justice and fairness between species I discussed in Chapter 5. Philosophers have mostly been standing outside the city gates arguing amongst themselves about the applicability to non-humans of highly abstract ethical concepts like intrinsic value and moral considerability, without ever getting up the courage to actually go through the gateway, enter the city and investigate or establish specific ethical relationships. But the concepts of intrinsic value and moral considerability that have concerned philosophy so much are no more than gateway concepts for environmental ethics, abstract preliminary concepts that speak of our stances of preparedness to enter into ethical relationships with earth others rather than shedding light on the ethics of specific kinds of relationships. Such debates are empty to the extent that they evade the real moral task of developing an adequate ethical response to the non-human world, which they do not address in any specific, rich or useful way. These responses include for example developing narrative and communicative ethics and responses to the other, developing care and guardianship ethics, developing alternative conceptions of human virtue that include care for the non-human world, and developing dialogical ethical ontologies that make available richer and less reductive ways to individuate, configure and describe the world that 'make the most' of the non-human other. They include developing the stances of openness and attention that are preliminary to dialogical and communicative relationships of sensitivity, negotiation and mutual adaptation of the sort we need in the context of the environmental crisis.

Ranking, dualism and heterogeneity

One of the legacies of human/nature dualism is the oppositional way the ethical contrasts are drawn in terms of homogenised species classes treated as contrasting or oppositional. Breaking down this dualistic construction would open the way for an interspecies politics and ethics which does not configure the world rigidly in terms of human and other, or its hegemonic variants in the moral extensionism of contemporary philosophy of human or lesser, and human and similar. This also means demoting the ethical centrality of species and general species ranking, and avoiding compulsive and singularistic human-centred rankings. This is not to say that we can never make any kind of ranking between species or judgement that something is better than something else, nor that nothing should or ever could be ranked along an axis from simple to complex. Ranking between species in specific contexts is not always avoidable, but generalised species ranking can be minimised or given a different role in a less centric context. We can avoid those especially problematic forms of generalised ranking that position earth others in an unnecessary valuational order of sacrifice.

Brian Luke (1995) has argued against the tradition of species generalism he calls the 'Great-Chain-of-Being' in which we discover a descending order of species merit of the kind that many philosophers still find intuitive, often arranged in terms of alleged gradations of rationality. This 'Great Chain' approach assumes the inevitability of interspecies choice and conflict, and of attempts to resolve it by selecting a few general species properties that are used as qualifications for picking out winning and losing species. But such choices are not inevitable, nor is the underlying assumption that the centrally determining and crucial thing about an ethical context is what species one belongs to. A better approach tries to avoid these kinds of homogenising ethical configurations and invariant species rankings by giving a larger role to other features of the ethical context, and therefore to context generally. This is in accordance with the methodological obligation, argued for in the preceding chapter, to minimise species conflict, and thereby ranking and choice contexts.

For example, the ethical perplexities and strategies for dealing with a strange highly venomous snake who has just moved onto your veranda may not be all that different from those involved in dealing with a difficult human stranger who has done the same. There may be some overriding reason to share and to prioritise the other's needs (perhaps you have some responsibility for their homelessness, or it is an emergency and temporary situation, a flood for example, where some charity to both snake and person would be in order). But suppose this is not the case; this difficult other has moved in for an indefinite period. If you have reason to believe that the result will be an unfavourable environment for both of you, one that is unlikely to accommodate both of you in the long-term without danger or conflict, then as the prior occupant you may be entitled to make it clear that this is your space, and to encourage the other to move on. Different methods of encouragement and different levels of responsibility for finding other accommodation may apply, depending on the context. But in neither case, *as a matter of justice*, are you entitled to initiate unnecessary and disproportionate violence, shooting the snake, or the difficult human, for example, just on the grounds that they may become a problem, and without trying less punitive solutions. Often we don't need to resort to major human/nature contrasts or hierarchies to illuminate such cases, and the same sorts of general ethical approaches can be applied in each case. If concepts of justice have an application in a comparable human case (your treatment of the abusive tramp camped on the veranda), there is no good reason to refuse them application in the interspecies case, (your treatment of the venomous snake camped on your veranda), contrary to claims made by many moral philosophers.

The motivation for a ranking in terms of invariant species value and order draws much of its strength from the felt need to validate the use of non-humans in human lives. Western philosophy has traditionally validated human entitlements to use earth others in terms of a valuational order of rational hierarchy, which entitles 'more rational' humans to dominate and sacrifice non-humans whose lives are supposedly cheaper. In a universe of ecological embodiment our lives, even at their most considerate, must deliver some destruction to members of other species. But there are better frameworks for thinking about the inevitable displacement of other embodied lives than those which derive from a superior positioning in a species value hierarchy invoked to validate our entitlement to displace others. A ranking system based on species sacrifice of this kind is avoided, for example, in the world-narratives which figure nature and life in gift-exchange terms as an egalitarian ethical system of reciprocity in which all benefit, participate and are ultimately themselves in turn consumed.[3] The seeming inevitability of sacrificial ranking rests on an unexamined suppression of important alternatives to this highly problematic 'Great Chain of Being' tradition which remains as an influential background to western thought.

Whereas the traditional rationalist hierarchy of the Great Chain of Being ranked creatures in broadly homogenised kinds according to alleged possession of rationality or proximity to the opposed order of materiality, the neo-Cartesian model which currently dominates environmental philosophy uses consciousness as its hegemonic 'sameness' axis of moral consideration. This transparently hegemonic conception that denies to others the potential for 'excellences of their own' creates several specific problems. The first is that it tends to produce generalised contextually invariant rankings which are pervasive, unnecessary and damaging, effecting various kinds of closure to the other's potentialities. The second is that it cannot allow adequately for incommensurability of abilities and difference in kinds of minds. This is a serious problem because recent evidence of elements of heterogeneity and incommensurability in mind points to the scientific inadequacy of frameworks based on obsessive and singularistic human-centred rankings.[4] I discuss these problems in sections below.

Ranking and interspecies egalitarianism

Interspecies (which some call biospheric) egalitarianism is sometimes portrayed as the thesis that 'all natural entities whether human or non-human should have equal moral weight'.[5] In this simple form however it is both implausible and unworkable. We might note, first of all, that even in the human case there are lots of problems in characterising equality as allocating to all within the field the same moral weight, especially if we mean by this that we have to give exactly the same weight to each persons' needs and interests in all our moral deliberations.[6] If this simplistic formula will not do to explicate equality for humans (except in some very limited contexts), it is hardly likely that it will explicate what is defensible in a larger and more complex notion like biospheric equality. Furthermore, the concept of equality is expressible both along the axis of sameness and along that of difference. Equality on the axis of the Same yields scalar equality, while equality along the axis of Difference yields the completely different concept of incommensurability or non-ranking. While critics of egalitarianism focus exclusively on the first concept, it is the second concept we need to give expression to what is valid in the idea of interspecies equality.

It is often assumed that a hierarchy with humans at the top is inevitable because the alternative is treating all individuals of whatever species as having the same value. This is only true however if items are ranked in a scalar way as either superior/inferior or as equal to one another. The options of ranking as superior/inferior or as scalar equals leave out a critical further alternative, namely not ranking at all. Both ranking as scalar equals and ranking in a simple hierarchy are forms of ranking, and there are a number of contexts where ranking itself is unnecessary and either logically or morally problematic. One of the logical cases is the case of incommensurability between beings, where we can neither rank as equal nor rank in a hierarchy: between beings with very different and only intersecting capacities, ranking is not possible in any accurate or meaningful way. Consider the idea of ranking yourself in relation to a mountain, for example. Between categories of very different beings, many of whose capacities the ranker may not be in a position to know, insistence on ranking (on a scale of superior/inferior which includes the case of equality) is both poor methodology and symptomatic of an arrogant stance of closure which is impoverishing and limiting for both human self and non-human other.

Ranking itself is open to moral and political evaluation as an activity, and in the human case at least, is widely recognised as being often morally problematic, especially where it involves unnecessary and invariant, context-insensitive rankings of human beings by broad categorial types, for example by 'race', class or gender. Colonialist, racist and fascist thinking is especially notable for its invariant categorisations and obsessive type-rankings of superiority between human groups, often based on morally irrelevant characteristics. While we are usually prepared to find ethically acceptable the ranking of very specific characteristics and skills not closely tied to large judgements about individual or class worth or connected too directly with moral or social value, the more generalised a ranking is, and the more direct the connection made with moral significance, the more reason we have to suspect it of carrying unacceptable hegemonic agendas. For example, we can compare ourselves with respect to susceptibility to heart disease or pneumonia, for these are not (at least not yet) indices of moral superiority, but an important element of democratic struggles is the attempt to arrange things so as to avoid large and invariant type-rankings of social or moral value, which are rightly seen as open to many kinds of abuse and distortion.[7]

In contexts where scarcity means that ranking of individuals is unavoidable, for example in medical triage, we recognise its morally problematic character by seeing it as less than ideal. We set up ethics committees who make triage decisions contextually, and by other means. We also recognise that a good, 'humane' medical system, if it cannot due to scarcity entirely avoid ranking, is one where the need for such rankings is kept to a minimum. Non-ranking, in the sense of avoiding or minimising ranking, is, I suggest, an important part of the content of human equality and respect, rather than the scalar kind of equality that assigns equal weight on some ethical scale in moral deliberations. Simone Weil writes 'Respect is due to the human being as such and it is not a matter of degree'.[8] But ranking on a scale as equal, to the extent that it opens up also the possibility of ranking as greater or lesser than, is 'a matter of degree', and thus cannot be the basis of this kind of respect. What is required here is not scalar equality but avoidance of ranking, or non-ranking, especially in the form of narratives and social arrangements which make ranking unnecessary.

Non-ranking, as the meta-ethical principle of minimising ranking and dealing with conflict and scarcity of resources cases contextually in ways that avoid invariant categories and type ranking between broad classes of beings,[9] is also applicable to interspecies ethics, comparisons and choices. Non-ranking is a much more plausible way to interpret the concept of interspecies egalitarianism than ranking as equal in a scale of moral worth. Non-ranking extends the recognition of the morally problematic character of value-rankings between highly general categories of humans to similar rankings between broad species types, and holds that we should generally aim, in our philosophies, individual interactions and through our social arrangements, to avoid ranking and to minimise contexts in which we have to adopt highly generalised value-rankings of ourselves as members of particular species. Non-ranking is a counter-hegemonic virtue, similar to and connected with the other counter-hegemonic virtues of openness, active invitation, attentiveness,[10] and intentional recognition, which I discuss below, and is like them important in encouraging the potential for communication and avoiding the arrogance and inevitable closure involved in making pervasive judgements of species value.

In any deeper interrogation, the ethical status of ranking must itself be scrutinised. As in the human case, there are many interspecies contexts for which ranking can be avoided, can be structured out, is irrelevant, does not arise, and in which its introduction across species would be gratuitous, ugly, limiting and impoverishing, blinding us to certain possibilities of interaction and exchange with earth others.[11] We should try to ensure that there are more such contexts. Even for conflict and scarcity cases, as Brian Luke points out, there are more context-sensitive ways to proceed than through the method of constructing general principles which designate classes of 'inferior' beings who are always available to be sacrificed to other 'superior' beings who must invariably count for more in some generalised scalar ranking of the moral universe.[12]

Framework stances and the myth of mindlessness

The program of conceptual work needed to counteract ethical hyper-separation must includes a program of expanding and decentering philosophical vocabularies to eliminate unwarranted and unnecessary rationalism and intellectualism.[13] These function (in much the same way as the old literacy tests that were used in the past to exclude blacks and minorities from voting) to exclude non-humans from the basic concepts and descriptions necessary to applying ethical vocabularies. Narrative and communicative approaches to environmental ethics are ruled out when philosophers or scientists insist on such unwarrantedly reductionist and hyper-separated philosophical vocabularies. For these we must re-admit the rich intentionality we attribute to the natural world in ordinary, unself-conscious and un-'rationalised' speech contexts. The intentional recognition stance I outline below of recognising earth others as fellow agents and narrative subjects is crucial for all ethical, collaborative, communicative and mutualistic projects, as well as for place sensitivity.

As I have argued, to the extent that there are framework choices here, there are good reasons (including the reason of prudence in our current context) to choose more generous conceptual stances that maximise our sensitivity to the non-human world, and to chose them over the traditional reductive frameworks that maximise insensitivity. People have been taught to identify rationality – wrongly – with human-centredness, reductionism and meanness (parsimony) towards the non-human world. Framework choices for explaining and relating to the non-human world are not unconstrained by the way the world is, but even conservative philosophy of science concedes that there is significant scope for choice because theories are inevitably underdetermined by this factor. Major framework choices like those between neo-Cartesian and counter-hegemonic stances towards the non-human are still more radically open to choice, because such theories have radically self-reinforcing and performative aspects. An honest assessment would recognise how our possibilities for interaction with and perception of the world are influenced in major ways by the postures we ourselves choose to adopt. Innumerable examples from the history of racism and sexism show how significant expectations and prior stances of closure are for what we can experience and perceive about another who is conceived in hegemonic terms.[14]

In the non-human case, if our dominant theories and reinforcing cultural experience lead us to stereotype earth others reductively as mindless 'objects', non-intentional mechanisms with no potential to be communicative and narrative subjects, as lacking potential viewpoints, well-being, desires and projects of their own (all intentional concepts), then it is quite likely that we will be unable to recognise these characteristics in the non-human sphere even when we are presented with good examples of them. What is required in order to be 'a receiver' of communicative and other kinds of experience and relationship is openness to the other as a communicative being, an openness which is ruled out by allegiance to reductive theories. To view such differences as simply 'theory choices' is to overstate the intellectualist and understate the performative aspects involved, which is captured somewhat better in the terminology of posture or stance. Is it to be a posture of openness, of welcoming, of invitation, towards earth others, or is it to be a stance of prejudged superiority, of deafness, of closure?

This said, there are still some aspects of theory choice that turn on comparisons between intellectual outcomes and explanatory power, even if they do not exhaust the meanings here. The theory choice approach I advocate here would situate our allegiance to a particular theory in the context of competing frameworks, which includes a choice between a narrowly human-centred Cartesian-based account of mind as consciousness that carries severe limitations for understanding other species, and a potentially de-centred but still largely undeveloped alternative of intentional recognition that can allow the concept of mind to take radically different forms. Its greater breadth offers a way to counter hegemonic and over-centralised concepts of mind and to avoid singularistic, unnecessary and over-determined rankings of broad categories of beings.[15]

Science fiction stories abound with Terran characters who are unable to recognise the radically different forms mind takes when they visit the alien ecology of outerspace worlds. It seems to me that a more immediate Terran problem is that, under the influence of our grossly reductive, human-centred theories and culture, we are unable to recognise the radically and even not-so-radically different forms mind can take with other species right here on earth. And if we are insensitive to this potentiality for different kinds of minds here on earth, we will hardly be sensitive to it when it occurs in the environment of even more ecologically different and alien worlds. Is there any prospect for refining and/or recovering a concept of mind that allows for more recognition of the diversity and diffusion of forms and elements of mind among the earth's species? Or must we, like the sci-fi human, be compelled forever to wander a lonely universe bereft of other species-minds, a fate made doubly tragic to the extent that it is not the result of our own genuine uniqueness but of our own centric limitations and insistence of a reductive framework of self-enclosure?

I argued in *Feminism and the Mastery of Nature* that we could avoid this self-made tragedy through a post-Cartesian reconstruction of mind that allows us to emphasise other marks of mind than the on/off concept of consciousness selected by Descartes precisely in order to effect the wholesale exclusion of non-humans, and that this choice of a more generous framework is not only equally rational but more rational. A post-Cartesian reconstruction of mind that emphasises intentionality, for example, could enable us to extend our recognition of mind-like qualities much more widely into the world and give better recognition to radical difference. To garner the benefits of such a reconstruction we will need to apply some of the courage and daring of the sci-fi hero in the intellectual area, the courage to accept an older, more inclusive way to talk we have been told is irrational, and the adventurousness to explore alternatives to the enormously well-entrenched human-centred paradigm of mind that treats it as unique to the human and views earth others in exclusively reductive terms.

Adopting the intentional recognition stance is one of a number of counter-hegemonic practices of openness and recognition able to make us aware of agentic and dialogical potentialities of earth others that are closed off to us in the reductive model that strips intentional qualities from out of nature and hands them back to us as 'our projections'. While the reductive stance aims to minimise the intentionality of earth others in order to allow for the greatest possible measure of exploitation (an explicit aim of much modernist science), the recognition stance aims for the greatest range of sensitivity to earth others, and in that sense to 'maximise' them, as a measure designed to counter the standpoint distortions of human-centred culture. The intentional recognition stance allows us to re-animate nature both as agent in our joint undertakings and as potentially communicative other: we can join scientists like Humboldt in hearing basalt cones and pumice speak their past to the well-versed observer who stops to listen.[16] We can re-join the poets in hearing the voices of the pines playing with those of the wind, and agree with the forest-caretaker in thinking of these same pines as needing adequate rainfall and as liking to get their feet wet.[17]

Some of the minds we encounter are able to tell us basic ecological things long forgotten or grown oddly unfamiliar, things we need to know about ourselves. They include those of canny animals who gaze back, size you up and tell you who you are – a dangerous predator! – and where you get off. To stay alive and reproduce they have to – and to all but the most reduction-blinded observer patently do – think ahead, try to outsmart you, work out how to escape your reach, and fool you with successful attempts to distract your attention.[18] The rich intentionality the reductive stance would deny to the world is the ground of the enchantment it retains in many indigenous cultures and in some of the past of our own, the butterfly wing-dust of wonder that modernity stole from us and replaced with the drive for power. Being able to conceive others in intentional terms is important to being open to them as possible communicative, narrative and ethical subjects. Extending intentionality to the non-human is crucial for extending to them a narrative conception of ethics.

Human-centred and reductive models of the other structure out these alternatives, direct and reduce our perceptual possibilities. A hegemonic narrative that structures the world as a human monologue will leave us little chance to perceive the other as another narrative subject, potential communicative partner, and agent.[19] Intentional description is essential to being able to represent agency, the view of the other as an originator of projects that demand our respect. Since recognition of the other's agency is in turn central to any kind of negotiation or mutual adjustment process, it is important to cultivate the ability and the conceptual basis for such recognition.[20] The stance of openness to nature's intentionality is important then for developing a whole range of alternatives to the dominant reductive and monological view which has so greatly impoverished our perception of and sensitivity to earth others. Acknowledging the legitimacy of intentional modes of description of the non-human world is also necessary if western philosophy is to avoid its implicit eurocentrism in dismissing as 'primitive' or less than rational the non-western cultures that often frame the world in thoroughly intentional and expressly narrative, communicative and agentic terms. But when we consider all these factors in our choice of frameworks, it is clear that adopting a stance that allows us to experience an intentionally rich world is not only just as rational as the reductive stance, (the position I argued for in Plumwood 1993a), it is in our present circumstances *more rational.*

The intentional recognition stance, as I argue in Plumwood 1993a, vindicates weak panpsychism, the thesis that elements of mind (or mind-like qualities)[21] are widespread in nature and are not confined to the human sphere or form. Weak panpsychism revises the mind–body hyper-separation and polarisation of Cartesianism to conceive of mind in more 'diverse, continuous and graduated ways' (p. 133) than in the Cartesian model of mind, in contrast to strong panpsychism, which expands the extent of one of the dualistic partners and holds that mind in a form close to the Cartesian conception of consciousness and experience permeates the natural world.

Feminism and the Mastery of Nature made a case that weak panpsychism gives a more thorough rethinking of the Cartesian model than strong panpsychism. Strong panpsychism tries to treat the world as permeated by mind still conceived according to human-like thought processes and the on/off Cartesian idea of consciousness (in which case it usually has to find an unacceptably centralised surrogate source for this mind); a further alternative commonly encountered these days revamps the old rationalist 'Great Chain of Being' through a neo-Cartesian mind meritocracy in which humans occupy the extreme end of a graduated experiential spectrum and exhibit mind's fullest and most complete expression. We should reject these approaches, first because of the tendency to re-centralisation, and second because they involve a moral extensionism which leaves unremedied many of the closure and hegemony problems of the Cartesian model. A simple ranking along a single spectrum of 'consciousness' is unable to allow for the heterogeneity present in mind, or to represent adequately the different kinds of mind-like qualities and expressions we can discern in nature, retaining the dualistic human/nature break of Cartesianism but relocating it elsewhere. If we take the intentionality criterion of mind seriously, treating it as a mark or indicator of the presence of elements of mind, we can find support for the thesis of weak panpsychism, and a route to words representing heterogeneity and towards breaking down some hyper-separation aspects of mind/nature dualism. (I will call this fuller thesis intentional panpsychism). Intentionality can provide both a ground of human continuity with and also a basis for recognising heterogeneity in mind and nature.

The project which situates this account of panpsychism and intentionality is that of post-Cartesian reconstruction of concepts of both mind and nature, aimed at throwing off the legacy of hyper-separation that affects contemporary forms of mind–body and human–nature dualism. I have analysed this mechanist hyper-separation as involving the stripping of intentional description from the material level of description and its concentration in a singular organ identified with the narrow, on/off concept of consciousness, leaving two hyper-separated orders of mind and body, or of mind and nature. A project aimed at undoing this form of dualistic construction would have as one of its major aims the rapprochement and mingling of these orders hyper-separated in Cartesian thought; this gives rise in turn to two subsidiary projects which attempt to rebuild the severed bridge of mind–body continuity from both ends, as it were.

The first project, which has been the focus of a number of philosophers, is that of rediscovering the 'body in the mind'.[22] The second, the complementary project that concerns our discussion here, is that of rediscovering the elements of mind in the dualised contrast class of materiality, the body and nature.[23] A further closely related post-Cartesian project is that of recovering a conception of 'speaking matter', as suggested by feminist philosophers such as Luce Irigaray. This project aims at restoring the intentionality stripped from the material sphere in Cartesian construction, in the process locating 'an alternative basis for a non-reductive account of continuity between mind and nature' – alternative that is both to Cartesianism itself and to several less satisfactory attempts to rediscover the mind-like elements the Cartesian model ejects from nature. But it also involves taking more seriously the diversity of marks of the mental and of elements of mind that are so thoroughly singularised, denied and reduced in the Cartesian and neo-Cartesian concentration on consciousness.

A simple spectrum or scalar concept like consciousness has the disadvantage, additional to unclarity and obscurity, of having little capacity to recognise incommensurability or difference, and none at all if interpreted in terms of hegemonic otherness. Intentionality can allow us to take better account of incommensurability because there is enough breadth, play and multiplicity in intentionality to allow us to use diverse, multiple and de-centred concepts that need not be ranked relative to each other for under-standing both humans and more-than-humans as intentional beings. For example pheromone-based, sonar-based and pollen-based sensitivities[24] and chemical communication systems such as those used by cells might appear as heterogeneous intentional capacities that cannot be treated as extensions of the paradigmatic human case, as narrow concepts like consciousness tend to be. In such a context, difference can be represented in more de-centred ways: difference, or incommensurability in the evolu-tionary context, does not have to be represented cumulatively in terms of graduation along a single axis. Incommensurability or difference-in-kind can be represented as well as difference-in-degree, and to that extent inter-species ranking can be de-emphasised. In short, we can allow for mind to take radically different forms, and thus allow for the incommensurability between the abilities of certain species and groups that is now increasingly attested by evolutionary theory and scientific study,[25] thus providing a viable and rational interspecies option to the usual human-centred ways to think about mind.

Intentionality and moral value

These are the aims of the intentional panpsychism as a project disruptive of human/nature dualism. Now it is possible, under assumptions drawn from the dominant doctrines about species ranking, to misunderstand the project involved in weak panpsychism, as one in which intentionality provides the criterion of intrinsic value, moral significance, or criteria for 'respect' or consideration.[26] As we have seen, concepts like respect and intrinsic value are just preliminaries to the ethical concepts we would need in order to develop an adequate ethical response to the non-human world, and there are large parts of that moral task they do not capture in any sufficiently specific, rich or useful way. The intentional recognition stance is highly relevant to this further complex of ethical tasks this book tries to advance. It would be a major misunderstanding to see the task of the intentional recognition stance as that of enunciating criteria for allocat-ing degrees of moral worth or considerability for individuals within it.[27] This would return us to the highly human-centred conception of what our ethical task might be I have called 'studying-down'. It would attempt to fit intentional recognition into the associated project of finding out which parts of nature are well enough qualified to deserve ethical status, substi-tuting intentionality for the rationalist-inspired properties of rationality or consciousness as the criterion for what counts for more in an ethical and value ranking of species and beings. Any project of trying to use intentionality as the criterion of the moral superiority of beings would be misconceived for several reasons, for example the reason that degrees of intentionality and consciousness are poorly correlated with degrees of value. We cannot plausibly claim that a greater degree of consciousness or a higher order level of intentionality corresponds to a greater degree of value in the human case. We do not become more respect-worthy humans by adding another layer of intentionality on top of the previous one, a higher-order level of thought, another thought about that thought, a wish about a thought – especially if that extra level or higher-order of thought involves thinking about how to deceive or to get the better of somebody else. And the teachings of Zen Buddhism, among other things, have helped many of us to see that certain kinds of compulsive or excessive consciousness can be a vice that can block peace, openness and receptivity to others. They may add intentional complexity, but as the case of deception shows, complexity is certainly not an unambiguous blessing or virtue, and is not to be equated simply with greater value or ethical superiority. But if we cannot make the claim that greater intentional complexity corresponds within the human group to greater moral worth, why should we be able to make a similar claim with respect to the superiority of humans as a group to non-humans as a group?

It is important to distinguish then between the use of intentionality as a criterion of individual moral worth (higher placement in a ranking of value or consideration) and what is more inclusive and different, the importance of our openness to the non-human other's potential for intentionality, including their potential for communicative exchange and agency. It is not that their degree of intentionality acts as a criterion of their qualifications or deservingness for receiving moral consideration from us, but that our willingness and ability to recognise the other as a potentially intentional being tells us whether we are open to potentially rich forms of interaction and relationship which have an ethical dimension. So it is not to this human-centred conception of ethics as 'studying down' but to the counter-hegemonic conception of the ethical task as 'studying up' that intentionality, in the form of the intentional recognition stance, is relevant. Intentional recognition is important ethically not as evidence of 'qualifications' for moral status but primarily because it is part of providing a counter-hegemonic alternative to the hegemonic stance of reductionism and closure, and because preparedness to adopt the intentional recognition stance reveals much about our own ability to develop ethical relationships.

A line is often drawn here between humans and non-humans in terms of orders of intentionality, with the claim that non-humans lack second-order cognitive or reflexive abilities. I think there are very strong reasons to think that some non-humans do have such abilities, evidenced for example by widespread deceptive and so-called 'imitative' behaviours.[28] A ringtail possum that used to gallop noisily across my roof to reach the ornamental trees next to my study they were regularly stripping learnt after a few encounters with an angry torch-wielding human alerted by the loud footsteps that a stealthy approach, moving quietly across the roof, was best. A young wombat I used to play vigorous chasing games with would sulk if he did not win; he was an expert at feinting and at manipulating a playmate's expectations, often feigning deceptive disinterest prior to mounting a surprise attack. All these behaviours require sophisticated higher-order intentionality; there are so many examples of this kind, which so many people experience, that one has to wonder whether theorists who strive to dismiss them have any knowledge of animals outside the laboratory. I think some non-humans may lack certain kinds of second or higher order desires characteristic of humans, (such as the desire to be a better wombat), but on the other hand, we humans may well lack some of their characteristic kinds and regions of desire and intentionality. Conclusions here must make allowance for several things: the possibility of providing alternative explanations for some of these apparent lacks, in terms of social organisation, for example; for the high level of human incompetence in understanding animal communication, and for our well-evidenced tendency to treat animals and other non-humans in hegemonic fashion as much simpler than they really are.

Even if we do grant that human minds are distinguished, for example, from those of non-human animals, by greater capacities for a higher-order of intentionality in human mental life, it is entirely unclear how this can support the idea that non-humans should count for less. The most it could show is that certain kinds of higher-order moral capacities and complexities could not occur among some non-humans, but if these sorts of capacities have negative ethical potential as well as positive potential, we can draw no clear conclusions favourable to human moral supremacy from greater human intentional complexity, if indeed it exists. Although we may be able to argue that some kinds of ethical dilemmas and dimensions would be lacking in those kinds of beings who did not have certain kinds of higher-order intentionality, this can surely at most lead to further conclusions about ethical complexity. The factor of incommensurability suggests the need for great caution in making any generalised mapping of intentional and ethical complexity onto the human/non-human distinction, and even more so for degrees of value.

The intentional recognition stance and non-humans

Being able to see earth others as intentional beings is important for breaking down human-centred forms of subject/object dualism and for recognising them as potentially communicative beings. Our everyday parlance is very generous in this regard, admitting intentional description very widely and broadly. But should we take this generous intentional attribution seriously or restrict our recognition in line with the exclusionary programs of philosophy? The fact that we can only do so by imposing complex and artificial restrictions provides good reason to be suspicious. The counter-hegemonic methodological principles I have suggested would recommend following ordinary parlance here and recognising intentional description as legitimate for a large range of earth beings and processes.

However, some philosophers have suggested that their apparent intentionality is merely a projection of our own, not to be taken seriously, as when we speak of the 'brooding mountain'. Now some forms of intentional attribution *are* more or less projections: for example, the locution clearly says more about us than about the mountain when, because of a change in *our* mood, the brooding mountain is transformed the next morning into a beckoning one. But not all non-human intentional attributions are of this purely 'projected' type that present disguised ways of saying something about us. The fact that there is such a distinction and that we do have a sense of the difference between more and less veridical attributions here shows that we cannot write off intentional attributions to non-humans as universally of the 'projection' type, in which there are no criteria for accuracy. Such attributions can also be part of more veridical narratives which are sensitive to the states of the other instead of (or as well as in relational cases) to our own states – the observation that the mountain is preparing to erupt for example, is not dependent for its accuracy on the observer's state of mind, although it is equally intentional. Neither can we see as arbitrary fancy Aldo Leopold's beautiful elegy to the Passenger Pigeon: 'Men still live who, in their youth, remember pigeons. Trees still live who, in their youth, were shaken by a living wind. But a decade hence only the oldest oaks will remember, and at long last only the hills will know' (Leopold 1949: 109).

An alternative compromise idea is that non-human intentionality is not real but we should treat such intentional attributions as if they are because it is a better predictive strategy. The 'as if' strategy deriving from Dennett (1996) and Searle that justifies much contemporary philosophical defense of reductive rationality is a strange animal, and there is a curious doublethink in the idea that the non-human world should be treated as if it had properties it does not 'really' have as part of a 'strategy' for prediction and control. The doublethink of the 'as if' convention has had one positive outcome anyway: it has allowed a wider recognition, in Dennett's case quite wide indeed, of the extent of intentionality in the non-human world (if not fully of its diversity) and of some of the advantages to be gained from 'recognising' it – or rather of the enormous predictive disability attendant on the naked reductive or Cartesian strategy of totally denying it.

But in the Dennett–Searle 'as if' methodology, what is given with one hand is taken away with the other: this advantage is offset by a negative feature, for this liberation of recognition is only possible because it is accompanied by a refusal to take intentionality seriously in ethical terms and by the insertion of Dennett's version of 'the intentional stance' into an essentially monological ethical framework based on human supremacism and minimising non-human intentional recognition in the interests of maximising the human share of the world. This means that rather than being a strategy for meeting the other, the 'pseudo-recognition' of the other as an 'as if' intentional being it permits becomes instead a strategy for domination in the form of prediction and control – the overly narrow objectives for rational theory construction Dennett's account adopts, in which narrowly self-interested projects oriented to control are the only concern, and other possibilities for a richer relationship are neglected.[29]

Dennett's 'as if' version of the intentional stance has moved beyond reductive-Cartesian rationality and taken one important, if tentative and still floundering step, towards recognising the extent of mind in the non-human sphere, but it insists on keeping a foothold still in the old reductive rationality and distancing from the implications of the new as merely another 'strategy'. The 'as if' strategy is fed by an essentially positivist methodology that insists that all that counts are 'the bare facts' and which ignores the way the philosophical and ethical frameworks that legit-imate our perceptions of the other influence what we will be able to experience and what kind of relationship we will be able to build. The fear of abandoning the terrain of reductionism and human supremacism that is lodged so deep in the traditions and identity of science lies behind Dennett's strange vacillation on the meaning of the intentional stance, and his insistence that any movement beyond the everyday Cartesian convic-tion that only humans have minds has to be rigorously 'proved'.[30] But you don't 'prove' a stance, you choose to adopt it!

Philosophy of mind needs to pluck up the courage for a further, more decisive step beyond the lingering Cartesianism of the 'as if' position, and abandon the claim that objectivity and rationality somehow require that we minimise our intentional recognition of the non-human world.[31] The question of whether there is or is not 'someone there', someone we refuse to recognise in an adult pig or gorilla but do not refuse to recognise in a 5-day-old human baby, is not a matter of 'proof' in the sense of being forced on us by some set of objective observations and singular structure of rationality, but at least in part a matter of making a choice about adopting a framework for ethical interaction.[32] This is one of the important insights of the idea of 'the intentional stance' that is not being followed through. In the case of animals, for example, we must recognise how much our 'observations' are influenced by choices and stances about who or what we 'invite in', (as Dennett himself seems to recognise for the case of dogs), and who we deny and reduce, usually for reasons that have little to do with differences in animal minds and abilities and a lot to do with our own choices about which others to subsume under an instrumental and reductive rationality in order to free ourselves from ethical constraints in our treatment of them.

If the onus is placed on scientific methodology to legitimate the lingering resistance to inviting in the non-human, it is open to us to inquire further as to why the 'real' hypothesis for non-human intentionality and the alternative 'as if' hypothesis are not treated as on an equal footing from the perspective of scientific proof. Why should the onus of proof be assumed to lie with the 'real' hypothesis just for the non-human case, but never for the human?[33] An appeal to the principle of parsimony here is question-begging if it is not applied in an even handed way to both the human and non-human cases.[34] There are of course many difficulties in applying parsimony principles to alternative hypotheses with very different consequence sets, (which it is reasonable to assume we have in the case of competing reductive and intentional frameworks), and this is only one of a number of reasons why we should consider parsimony a simplistic and highly problematic framework for theory selection. Another is that the parsimony concept as invoked here will not do the advertised job of minimising our 'theoretical assumptions' about the world, (since it is entirely unclear how there are 'more assumptions' in the idea that non-humans have minds than in the idea that they do not),[35] but rather does the undercover job of minimising our sensitivity and generosity towards the more-than-human sphere. This approach to framework selection follows the pattern of the monological model that is, as I have argued, in the present context ecologically irrational.

It is an alarming feature of the current 'philosophy of mind' approach to these problems of understanding non-human minds that the ethical and political choices and potentially hegemonic aspects of this account remain largely unexamined, and that it attempts increasingly to draw around itself the commanding robes of scientific singularism and detachment in its new guise of cognitive science. A philosophical account of the non-human mind so identified is adrift with no critical ethical compass to guide it except allegiance to the intuitions left over from a deeply human-centred, Cartesian past which are strongly embedded in the approach to non-human animals in dominant forms of science. To be sure, Dennett advises us to watch out for illusions, but provides no useful critical guidance about where these might lie or what we might do about them in the way of a counter-hegemonic program of the sort I have suggested. Unless it develops better critical guidance, this kind of scientised 'philosophy of mind' cannot consider and try to guard against the obviously enormous potential for such accounts to harbour the typical illusions of human uniqueness and superiority we have been dissecting.[36]

Opening up interspecies ethics

As I have argued in Chapter 6, the idea broadly expressed in the concept of intrinsic value, that the value of the more-than-human sphere cannot be arrived at by consulting human interests alone, that the larger-than-human world counts for something in its own terms as well as in terms of our relationship to it, forms a sort of gateway into environmental ethics, not just in historical terms, but in the sense that if nature counts for nothing, more specific questions of ethics cannot arise. Yet beyond an affirmation of the applicability of ethics, an abstract affirmation of nature as deserving bare respect or as having non-instrumental value, (or as some would have it, intrinsic value) fails to arouse the imagination or supply plausible narrative contexts for these attributions, let alone providing useful material for dealing with practical ethical problems. Such abstract affirmations actually do very little to put flesh on the bones of an environmental ethic, leaving us still with many detailed tasks of construction and recognition. It must be this narrative failure, together with the related factor of the extremely truncated nature of the relationships many people now have with animals and nature, that has given certain philosophers the idea that there is any *question* about the possibility of interspecies ethics, which to anyone who lives in close proximity to wild non-human communities is something that seems hardly possible to doubt.

For example, philosophical contact with animals these days is mostly attenuated, and where it occurs is almost always with dependent animals that are individualised and highly disembedded from any wild communities. This paucity of experience may help explain why highly individualised and disembedded accounts like rights and utilitarianism seem plausible as frameworks for interspecies ethics. These features plus the growing scarcity in our lives of relationships to communities of free-living creatures make it hard to imagine egalitarianism as something to aim for in interspecies relationships, as in intrahuman ones. They also make it hard to envisage circumstances where interspecies care and justice conflict in ways directly related to the differences in the kinds of particularistic ethical relationships we bear to other species. But someone who lives in a rich interspecies community may often have not only to imagine but to deal with the moral demands and dilemmas of justice and care very similar to the ones that can appear in the human case. This may include conflict for example between the needs of creatures varying between being much-loved familiars, mysterious strangers, and larger communities of free-living animals strongly embedded in their place. All these things can be directly and powerfully experienced – may indeed be unavoidable – where richer interspecies relationships are possible.[37] Philosophical tradition, unfortunately, seems to enjoin scepticism of any experience that cannot be immediately conveyed to a rationalist who has never left his armchair.

Feminist philosophers have identified the 'universalist/impersonalist tradition' of rationalism as androcentric. Virginia Held has seen its excessive concern with abstraction and universal principle to the exclusion of more relationship-based forms of ethics as a major reason for the inadequacy of moral philosophy for feminist concerns.[38] Carol Gilligan has argued that the ethics of special relationships, as well as the contextual and narrative aspects of ethics, have been undervalued or suppressed in rationalist and androcentric treatments that focus on the rational, abstract and universal.[39] Also neglected or excluded in rationalist ethics are virtue ethics and moral epistemology, especially the ethical requirements in certain contexts Margaret Walker and Iris Murdoch have noted for attention and openness,[40] and for 'patient and just discernment'[41]. Walker outlines an alternative feminist paradigm which treats ethics as a 'lattice of similar themes — personal relationships, nurturance and caring, maternal experience, emotional responsiveness, attunement to particular persons and contexts, sensitivity to open-ended responsibilities'[42] As Walker explains 'This view does not imagine our moral understandings [as] congealed into a compact theoretical instrument of impersonal decision, [such as rights or value] but as deployed in shared processes of discovery, expression, interpretation, and adjustment between persons.'[43]

Dominant rationalist and universalist biases are reasons for the inadequacy of much contemporary philosophy for non-human lives as for women's lives. There is no good reason to think that the particularistic kinds of ethical relations feminists have discussed are any less relevant to interspecies ethics than to intrahuman ethics, that these interspecies relationships are of necessity any less multidimensional, complex, rich and varied than our relationships with humans, or any more reducible to single parameters like rights. Interspecies ethics can, for example, involve both more generalisable relationships involving considerations of fairness and justice and deeply personal relationships involving care, and the conflicts and connections between these dimensions. By the same token, they can exhibit much the same and sometimes (often because of lack of information due to lack of attentiveness) a greater level of conflict, dilemma, and perplexity. The very heavy, and often exclusive, emphasis academic philosophy has given abstract and formal questions of value is an impoverished approach for issues and contexts that call for a wider and richer range of specific ethical approaches such as virtue ethics, care ethics, solidarity and friendship ethics, ecological and food web ethics of reciprocity, and communicative ethics. This suggests a broader way to interpret the concept of respect than in terms of economically cooptable concepts such as value: as being able and willing to hear the other, to encounter them dialogically and not just in terms of economically cooptable concepts such as value as presences, as positively-other-than, as subject rather than object, and to consider their welfare, as both individuals and communities, in all that we do.

None of this is universal, in the sense that it offers a complete ethic generalisable to every context. For example care and guardianship ethics are appropriate for some contexts and not for others; a well developed ethical sensibility helps us to pick the appropriate ethic for the context. In making such decisions, it is usually not just nice but crucial to know something of the other's context and circumstances, something which may often be easier in the human than in the non-human case. For example, people who have little knowledge and experience of snakes and little access to community experience are much more likely to overreact with unnecessary violence that is both dangerous for them and unjust for the animals under attack. Narrative ethics, supplying context and identity, can help us configure nature as a realm of others who are independent centres of value and need that demand from us ethical relationships and responses. As many theorists have noted, narrative is important for constituting the moral identity of actors and actions;[44] intentional description is in turn crucial to legitimating rich narrative description of the non-human sphere. In the interspecies as well as the intraspecies case, narrative can supply crucial information about context, and reveal the complex interplay of different ethical concepts and relationships.

Once we get up the courage to go on through the gateway into the interspecies ethical community, we will need a range of ethical frameworks suitable for the contexts that we will encounter and the relationships we may establish. The first thing we are likely to need in our philosophical toolbox is a communicative ethic, for we will need to ask permission to enter the interspecies community, and once inside we will need such an ethic to pursue negotiation and participation in dialogical relationship with the other inhabitants. The interspecies politics a freer conception of ethics can make possible could create alliances across species that de-emphasise the importance of generalised and stereotypical species frameworks and differentials and open the door to new kinds of communicative experience, (new, that is, for western culture), which might just begin to frame the world in more sensitive and nuanced terms than we can imagine while wearing the simplifying blinkers of human superiority.

Communicative interspecies ethics

Perhaps the most important task for human beings is not to search the stars to converse with cosmic beings but to learn to communicate with the other species that share this planet with us. The interspecies relationships I have discussed above presuppose high levels of interspecies communication, but this need not be limited to communication in the narrow sense of 'rational' verbal or symbolic discourse. The possibility of interspecies communication is of course just as contested as that of interspecies ethics. Attempts at cross-species symbolic communication are usually regarded in the dominant culture of the west as signs of mental disturbance, as in the phrase, 'She talks to the birds!', (although trying to talk to plants is regarded still more seriously). Attempts at serious communication between humans and other species are almost completely precluded by the arrogance and human-centredness of a culture that is convinced that other species are simpler and lesser, and only grudgingly to be admitted as communicative beings. Methodology based on these assumptions more or less guarantees that communication will not take place. Or alternatively, that when it does occur, it takes place on exclusively human terms such that the non-human species is required to learn a human language but not vice versa. This arrangement severely disadvantages the non-human party and allows us to confirm our delusion that other species are inferior. Thus ethical and political aspects are in the picture from the very beginning, in the question of how the communicative situation is arranged. The real communication challenge at this level of interspecies communication is for we humans to learn to communicate with other species on their terms, in their own languages, or in common terms, if there are any.

Most people have had some experience of communication with animals even if they do not call it by that name. Nevertheless communicative acts, models, projects, virtues and concepts of communicability have application and virtue in relation to a much wider group of communicative beings than animals. I will be arguing in this section the case for spreading the category of potential communicants and the concept of communication and communicability out very widely beyond the human to take in not only living inhabitants of the earth and of space, but also places, experiences, processes, encounters, projects, virtues, situations, methodologies and forms of life. In a dialogical methodology, the other is always encountered as a potentially communicative other. This is part of what is involved when we move from the reductive subject–object models of relationship characteristic of mechanism to subject–subject models of an alternative communicative paradigm. Self-maximising modes of interaction are monological – the other is not encountered as an independent other but is encountered reductively as a reflection of self and self's needs, as a resource or shadow. To treat the other as a potentially intentional and communicative being and narrative subject is part of moving from monological modes of encounter (such as those of anthropocentrism) to dialogical modes of encounter. Communicative models of relationships with nature and animals can improve our receptivity and responsiveness, which clearly need much improvement. They seem likely to offer us a better chance of survival in the difficult times ahead than dominant mechanistic models which promote insensitivity to the others' agency and denial of our dependency on them.[45] This clash of models is critical for our times.

The politics of communicative concepts is one of conflict between tendencies to try to shrink and opposing tendencies to expand the extension of the concept.[46] I myself am of the second persuasion, as will be clear. On the other hand, shrinkage strategies suit those motivated by the desire to maximise the category of exploitable resources, to maximise what is available for unrestrained and reductive forms of use. Like the closely related reductive manoeuvres of subject/object dualism, reducing or minimising the category of potential communicants licences forms of use that are unconstrained by considerations of the other's well-being, that are unreflective (because as object or resource the other does not need to be given an account of), and reductive, because the less the other is perceived to be the less the perceived injustice in their treatment as reducible to mere commodities. The universalist/impersonalist tradition is used to support shrinkage of the potentially communicative class.[47]

Moral dualism is one of several philosophical stances that minimise the potential for interspecies communication. The subject/object framework associated with anthropocentrism and mastery is another anti-communicative framework. The dominant framework of rationalism also serves to legitimate reduction and exclusion, and to obscure the alternative of applying concepts of communication more widely than to animals (and has also hindered applying them to animals). Rationalistic accounts of communication background the body and foreground supposedly mentalistic and linguistic aspects, treating communication in intellectualist terms as a matter of high level verbalised exchange with no significant bodily or emotional components. But these same features make rationalist accounts highly problematic frameworks for many intra-human forms of communication, most obviously those with pre-linguistic humans such as babies and small children. Rationalist models which treat communication in intellectualist terms as an exercise in pure, abstract, neutral and universal reason, and which delegitimate the more emotional and bodily forms and aspects of communication, operate to exclude non-humans from full communicative status just as they exclude various human others accorded lower human status as further from the rational ideal. These disembodied rationalist models exclude the forms of communication associated with animals along with the forms of communication associated with women, with non-western cultures and with less 'educated' classes.[48]

We do not have to understand communication in these exclusionary and human-centred ways, and doing so runs counter to the observation that non-humans communicate with one another (and we with them) by a great variety of methods other than through narrowly-conceived 'rational' communication – that is, abstract, linguistic and symbolic forms. As Lynda Birke points out, the conclusion we should draw from the story of the famous counting horse 'Clever Hans' is not that customarily drawn, that non-humans lack communicative abilities or that only linguistic abilities should be counted as yielding knowledge, but rather that the (possibly non-linguistic) communicative abilities Hans apparently did make use of in correctly reading his human partner's bodily cues are indeed a remarkable and discounted route to knowledge.[49] Biologist Marian Stamp Dawkins[50] critiques the widespread intellectualist fallacy that language is so central to mind that in its absence there can be no knowledge of others' experience and no communication. Even in the human case, where language is important, not only do we have other means of finding out about what other people are thinking and feeling than language, we often give these other methods – including 'reading' dramatic action and forming judgements on the basis of dispositions and general behaviour – more weight than language, choosing to correct judgements about people in the light of what they say by judgements based on what they do. Stamp Dawkins argues that the absence of language may be a slight handicap in our knowledge of non-humans and in communication with non-humans, and may challenge our ingenuity more, but it is by no means the insuperable difficulty it is often made out to be. Her own work revealing the strongly expressed preferences of laying hens for pecking opportunities, dustbaths, nestboxes and choice about sociality – all things they are deprived of in intensive rationalist agriculture – exemplifies very well this communicative ingenuity about determining the views of non-humans and entering into their 'inner' worlds. Through experimental design and manipulation it is able to meet an exacting standard of proof about what laying hens find attractive and comfortable that should be sufficient to satisfy any sceptic. Many similar conclusions at less exacting standards might be reached without manipulation by sympathetic and attuned observers capable of open interaction who respect non-humans as agents and choosers – after all, not all our reasonable beliefs and conclusions can or should be formed at the highest level of proof. The fact that there are many perfectly good ways of finding out about animal experience also reveals how much of our ignorance is calculated and cultivated; we do not know what non-humans experience because we do not want to know, since doing so would oblige us to challenge accepted and profitable practices that inflict immense deprivation on commodified animals.

Freed from rationalist assumptions, communicativity can be understood broadly rather than narrowly, allowing for the great variety of expressiveness associated with the great diversity of mindfulness in the world. Nerve cells communicate by transmitting chemical messages, as do certain insects and probably plants. Embodied communication involving dramatic action is the primary method of communication in many intrahuman and interspecies animal contexts: we do not rely on just *telling* a small child not to run onto the road; we supervise it closely, ready to snatch it up if problems arise, and show by our concern and our embodied actions the danger to be avoided. To command a wombat not to open a cupboard door would be a complete waste of time, but a gentle but determined push that sends the attracted animal in the opposite direction will get the point across nicely that attempts to open the door will be resisted. When I found a large and highly venomous tiger snake sunning itself on my patio morning after morning, I was able to convey my own counter-claims to the space effectively by throwing some sandshoes to land within a foot or so of the sleepy reptile, who slithered off promptly and never returned. Of course it helps to know how the other will read one's actions, what the etiquette[51] of an interspecies encounter is likely to be: you must never look a lyrebird too boldly in the eye as it steps past you at close quarters, or it may interpret your interest as evil intent and take fright; if you want to avoid alarming it, feign boredom and take an occasional sideways or casual glance from under your lashes. Reading embodied action is part of all our lives, and is the common language of embodied beings.

Communicative models which allow us to overcome rationalistic biases and exclusions for the human case will also help us to recognise non-human animals in their denied aspects as communicative beings. But an emphasis on communication and its use as a criterion of moral worth or value could remain problematic for non-humans to the extent that it failed to recognise diversity, was biased towards communicative capacities that are characteristic of humanity, and recognised as communicative only those species most similar to ourselves. To overcome this risk of implicit anthropocentrism, we should understand communication broadly and with due respect for difference, treating communicative behaviours as highly diverse and as part of plural set of grounds for relationship, rather than its unique and exclusive basis. We must cultivate sensitivity to communicative capacities *within species* as well as to their capacities for communication with humans.

It is however important not to over-idealise the communicative model. Communicative relations have much promise in healing the crisis in human/nature relationships: they open up new moral possibilities for organising life in ways that can negotiate conflicts of interests, build agreement, trust and mutuality, and allow us to avoid instrumentalism and the imposition of the will of one party on the other by force. Communicative relations don't necessarily follow out those possibilities, however, and it is important not to romanticise the communicative model, which does not automatically eliminate the dynamic of power, either in terms of equality of access, of hierarchy in forms of communication, or of the structuring of communication in hegemonic ways. Any particular act of communication can take place in (be nested in) a variety of contexts, some of which may be monological. The important thing is communicability, respecting others as agents and choosers and as potentially communicative subjects, which is part of treating them as subjects proper, the other crucial ingredient being intentional recognition.

There are several further philosophical and rationalist obstacles to developing frameworks for an interspecies communicative ethic. One is the insistence we met in Chapter 2 that we must use separate vocabularies for humans and non-humans in order to keep basic mentalistic, narrative and communicative concepts confined to the human. This demand for hyper-separation of human and non-human description is often legitimated by the concerns about 'anthropomorphism' we analysed in Chapter 2. But it can also be based in a philosophical form of rationalism that insists on an over-intellectualised analysis of intentional concepts that creates barriers to applying the same kinds of ethical and mentalistic concepts to non-humans as to humans. An example is the claim that sophisticated higher order intentional functors, especially belief, must be present before we can correctly ascribe any kind of intentionality at all to anyone, even though most intentional description can be analysed better in much less intellectualist ways.

Important resources for recognising and sustaining relationships are the communicative virtues. The virtues, writes Anthony Weston, are 'those traits that sustain and deepen relationship', while Carol Gilligan speaks of morality as arising 'from a recognition of relationship, a perception of the need for response'.[52] In the context of strong centric traditions, counter-hegemonic virtues can be emphasised as corrective. These are ethical stances which resist distorting centric constructions, helping to counter the influence of the oppressive ideologies of domination and self-imposition that have formed our conceptions of both the other and ourselves.. These counter-hegemonic virtues include philosophical stances and methodologies that maximise our ethical sensitivities to other members of our ecological communities and openness to their agency; they are antagonistic to stances of reduction, superiority and scepticism that minimise the kinds of beings to whose agency and communicative potential we are open. Counter-hegemonic stances include especially communicative virtues:

- recognising continuity with the non-human to counter dualistic construction of human/nature difference as radical discontinuity;
- reconstructing human identity in ways that acknowledge our animality, decentre rationality and abandon exclusionary concepts of rationality;
- acknowledging difference, non-humans as 'other nations', as 'positively-other-than', including a non-hierarchical conception of more-than-human difference;
- decentring the human/nature contrast to allow a more inclusive, interspecies ethics;
- de-homogenisation of both 'nature' and 'human' categories;
- openness to the non-human other as potentially an intentional and communicative being (the intentional recognition stance);
- listening to the other (attentiveness stance);
- active invitation to communicative interaction;
- redistribution (generosity stance)
- ethical consideration without closure directed towards an excluded class;
- non-ranking stance minimising interspecies ranking and ranking contexts
- 'studying up' in problem contexts (self-critical stance);
- negotiation, a two-way, mutual adjustment stance;
- attention to the other's complexity, outrunning of our knowledge.

One of the most important among these virtues is listening and attentiveness to the other, a stance which can help to counter the deafness and backgrounding which obscures and denies what the non-human other contributes to our lives and collaborative ventures. Openness and attentiveness give us sensitivity to the world as 'alive, astir with responsive presences that vastly exceed the human';[53] they allow us to be receptive to unanticipated possibilities and aspects of the non-human other, reconceiving and re-encountering them as potentially communicative and agentic beings with whom we ourselves must negotiate and adjust. Closely allied stances are those of invitation, which risks an offering of relationship to the other in a more or less open-ended way,[54] and receptiveness to presence and response. These counter-hegemonic virtues help us to resist the reductionism of dominant mechanistic conceptions of the non-human world, and to revise both our epistemic objectives of prediction and control and our denial of non-human others as active presences and ecological collaborators in our lives.

Overall, what is involved here is a movement from a monological to a dialogical conception of the human self and its possibilities for relationship to the non-human world. These reframings prepare the ground for movement from monological and dualistic types of relationship with nature towards the kinds of structures of relationship we need to develop to begin addressing the environmental crisis at the level of culture. They can open the way for a culture of nature that allows for much more in the way of contextual and negotiated relationships of communication, balanced dialogue, and mutual adjustment between species, starting with our own, in what could become a liberatory blending or mingling of nature and culture.

9 Unity, solidarity and deep ecology

The basis of solidarity – identity or difference?

Recent environmental thought has presented a popular alternative to the moral dualist constructions of academic philosophy that circumvents the seemingly endless argument over whether humanist ethical and value principles can somehow be stretched to extend to some non-humans. This alternative, deep ecology, has been to a large extent based in activism and oriented to justifying and explaining the political solidarity with earth others of those who act to defend nature. The objectives and sympathies of activists who stand in front of bulldozers or do tree sits are usually much broader than the widest aperture moral extensionism can be stretched to cover. For these concerns we need an open ethics that covers trees, mountains, wild rivers, wilderness areas and endangered species, all of which are left out in the cold by moral extensionist and dualist forms of argument – or at least, they are left just where they were before the intervention of these forms of environmental ethics, conceived instrumentally as resources for the need, pleasure or spiritual uplift of a privileged group of humans or honorary humans.

Deep ecology, and especially the work of Arne Naess, has helped shift the discussion away from conventional extensionist ethics towards activist-inspired issues of how we can account for and develop our capacity for solidarity or 'standing with' earth others, and also towards the broader and more philosophically productive ethico-ontological issues concerning the analysis of human identity, alienation and difference from nature that underlie many ethical stances. For his account of solidarity, Naess appeals to features of the human self, and to concepts of unity, identification and self-realisation to provide a foundation for activist concern for nature that avoids the scope problems of moral extensionism and dualism. The resulting theory certainly gives a wide enough coverage for all activist concerns and moves decisively beyond instrumentalism. But one problem is that it is now too wide; few identifications, including those with problematic causes and with items such as bulldozers, are excluded by such psychological mechanisms, as I argued in *Feminism and the Mastery of Nature*.

There are other problems too: to the extent that criteria for inclusion are based on similarity to or unity with the human and give poor recognition to nature's independence and difference, it retains many of the problems of moral extensionism. Such a philosophical foundation for activism and solidarity can remain in a subtle way human-centred, since again it makes solidarity turn on conceptions of unity with, similarity or difference to the human centre instead of on independent relationships. If we work mainly with concepts of identification it can be very difficult to get the right balance between continuity and difference, while trying to base our methodologies on concepts of unity opens up some very problematic territory indeed. Naess's formulation of this basis in terms of the concept of unity or fusion of interests makes the fundamental ethical form implicit in deep ecology essentially a one-place relationship. This makes it un-suitable as a basis for ethical models, such as that of communication or negotiation, which require explicit recognition of at least two places in the human/nature relationship. Such an ethic cannot address the other as a communicative or potentially communicative subject, and hence is parti-cularly unsuitable for animals. Since a communication model offers a potentially powerful new image and mutualistic model to replace that of the dominant mechanistic worldview, we have to forgo rather a lot in the interests of maintaining an account based on unity. I discuss these problems below, and present an alternative analysis of solidarity based on feminist theory that I think is more useful for environmental activism.

One useful route into exploring the diverse answers available to the question of how to ground solidarity with and respect for the value of nature is the debate between Arne Naess and fellow Norwegian mountai-neer Peter Reed. Despite their commonalities in the search for a ground for a new (for the humanist west) ethic of respect, Reed and Naess differed profoundly over the question of whether the abstract foundation for the desired new relationship will be found in human unity with and embedd-edness within the natural order, or in the 'existential gulf', our disconti-nuity and difference from nature. Naess proposed foundations formulated basically in terms of identity and unity: Reed's counter-advocacy, in a powerful essay published posthumously, of basing respect not on sameness but on difference, could hardly have presented a stronger contrast. I argue in this section that the criticisms both disputants make of each other are valid, which points to resolution via a third position which would allow us to combine elements of both continuity and difference, self and other, in dynamic tension.

Naess, focussing on human alienation from nature, elects for identification with nature and the realisation of the Self based on the totality of these identifications as the foundation for respect for and defence of nature. This position created a useful alliance with those forms of Buddhist thought which cast the sense of personal separateness as the ultimate illusion, contributing in no small measure to the political success of Naess's version of deep ecology. 'Identification', used in examples as synonymous variously with sympathy, loyalty, and solidarity, is given a technical gloss by Naess (in his reply to Reed) in terms of interest fusion or identity, 'the process by which the supposed interests of another being are spontaneously reacted to as our own interests' (Naess 1990: 187). The position, in spite of the careful qualifications in terms of interests Naess gave it, ultimately draws on sameness and identity as the basis of the respect relationship. As Reed saw it, respect could only be based on the very existential gulf Naess's work sought to remove. It is, he argued, 'our very separateness from the Earth, the gulf between the human and the natural, that makes us want to do right by the earth' (Reed 1989: 56). There was an alternative to Naess's account, Reed argued, based on taking the other –nature – and not the human self to be basic: 'one approach sees humans as part of nature, the other sees nature as part of humans' (Reed 1989: 54).

Relying on Martin Buber's theory of 'I-Thou' relationship, Reed declares the other that is nature to be not part of the self but 'a self-sufficient being of whom we have an inkling'. It is 'the Wholly Other', 'a total stranger', 'radically apart' (Reed 1989: 57). In the right spirit, we can meet this other, but only as 'two ships that pass in the night', since the 'I' and the 'Thou' do not depend on each other. Naess is certainly right to criticise Reed's dualism and failure to address the problem of alienation. Reed does not merely stress difference, he retains the existential gulf of the dominant dualistic tradition in its full form. This gulf yawns between humans and nature, according to Reed, because all we humans have in common with it, our merely physical nature, is an inessential and accidental element of our identities. Reed's absence from the present debate seems to me to do something to undermine this view of the physical as an unimportant element in human identity. Reed's reaffirmation of the existential gulf, a key and especially problematic part of the western tradition, leads him to treat physical nature in a deeply ambivalent way: physical nature is both 'mere' (in the human case) and the object of what amounts almost to worship (in the case of the other). We are left wondering why the supposed radical difference of the other should be a basis for awe and wonder in the one case and something like disdain or indifference in the other.

Reed's account is strongly oriented to wilderness. In contrast to Naess, who often focuses on mixed communities, Reed is plainly one of those who believe that it is only the 'pure' landscape of human absence that represents nature. It is not only the otherness but the huge scale and indifference of wilderness landscapes that evokes awe, and leads to revelations of intrinsic value in nature. When nature is terribly dominant, says Reed, we have a sense of fear and of wonder which is missing in contexts too familiar and humanised. Nature is both related to us and other, but it is difference alone, it seems, which is the basis of the intuition of value. It is hard to see how this kind of orientation to 'the Wholly Other' can provide a basis for consideration of nature in the large number of situations where it is less impressive and more vulnerable – precisely the kind of context, one would have thought, where activists especially need a respect ethic. In contrast to Naess's position and its politically useful alliances with the perennial philosophy and with Buddhist thought, the austerity, almost self-revulsion, of Reed's account, with its stress on human insignificance and final, frankly misanthropic, suggestion that the world might be a better place without human beings, seems unlikely to generate widespread appeal (especially at the ballot box).

Nevertheless, Reed's critique of Naess points up some important problems and tensions in the use of identity as the foundation for an environmental ethic. On first glance, Naess's account does not appear to appeal to either fusion or to egoism – since we are supposed to defend not the self but the big Self as 'the totality of our identifications'. But, says Reed, there seem to be inconsistent requirements hidden here: we are supposed to retain a sense of our individuality as we work to save the big Self from destruction – but at the same time we are supposed to lose interest in our individuality as we cultivate our identification with the big Self.[1] We are required to be egoists and also not egoists, to retain the intensity and defence drive of egoism, but also to abandon certain key differentiations between ourselves and others, in order to establish that equivalence between self and other which enables a transfer of our self-regarding motives. Naess's position, on closer inspection, ultimately *is* based on a kind of self-interest and upon a form of fusion or expulsion of difference – taking the form, as Naess explains in his reply, of *identity of interests*. 'Identification' writes Naess, is a process 'through which the supposed interests of another being are spontaneously reacted to as our own interests' (Naess 1990: 187). Selves may not be fused, but interests are, and the other is included ethically to the extent that a kind of equivalence to self is established through identification.

But analysis in terms of interest identity won't enable us to dispense with difference. We may identify in solidarity with an animal, say a wombat, expressing our solidarity by being willing to undertake political action on their behalf (working to remove them from 'vermin' status for example), but we do not thereby acquire identical specific interests, in grass eating, for example. Although we may (as relational selves) assume the overarching interest of the other's general well-being and react to that as bound up with our own, it is crucial to our being able to defend that well-being that we retain a clear sense of them as distinct beings with different, perhaps entirely different, interests from ours. We must attain solidarity with the other *in their difference,* and despite the ambiguity of the term 'identification', solidarity here cannot be interpreted as identity; solidarity and respect cannot be understood as processes of overcoming or eliminating otherness or difference, and neither ethics nor motivation can be derived from establishing ethical equivalence to self or from extending egoism to a wider class of big Selves. Even though Reed goes on to develop his account of otherness in ways that turn out to be rather problematic, he is, I think, importantly right on what I take to be his main point, that an account based entirely on unity and identification with Self provides a problematic basis for respect for the non-human world, and one particularly inadequate for those issues, such as wilderness, where the otherness of nature is particularly salient and striking.

It is tempting to conclude that both Naess and Reed remain within the 'solipsistic omnipotence of the single psyche'.[2] Reed's pure other-based account is a reversal of Naess's pure self-based one, but both seem to miss the importance of relational dynamics, the precarious balance of sameness and difference, of self and other involved in experiencing sameness without obliterating difference. Reed's positing of self and other as utterly disconnected, as 'ships that pass in the night', misses the conceptual, energetic and material dependence of self on other: if the other plays an active part in the creation and maintaining of self, there can be no 'pure other' and no 'pure self'. Reed reaffirms the western tradition of denying nature and the radical distancing between humans and nature an environmental ethic must aim to counter. Naess is right to reject this picture as reproducing a key part of the problem. However, the pure self/pure other choice presented by Naess and Reed and the underlying metaphysical choice of Same/Different is a false dichotomy: both continuity with and difference from self can be sources of value and consideration, and both usually play a role.

Some of the problems in each other's work Naess's and Reed's mutual critiques point up can be resolved in a larger critical framework, employing resources from feminist theory and postcolonial theory (defined in During (1987) as 'that thought which refuses to turn the Other into the Same'). To deal with the problems of identity the present form of human colonisation of nature generates, an adequate environmental ethic needs to provide an (usually sequenced) affirmation of both continuity and difference between humans and nature, as appropriate to the context. As we have seen, in the western tradition especially, there is a need to stress continuity between self and other, human and nature, in response to the existential gulf created by dominant hyper-separated (radically distanced) and alienated anthropocentric models of nature and of human identity. We stress human continuity and ecological vulnerability in response to those aspects of centric models that define the truly human as (normatively) outside of nature and in opposition to the body and the material world, and conceive nature itself in alienated and mechanistic terms as having no elements of mind.

But we also need to stress the difference and divergent agency of the other in order to defeat that further part of the centric dynamic that seeks to assimilate and instrumentalise the other, recognising and valuing them only as a part of self, alike to self, or as means to self's ends. What makes it possible to combine this joint affirmation of continuity and difference consistently is the distinction between hyper-separation and difference. This distinction is reflected in a corresponding distinction between continuity and identity which enables us to say that although we need to affirm continuity with nature to counter our historical denials, doing so does not require any simple assumption of identity. Neither Reed nor Naess distinguishes sufficiently between difference and normative hyper-separation, an emphatic form of differentiation associated especially with the view of the other as inferior. The outcome is that Reed treats difference, on his account the basis of the other's value and of their ethical recognition, as implying the denial of continuity and the maintenance of the existential gulf, while Naess treats removing the existential gulf as meaning the expulsion of difference and the basing of value on forms of identity or equivalence to self. We need a concept of the other as interconnected with self, but as also a separate being in their own right, accepting the 'uncontrollable, tenaciousness otherness'[3] of the world as a condition of freedom and identity for both self and other. Feminist theory can help us here because it has developed logical and philosophical frameworks based on maintaining the tension between Same and Different rather than generally eliminating difference in favour of sameness or vice versa.

Solidarity and oppressive concepts of unity

The choice these two frameworks offer us, of valuing nature either as Same or as Different, is ultimately an anthropocentric one, since to base value exclusively on either sameness or difference to the human implicitly construes the human as the centre and pivot of value – either as the positive (same) or as the negative (different) source of value and recognition. A framework bringing all value and recognition of the other back to identity with or difference from the human self still conceives the human as hegemonic centre, and presents only a variant on the moral extensionism that is now a standard part of the contemporary neo-Cartesian consensus in philosophy. We need an alternative basis for ecological action that recognises the other's incommensurability and does not define the other's worth in hegemonic terms that relate it always back to the human as conceptual centre.[4]

The popular interpretation, based on Naess's account, of the central concept by which we relate ethically to nature as that of sameness or unity – and of psychological and self unity as the central meaning of 'identification' – creates a number of serious problems of merger and boundary recognition. Vague concepts of unity and identity provide very imprecise and inadequate correctives to our historical denial of continuity with and dependency on nature. Ethical theories based on unity cannot provide a good model of mutual adjustment, communication and negotiation between different parties and interests, is unhelpful in the key areas where we need to construct multiparty, mutualistic ethical relationships. Recovering multiplicity and difference requires a dual project of rejecting hyper-separation and also affirming difference, as responses to different parts of the logic of the One and the Other and to the Othering of nature. Affirming continuity counters the construction of human identity as emphatically separate from an homogenised passive nature whose works are similarly hyper-separate. But the confusion of continuity with identity and the construction of unity as the basis of relationship prevents us from combining this countering of hyper-separation with the recognition of difference and of the other as a distinct centre of needs and projects.

Naess's formulation of the basis of activism in terms of the ambiguous concept of 'identification' obscures the fact that the basic concept required for an appropriate ethic of environmental activism is not that of identity or unity (or its reversal in difference) but that of *solidarity* – standing with the other in a supportive relationship in the political sense. But there are multiple possible bases for solidarity, and the politics of solidarity is different from the politics of unity. Solidarity requires not just the affirmation of difference, but also sensitivity to the difference between positioning oneself *with* the other and positioning oneself *as* the other, and this requires in turn the recognition and rejection of oppressive concepts and projects of unity or merger. 'Identification' has also made it easy for some transpersonal ecologists to import into the concept of solidarity various problematic themes of egoism, self-expansion and self-defence along with a masculinist and pseudo-rationalist agenda of inferiorising particular emotional attachments and advocating a version of disengagement.[5]

One of the main difficulties in interpreting solidarity in terms of vaguely specified concepts of unity is that this interpretation does not theoretically rule out some possibilities that ought to be ruled out. Oppressive projects of unity abound in the human case, especially in the case of hegemonic relationships of colonisation. To the colonising mentality, these projects of unity often appear in quite a different light to the way they appear to the subordinated group; what appear to the coloniser as improvements or as support appear as imposition and cultural destruction to the colonised. Recent Australian culture has provided many examples, in the literary and artistic frauds perpetrated by people of settler culture pretending to be Aboriginal, of assimilating or incorporating projects of unity which deny the indigenous other's difference or transgress the other's boundaries. Some of those who adopt these oppressive projects of unity lay claim to Aboriginal identity, culture and knowledge on the basis of alleged empathy, while others appear to regard indigenous culture as a free good, available to all, and others still are clearly intent upon harm. But even where the motivation is sympathetic, the oppressive and transgressive character of these projects of unity is usually fully evident to the indigenous people concerned.

Similarly, colonial history in Australia and elsewhere abounds in projects of cultural assimilation of indigenous peoples which succeeded the attempt at genocide and which had as their aim an oppressive form of unity, namely incorporation, in which the subordinated party is produced as an inferiorised version of the dominant party ('pidgin') or is denied any voice of their own. The incorporative self uses unity in a hegemonic fashion to absorb the other or recreate them as a version of the self. To the extent that the colonising project is one of self-imposition and appropriation (literally 'making self'), the incorporative self of the colonising mind is insensitive to the other's independence and boundaries, denying the other's right to define their own reality, name their own history, and establish their own identity.[6] This insensitivity extends to include the other's epistemic boundaries; it often assumes that the other is transparent – that they can be grasped and known as readily as the self – or that they are too simple for anything to be hidden, or outrun the coloniser's knowledge. To the incorporative self, the other can be taken (appropriated) and taken for a benefit which is expressed exclusively in terms of the self, of the One, about whose beginning and end we are encouraged to be unclear. These examples show us that respect for the other requires recognising their difference and boundaries – not claiming to be them or to encompass them. Oppressive projects of unity like this can arise from the failure to distinguish unity (positioning the self *as* the other) from solidarity (positioning the self *with* or in support of the other).

Now I am not saying here, as some supporters of deep ecology seem to think[7], that all deep ecologists or others who have theorised the basis of solidarity in terms of unity are selfish male chauvinist pigs, that they all wish to incorporate nature into the self, or are all megalomaniacs aiming at control who take their own interests to be those of nature or the universe at large. Nor am I insisting that we must treat deep ecology according to its worst possible interpretation, as the incorporative self. What I am saying is that assumptions of unity of interest are especially liable to hegemonic interpretations, and that in the absence of a critical analysis of power are open to cooption by existing dominance orders and by the dominant Lockean account of the incorporative self upon which capitalism is based. I think the wish to stand in solidarity with nature can be given an alternative theoretical development in terms of elaborating more carefully a concept of solidarity that does not confuse solidarity with unity, the relational with the incorporative self.[8] Replacing the concept of unity with that of solidarity would no doubt displease some deep disciples and displace some alliances,[9] but potential for a different set of alliances opens up as those with others are de-emphasised. Deep ecologists can learn much from feminist theory and anti-colonial theory about how to go about the theoretical task of rejecting hyper-separation and elaborating a concept and ground for solidarity with nature distinct from unity, one which at the same time allows us to affirm continuity and to respect nature's difference.

There are, I have suggested, multiple bases for critical solidarity with nature. One important critical basis can be an understanding that certain human societies position humans as oppressors of non-human nature, treating humans as a privileged group which defines the non-human in terms of roles that closely parallel our own roles as recipients of oppression within human dominance orders. Our grasp of these parallels may be based upon imaginative or narrative transpositions into locations paralleling that of the oppressed non-human other: artistic representation has an important place in helping us make such transpositions. Literature has often played such a transposing role historically, especially in the nineteenth and early twentieth century, in relation to the class system, slavery, women's oppression, and animal oppression. In recent decades science fiction narratives that imaginatively position humans as colonised or exploited reductively as food by alien invaders have provided very powerful vehicles for such imaginative transpositions into a place that parallels that of the non-human food animal. So have those cartoonists whose 'absurd' humour depends upon exploiting parallels in the condition of the human and non-human oppressed. A chicken coming from a human house carrying a baby passes a woman coming from a chicken coop carrying a basket of eggs, for example.[10] A Larson elephant is outraged when he notices the ivory notes on a piano keyboard at an interspecies party and makes the connection to the fate of his own kind.

The leap of recognition that is often described and explained in terms of an unanalysed and capricious emotion of 'empathy' or 'sympathy'[11] is often better understood in terms of a concept of solidarity that is based on an intellectual and emotional grasp of the parallels in the logic of the One and the Other. Since most people suffer from some form of oppression within some dominance order or other, there is a widespread basis for the recognition that we are positioned multiply as oppressors or colonisers just as we are positioned multiply as oppressed and colonised. This recognition that one is an oppressor as well as an oppressed can be developed in certain circumstances to become the basis for the critical 'traitorous identity' which analyses, opposes and actively works against those structures of one's own culture or group that keep the Other in an oppressed position.[12] Traitorous kinds of human identity involve a revised conception of the self and its relation to the non-human other, opposition to oppressive practices, and the abandonment and critique of cultural allegiances to the dominance of the human species and its bonding against non-humans, in the same way that male feminism requires abandonment and critique of male bonding as the kind of male solidarity that defines itself in opposition to the feminine or to women, and of the ideology of male supremacy. These 'traitorous identities' that enable some men to be male feminists in active opposition to androcentric culture, some whites to be actively in opposition to white supremacism and ethnocentric culture, also enable some humans to be critical of 'human supremacism' and in active opposition to anthropocentric culture. 'Traitorous' identities do not appear by chance, but are usually considerable political and personal achievements in integrating reason and emotion; they speak of the traitor's own painful self-reflection as well as of efforts of understanding that have not flinched away from contact with the pain of oppressed others.

What makes such traitorous identities possible is precisely the fact that the relationship between the oppressed and the 'traitor' is *not one of identity*, that the traitor is critical of his or her own 'oppressor' group as someone from within that group who has some knowledge of its workings and its effects on the life of the oppressed group. It depends on the traitor being someone with a view from both sides, able to adopt multiple perspectives and locations that enable an understanding how he or she is situated in the relationship with the other from the perspective of both kinds of lives, the life of the One and the life of the Other.[13] Being a human who takes responsibility for their interspecies location in this way requires avoiding both the arrogance of reading in your own location and perspective as that of the other, and the arrogance of assuming that you can 'read as the

Other', know their lives as they do, and in that sense speak or see as the other. Such a concept of solidarity as involving multiple positioning and perspectives can exploit the logic of the gap between contradictory positions and narratives standpoint theory appeals to.[14]

The traitorous identity implies a certain kind of ethics of support relations which is quite distinct from the ethics involved in claiming unity. It stresses a number of counter-hegemonic virtues, ethical stances which can help to minimise the influence of the oppressive ideologies of domination and self-imposition that have formed our conceptions of both the other and ourselves. As we have seen, important among these virtues are listening and attentiveness to the other, a stance which can help to counter the backgrounding which obscures and denies what the non-human other contributes to our lives and collaborative ventures. They also include philosophical strategies and methodologies that maximise our sensitivity to other members of our ecological communities and openness to them as ethically considerable beings in their own right, rather than ones that minimise ethical recognition or that adopt a dualistic stance of ethical closure that insists on sharp moral boundaries and denies the continuity of planetary life. Openness and attentiveness are among the communicative virtues we have already discussed; more specifically, they mean giving the other's needs and agency attention, being open to unanticipated possibilities and aspects of the other, reconceiving and re-encountering the other as a potentially communicative and agentic being, as well as 'an independent centre of value, and an originator of projects that demand my respect'[15] A closely allied stance, as Anthony Weston points out, is that of invitation, which risks an offering of relationship to the other in a more or less open-ended way[16]

There is a considerable convergence here between the counter-hegemonic virtues of solidarity and mutuality and the kinds of virtues of openness Naess's form of deep ecology has itself recommended. Deep ecology however has tended to stress recognising value rather than agency: valuing nature is somewhat the stance of someone looking on at nature, whereas the stance of recognising agency is important for all collaborative, communicative and mutualistic projects. Although the term 'virtue' would probably not be acceptable to deep ecologists who have followed Arne Naess in treating ethics as unnecessary, authoritarian and passé, it is, as I have argued[17], clear that the theory of deep ecology has not succeeded in eliminating ethics, but rather in disguising its ethical assumptions as psychological assumptions. The ethics of solidarity provides an alternative basis for many deep ecological insights which avoids the implicit positivism of the 'no-ethics' approach, enables the development of stronger connections to human liberation movements, and avoids the many difficulties of the unity interpretation.

Unity and the political theory of deep ecology

In the area of political theory similarly, deep ecology has the possibility of different routes of development which are allied with divergent political choices. Again, it is in part a question of deciding whose company you want to keep – a choice which deep ecology cannot now say 'pass' to as it did in the early days, especially as questions of political organisation have come so much to the fore in contemporary discussion in environmental theory. Since virtually every political position now claims to be green, (or has a green-dyed form, sometimes where the dye will clearly come out in the first wash), the question can't be declined via some version of a Principle of Tolerance, which is the way Naess's work suggests for dealing with it, or by appeal to individual consciousness change. Deep ecology's political thinking in response to this problem has so far been strikingly shallow: initially it employed the concept of unity between person–place and person–community to embrace bioregionalism and small-scale communitarianism, without any clear indication (beyond individual consciousness change) of how this was to be achieved or what political structure would maintain it or guarantee its ecological character. This early fantasy phase of unity has now been succeeded by theoretical developments I discuss below – also based on unity – that are more explicitly accommodating to existing power structures.

In the earlier sections, we noticed how the theoretical possibilities associated with unity and individual consciousness change have assumed a privileged role over the solidarity and structural analysis allied with feminist-postcolonial theory and other politically radical movements. Just as deep ecology failed to provide alternatives to an ethical theory based on unity, it has failed to provide political alternatives to political theory based on unity. This pattern in the political area provides the basis for the seduction of deep ecological political theory by a conservative paradigm endorsing capitalism, private property and small government, and by a notably shallow and elite-accommodating deep pocket strategy that seeks the ecological enlightenment of the Man of Property as its main objective.[18] The unity interpretation, which has the potential to provide support for both totalitarian and capitalist positions, once again provides the means by which this hegemonic accommodation is constructed.

Several recent theorists have pointed to the ecological history of Nazism to argue that deep ecology has a certain potential to support nazism and fascism. This danger is variously attributed to its tendency to question modernity and humanism and to display elements of romanticism[19], and to undermine private property and individualism.[20] I shall argue that these arguments rest on shallow analyses of fascism and Nazism, as well as of what is of political relevance today. While it is important to acknowledge the potential of environmentalism in general and deep ecology in particular to support undemocratic forms of politics, these arguments misidentify the ways in which this potential arises. The main danger comes from a different direction, not so much from its alleged romanticism and critique of humanism or from its holistic understanding of ecology, but through the potential of the unity interpretation to support the idea of community as a unity or fusion of interests and the associated idea of a pure home devoid of alien elements.[21] The unity interpretation at the institutional level involves the attempt to seek the political along with the ethical inclusion of non-human nature in terms of the Naessian concept of unity of interests, expressed at the level of political theory by concepts of coverture and community.

Luc Ferry is one of a group of recent critics of deep ecology's authoritarian potential.[22] Ferry identifies 'shallow' forms of ecology with humanism and a progressive affirmation of modernism, and blackens any deeper form of ecological thought which tries to challenge human/nature dualism in a more thorough-going way, through the alleged association of deep ecology with Romanticism, anti-modernism, anti-humanism and even Nazism. But the crudeness of such an analysis is apparent when we consider that all these positions have multiple faces which must render all such simple equations suspect. The analysis ignores the oppressive and problematic aspects of modernism and humanism, especially where humanism defines itself against or in opposition to the non-human, and relies on the dubious assumption that more ethical consideration for non-humans necessarily means less for humans.[23] While it is important to note the role of those forms of Romanticism corrupted by the desire for unity and other oppressive forces, any analysis which puts all its stress on this factor ignores the diversity and liberatory aspects of some forms of Romanticism[24], and the well-documented complicity of the worst aspects of Nazism with modernism and rationalism.[25] At present the danger from deep ecology's political naiveté comes from quite a different direction, from capture by the liberal right rather than the fascist right.

Michael Zimmerman also reaches perverse conclusions from his interrogation of Nazi ecologism because he too adopts oversimplified accounts of fascism and Nazism: he favours the 'irrationality' explanation that overlooks the ambiguity of the Nazi relationship to modernity and casts it as the evil throwback to mindless collectivity and blood and soil tribalism, the dark binary of the White Knights of individualism, private property, liberalism and Enlightenment rationality. But, as recent critical theorists have shown, this portrait of Nazism as an irruption of 'premodern irrationalism' obscures as much as it illuminates. Zimmerman's binary account assumes that the Nazi form of fascism remains the chief political danger we have still to fear, and that it is just in their critique of modernity that we should seek the primary source of Nazi horrors. But this too overlooks analyses such as Bauman's, suggesting that the extermination programs were in many respects an extreme *expression* of modernity and its rational capacity to scapegoat, marginalise and eliminate; both the programs and Nazi thinking in general involved strong modernist elements of human/animal dualism, instrumental/bureaucratic order and hyper-rationalism.[26] It was less the fledgling science of ecology, as Zimmerman (1995: 248) claims than the very well-established modern science of biology in which Germany led the world[27] that helped to supply the intellectual foundations for Nazi racist practice and the biological rationalism that underlay the extermination programs. But Zimmerman's shallow analysis also fails to note that Nazi doctrines of racial purity were in many ways an intensification of the 'normal' doctrines of white racial superiority that had accompanied the colonising and 'civilising' process undertaken in the Americas, in Asia, Africa and Australia – doctrines which provided the justification for dominant global property-formation regimes.[28]

Zimmerman's analysis not only misidentifies the political problem in deep ecology and offers a mistaken analysis of where it lies, it uses the mistake to promote solutions for ecological problems in line with the conservative paradigm of strengthened private property and 'small government'. Thus Zimmerman argues that deep ecology is in danger of providing support for Nazism and fascism, and that environmentalism will avoid this to the extent that it avoids any critical engagement with private property and avoids calling on government intervention or supporting institutional arrangements which require it. Zimmerman's identification of individualism, private property and small government as the most important bulwarks against the fascist potential he discerns in deep ecology demonstrates the narrow range of his political focus.

Nazism is an important test for any theory (although given its contested interpretation hardly a neutral and unambiguous one), but for a relevant and widely-informed political ecology it would surely be advisable to plot in a few more points on the political map, as well as to plot them more accurately. Plotting in more points would show that individuality (or the liberal-capitalist form that Zimmerman equates with it) and associated private property in its liberal-capitalist extreme have their own burden of human (and non-human) death and suffering to answer for. If Zimmerman's narrow focus on and shallow interpretation of Nazism allows a stress on collectivism/individuality as the major relevant axis along which we should judge fascist potential, a broader focus would note the liberatory ambiguities of individualism and suggest placement on a unity/difference axis as a more reliable index of authoritarian potential.

In a number of recent contributions, another political theorist associated with deep ecology, Gus diZerega, provides a very useful account of individuals as members of multiple intersecting communities or relationships of mutual interest. These include the political sphere, the family and the ecological community, and all of these should respect their members, who should never count for nothing.[29] This model of community membership is developed in some illuminating ways to show the problems of instrumentalism and rights theory, but what is of concern is diZerega's suggestion that the family, and by implication the ecological sphere, can ideally be envisaged not as a community of multiple and mutual interest but as a community of natural harmony or unity of interests governed not by considerations of justice but by those of love. diZerega aims to develop a liberal green Jeffersonianism that lauds the market but hopes to keep what is valuable beyond its reach; despite its splendid efficiency, we wouldn't want anything of real value, such as family relationships or magnificent natural areas, to be subject to it. This approach fits with a dynamic of setting some 'special areas' apart that goes with moral dualism and extensionism. Zimmerman and diZerega diverge however on the question of institutional modifications to property. Zimmerman opts for a future liberalism that evolves into an ecologically benign form where through consciousness change ecologically enlightened individuals who have unified their interests with those of nature participate in the market without commodifying nature. diZerega, however, opts for the better alternative of more accountable forms of public and private property.[30]

Zimmerman adopts the unity interpretation in a stronger form than diZerega. As feminist political theorists such as Susan Moller Okin (1989) and Carole Pateman (1989) have shown in the case of women, models of a community such as the family as a natural unity or harmony of interests are hegemonic, allowing the weaker elements in that community to be dominated without recourse by the more powerful – normally the husband – and in the event of justice conflicts tending to throw the ideological and economic burden of introducing 'disharmony' back onto the wife and other weaker members. Without institutional modification to recognise the multiple and potentially conflicting interests involved and to protect equality structurally, this in effect provides a form of coverture. The political equivalent of coverture for nature seems to be what is being advocated in Zimmerman's thinking – nature's interests will be 'covered' not by 'big government' public institutions but by the property owner, who safeguards its interests through fusion when enlightened just as the husband as enlightened household head was assumed to include and safeguard the interest of the wife under coverture. This is like emphasising that wives are loved and provided for in marriage in place of recognising the wife as a separate political and economic actor whose interests require recognition as equal in institutional arrangements. The property form advocated by Zimmerman appears similarly to decline institutional modification, envisaging instead a form capitalism in which ecologically enlightened individuals who have changed their consciousness according to the prescriptions of deep ecology unify or fuse their interests as property owners with those of nature and show the way to an ecologically benign capitalist marketplace.

In the present climate of stingy government, many environmental groups are obliged to find wealthy private donors, a source of funding which is tapped with varying degrees of reluctance but which is always a potent threat to their democratic vision and political integrity.[31] Some groups with allegiance to deep ecology have specialised very strongly in courting the so-called 'deep pocket', the wealthy individual who can be converted to the ecological cause and whose 'generosity' finances campaigns and protects 'special' lands from the much-praised efficiencies of the market. Reliance on this strategy has a demonstrated potential to defuse or blunt opposition to and engagement with the general system of nature-commodification and property-formation capitalism represents. Most environmental groups see this as a temporary expedient justified by their sense of urgency and desire to save as much as possible within the existing framework, rather than as an ideal situation. But a deeper and more systematic ideological commitment to this and other elite-supporting strategies seems to be emerging in certain deep political theorists, based upon deep ecology's dominant unity interpretation and its narrow focus on individual consciousness change. This is a commitment to defending capitalism and refusing any critique of or systematic modification of the institutions of property that have commodified the earth in favour of accepting the political coverture of nature and strategies aimed at the ecological enlightenment of the Man of Property.

Thus the final pages of Zimmerman (1994) reach the conclusion that the best the ecologically-challenged can legitimately hope for, given the political constraints of supporting 'individuality' his argument defends, is some eventual development toward Atman consciousness on the part of a few rare and privileged individuals, (who, if they are going to be able to make a difference in the real world of ecological destruction, will need to be not only ecologically-enlightened but powerful as well). This strategy seems to support property concentration and inequality, (since the more each Enlightened individual owns, the fewer individuals will need to become enlightened in order to save nature) which, as we have seen, is unlikely to foster effective action on environmental problems.

The ecological enlightenment of the man of property

Those deep ecology theorists who employ the unity interpretation in this way are developing an account which is in deep complicity with the system of commodification of nature and its founding fathers. If Zimmerman explicitly deplores any casting of ecological aspersions on the sanctity of private property and holds out as the best hope for ecological salvation the conversion of more billionaires to deep ecology, a green model of the ecologically enlightened family landholder is in danger of offering a Jeffersonian solution in the fullest sense. The ecologically enlightened Man of Property seems to be envisaged on the model of Thomas Jefferson the slavemaster. For those familiar with Jefferson the rhetorician of republican freedom and revolutionary equality, it is an everlasting irony that Jefferson, although perhaps in some respects a more enlightened master than most,[32] nevertheless resisted freeing his slaves and never himself gave up the institutional power to abuse, despite his strictures on the effect of such power on the slavemaster's character.[33] In such a 'Jeffersonian' model, nature would occupy a position in the ecologically enlarged household of the Man of Property similar to the wife, the slave or the indentured servant. The enlightened land-holder will take care of the interests of the land as part of a sphere of familial harmony, protected like the family from the necessary if distasteful drama of capitalism going on outside the boundaries of the estate. A more realistic account would recognise that individual enlightenment and good will is not enough, that nature, as well as women and slaves, require institutional protection and guarantees which involve major modifications to the concept, formation and distribution of property itself.

The systematic deep pocket solution of the ecological enlightenment of the Man of Property discloses a nest of contradictions upon exposure and analysis. Is there not a contradiction (or two) between ecological enlightenment and the amassing of property? Is it not more likely that this source of funding will tend primarily to support wise use or other groups that aim to undermine or destroy green efforts? Although diZerega recognises that the market can be a destructive and instrumentalising form, the aim is to keep certain special areas of land away from it as exceptions rather undertaking any general modification of it in a more universally applicable way. This would represent an intensification of the current North American solution based on use/respect dualism. Where the means to protect special areas is obtained by the commodication of other areas, only exceptional areas can be protected. The area protected by coverture in this way is like the protected wife of the Man of Property – her enhanced security and comfort is obtained at the expense of increased impoverishment and vulnerability for a large group of subordinated others. The protection for the spaces and places of the Man of Property depends upon the degradation of places of less powerful others somewhere else, somewhere remote.

The deep pocket solution ignores at the spiritual level the corrupting influence of power, and at the ecological level neglects the way the ecological health of 'special' lands depends on the health of other lands that are subject to normal commodification and that cannot be protected in a similar way if the economic system of commodification is to function normally. But the ecological health of the special lands is interdependent with that of the 'ordinary' land that is commodified. We are already seeing the effects of this interdependence in the ecological decline of many areas like the Great Smoky Mountains National park and other 'protected' lands that are showing signs of degradation because of a general decline of ecological conditions and of the health of surrounding lands.[34] The outcome of systematic deep pocket strategies is likely to be a hegemonic form of protection – better protection for some lands under coverture near the main centres of wealth, but the progressive degradation of lands remote from centres of wealth, which may well be the places where the greatest need for ecological protection is located. Finally, the solution is one where for the sake of a consolation prize we forgo the opportunity to tackle the main critical problem: we give up the search to re-imagine our relationship to the non-human in communicative terms and to seek change in the main system of commodification that is destroying the earth.

In certain ways, as I have argued, this conservative political development within deep ecology has grown out of a set of historical circumstances which has provided key intellectual elements for it. Some of it is implicit in the dominant theoretical direction and characteristic theses of deep ecology; the stress on unity or fusion of interests, as we have seen, goes back to Naess himself. Other elements, including the strong emphasis on individual consciousness change and weak emphasis on institutional change, have been encouraged by political alliances with other groups such as eastern spirituality and the human potentials movement which must have seemed like a good idea at the time. Yet none of these problematic political developments follows from the basic ideas of deep ecology about the need to radically transform our concepts in ways that include nature ethically and politically; in this respect the developments I have objected to are contingent to deep ecology, and are in some conflict with certain of its basic insights. So deep ecology as a fundamental position is multiple and has the potential to develop some much more radical answers to some of these questions, some of which I will explore briefly now.

Is there an eco-socialist deep ecology?

The main question thrown up by the idea of Zimmerman and diZerega's 'evolutionary liberal' analysis seems to me to be: how can respecting nature be compatible with owning it? Individual consciousnesses may change, but the problem lies in the *institution* of private property which entitles the owners to do anything they like to the piece of nature they own, just as the 'kind' Jeffersonian slavemaster was entitled to do what he liked to the slave he owned. Doesn't respect and consideration for nature require a different conception of property? Doesn't it require an institutional framework not based on coverture, that recognises and represents all the 'non-owner' interests involved in property – including those of nature itself, as the invisible (or rather, conceptually disappeared) collaborator, and those of the denied social others who have contributed to it both directly and indirectly? And doesn't the idea of respecting nature require that it be recognised as an active presence and agent which contributes in a myriad of ways to our daily lives – its recognition as 'an independent centre of value, as an originator of projects that demand my respect'?[35] These ingredients could provide a sufficiently courageous version of deep ecology with the basis for a radical critique of capitalist concepts of property.

The task for a Green Jeffersonianism is to clarify its intentions regarding unity and coverture, showing how it can escape its Jeffersonian heritage and the alliance with the Lockean model of property, with its inbuilt assumptions of coverture for nature. The Lockean model of acquisition provides a major basis for the recipe for property formation which is the foundation of contemporary capitalism. In the context of the 'new world', it also provided, as Deloria (1970) notes, the basis for the erasure of the ownership of indigenous people and the appropriation of their lands. Locke's recipe for property formation allows the colonist to appropriate that into which he has mixed his own labour, as part of the self, transferring his ownership of self to what is laboured on, on condition that it falls under the category of 'nature', not under prior ownership. But since the colonist was either not able or not disposed to recognise either the prior ownership of indigenous others nor their different expression of labour and agency, the formula aided large-scale appropriation of indigenous lands by those who could visit upon them highly transforming and destructive European-style agricultural labour.

Applying the formula retrospectively led to a regress, a failure to recognise as conferring ownership indigenous hunting and gathering activities that did not transform the land significantly in ways European colonists recognised as sufficient 'labour' to qualify for past or present property ownership. (Even until very recently, as Deloria notes, it was held that the failure of indigenous people to make properly individualistic and maximally transformative use of their land was a sufficient reason why it should be taken away from them). To the extent that indigenous people were seen as 'nature', 'nomads' or 'parasites on nature' who were incapable of effective ecological agency or the kind of agricultural labour that was held, on the European model, to be the true mark of humanity, the Lockean formula helped in the deep cultural erasure of their claim to prior ownership. In the context of the hyperbolised autonomy and hegemonic conceptions of agency associated with western individualism, the Lockean formula is virtually an invitation to appropriate what others have made their own, often in much deeper and less appropriative ways than the western way of converting land to market-based uses.

But it is not only the deep erasure of indigenous people that is expressed and sanctioned in the Lockean concept of private property, but also in a similar way the deep erasure of nature. Deep ecology, to the extent that it can advocate countering this erasure and recognising nature as presence, agent, and collaborator in our lives, could also provide the foundation for a deep questioning of the Lockean form of property and for envisaging a different institutional form. Implicit in Locke's recipe for annexing new world 'nature' as European property, is an assumption of the emptiness and nullity of nature itself, which also serves as the foundation for the erasures of those human others counted as nature. For if nature and the land is itself active presence and agent, 'independent centre of value... originator of projects that demand my respect', the whole basis for the Lockean formula's use to support capitalism collapses. The outcome of working the land must be seen as the product of at least two (kinds of) agencies and interests, and not of a single one (the human one) who is entitled to appropriate it in accordance with the capitalist interpretation of Locke's formula. For if, as Locke's formula concedes for the human case, the outcome of 'mixing labour' in the land is the product of more than one agency and interest, it cannot be placed entirely at the disposal of just one of these agents, the human one, any more than a single agent is able to appropriate other joint products in which his or her labour is mixed with those of other human agents. Once the agency of nature has been recognised, this placement can only appear either as unjustified seizure or as a form of coverture, the assumption of unity or fusion of interest which we identified above, and is subject to the same kinds of objections.

In short, once we take the prior presence and agency of nature seriously, the most the Lockean formula can really support is a mutualistic or guardianship concept of property, as an institution which is of mutual benefit to both the human 'partner' and to the other human and non-human 'partners' in any collaborative product, which must include the land itself.

The seizure by just one of these collaborative partners of the whole product without any regard for the interests of the others is as unjustified in the case of non-human partners as it is in the case of human ones. But this seizure was what the capitalist interpretation of the Lockean formula in practice justified by treating nature as a mere productive potentiality rather than an independent centre of needs, by denying nature's prior agency as an originator of ecological projects in the land that demand our respect, and by backgrounding and nullifying the ecological labours of nature on which we depend for all we do.

Similarly unjustified is the concept of 'improvement' and 'progress' in the transformation of land where this is an 'improvement' from the perspective of and for the benefit and well-being of only one of the partners, a human one. Damage to other partners, including nature, would have to be compensated, for example by the provision of other benefits to that partner elsewhere. Property would have to be treated as very much more of a mutualistic partnership, to be used for mutual benefit of both nature and the human guardian(s) of the land, and would have to recognise and provide benefits for a much wider range of interests and collaborators, that include nature. To the extent that a similar case can be made for the institutional recognition of denied human others in the property relationship, more accountable and collective forms of property formation are also broadly indicated. Furthermore, it is not only in the area of land ownership that the Lockean formula delivers pernicious results for nature, and not just a question of decoupling some types of land tenure from the market, as diZerega seems to imply.[36] To the extent that we can read a similar erasure of non-human agency in other property formation systems based on the Lockean formula, there is a potential for nature and other denied agents to be similarly damaged. For example the legal award of ownership of genetic materials to individual patentees similarly employs the Lockean formula to effect a similar erasure of non-human (and some human) agency. In a truly deep ecology, capitalist systems of property formation would be seen as requiring a thorough and general rethinking.

In the case of land, the outcome would no doubt work out differently in different local contexts, depending on factors like political institutions, size, and the cultural representation of the non-human and so on.[37] Where size is small, the deep outcome might look more like those limited and joint indigenous land tenure systems that until recently accounted for much of the world, which allowed a high level of accountability in ownership, spiritual land relationship, community decision and responsibility, and greatly reduced possibilities for transfer and accumulation. In the context of larger systems, the kind of institutional structure that taking nature's agency seriously would suggest might be more like that of the land trust arrangement, whereby particular individuals or groups have use-title to land for certain limited purposes that is subject to serious conditions of respect for other interests (which would have to include those of nature and the land itself). Basic decision power in the land could be vested more broadly in larger continuing publics, who might represent nature politically via a system of accountability to trustees and speakers for particular places and for larger ecological systems including biospheric nature.

This can be part of a broader change in which systems and institutions take account of and give representation to the interests of our planetary partners. Although forms of representation could vary, no responsible system that takes nature seriously can afford to leave these denied and silenced partners in our lives out of account in the way capitalism and the dominant Lockean system of property formation does. This provides part of the case for a positive answer to the question: is there an ecosocialist deep ecology? A really deep ecology must rethink private property. Among the rest of the answer must be the construction of a robustly counter-hegemonic socialist theory and practice that takes countering human-centredness, its injustices and hazards, seriously. This is an ongoing project and process that is far from completed (if it ever could be) but to which we who care for the future of the planet should give our attention.

10 Towards a materialist spirituality of place

Is spirituality more fundamental?

When asked at a recent public lecture what to do about the environmental crisis and the failure of compassion for non-humans, noted environmental author Peter Mathieson told his questioner to join his local church. It didn't matter what church – spirituality was what mattered, and any kind would be helpful. Is spirituality really the answer? Are all its varieties helpful in the face of the ecological crisis? Or only some? Aren't some forms of spirituality and religion part of the problem rather than part of the solution? Neither Hitler nor St. Martin of Tours (who demonstrated the superiority of his Christian god by attacking sacred trees) are attractive spiritual guides for an environmental culture, yet on any broad definition of spirituality as faith each had a strong commitment to a form of spirituality. What has inhibited our dialogue about the politics of spirituality?

Some ecofeminists have also seen spiritual relationships as the most fundamental kind[1], and spirituality as the prime arena in which the coming struggle for human survival will be won or lost. It seems to me though that, as a general field, spirituality, far from being in some generalised and indiscriminate sense 'the answer' to our difficulties in coming to terms with nature, has many of the same ambiguities and potentials to foster better or worse relationships with nature as other kinds or theories and practices. The problems of reason/nature and mind/body dualism, human-centredness and self-enclosure, remoteness and use/respect dualism arise for spirituality in much the same way as for areas like ethics. A critical engagement with the political and ethical character of specific forms of spirituality is essential; spirituality itself is no substitute for engagement with ecological ethics and politics. Most ecofeminists have acknowledged this in calling for specifically ecological kinds of spirituality that are nondualist and immanent in orientation rather than transcendent and rationalist.[2] Spirituality as such cannot be the answer, for specific forms of spirituality can subvert key aspects of the dominant economic and political order or be complicit with it. Still, the concept of spirituality can be an important place to start questioning large parts of it. This is what I will argue for the spirituality of place.

How can spirituality contribute to the way critical political ecology theorises earth relationships? From the perspective of the urgent practical problem of developing a better earth ethic and culture, spirituality is certainly part of the story, but broad and generalised definitions and projects of spirituality are too indiscriminate to be particularly useful in this context – the more important question is: what kind of spirituality? The general concept of spirituality frames a quest in very general terms that are not very clearly directed to ecological forms of land connection. True, western culture in the past has had its own forms of land spirituality in the form of holy places, but its dominant post-Christian forms have been framed in terms that have opposed it to the earth and to the body, and seen the spirituality of place as something to be overcome or drawn into its larger scheme which figures the value of place accordingly, in the largely instrumental terms of leading us to a higher, non-earthly place. Historical Christianity, as John Passmore remarks,[3] often saw pagan place and nature reverence as its main enemy, and set itself the task of destroying pagan shrines or absorbing them into its own framework of transcendence. Usually such subsumption involved giving them a meaning contrary to the one they originally held, one in which their sacredness is entirely derived and secondary, merely reminding us of or leading us on towards a remote, higher immaterial world which is the real source of sacrality.

There is, in short, a definitional dilemma for appeals to spirituality. If defined very inclusively, as, for example, access to and pursuit of meaning, vision, value and deep purpose, it is clear that very many different kinds of earth philosophies count as spiritual on this definition. But this includes some varieties that have been deeply damaging and antipathetic to the earth and its systems of life. For examples, we can consider certain traditional forms of spirituality that are hostile to the body, to other species, to the earth, or to women, or that foster racial or religious hatred. Or we could consider certain types of 'blood and soil' land spiritualities that form the basis for ethnic exclusion and war. A similar problem appears if spiritualities are taken to involve locating human lives in terms of larger earth, galactic or universal processes, or if they are taken to involve faith in powers or presences (energy, force, being, deity or deities, God or Goddess) beyond one's own individual ego.[4]

For these projects can be pursued in ways that are more or are less life-affirming.[5]

We get a similar outcome if we define spirituality in terms of recognition of the sacred dimension of life. Again, we have to take into account problematic concepts of the sacred that define it in oppositional contrast to the profane or fallen, or which locate value and meaning in an immaterial abstract realm in a way that devalues the earth and embodiment. From the perspective of a land ethic, setting up a few special locations as 'sacred' may do little by itself to counter the devaluation, degradation and instrumentalisation of ordinary land. Again, from the perspective of the land, the problem is not so much that contemporary non-indigenous culture lacks a concept of the sacred, as that it has mostly located the sacred in the wrong place, above and beyond a fallen earth. The definition of spirituality that could vindicate the assumption that all forms of it are in opposition to the modes of existence destructive to the earth has yet to be supplied. On the inclusive side of the dilemma, the label 'spirituality' by no means allows us to suspend critical judgement and responsibilities to consider the ethical and political content of systems of beliefs and practices. It is crucial to consider what kind of spirituality is in question; but in order to do this we would have to go well beyond spirituality as such to outline a philosophy, and a politics to go with it.

On the other hand, the concept of spirituality may be given a less inclusive meaning (although the apparently inclusive character of the concept is certainly part of its appeal) that would aim to bring the content of systems of spirituality out in generally positive terms. For example we could define spirituality itself in dialogical terms, as a certain kind of communicative capacity that recognises the elements that support our lives. This makes a better connection with treating the earth in more considerate and sensitive ways, but we will then be obliged to recognise that many systems and positions that are usually counted as spiritual, such as traditional Christianity, may not emerge as spiritual at all on this criterion. For those many apparently spiritual forms where concern takes a human-centred form that is exclusively concerned with human well-being cannot then be counted as spiritual. There is no way to guarantee the soundness of spirituality simply by definition or good intention; this can only be established by the usual critical routes. Spirituality does not offer a personalised, faith-based shortcut around critical and philosophical debates.

The idea that spirituality can provide the answer in some more fundamental way than, say, politics and ethics seems to derive its strength from a series of common contrasts that draw on rationalist and dualistic assumptions. In one sense, spirituality is contrasted with modernity and especially with the reductionism of modernity. In this sense, spirituality can mean rediscovering the 'spirit' in things that reductionist views and discourses of nature have dispelled. This is important, but the language is dualistic, suggesting 'spirit' as an extra ingredient. We need to be more careful about just how reductionism is involved here. It is not just scientific modernity that has been reductionist and devaluing towards nature. Some pre-modern forms of spirituality were also reductionist, centralising all spirit and grace in a remote monotheistic deity and stripping it from the immediacy and particularity of earthly life and place.[6] There are, rather obviously, many different concepts of spirituality, as well as visions of what specific life practices are spiritual. Often we are presented with a choice between religion and science: spirituality is similarly contrasted with scientific outlooks, and opposed to the human-centred and reductionist forms of science that evict meaning from the world, permitting its return only in instrumental form. But the implicit contrast between reductionist science and restorative spirituality that returns meaning to the world is a false choice. First, as I argued in Chapter 2, human-centred and reductionist science is not the only possible kind of science, and second, some forms of spirituality are just as human-centred, instrumental and reductionist as dominant science where the natural world is concerned.

Indeed the conventional contrast of religion versus science obscures the extent to which they have in specific cases evolved jointly and share related ideals. In the spirit of the classical tradition of earth denial, Christian ideals of salvation subordinated the 'unimportant' earthly world of nature and material life to the immaterial celestial world beyond the earth. In the Enlightenment, this was transformed into the idea of subordinating nature to the realm of scientific law and reason as science began to rival and replace religion as the dominant belief system. So under the guise of objectivity, modern science, now with religious status, has tended to update rather than supersede these oppositional and supremacist ideals of rationality and humanity. In the scientific fantasy of mastery, the new human task becomes that of remoulding nature to conform to the dictates of reason and achieve – on earth rather than in heaven– salvation as freedom from death and bodily limitation. This project of reducing and rationalising nature involved both the technological-industrial conquest of nature made possible by reductionist science, and also the geographical conquest of empire which in turn fed the universal claims of scientific knowledge. The problem is neither religion or science as such, but rather the collusion of both in their dominant forms with projects of human-centredness and rational supremacy.

'Materialism' and spirit/matter dualism

A second contrast that is influential here is one in which spirituality contrasts with materialism, and this sense of spirituality is predisposed to draw terminologically and implicitly on the old spirit/matter dualism which runs so deep in western (and some non-western) traditions. This is the sense of materialism in which it is identified with 'consumerism', the belief that happiness or fulfilment requires more material goods or demands more material throughput. But the diagnosis here seems inadequate and imprecise: consumerists do not aim simply to accumulate material items per se (e.g. pebbles, leaves, potato chips, pieces of bark) but to accumulate items (both material and cultural) that give comfort, prestige or power. So it is not materiality itself that is sought for its own sake, and the aims of such accumulation incorporate objectives that are not in any straightforward sense 'material'. There seems, in fact, to be no good reason why we should not count them as spiritual in the inclusive senses, and enrol consumerist spirituality among the many kinds of spirituality that are not friendly to the earth. Why locate materiality as the main problem in consumerism? Surely the problem lies in the attitudes and practices of human consumers, which are not themselves tangible or material, or only partly so. Only the determination to bring spirituality out as always the better, ethically unassailable element and to devalue matter can explain why the material and embodied sphere has been so unquestioningly picked as the culprit in the rather ambiguous case of consumerism. Such terminology is not neutral but conforms to the mind/body, reason/nature, spirit/matter pattern of dualisms that are characteristic of rationalism and its Christian variants.

The main objection though I think to these terminological strategies of hyper-separating and elevating spirit against and above matter is that they continue to anchor our cultural dialogues in frameworks of great power and resilience that devalue the material world of the senses and the body, the world of 'coming-to-be and passing away', in short, the sphere encompassed traditionally in the west by the term nature. Because it is so vaguely targeted, this kind of devaluation of 'materialism' has the potential to revive elements of dualism, spiritual remoteness and other-worldliness that have been so problematic for nature. Its oppositional formulation of spirit versus matter renders invisible the important concept of a materialist spirituality which does not invoke a separate spirit as an extra, independent individualised ingredient but rather posits a richer, fully intentional non-reductionist concept of the earthly and the material.[7] Given the western tradition of devaluing and backgrounding materiality and identifying the human essence with disembodied reason rather than with the lower 'animal' body, there is an important sense in which what we need is more materialism, not less, a better awareness of ourselves as materially embodied beings in a material universe in which we are all material (e.g. food) for one another, and also as organised material beings rather than 'mere matter' in its unorganised state. In this sense, we have the option to ask for little in the way of a separate individual essence that persists after death, but be satisfied with a materialist spirituality which recognises that spirit is not a hyper-separated extra ingredient but a certain mode of organisation of a material body, unable to exist separately from it. This richer conception of materiality as intentionally organised and thus participating in mindfulness and transcendence is part of what is gained in the intentional recognition stance we outlined in Chapter 8, and is a big part of what is sacrificed in reductionist and minimising conceptions of the other as resource or commodity.

Human-centred spiritualities

The movement to give a positive content to spirituality beyond these traditional rationalist foci, distinctions and metaphors, suggests a focus on practices that aim to create a new sense of the meaning of human lives by putting them into the larger contexts of the universe. Spirituality is also characterised by typical themes which reflect on human life in the context of its great events of birth and of death, and in relation to more-than-human life. This is an area where there is inevitably a great deal of freedom, hence diversity, because most of the answers are beyond our certain knowledge, because there is no methodology for establishing a single correct one, or because what is involved is not factual and cognitive but primarily performative, perceptual and emotional – adopting a stance, a framework for welcoming and experiencing the world. So this is also a place where minds can stretch and free themselves, pirouette and leap, where ten million flowers can bloom.

I myself have never been drawn towards a singularity of worship directed towards a single transcendent god, since the idea of a single source of creation, meaning or purpose outside the immediate world which subsumes all others within it has always seemed too centralised and remote. For me, creativity, meanings and purposes have always been multiple, various and amply discernible in the world, not located above or beyond it. I have found insights from many cultural sources helpful and relevant in avoiding spiritual remoteness, but especially so the sort of concept of spirituality that is sketched by the Native American writer Carol Lee Sanchez, who defines being spiritual as being 'inclined to honour, respect, and acknowledge the elements of our universe (both physical and nonphysical) that sustain and nourish our lives' (Sanchez 1993: 222). Such a concept of spirituality is opposed especially to the delusions and ingratitudes of hyperbolised autonomy and associated delusions of disembeddedness that would ignore or deny these same supporting elements of our lives, which some might think of as ancestral beings or forces. Sanchez identifies the spiritual practices she discusses as a 'Tribal' spirituality common to many Native American peoples she learnt in her own context as a member of Lakota and Laguna Pueblo traditional communities. Her purpose is to make these available to a wider group of people. Her system is, I believe especially worthy of attention because it draws on a highly developed set of beliefs and practices that systematically reject human/nature dualism and sacrificial species hierarchies. Thoroughly tested over a long time by full communities in the demanding practical context of a pueblo life, it shows clearly the viability of other ways to think about interspecies spiritual relationships than those of the dominant culture. Although many elements of such counter-centric spiritualities can be found also in other indigenous cultures, among some individuals and in some non-dominant traditions in the west, they are I think particularly clearly elaborated and theorised here.[8]

Sanchez's discussion of her people's traditional spirituality illuminates for the western reader a truly dialogical concept that stands in opposition to human hyper-separation and 'out-of-nature' status. Sanchez' spirituality acknowledges human kinship to non-human beings and elements of the world, giving an important ceremonial place to phrases such as 'all my relations' whose repetition 'consistently reminds the speaker of her or his personal connection to the universe' (Sanchez 1993: 213). It is a spirituality that both locates human beings within nature and acknowledges ethical, personal and narrative relationships as extending to the more-than-human world. Non-Tribal western spiritualities, Sanchez argues, are usually human-centred because 'the emphasis...is on humans interacting with each other. Being a good person usually means being kind to your neighbours and friends and loving to your family; you are generous, helpful, pleasant, a pillar of the community doing good deeds for others. What is missing here is the distinct inclusion of non-humans. Being a good person in Tribal terms means your good behaviour and intentions are extended towards creatures, plants, and elements, as well as humans' (Sanchez 1993: 222).

Sanchez' 'Tribal' spirituality is counter-hegemonic, resisting the hubris and blind spots of human-centredness and human self-enclosure, and rejecting the use/respect dualisms and spiritual remoteness of dominant Christian-rationalist spirituality. Use/respect dualism characterises remote nobility spiritualities that define the sacred as the exceptional Sunday in contrast to the weekday or normal, conceived as profane or fallen. They treat the sacred as a special area or dimension of life or experience radically separated from dailiness, or as a special earthly place that is hallowed because of its association with human or divine figures whose essential abode is remote from the earth itself. The sacred is part of the abstract, ideal and universal dimension, while the profane inhabits the individually and physically intimate, the sensory and emotional, the homeplace where the embodied self is nourished. In Sanchez' account, as in some of the religions of Asia, sacredness can permeate daily life, applying generally to the universe and everything in it, which is held to be 'entitled to reverence and respect' (Sanchez 1993: 224).

Indigenous critiques

Sanchez is one of a number of indigenous philosophers who have mounted powerful critiques of the human-centredness of western spirituality and its denial of ecological inclusion and connection. In the earlier, perhaps less Christianised versions of Chief Seattle's famous speech, there is an important critique of the spirituality and environmental values of Christian-rationalism as expressed in its theories of death and accounts of the basis of property and land relationship. This critique, possibly more fully developed in the original to which these translations are little more than rough guides, was censored out of the later popularisations and strikingly omitted from the best known version of Chief Seattle's speech put out by the Baptist Church in America. 'Your dead forget you and the country of their birth./As soon as they go beyond the grave and walk among the stars./They are quickly forgotten and they never return./Our dead never forget this beautiful earth./It is their mother./They always love and remember her rivers,/Her great mountains, her valleys./They long for the living… And their spirits often return to visit and console us'.[9] Seattle portrays past generations now dead as retaining connection to and enriching tribal lands, remembering and celebrating particular loved places on the earth, and returning both to them and to the living in a spirit of friendship and love. The continuing connection of the dead to tribal lands is a source of strength, reassurance and continuity for the living.

Australian Aboriginal philosopher Bill Neidjie weaves his people beautifully in the ecological fabric of the world as connected beings, held by the land and its places of special sacrality, where the big narratives are centred. His dialogue is directed towards instructing the west, not only about his own people's wisdom, but about what is radically maladaptive in theirs. Neidjie locates the problem in our disregard for the land, our belief in our own individual immortality and our resistance to recycling ourselves back into the land and its communities of earth others. The world around Bill Neidjie is never the unconsidered background for human life – the land is in the foreground, as 'country' – a giver of meaning, a communicative source to be read as a book. 'Our story is in the land: it is written in those sacred places; my children will look after those places, that's the law'. He stresses our kinship with non-human elements of the world and our embodiment. 'Earth... like your father or brother or mother/because you born from earth. You got to come back to earth... That's your bone, your blood. It's in this earth, same as for tree.'[10] In this passage, Bill Neidjie shows the dominant spiritual culture of the west that it has not faced up to the basic facts about ecological life and death on earth, facts which, as he rightly perceives, it mostly behaves as if it does not know. We humans don't rise from the dead to join other blessed ones in disembodied regions remote from earth. Our spirits and bodies are united in death with the earth from which we came, which grew us and nurtured us, in the same way as those of animals and trees. We are not set apart. Chief Seattle too may be seen as critiquing a radical separation between the land of the living and that of the dead, corresponding to a dualism of spirit and matter, reason and nature, presupposed in Christian-rationalist accounts of both life and death. In this system, the dead are completely separated off from the land of the living and from all non-human life. Any return they might make is attributed either to miracles (theistic exceptionalism) or to corruption by the earth, in which case it is normally represented in terms of horror, as demonic. This is a dualism of life and death, corresponding to that between mind and body, with the dead destined for an immaterial realm that provides both their true abode and ideal form or essence, a realm in which there is salvation for humans alone. This vision of spiritual remoteness displays in extreme form the unhappy, earth-denying outcome of the vices of hyperbolised autonomy, denial and backgrounding of the elements that support our lives. If we aspire to continuity and union with the sacred at the end of our lives, we had best find the sacred in a form that is not spiritually remote or devaluing of our earthly lives, and that is available to unite with. The obvious choice seems to be the earth itself and its communities of life. As I have argued (in Chapter 8 and in Plumwood 1993a), intentional recognition provides the basis for a fusion of mind and matter, since materiality is already full of form, spirit, story, agency, and glory. It can provide the basis for the dialogical ways of thinking about the earth, other species and personal identity stressed in many wisdom traditions, and suggests a much more satisfying and earth-sensitive solution to the problem of providing personal meaning to life and continuity after death than does the traditional Christian-rationalist solution in which individual persistence is hyperbolised or overemphasised, and the ideals of reason and salvation are hyper-separated from the earth and from embodiment. Seen in this embedded way, the 'personal' is not to be equated with the solipsistic hyperbolised individual whose essential self identity can be maintained beyond death in a separate realm, but acknowledges essential links to nations and communities of earth others, including the more-than-human ancestors of the human. Since these communities of nature live on after an individual's death, a satisfying form of continuity for the fully embedded person may be found in the mutually life-giving flow of the self upon death back into the larger life-giving other that is nature, the earth and its communities of life. Some may feel they need more: for me, this recycling is enough.

Trickster spirituality: the world as agent

An important but often neglected aspect of spirituality is the propensity to relate our lives, both personally and in terms of our membership of some larger group, to the more-than-human world, and especially to be open to meanings available in the elements of contingency and chaos in the world. Spirituality may take a monological or dialogical form, a humorous or severe form. Human-centred spirituality is typically monological in its stance towards the world, seeing meaning as coming only from the human and human-designed. The idea that the larger world is meaningless and that only the human, the controlled and intended, can ever be meaningful is part of Enlightenment rationality, a part freeing us from what it called 'superstition' but also cutting us off from enchantment and from certain important kinds of openness to chaos and wonder at the world. Human-centred ideas of contingency support the mechanistic-rationalist obsession with mastery and control over a passive world conceived as transparent and incapable of agency. The dominant framework of rationality and spirituality writes these assumptions that deaden and impoverish our encounters with the world into the very concepts of rationality and contingency. As Lewis Hyde remarks, 'to speak of 'contingency' or 'coincidence' usually connotes a more or less meaningless convergence' (Hyde 1998: 97). In other words: 'Do not be tempted to look for any significance in the way the world works itself out – we know in advance that there is none there'.

In a dialogical framework, in contrast, where we view the world as another agent or player, meaning can be present also in the intricate contingency of the world, and is potentially at least as wondrous a gift from the more than-human sphere as it is from the human one. Hyde takes the ability to work with contingency to be a mark of the Trickster mind, the shape-shifting mind that 'pesters the distinction between accident and essence and remakes this world out of whatever happens' (Hyde 1998: 100). Trickster holds the secret of meeting the world always newly created, fresh, of being open to the unexpected, the revelatory, to signs and wonders, not necessarily addressed to you personally, but possibly open for you to read. But the ability to take coincidence seriously is not a gift we in the dominant culture admire: we condemn it and confine those who work with contingency to the margins of the dispowered realm of art, where it helps to define those disruptive of tradition, those who would break the acoustical seal around the music-hall and present noise as music, paint spattering as art.[11] Yet, as Donna Haraway has stressed, it is important to be able to see the world – even a glimpse can be life-changing – in the guise of another subject, even as a knowing humorous mind, a deceiver.[12] The dominant rationalist culture is closed to even a glimpse of this kind not only because of its objectifying and monological bent but because its human/nature dualism has hyper-separated the essence/intention pair from the contingency/chaos pair, identified essence with universality and timelessness, and accident with change, particularity and randomness. Then it has gone on to identify the goal of humanity with the prestige partner in each pair, that is, with design, intention, control, and with immunity or distance from the devalued part, conceived as accident and chaos. The outcome supports the idea of life in which the rational human confronts a world whose own organisation is accidental and inconsiderable, even unthinkable, another reduced to the raw material for desires and open to unconstrained manipulation in the processes of commodity production.

All these deadening associations are up for reworking by the philosopher sympathetic to the Trickster mind. Accident or coincidence may be seen as the reductionist analogue of mystery, for example, as the stripped down, radically reduced body is of the total personage. But the Trickster is just one persona of the world as communicative agent: the gift of meaning and communication from the world can be just as attractive and life-affirming when it aims at nothing more unfamiliar, sophisticated or devious than reproduction, the form, for example, of a nightly chorus by the pond. From spring to midsummer where I live, frogs take over the aural space of dusk and early evening for their annual production of the 4-hour opera 'Hylas and the Nymphs'. During the season these great tremolo-voiced anurans[13] (once – prior to their enchantment and amphibian transformation, it is rumoured – a famous Italian operatic troupe) tell of the seduction of the hero Hylas, the water carrier of Aphrodite, by Litorian water nymphs, and detail his subsequent erotic career as one of their number following his own enchantment by the angry goddess. Their poignant story is inscribed in the naming of their family, the Hylidae, by a science for once friendly and not opposed to the richness of mythic narrative that is the outcome of meeting the world dialogically.

Access to collective spiritual imagination and experience that is inherited and elaborated over generations rather than individually chosen and developed is always richer, especially in the dialogues of place. Individuals isolated from such sources and stuck with spiritual multiplicity and choice do not of course need to follow any established 'brand' practice with respect to any of these philosophical dimensions of spirituality. They can however apply counter-centric criteria to help them make imaginative choices, both individual and collective, with a view to achieving more earth-friendly and counter-hegemonic forms of spirituality. I have argued that we can see in the centric features of cultures, whether considered as individuals or as particular gendered, racialised, species or national-economic groups, a common pattern or logic of oppression, and that these can also be resisted by disrupting that common pattern and its logic, that is, through counter-centric strategy. Applying the same thinking to spirituality, we can similarly discern a general pattern for selecting kinds of spirituality that are earth-positive rather than earth denying, and that disrupt the dualistic choices and frameworks that have so often narrowed and impoverished the spiritual vision of the west. We can say that the pattern of an ecological spirituality should be one that shows friendliness to the earth, envisaged as a place of positive, intrinsic value rather than as a corrupted and instrumentalised way-station to the next life or as a 'vale of tears'. It will be materialist in avoiding spiritual remoteness, aiding awareness of and honouring the material and ecological bases of life, and it will be counter-centric in affirming continuity and kinship for earth others as well as their subjecthood, opacity and agency. It will be dialogical, communicative,[14] open to the play of more-than-human forces and attentive to the ancestral voices of place and of earth.

Place-based spirituality as oppositional practice

Different cultures have different bases for ownership of the land: these differences can be so radical that they amount to different paradigms of land relationship, incomprehensible to those from a different framework. In some cultures it is the productivist and human-centred paradigm of expenditure or mixing in of human labour that validates the claim to own the land. This Lockean position, validating capitalist and colonial models of appropriation and ownership, is, as I have argued in Chapter 9, another project of hyperbolised autonomy, a one-way, monological form of relationship in which nature's agency and independence is discounted and the land conceived as an adjunct to, or resource for, human projects. But land ownership can be based on far more communal and narrative criteria that yield relationships that are two-way and two-place, in which you belong to the land as much as the land belongs to you. In these it is not just a few exceptional pieces of land that are revered, but the land of belonging generally that is meaningful, filled with history, stories and the presence of ancestors. An alternative paradigm is communicative, making ownership out in the essentially narrative terms of naming and interpreting the land, of telling its story in ways that show a deep and loving acquaintance with it and a history of dialogical interaction.

A world perceived in communicative and narrative terms is certainly far richer and more exciting than the self-enclosed world of meaningless and silent objects exclusionary, monological and commodity thinking creates, reflecting back to us only the echo of our own desires. The communicativity and intentionality of more-than-human others is often the key to the power of place. As dusk gathers beyond my desk and the light glows green, the forest around me comes alive with a sublime and delicate sound like the chiming of countless little silver bells. The sound is almost the only sign to human senses of the innumerable tiny rainforest tree crickets who rub their wings and legs together to make it. It evokes the enchantment of late summer in the cool, misty mountain forest of my Australian home more richly and sensually than any human description, any photograph, map or calendar. As the year turns, this dusk song gives way to others, in regular succession, for the twilight is a sensory and communicative space of much significance for forest dwellers. The erotic tinkling of the crickets holds the space until the first cool weather. That is the time for the squeals of the Little Red Flying Foxes feeding on nectar-filled white Pinkwood flowers. Then, in the chilly violet twilights of late autumn, the silence may be broken by a Lyrebird calling late from nest or perch. Or, if you are lucky, you may hear a distant Powerful Owl hoot and cry for love. In the frosty stillness of moon-silver nights in May or June, you should listen for the Sooty Owl's shuddering, ghostly, scream, and for the questing bass of a male Barking Owl from June to August, while the courting Mountain Thrushes still play their early evening flutes. August brings forth the first Boobook Owl duets – his baritone to her soprano – that signal spring, foreshadowing their cheerful but impassioned mating operettas of September and October. November to January is the best time for the great frog choruses, although these in turn have their negotiated spaces and species successions throughout the year. But from midsummer onwards the lusty tree frogs retire and dewfall brings out whole droning orchestras of mole crickets, each drone, it seems, equipped with an ear-splitting vibrator designed to guide in a flying evening mate. When they too begin to retire in February, the cycle starts once more as the gentle love-songs of the dew-crickets fill the twilight autumn air again until the first cold spell.

What I have described is the experience of twilight communication in southern Gondwanic rainforest, a succession that gives a glimpse of a community whose sharing of communicative space is negotiated through the same processes that shaped its species diversity. Through such subtle and exacting sensory rhythms the land itself can speak to us and place anchor our lives. Space becomes place not only through its human but also through its non-human inhabitants. Without the richness of narratives and narrative subjects that define and elaborate place, the connection between our lived experience and our sense of space and time is reduced, and life lacks immediacy, becomes flat, impersonal and placeless. Place loses agency along with salience, and places themselves become interchangeable, irrelevant and instrumentalisable, neutral surfaces upon which 'rational' human projects can be inscribed. The dullness and dislocation that is associated with placelessness has been remarked as an impoverishing feature of rationalist culture (Relph 1976, 1981). From inside a culture that destroys such narratives, space and time are silent, the province of experts equipped with charts and theories.

To understand such a language of the land requires a deep acquaintance with some place, or perhaps a group of places. It also requires a capacity to relate dialogically to the more-than-human world, since this is a very important source of narratives and narrative subjects defining the distinctiveness of place. But mobility rules modernity, and for most people in urban contexts both place and the more-than-human sphere are disempowered as major constituents of identity and meaning. This loss in turn selects, stores and experientially supports the hegemony of the universalising and minimising conceptual frameworks that are so important a part of the modern rationalist inheritance. A spirituality of place is challenging because it is at odds with the western system of dualisms that has made the particular and immediate, the bodily, the sensory, the experiential and the emotional the inferior 'others' to the abstract, the mental and the rational-dispassionate. A spirituality of place is not then something that will just fall into the laps of people with these kinds of traditions behind them. Because its dominant traditions have been hostile to or remote from nature and place, locating the sacred in a transcendent higher world beyond the fallen earth, the development of a non-superficial spirituality of place that locates the sacred as immanent in particular places is highly problematic for western culture, and requires major rethinking and re-imagining.

The concept of a spirituality of place is often interpreted to mean that the problem of placing ourselves can be addressed at the purely individual and private level of personal quasi-religious feelings, observances and rituals relating to places. Narratives of individual attachment to places are important, but often leave unidentified and unchallenged the larger *structural* obstacles to developing a place-sensitive society and culture. Although in fact it seems unlikely that land attachment would be able to develop as strongly in a system which gives no adequate structural recognition to such relationships, the key question here is the extent to which the land spirituality of individual subjects is typical or able to be made general or 'normal'. If such individual sensitivities exist in the counter-spaces and are unable to be generalised, they may tell us little about the place-sensitive character of a culture as a whole and its structural constraints on, and denials of, attachment to place.

Spiritual systems can be 'placed' in different ways, as for example, place-centred (some indigenous societies), place-bound (feudal society) and place-sensitive. Only the last may be an achievable cultural project for the western present, but the others are instructive. 'No traditional Aboriginal myth was told without reference to the land, or to a specific stretch of country where the incidents it relates were believed to have taken place. No myth is free-floating, without some local identification....the land and all within it was irrevocably tied up with the content of a myth or story, just as were (and are) the people themselves....It is, then, the land which is really speaking – offering, to those who can understand its language, an explanative discourse about how it came to be as it is now, which beings were responsible for it becoming like that, and who should be responsible for it now' write anthropologists Catherine and Ronald Berndt (1989: 5–6). Such a society, which might be termed place-centred, represents the other extreme to the contemporary extreme of an increasingly place-denying global society.

Many different cultures can support powerful attachments to place, but in structurally different ways. Although fortunate individuals from cultures which are unsympathetic to or merely tolerant of place-attachment may still be able to develop strong ties to place, there are important structural differences in the way respective cultures treat those attachments. If in a place-centred culture social customs, etiquette, and institutions in every way nurture and recognise relationships to place, modernist culture and its institutions conversely and systematically neglect, frustrate and deny these relationships. The survival requirements of economic availability as an employee in the labour market, for example, require each of us to spurn and set aside our place of extended family attachments. They demand of each of us, in the normal case, that we renounce our first love – the maternal place – ask us to leave and to forget, and this will be only the first of many such betrayals required of us. The sacrifice of place attachments foretells the sacrifice or familial and other close attachments in more developed stages of capitalism. Clearly, in these circumstances, it is not enough to produce tales of contemporary individuals who have by good fortune been able to ignore or beat dominant structural constraints on place sensitivity and place relationship.

Place attachment and place-sensitivity are vitally important ingredients in personal and community identity formation and in a good human life, much frustrated in current lives of excessive mobility and time-poverty. However, the goal of place-conscious and place-sensitive culture need not dictate a place-bound, stationary lifestyle of monogamous relationship to just one place, organised around singular ideals of attachment and fidelity. (For place too, ideals of unity can mislead us). Place sensitivity requires both emotional and critical approaches to place, and this must include an understanding of place that is rooted in memory (including community memory) and experiences, and an understanding of the hegemonic social relationships expressed in places and between places.[15] Neither are singular: both spiritual and critical projects require that we acknowledge caring relationships to multiple places, as does any achievable goal of recognising the 'ecological footprint' of daily living. An excessive focus on attachment to the immediate 'home-place' as the singular locus of our care for and knowledge of place can desensitize us to the vital role of these other place relationships. In the practice of pilgrimage or journeying between places, place is encountered as an end and not primarily as a means to some other 'holiday' end, such as improving one's income or health prospects, gaining exercise or relaxation, escaping the problems of dailiness, or meeting the right people. The orientation of journeying, as a project of multiple place-encounter, is dialogical rather than monological, as a communicative project to explore the more-than-human as a source of wonder and wisdom in a revelatory framework of mutual discovery and disclosure.[16] Journeying is an important dimension of life in which we can escape the instrumental mode to encounter the earth as another agent and locate ourselves in the narrative of its history and power. A spirituality thus open to taking places and ancestral elements of the land as sources of revelation can bring these modes of knowledge back to inform and inspire the understanding of the home place, now 'known for the first time' as part of this encompassing context. Where the dominant mode of land relationship is place-bound, or is mainly instrumental and propertarian, it may be difficult even to begin these important spiritual journeys.

A place-sensitive society would do more than minimally tolerate a taste for place in those who can afford to indulge it: it would nurture relationships to place structurally as the normal case, not the exception of privilege. Over-individualised accounts which suggest modern liberal capitalism can promote place attachment, overlook the way relationships to place are differentiated and structured through various gendered and racialised relationships, and are affected also by class and colonial status. Those who are most vulnerable and powerless are most at risk of losing control over their ability to remain in a home place or place of attachment. In many contemporary welfare systems, for example, the unemployed are legally required to move on bureaucratic demand: their attachments to place are given no weight at all. Similarly, indigenous people as colonial subjects lost their power to maintain their relationships to place and were required to relocate to the places their colonial masters specified, in ways which did not recognise their traditional tribal or place relationships. In the recent past of the west, we may think of the enclosures, which created an unattached urban working class and the conditions for the commodification of labour, precisely by commodifying, and hence destroying, traditional peasant land and place relationships.[11] Generally speaking, those groups who are already well enough provided for to resist the imperatives of the market in labour have the best chance of developing or maintaining a relationship to place, but this relationship then usually suffers from the problem of being framed in the monological terms of property ownership.

Other structural obstacles to belonging to place include the constituents of modern capitalism that envisage the earth in terms of private property and accumulation, so that places become interchangeable units of the underlying economic substratum of property. This is a framework that envisages place in instrumental terms, reduces attachment to profitability or other market benefits and reduces the value of land to a potential for accruing these benefits. There are many levels of alienation from place-attachment widely-shared across modern cultures; the most basic are insensitivities to the more-than-human aspects of place born of human-centredness, and human (and especially urban) self-enclosure. For the neo-Europes, factors strongly associated with neo-European colonial origin, eurocentrism and nostalgia for a European homeland, lead to a view of the new country as inferior to, or as an extension of, the old centre or 'home', to be experienced and judged primarily in relation to that centre, or as to be re-made in the image of the centre, rather than as an independent presence to be engaged with on its own terms. High levels of urbanisation and mobility discourage deep contact with the non-human aspects of place. These require time in that place, time for the experience of seasonal change, and time to make contact with its non-human voices, and time is what we increasingly lack. We have taken a quantum leap further in insensitivity to place with the current form of globalisation, which increasingly demands such a heavy investment of time for the work of survival that attachments of any sort become problematic, and now demands that we prioritise a global standpoint of place which is the standpoint of no place or of abstract, virtual space. The quest for a nature and place-sensitive society, like the quest for a better quality working life and a genuinely communicative democracy, unveils a project that is radical in the sense that its fulfilment as the normal case would challenge the existing order very deeply and fundamentally at many levels.

Conclusion

The illusions and blindspots of the centre about the extent of their power have caused many empires to crumble. Masters of the universe suffer from systematic distortions in their perceptions of safety, vulnerability, dependency and autonomy. Just as autonomy reduces points of vulnerability, so illusory autonomy gives a false sense of invulnerability. If privilege (which, as I have argued, is associated with perceptions of autonomy) fosters illusions of disembeddedness and remoteness, security is likely to be perceived as lying in tightening control over the hyper-separated and subordinated other rather than in achieving mutuality with them based on negotiating our interconnected needs.

The Empire of Men over mere things, which some call modernity and others rationality, will topple along with the other empires. The illusion of Reason's absolute power over and remoteness from nature it is built on may take somewhat longer to self-destruct than most illusions of empire, but its eventual demise is unavoidable. Although privilege confers a degree of remoteness from certain kinds of environmental damage, and fosters a sense of invulnerability, remoteness from the consequences of destroying nature is the ultimate illusion. If the world of nature dies, Wall Street dies too. Even if the machinery of Reason has become mainly a ghost empire of institutions for enforcing rules that entrench a hazily discernible centre through the destruction of nature (as 'resource') and the immiseration of the less reasonable people it counts as nature, it must still depend on what it destroys for its ultimate survival. Its rationality is ultimately suicidal. We have traced how it has come to these illusions, and by what conceptual means they are developed and shored up, especially in the spheres of economic, scientific and ethical rationality. This casts some light on the reasons why the environmental crisis arose, why it persists, and why the dominant culture seems for the most part to be unable take effective action against it.

Using the materials we have developed, we can now cut through several debates in environmental theory. First, the debate about whether the failure of reason in the ecological crisis lies in inadequate knowledge (ignorance), poor political structures (interest), or badly adapted and human-centred ethical, philosophical or spiritual worldviews (illusion). I have argued that the roots of our current form of ecological irrationality are to be found in all of these things – ignorance, interest, and illusion – and that these different elements work together and reinforce one another to create a larger ecologically irrational response that is embedded in the very framework and structure of our thought systems. The ecological rationality failures of the dominant culture of capitalism occur at several levels, including those of economics, politics and governance. At the economic level, the neo-liberal order profits from and normalises ecologically irresponsible and unaccountable systems of production and consumption that inflict massive biospheric degradation and suffering, simultaneously eliminating or co-opting potentially critical and corrective systems, including scientific and political ones. At the level of politics and governance, the increasingly unequal distribution of power under neo-liberalism propels us toward ecological collapse because it skews decision-making against changing destructive practices and disables corrective forces.

Under the dominant system, the biggest say in decision-making and policy goes to the one fifth of humanity who gain from the present system and who have the least motivation to support change. Since these gains apparently give the privileged the ability to make themselves remote from the negative consequences that afflict the other four fifths, and they calculate their gains to outweigh their losses, it seems 'rational' for them to ignore environmental consequences. Our present course may be 'rational' (in the sense of self-interest), for these elite groups, but it is entirely irrational (in all senses) for the rest of us. Eventually, no doubt, it will be irrational for them too. But we in the losing 4/5ths cannot pin our hopes on waiting until the abuse of the earth catches up with these 'winners', as it eventually must, because, given the abilities of elites to evade or postpone negative consequences and move assets, they may well be the last to feel its fatal effects. In this version of the Titanic, the rich seize the lifeboats by allowing the market to decide who can get in them, but it can only be a short time before they are overtaken by the same fate as the others.

Remoteness, or the sense of it, and irresponsibility are greatly worsened under the dominant global order. This allows privileged subjects to harbour illusions of ecological disembeddedness and invulnerability to an extreme degree, far greater degree than for other subjectivities. Political structures that allow the privilege and short-sightedness of the rationalist economic sphere to dominate other spheres, with few independent avenues for correctiveness, are poorly adapted to deal effectively with ecological realities. Our analysis suggests that in the environmental crisis these distortions have created we have to deal not only with failures of ecological rationality stemming from interest and ignorance but also with forms of irrationality stemming from the delusions of human-centredness. As we have seen, human-centredness permeates the dominant culture, fostering illusions of disembeddedness and invincibility, which are likely to be especially strong among privileged decision-makers. At the level of science and reason, an anthropocentric logic of human self-imposition has been masquerading as rationality since at least the Enlightenment, as conceptual machinery for commodifying and getting the most out of the radically reduced Other that is nature. Ethical systems that would reduce the more-than-human other and minimise what is owed to them, leave that other maximally open to regimes of commodification that in turn support privilege and its typical illusions of power over and apartness from nature. The cultural anthropocentrism and insensitivity to ecological embeddedness of the rationalist west is a general background hazard, again greatly worsened under a global empire that strengthens the west's cultural dominance. We are confronting not just interest and ignorance here but also various forms of illusion and irrationality.

We can also cut through the long-running and increasingly repetitive 'prudence versus ethics' debate in environmental ethics on whether our attempt to cut the more-than-human world down to our size is is wrong because it is unethical or because it is against our own interests. It is both. Our ethical and spiritual failures are closely linked to our perceptual and prudential failures in situating ourselves as ecological beings. To the extent that we separate ourselves radically from nature in order to justify its domination, we lose the ability to respond to it in ethical and communicative terms. We also get a false idea of our own character and location, including an illusory sense of our independence from nature. This is a prudential hazard because it makes us insensitive to ecological limits, dependencies and interconnections. Following out this anthropocentric logic that has been mistakenly identified with reason will be destructive to the extent that it encourages us to be unaware of the way other organisms and more-than-human presences support our lives, and imprisons us in maladaptive ideologies of self-containment and hyperbolised autonomy.

We need a cultural paradigm shift in many linked areas to adopt a partnership or dialogical model of relationships with nature in place of currently disabling centrist control. Ultimately our survival depends on our preparedness to undertake in many areas and at many levels a project of profound cultural remaking and renewal that addresses these failures of ecological rationality. This task is urgent. Not only existing forms of environmental degradation but the tightening of control over nature in the further development by capitalist science of biotechnology, bioprospecting and intensive agriculture promise to produce an unliveable world in short order unless there are major changes in direction The impact of this deepening control and instrumentalism on the future lives of animals and other nonhumans is a vitally important consideration that is being largely omitted from contemporary debates over biotechnology. These forms of technology are built on the same assumptions of apartness and invulnerability that blind the centre, and whose failure we see in phenomena like BSE. Rationalism and consequent over-valuation of human technological ingenuity mean that the downsides of such technology catch us perpetually unawares, are never anticipated or properly evaluated in advance. Our well-confirmed tendencies to overestimate and overvalue our own technological control and to vastly underestimate their potential for negative impacts on us and on the more-than-human world are fed by the same dissociations. We encounter these blindspots of rationalist hubris repeatedly in the introduction of new technologies of control.

We have reached a point of technological power where such mistakes and blindspots have grave implications for our survival. For this reason alone we must undertake a profound rethinking of rationalist culture and move towards democratic economies and forms of science. The historic task of cultural change is to resolve throughout the dominant culture the distortions of rationalist human/nature dualisms that deny our ecological embodiment and membership of the global ecological community. We must counter those maladaptive forms of reason that radically distance us from the non-human sphere and disguise or disappear our ecological embeddedness and vulnerability, in order to develop a communicative, place-sensitive culture which can situate humans ecologically and nonhumans ethically. Strengthening the democratic and corrective forces means eliminating the radically unequal distribution of power and resources, remembering too that many rational distortions have their source in privileged denial and backgrounding of the fundamental supporting and nurturing roles of excluded and devalued groups, especially women. Challenges to human-centred and rationalist culture and consciousness will not be effective unless they also challenge their bases in current structures of power ; the ecological message, no matter how persuasive to people at large, will never change policy while this is made by ruling elites who have a powerful stake in keeping the systems we have to change. Our best hope is to change the basis of democracy so that more fully egalitarian forms of democratic economy and culture can give everyone an equal stake in benefits and an equal risk of adverse consequences. We must aim for fairer inputs in steering the ship, determining its directions in ways that are rational for everyone. We need too structures of working life that encourage us to exercise responsibility and care for one another and for the natural world.

Rationality failures in many areas mean there are many productive ways to work for change. We need skills and structures at all levels of our lives that can make us aware and responsible for our ecological impacts – economic structures that reduce remoteness that are among the strategems of ecological economics, dialogical skills that increase our ability to modify and negotiate our goals in the light of the other's needs and responses, and many more. Ecological forms of both spirituality and rationality would help us recognise the way both human and earth others nourish and support our lives, would remind us that nurturers must in turn be nurtured, and prevent us from taking from that capacity to nourish more than we put back. It would caution us to abandon further projects of rational conquest that depend on flouting this basic wisdom, such as of space colonisation. Space colonisation is an extreme example of a rationalist project that misunderstands our nature as earth beings. Hyperbolised autonomy and the backgrounding of the earth here create an illusory sense of detachability from the earth, and present as "rational" a project where every venture outwards further damages the earth we depend on. When we have learnt the true nature of our being as earth-dependent and have learnt both to cherish the earth and to go beyond it without damage, it may be time for us to try to leave for the stars – but not before.

Notes

Introduction

1 Gross (1993), my italics.

2 According to some proponents of the population hypothesis, the trouble is that we breed like animals, or more precisely, like rabbits. I do not contest the view that the planet is excessively dominated by the human species. From the perspective of those non-humans that are being driven from the face of the earth, (and this is a standpoint like other oppressed standpoints that we can and should cultivate) either by direct human assault or by being deprived by humans of the share of the earth territory they need to reproduce their kind, there is indeed too much of humankind around. Nevertheless this excess can be seen as a symptom, one relating excessive numbers to a global culture that treads in an excessively heavy way upon the earth, and that has insufficient regard for the lives of the others with whom we should share it. That is, it can be seen as composed of both natural and cultural elements, intermingling and infusing one another, rather than as 'human nature', or as the ultimate explanation.

3 For the term 'technical fix' see Lovins (1977).

4 Lovins (1976, 1977, 1999).

5 See Brennan (2000).

6 Yencken (2000).

7 Especially in the light of work like Dryzek (1992) suggesting that administrative reason is generally hostage to global economic forces, and resists relevant changes to the hilt.

8 Lovins (1977: 11, 1999).

9 On the question of partiality as an obstacle to justice see Friedman (1993).

1 The ecological crisis of reason

1   UNEP (1997, 1999).
2   Brennan (1993, 2000).
3   Price (1999: 200).
4   Plumwood (1995b).
5   Mary Midgley characterises scientism as 'the undiscriminating faith in science as the cure for all ills and the right way to answer all questions' (Midgley (1996: 140).
6   See hooks (1994) and Frank (2001).
7   Brennan (1993).
8   Pusey (1991).
9   Jennings A.L. (1993).
10 See Plumwood (1993a) and England (1993).
11 The term is now contested by economic rationalist economists who prefer the more neutral but quite uninformative 'market reform'. Dryzek (1997: 102) uses the term 'rationalist', in a sense somewhat at variance with the widespread philosophical and economic sense used here, to mean 'entailing substantial cogitation, calculation, and design on the part of policy makers'. This makes 'economic rationalism' a matter of 'the intelligent deployment of market mechanisms to achieve public ends'.
12 See for example Ralston Saul (1993) and Frank (2001).
13 Such an approach is clearly no more truthful (since the rationalist market is by no means free of intervention) than it is contextually sensitive and compassionate, and it is spreading poverty and desperation around the world. See Chassudovsky (1997).
14 Polanyi (1994).
15 This form of denial, on which I elaborate in Chapter 3, has been extensively discussed by feminist philosophers such as Elizabeth Gross (1993).
16 See FAO (2000).
17 As David Orr has pointed out (Orr 1992, 1994) most ecological damage is planned and carried out by the highly educated products of western universities and education systems, often well-intentioned but schooled precisely in these forms of rationality.
18 See Harris (1998).
19 The evolutionary and historical importance of oceanic and shoreline ecosystems to the development of human culture suggests that the great decline of these supporting systems through pollution and over-harvesting in our time, possibly in many cases past the point of recovery, represents a major ecological watershed for our species.
20 See Wood (1998) and Plumwood (1992b) on some of the further economic impacts of fish farms.

21 Ominous further examples are Biosphere 2 (Tilman and Cohen 1996) and, coming next, the products of genetic engineering (Shiva 1994, Steinbrecher and Mooney 1998).

22 The view of the non-human world as rationally replaceable and inferior and the superior status accorded the substitutes produced by reason also helps explain why machines are often now accorded more value and legitimacy as possessors of mind than animals, for whose mindfulness and agency we are assumed to require stringent proof.

23 Lorraine Code (2000: 184).

24 Lorraine Code (2000: 184).

25 See Waring (1988) and Okin (1989).

26 Mies (1986) and Shiva (1988).

27 See Waring (1988).

28 England (1993).

29 See Jennings (1993) and Fraser (1997).

30 See Plumwood (1993b, 2002). Here the monological/dialogical distinctions is linked to contrasting treatments of negation and otherness.

31 Newman (1995).

32 It follows that 'white-supremacist capitalist patriarchy' remains an incomplete specification, but the idea of identifying such a system by giving a list is in any case severely problematic.

33 Theorists include Tronto (1993) and Held (1995).

34 See Tronto (1993). On the history of the private sphere as the sphere of women and morality, see Price (1999) and Nicholson (1986).

35 Jennings (1993). We can take the reproductive sphere to include the ecological, as in Merchant (1980).

2 Rationalism and the ambiguity of science

1 Haraway (1997).

2 See Rogers (1995) and Harris (1998).

3 Wood (1998: 52).

4 Rogers (1995: 99).

5 Quoted in Wood (1998; 52).

6 Wood (1998: 52).

7 See Harding (1986, 1991, 1993).

8 See Rogers (1995: 102).

9 The fate of scientific regulators such as the US Environmental Protection Agency is also relevant here. See Dryzek (1996b: 26).

10 Donna Haraway (1997) adopts the terminology of 'technoscience'. A broader understanding of science as 'technoscience' brings out the relationship between science and capitalism as much closer than suggested by

the metaphor of capture. Strategic boundary shifts between 'science' and 'technology' or 'politics' help maintain the ideology that 'science proper' can do no wrong by displacing attention and responsibility for any ill-effects onto externalised activities or parties identified as 'outside' science proper (for example, onto 'technology', or 'society' or 'politicians' and its 'use' of science).

11   As Carol Gilligan puts it: 'Seen as responsive, the self is by definition connected to others .... Within this framework, detachment, whether from self or others, is morally problematic, since it breeds moral blindness or indifference – a failure to discern or respond to need' (Gilligan 1987: 24).

12   See Kuhn (1962), Feyerabend (1975), Latour (1987), Latour and Woolgar (1979), Merchant (1980, 1989), Johnson (1987) and Haraway (1989).

13   See Bordo (1987: 89).

14   Bordo (1987: 27).

15   Hayward (1998).

16   See Haraway (1991a,b).

17   This is one meaning of the term 'hegemonic'.

18   See Harding (1991).

19   See Harding (1991, 1993a).

20   Harding (1993b: 69).

21   For example, as Carter (1999) points out, the state, the techno-bureaucratic class and the military all have a motivation to maximise economic output.

22   The term 'dualism' is reduntant in this instance because the term 'object' is usually already a dualised term, and the subject/object relationship is already a dualised relationship which allows no other construction. The logic of the object term exemplifies the characteristics of dualistic thinking as I outlined them in Plumwood (1993a). There are of course more harmless logical ways to use these terms and to think about the distinction, for example as marking the difference between extensional and intensional places in an intensional relationship such as 'I know the animal you mean', where the animal is the 'object' of thought. In this case it need carry no exclusionary implications that the internal 'object' is objectified, or is taken to lack subjective, mind-like or intensional characteristics itself.

23   *Love and Sex in Plato's Epistemology* in Evelyn Fox Keller (1985: 21–32).

24   Fox Keller (1985: 21).

25   Plato in the Republic distinguishes higher and lower forms of knowledge in these terms.

26   As Fox Keller (1985: 32) puts it, Bacon 'remains faithful to the funda-

mental categories of his predecessor [Plato]'. One might also note that the insistence of many forms of empiricism on purity of observation unmixed with theory makes it the dualised opposite of rationalism, which is thus preserved in the binary form of denial, as it were.

27 Bacon's images in Anderson (1960: 29).
28 See Merchant (1980).
29 Bacon, quoted in Fox Keller (1985:35).
30 At least, the privatisation process, which is reaching its zenith in our time, is begun in this period. See Longino (1992).
31 Bacon quoted in Fox Keller (1985: 35).
32 Although religion may be retained as a harmless or politically useful adjunct, its salvational project is essentially usurped by science.
33 See Harding 1993b, Gould 1981.
34 There is of course more than one alternative here. For example, reductionist and rationalist empiricism is not the only arrogant knowledge position which evolved following the empirical turn; history has as usual obliterated the record of the losers in the competition to evolve the modernist scientific worldview. The reductionist worldview of Cartesianism had in turn its scientific critics in the Romantic rationalism of nineteenth century intellectuals such as Coleridge, Carlyle and Emerson, and of the Cambridge Platonist school. Modern Romantic rationalism, like empiricism and unlike classical rationalism, wanted to find a way to accommodate some form of empirical observation, but retained rationalist elements by resisting reduction of the objects of scientific knowledge to material phenomena. It did this by conceiving science, in the guise of agent of reason, as the ultimate underlying moral truth, and material phenomena themselves as the creations of reason, which is 'antecedent to all, determinative of all'. The result lifts the status of what is known, but only by ceasing to view the material sphere as the real objects of knowledge. The outcome is equally anthropocentric: human knowers, as the representatives of reason, have a duty to humanise the world and remake it along rational lines. Modern romantic rationalism then allows modern science, now with religious status, to update rather than supersede the oppositional and supremacist ideals of rationality and humanity inherited from classical rationalism. The modernist project of 'saving' or rationalising nature, then, is justified differently but remains common to both modern materialist and modern rationalist positions. Both presuppose the technological–industrial conquest of nature encouraged by reductionist science, and the colonial conquest of empire which in turn fed the universal claims of scientific knowledge. See Walls (1995).
35 And thus perhaps the unravelling of the enduring exclusionary tradition which 'bears witness to the fact that men are united by love and esteem for

their own sex, and can thus produce a symbolic order that perpetuates a kind of autistic self-absorption originating in their ancient envy of maternal power' Cavarero (1995: 107).

36 Strictly speaking Ockemism is a principle of minimising assumptions, but it is certainly often and illegitimately used as a justification for adopting minimising methodologies of reductionism.

37 The 'two cultures' terminology originated with Snow (1959).

38 The post-modern tendency to reduce nature to culture is encouraged by the assumption that non-human nature can be treated in just the same way as the human body (see for example Prokhovnik 1999), despite the fact that the human body is clearly much more closely integrated in human culture than is the non-human sphere.

39 Of course this is a simplified picture. Each realm has its strongholds and spies within that of the other, for example, much philosophy is concerned with justifying and interpreting the science side of the divide, while skill in blending scientific and literary forms of expression is being accorded more value within science. Nevertheless, these forms of addition, interpenetration and hybridity rarely go deep enough to challenge the fundamental epistemological and philosophical structural dualism.

40 Awareness of these limitations provides the basis for Harding's concept of 'strong objectivity'. See Harding (1991).

41 See essays in Soule and Lease (1995).

42 I have used the term 'subjectivise' here but as I argued in Plumwood (1993a) the more accurate and less restrictive term is 'intentionalise', since many aspects of nature which are only doubtfully experiential and conscious subjects (one often assumed meaning of 'subjectivity') are much less doubtfully intentional subjects. Intentionality bridges the radical gulf between subject and object.

43 In the natural sciences, these have included that of von Humboldt. See Walls (1995 op. cit.). For a recent model from feminist science, see Evelyn Fox Keller's (1985) account of the work of Barbara McClintock.

44 Of the manipulative and control orientation, Freya Mathews has written: 'The role of science in the environmental crisis is undoubtedly ambiguous. On the one hand science acts as an advocate for the environment, identifying environmental problems and devising fixes for them. On the other hand, even the most sympathetic science tends to remain radically interventionist... this control of the natural world – even for the purposes of protecting it – would appear to confirm the view that nature is an 'object' for science, to be manipulated and appraised accordingly...given the ecological traumas occurring on all sides, environmentalists can ill afford the ideological purity of refusing the services of science. But even as we bow to this necessity, I think we must constantly bear in mind the role

of science in the genesis of the crisis, and commit ourselves in the long term to the development of a genuinely biocentric science which would aim at understanding nature rather than subduing it. Such scientific understanding would be gained through empathy, dialogue and receptive and engaged interaction with the natural world, rather than through the detached observations and manipulations of a disengaged 'spectator' (Mathews 1991: 9–12).

45　See Walls op. cit.
46　Adams (1992).
47　Cohen (1995: 239).
48　Midgley (1983).
49　This sense is closely analogous to the concept of weak anthropocentrism outlined in Plumwood and Routley (1979).
50　See Quine (1960, 1960).
51　Stamp Dawkins (1998).
52　Benjamin (1990).
53　See Haraway (1989).

3 The politics of ecological rationality

1　For this rational reproductivity they choose, not the Platonic method of selecting promising young rationalists from among the subordinated and devalued non-Guardian population, but the more rationally-appealing method of cloning themselves. Cloning offers a higher degree of control over the chaotic and troublesome sphere of nature and the body and eliminates the need for any immediate affective community other than the EcoGuardians themselves.
2　Aditjondro 2001.
3　Ibid, p. 3.
4　Not to mention ecological Platonists. See Mahoney (1997).
5　For some further reasons why such a regime is unlikely to retain its initially noble ideals in the longer term see Carter (1999: 25–26).
6　On the general complexity of the factors involved in rainforest destruction, see Plumwood (1982), Plumwood and Routley (1980).
7　See also Skocpol (1979). Unless they are strongly democratic and egalitarian, spreading risks evenly across all groups, states have as much potential for generating remoteness from consequences for their decision elites as any other form of power.
8　On 'satisficing' see Routley (1984).
9　Bartlett (1986), Dryzek (1987, 1990), Hayward (1994).
10　Haraway (1991), Harding (1991).
11　Which is not to be identified with instrumental reason. See Plumwood

(1996). Indeed, since anthropocentric culture contributes in a major way to remoteness, such a prudential inquiry must go beyond concern with the arrangement of existing ends and extend to questioning the instrumental treatment of ecology and nature itself.

12 On Prometheanism, see Hayward (1995). For a feminist critique of rationalist interpretations of reason, see especially Lloyd (1984).

13 Harding (1991, 1993).

14 Although culture, epistemology, ethics, and rationality itself are all implicated in questions of ecological rationality, and not only questions of political structure (contra Pepper 1993).

15 Dryzek (1987).

16 Martin (1995).

17 The interpretation of flexibility is plainly highly politically inflected and defined relative to larger political choices and parameters: thus an alternative interpretation of flexibility suitable for a democratic polity might see it as best realised in conjunction with features such as basic income security and democratic workplace responsibility.

18 Thompson (1996).

19 An appeal to science will not solve the problem raised by ecological rationality. Unless we make the assumptions that the initial knowledge and judgement of the Scientist King is perfect, and that there is a method for perfectly reproducing and perfectly applying this body of knowledge, science itself cannot escape the need for epistemic, political and social structures which enable good ecological correctiveness. To the extent that environmental oligarchy assumes that 'objective science' can itself provide a reliable source of correctiveness, its proponents depend on ignoring the substantial body of work showing how power distorts conceptual frameworks and knowledges, and how science produces for the needs of the powerful. Recent work on the way such distortions in science are generated by forms of power and oppression includes Sandra Harding (1991).

20 This formulation aims to avoid the ecological reductionism that haunts bioregionalism, and the implication that ecological consequences are automatically privileged or are the only ones that must be considered.

21 John Dewey (1961).

22 Hayward (1995: 209).

23 Walzer (1983).

24 Sale (1980, 1992), Plant (1992).

25 Marglin, S. and Apfel-Marglin, F. (1990).

26 Plant (1992: 2) sees the problem in appropriately general terms as 'how to put the power of decision-making in the hands of those who will bear the

consequences, and how to keep it there'. However, the rest of the book assumes that this boils down to questions about spatial remoteness.

27 It cannot without endorsing strong, reductionistic ecological priority empower those who bear the ecological consequences over those who bear other consequences, since ecological consequences are not the only kinds of consequences that will flow from a community's decisions. Not silencing and disempowering those who bear the consequences is a minimum condition, although some way might be found to supplement it by reflecting basic ecological priority.

28 The connection between trade, transport and damaging forms of energy use such as fossil fuels is contingent rather than necessary, since alternative transport systems using wind and aerofoil technology such as dynaships could greatly reduce the ecological costs of trade and transport. This means that trade is not inevitably damaging on the grounds of excessive energy use, and again demonstrates that consequential rather than spatial remoteness is the key concept.

29 Autarchic bioregionalism tends to assume a reductionist rather than a basic form of ecological priority that privileges ecological relationships automatically over other kinds of relationships. Thus decision-making communities are to be formed to coincide exactly with important ecologically boundaries, although there must on a non-reductionist view be other important components to community formation than ecological ones.

30 Dryzek (1996).

31 Galtung (1986: 101).

32 Some theorists, for example, libertarian municipalists like Murray Bookchin, recognise that certain political conditions must be specified before we can decide whether or not a given small-scale autarchy is ecologically viable. But the question of how far the larger political networks they propose, such as federations, preserve remoteness principles remains to be considered.

33 Plumwood (1993a, 1991a).

34 Galtung (1980, 1986).

35 Galtung (1986, 1979).

36 Galtung argues for forms of exchange that follow the principle of cancelling externality and treating all others as internal sectors, as for working from the other direction as well to expand economic accounting to take into account more impacts.

37 The term is of course fatally ambiguous between global organisation and the present form of global organisation.

38 There are plainly some serious tensions in taking both egoism and detachment as rational, but concepts of disengagement are formulated to paper these over.

4 Inequality and ecological rationality

1 This was the argument recently employed by World Bank officials to justify third world waste dumping.
2 Walzer (1983).
3 This is a bit narrow, of course, since not all ecological issues and areas of degradation or concern can be reduced to 'ecoharms'.
4 Dowie (1995), Plumwood (1995b).
5 This is at least in part because it prioritises interests according to a completely different political logic than that involved in ranking ends according to whether they are pre-conditions for other ends.
6 Fraser (1989: 80).
7 This is the normal form of the lobbying contest between powerful economic interests and vocal green organisations the interest group model generates.
8 Jennings and Jennings (1993).
9 Many of these forms also impact on future people, who, in terms of exclusion from decisions which impact on their welfare, have to be considered highly disadvantaged.
10 So although we have the term 'environmental racism' established to cover such issues of redistribution, these points provide reasons for thinking that, contra Beck, we still need concepts of class if we wish to understand them, and that we cannot work exclusively with the racialised 'difference' discourses which are often used now as surrogates for suppressed concepts of class. Perhaps we can even regard class privilege as partly constituted by access to such forms of remoteness, and as having multiple determinants depending on the form at work.
11 Pateman (1989: 163).
12 Of course not all environmental issues have this association with marginality. Theorists of ecojustice have noted that those that have associations with more privileged groups, such as wilderness and biodiversity, tend to have a better public profile (Jennings and Jennings 1993). I do not intend to suggest that these more prestigious forms are less important or are negligible, but rather that the consequential remoteness of privileged groups is often reflected in what counts as an ecological issue in the public sphere. The divide coincides roughly with the difference between a concern about damage to 'good' nature versus a concern with repairing or avoiding further damage to 'bad' (already damaged) nature.
13 This is one among a number of reasons why the privileged may appear in opinion polls and the like as more environmentally concerned, a result which should clearly not be taken at face value.
14 Jennings and Jennings (1993).

15 Young (1995), Dean (1996).

16 I assume here neither that all ecoharms can be dealt with via party negotiation nor that these should take the form of 'bargaining sessions', judicial or otherwise. Although consensus-oriented deliberation might deal better than liberalism with cases where there is agreement about what constitutes a collective ecological good, it will face problems in situations where there is no consensus about different conceptions of the ecological good, as in the case of different cultural conceptions of 'the best state' of nature.

17 This condition seems to me to rule out individualist forms of capitalism and to point to community control of investment decisions, since the power to control these decisions so crucial to community well-being would tend to make entrepreneurial interests sponsoring a polluting or damaging process highly privileged in any dispute resolution or communicative process.

18 Walzer (1983), Young (1991, 1995), Dean (1996).

19 Young (1999).

20 See Pateman (1989).

21 Fraser (1997).

22 Young (1995).

23 Walzer (1983).

24 Plumwood (1995b).

25 Young (1995: 141).

26 Young (1995).

27 Habermas, quoted in Dean (1996).

28 See also Phillips (1991), who argues that class differences require better parliamentary representation, but does not discuss the paradox of making an allegedly equal political form complicit in representing differences of subordination.

29 Nancy Fraser has written insightfully of the need to discriminate among differences, only some of which are to be affirmed (Fraser 1995, 1997).

30 Fraser (1997).

31 Fraser (1997).

5 The blindspots of centrism and human self-enclosure

1 Snyder (1990). Snyder's claim can be verified by checking the amount of time newspapers and news reports spend on each 'world'.

2 On the relationship between reason-centredness and human-centredness, see Plumwood (1997a).

3 We might also see this form of centredness as reason-centredness. There is a great deal of overlap between these forms, which assist and support one

another, but they are strictly speaking different although they have the same logical structure. Many transcendental forms of rationalism are reason-centred and to a lesser extent human-centred, as are rationalist forms of Christianity.

4   See Seidler (1994).

5   I use the general term centrism rather than phallocentrism because the relevant pattern identified is not limited to gender or genderised relationships, although dominant gender relations in many societies are prime examples of centric patterning. There are important questions about whether all centrisms are hegemonic. I think that although centrisms may share a common logical structure (a conjecture that remains to be closely investigated), only a certain class is hegemonic. Thus some concepts in some contexts can get to be treated as the norm or as privileged in terms of expectations of occurrence, and their contrasts as exceptions, without our being able to say that the outcome is 'oppressive' or involves power (for example, 'clear' in contrast to 'cloudy' for those living in the desert). A hegemonic centrism would involve a larger range of contexts than normalcy of occurrence, privileging one term over the other for example as a source of value, meaning, agency, identity, etc. To allow for this, I prefer the terminology 'hegemonic centrism'.

6   Hartsock 1990: 161).

7   I don't want to suggest that this hegemonic centric structure gives a complete account of oppression or of the concept of the Other, to deny that there may be other kinds of oppression or features specific to particular kinds of oppression, or to claim that race, class, gender and nature hegemonic centrisms constitute a complete list of oppressions. Elsewhere I argue that these forms of centrism acquire cultural centrality in the specific political system of liberalism as the major exclusions of the liberal master subject (see Plumwood 1995a).

8   Plumwood (1993a).

9   See Plumwood (2002a).

10   Any institutionalised system of domination that aims to avoid arbitrary elements and take full advantage of cultural potential for its reproduction must aim to separate the dominating group from the others, and will tend to adopt cultural means which define the identity of the centre (usually cast in the west as reason) by exclusion of the inferiorised qualities of the Other. Hyper-separation maximises security for the dominating group.

11   Jones (1994).

12   Hartsock (1990).

13   Memmi (1965).

14   Said (1978: 38).

15 Frye (1983: 32).

16 Said (1978: 40).

17 Also for the more general reasons that appear in Hegel's master-slave dialectic.

18 Incorporation is also termed assimilation and 'conversion' (Mazama 1994).

19 Memmi (1965).

20 Although I use the expression 'instrumentalism' here to name this specific feature of denial of agency and the use of the periphery as the means to the centre's ends, the term is also often used to designate the entire centric complex of thought, for example as 'instrumental rationality'.

21 Ruether (1975), Warren (1990), Stepan (1993).

22 As I discuss in detail in Plumwood (1993a).

23 See Marglin (1974).

24 See Marglin and Marglin (1990).

25 On the need to demassify and de-homogenise concepts of nature, see Plumwood (2001).

26 This aspect of the account reflects some of the unease with the deep/shallow distinction, but continues to allow a form of the distinction some critical role in distinguishing thorough going and framework challenges from other more superficial and partial challenges.

27 On the question of partiality as an obstacle to justice and justice as giving others their due, see Friedman (1993: 66).

28 Both liberal capitalism and the Marxist productivist model (Benton 1989) fall in with this framework of ecological denial, the latter denying the agency of nature by treating it as the passive object of labour, the former also denying its agency in the creation of value, as in the Lockean story.

29 Unless they've really had all spark of resistance and independent thought squeezed out of them, it is hard for the oppressed party to see their own labour contributions for example as inessential, or to acquiesce completely in its disappearance or devaluation in the dominant framework. Thus even conservative women who otherwise seem to accept the Othering structure often resist the idea that their work as inessential, and refer to this explicitly as a male illusion they and other women can see through. Scepticism about the position of the Other does not, however, come automatically to the oppressed – it is a major and difficult achievement but one often precipitated by the perception of a certain incongruence between oppressed experience and hegemonic perspectives. The perspectival difference is another reason, in addition to the effects of redistributing ecological ills downward, why it is problematic to have decision-makers drawn heavily from privileged groups. This is also why

successful rulers must know how to draw on advice from those less out of touch.

30 Although the concept of 'ecosystem services' can be dangerously human-centred if it fails to recognise that such services have a much wider range of beneficiaries than the human and if it supports instrumentalising and servant-like conceptions of the non-human sphere.

31 See Tilman and Cohen (1996).

6 Philosophy, prudence and anthropocentrism

1 The general outlines of a partnership ethic can be found in Carolyn Merchant (1995).

2 On the universalist/impersonalist tradition in ethics, see Walker (1995).

3 Especially Norton (1991), Dobson (1990), Hayward (1998).

4 There is a clear counterfactual difference, at least, between an anti-anthropocentric stance which provides consideration for non-human interests and the more limited stance Norton advocates, since an anti-anthropocentric stance provides at least a stronger set of counterfactual guarantees of consideration for nature over a wider range of circumstances.

5 Norton (1991: 233)

6 John Passmore (1974) and Don Mannison (1980).

7 Dobson (1990) and Norton (1983, 1991).

8 Hayward, whose terminology is rather idiosyncratic, is able to declare that instrumentalism is not a problem because he employs the term 'instrumental' in the low redefinition sense of simple use. Hayward then finds himself obliged to go on to say things like 'the problem lies not with the giving of instrumental consideration as such to non-human beings, but in according them only instrumental value' (Hayward 1998: 47). This very weak way of using the term 'instrumental' is at odds with its established meaning in the most important contemporary contexts of its use, for example in the philosophical critiques of instrumentalism and instrumental rationality developed by the Frankfurt School and their heirs. See for example Baumann (1989).

9 See William Grey (1993), and for an earlier argument along similar lines see Thompson (1990).

10 Grey (1993: 470).

11 Grey (1993: 464) Grey's thesis that only humans count morally implies that even other animals we know to be fully conscious and capable of communication, such as other primates, have no right to moral consideration. Grey's claim is certainly a much stronger one than most critics of the ideal of escaping human-centredness have wanted to assert, and its implication that non-human animals do not require moral consideration

from us is widely rejected by theorists from many different ethical and political positions as arbitrary and unjust. But Grey gives this extremely counter-intuitive consequence of his claims concerning animals no attention. The first question Grey's claim that anthropocentrism is benign raises is: 'Benign for who'? Grey does not explain how a position which so downgrades the ethical claims and visibility of animals and nature can possibly be *benign for them*, especially in the present circumstances in which they are increasingly denied any free place on the earth.

12 Ibid, p. 473.

13 Ibid, p. 473.

14 An exception to this claim is Hayward (1998), who considers several senses of human-centredness, although again without reference to the classic critiques of centrism. Hayward bases his conclusion that human-centredness is inevitable and non-problematic on what I have called cosmic anthropocentrism. Hayward does object to speciesism, which he defines as 'arbitrary discrimination on the basis of species' (p. 46), but this is as limited a critical approach as trying to treat issues of gender domination in terms of 'discrimination' rather than in terms of a more encompassing concept like androcentrism.

15 From this, Grey assumes he is entitled to go on to draw his further corollary conclusion: Only human interests are directly morally considerable – non-human interests can count only indirectly (as they affect human ones) in determining the morality of an action.

16 Young (1991: 105).

17 Butler (1726).

18 See for example Fox (1990: 20–21).

19 Although the view that avoiding anthropocentrism demands eliminating all human bearings and extending concern impartially to all times and species is attributed by Grey to a group specified vaguely as 'environmental philosophers', this attribution not only buries a major area of contest but obscures the fact that concern with cosmic anthropocentrism is closely associated with one particular group of environmental philosophers – deep ecologists, and reflects their orientation to transpersonal and transcendence-of-self philosophies. Thus Fox establishes the basis for his subsequent adoption of the perverse cosmic sense by an early appeal to the Copernican model, and glosses anthropocentrism repeatedly as 'human self-importance', which leads smoothly on to the idea of detachment from self. It is a short step from the accounts of the ecological self as the overcoming of 'selfish' attachment and particularity which especially characterise deep ecology to demanding detachment from epistemological location. These pseudo-rationalist versions of deep ecology have therefore themselves helped to generate the perverse cosmic understanding of

anthropocentrism. There is a similar problem in the reverse direction about concepts of ecocentrism and biocentrism, whose terminology can be confusing. In the injunction to replace anthropocentrism by ecocentrism (Eckersley 1992) 'centrism' must be taken to indicate standpoint location and not a hegemonic centrism, since it would hardly be helpful to replace one form of hegermonic centrism by another.

20 See Kheel (1990) and Plumwood (1993a).

21 It is cultural rather than geographic eurocentrism that is in question here and this concept of cultural 'Europe' would normally be taken to include the neo-Europes such as North America and Australasia.

22 Said (1978), Asante (1987). A polycentric world has many centres, whereas an acentred (decentred) one has none. Depending on how it is developed, a sufficiently inclusive and flexible polycentrism might also be described as a (relatively) de-centred world. A strong current of African-American thought advocates Afrocentrism, which celebrates an African cultural heritage, as a cultural home or 'centre'. Contemporary African scholarship has distinguished between on the one hand claiming an Afro-centric epistemic home or cultural location and on the other asserting a single dominant centrism. According to Molefi Kete Asante, this distinction corresponds in part to the difference between the viewpoint of 'cultural appreciation' which celebrates a particular cultural consciousness or heritage on the terms of a polycentric model, and the mono-centric viewpoint of 'cultural deficiency' which defines other cultures as inferior or deviant in relation to one's own which is privileged as the single centre (Asante 1987). (The feminist distinction between otherness as deficiency and as 'positively-other-than' occupies the same logical ground.) It is because polycentric forms of centredness and dominating forms of mono-centrism are different that Afrocentrism in this polycentric form does not necessarily imply the assertion of a new dominant or 'hegemonic' centre. Polycentric emphasis on recovering cultural location is in part a political response to being subsumed within a dominant colonial centre. It is precisely because this colonial model has defined non-European cultures and races in relation to itself as Other, as periphery to centre, that it is now seen as necessary to embrace a form of Afrocentrism, as a positive cultural assertion 'removing African people from the periphery of the European experience to restore them to their own centre' (Mazama 1994).

23 Mackinnon (1987), Young (1991).

24 For many psychological theorists, this is also an account of the masculinised self. See for example Frye (1983) and Chodorow (1985).

25 For useful discussions of selflessness, self-denial and the place of prudence see Hampton (1993) and Grimshaw (1986). As Hampton

writes: 'Moral people do not put themselves to one side; they include themselves in the calculation and give themselves weight in the determination of the right action to take' (Hampton 1993: 165). Not however exclusive weight.

7 The ethics of commodification

1 See Plumwood (1993a).

2 As I argued in Plumwood (1993a).

3 Expressions of concern for abused animals are often greeted with the comment 'How can you be so concerned about these (mere) animals when there are all these oppressed humans who need your concern?' Thus Murray Bookchin comments (Bookchin 1982) that to be concerned with animal suffering and death in nature 'cheapens the meaning of real [human] suffering and death' (p. 362). To the extent that such remarks point up some (real rather than imaginary) excessive exclusiveness of concern with animals, they can have a point, but this exclusiveness is not demonstrated by the mere fact of concern with animals. Such arguments for excluding non-humans from a justice focus are of course circular, and the further assumption that moral concern is a limited good such that concern for one group must mean less for another group is, as Mary Midgley op. cit. (1983) points out, quite unwarranted.

4 Singer (1997).

5 See Rogers (1997).

6 On the extension to primates see Goodin *et al.* (1997). The moral extension proposed is problematic to the extent that it is based exclusively on the overall similarity of simians to humans, on their being 'our nearest relatives'. The assumption seems to be that simians are clearly superior to all other species in ethically relevant capacities, including cognitive capacities. However, the experimental data cited by Lesley Rogers (1997) on the cognitive abilities of some bird species suggests that their abilities in some areas may exceed that of simians (including humans), leading to problems about just who does count as a 'relative' and why we should be prepared to recognise only primate relatives. This points up the difficulties in employing a purely familial ethical metaphor here.

7 One measure of genuine ethical progress in this century has involved declining the nineteenth century colonial obsession with imposing a priori ethical rankings on diverse human groups – especially races, genders and civilisations. In my view it is time we began to apply the same principles of non-ranking to other species.

8 This idea is now largely discredited among philosophers, although it

clings on remarkably among scientists, especially those making experimental use of animals.

9   It may be that some limits are imposed by the viable logic of concepts of
respect and other ethical concepts themselves, but this kind of closure
does not require that we draw a special boundary of moral exclusion in
minimising ways. See Luke (1995), Birch (1993) and Weston (1998).

10   Taylor (1996: 260).

11   Some other rationalist elements of Singer's position such as the strongly
calculative rationality of his utilitarianism and his strong exclusion of
feeling as ethically relevant have been critiqued by feminist thinkers.
See McKenna (1995). One might also include the adoption of a Cartesian
concept of consciousness, as the self-transparency of the rational subject,
as the criterion of moral considerability. For further discussion of Singer
and Regan's moral extensionism see Cuomo (1998).

12   Singer (1980).

13   Personally, to my sensibilities Singer's proclaimed indifference to plant
lives is deeply shocking. I have concern for plants and old trees I know
well as individuals and feel regret and loss when they die or are harmed. I
cannot see why my experience is any less rational, ethically valid or
relevant than Singer's, and I certainly cannot see any rational case, in
the present dire ecological context, for making a virtue out of callousness
and insensitivity to other species' lives.

14   See Singer (1997). Humanism, like these other positions, is multi-
faceted and includes potentially positive elements such as human solidarity. But the position has long been open to distortion and subversion
in several respects: first through the tendency to build concepts of
human equality and solidarity on an exclusionary form of bonding
which defines the human in dualistic opposition to its Other, the dualistic contrast class of the non-human; second, by the legacy of an older
elite-based rationalism which continues to whisper its interpretations of
leading concepts into the receptive ear of Enlightenment, converting its
disarming declarations of equality into programs for the benefit of a
rational meritocracy. Included here is the idea of impartiality, universality and objectivity as the exclusion of care, compassion and emotionality. Third, the doctrines of equality and justice these positions have
enunciated have been subverted by the insistence on a boundary to their
inclusiveness. All these human-supremacist features rebound against the
project of human solidarity, and have been mobilised against those
human groups associated with the excluded non-human class. Thus
the third element has long done battle with the first element of equality
and solidarity. None of these problematic elements of humanism can be
adequately challenged in the Minimalist program, as we have seen.

15 See Plumwood (1995a,b).

16 See for example essays in Bok and James (1992).

17 See for example Singer (1997, 1998).

18 Benton (1993: 92).

19 The politics of individual virtue which issues from the rights approach to food also promotes an excessively polarising focus on absolute abstention from rather than reduction of animal consumption, even though, as Mary Midgley notes, the former is likely to be less effective than the latter in actually reducing animal suffering. In the context of the ecological community with its mixed relations of carnivores and others, rights conflicts between rights to eat and rights not to be eaten are in fact the standard case.

20 On the ethnocentrism of uncontextualised vegan positions, see Plumwood (2000).

21 I outline the alternative contextual and ecological vegetarian position in Plumwood (2000).

22 It is true that certain boundaries are important for ethical treatment and that being eaten or used can be a much greater harm to some kinds of individuals and species than others, something we need to take into account for ethical eating. I am not suggesting that there are no significant ethical boundaries in non-human ethics. But the salient distinctions here do not coincide in any simple way with the boundary between animals and plants as Minimalism assumes, but turn on such features as individuality, species-life, attrition and wastage rates, sensitivity to and care for others of the same species, and so on. In this situation some animals are much more like some plants, for example flies, some fish, corals, insects, and other species with naturally high attrition rates and no offspring care. And of plants, especially long-lived plants, there is much that we have still to learn about how individuality is expressed. The emphasis upon individuality could also be argued to be a form of assimilationism or valuing sameness. As Carol Gilligan (1987: 24) notes 'The question of what responses constitute care and what responses lead to hurt draws attention to the fact that one's own terms may differ from those of others. Justice in this context becomes understood as respect for people in their own terms.' The point has an important application to species life.

23 With the help of modus ponens. Of course this ease is more apparent than real, since a host of problems about rights not to be eaten conflicting with rights to eat then arise.

24 Adams (1990, 1994).

25 Adams (1990, 1994).

26   This emerges clearly when we transpose a human subjectivity into a reductive situation, as in 'The Planet of the Apes'.

27   The term 'construction' is appropriate here because a reductive conception of a being will often result in their becoming reduced, by denying them the opportunity to develop potentials they would otherwise have. Reductive construction correspondingly stunts potentials and sensitivities in those who so reduce them (see Weston 1996). The construction locution is also useful in circumventing the false dichotomy often presented between materialism and idealism. Thus reductive views of animals help construct the practices of the factory farm, while the reductive practices of factory farming help to select and maintain reductive views of animals. Conflicting as well as supportive relations are also possible.

28   Shagbark Hickory (1996).

29   See Wittgenstein (1953).

30   An alternative approach to food is outlined by Shagbark Hickory (1995):

> For most or all American Indians food (plant as well as animal) is kin. Relationships to plants and animals as, on the one hand, food and, on the other hand, kin creates a tension which is dealt with mythically, ritually, and ceremonially, but which is never denied. It is this refusal to deny the dilemma in which we are implicated in this life, a refusal to take the way of bad faith, moral supremacy, or self-deception which constitutes a radical challenge to our relationships to our food. The American Indian view that considerability goes 'all the way down' requires a response considerably more sophisticated than those we have seen in the west, which consist either in drawing lines of moral considerability in order to create an out-group, or in constructing hierarchies of considerability creating de facto out-groups in particular cases.

31   This move of using the commodity term 'meat' as universal is sanctioned by terminological practice in the west, which to that extent expresses cultural imperialism.

32   See Adams (1994: 103).

33   This is often only relatively a privileged fate, relative to that of the meat animal. The story of the happy, privileged private pet is idealised for the housebound animal in much the same way as it is for the housebound wife. In practice both suffer and are vulnerable under a form of coverture which allows the household head many opportunities to abuse them with little redress (Adams 1994). Both can suffer endless ennui, confinement and the indignity of underemployment or uselessness, and both may be limited and distorted in their development by their role of

supplying emotional support for hyperrational masters. At the same time, the need to integrate and confine the animal companion to the space of the individual private household is a further source of limitation, deprivation and assimilation for the animal and of corresponding stereotyping and limitation for human knowledge of companion animals, since it both limits what the pet animal can become and greatly contracts the range of suitable companion animals. The pet's positioning within this privatised structure also supports its infantilisation.

34 The farm wife too had an important economic role, and although that hardly amounted to equality, had to be accorded some respect on account of it.

35 So bringing animals back into human lives cannot just be a matter of better planning and design, but also requires more far-reaching changes.

36 The dualism of the Modern Contract forms the background to such abuses as the dumping of domestic cats in the wild by 'animal lovers', to become a menace to indigenous animals in contexts like Australia where there are few checks and balances.

37 I have not proposed a New Contract to replace the Old and the Modern Contracts because I think, with Mary Midgley (1983) and Carole Pateman (1989), that the contract framework is highly problematic and exclusionary.

38 On the reasons for not defining 'wild' in terms of human absence, see Plumwood (1998d).

39 Individualisation is another factor that makes such relationships of familiarity difficult to achieve in the contemporary West. The reduction of the domestic animal's living possibilities to that of being an individual human household member on the one hand or gulag inhabitant on the other leaves out the possibility of animals inhabiting the larger shared common world of the mixed community– as the village-common geese do, for example, occupying a role which shades off into that of the wild, free-living animal (Benton 1993).

40 For an example of such an alternative, see Mathews (2000).

8 Towards a dialogical interspecies ethics

1 A reversal scenario based on self-revulsion instead of self-love might treat the other as of worth just to the extent that they are different from the self, but this would be equally centric.

2 The distinction between studying up and studying down is well established in feminist methodology. Very roughly, in 'studying down' the investigator looks for the source of an ethical or social problem in the

oppressed, (often someone who is their social inferior), whereas in 'studying up' he or she looks for it in the oppressor. Studying up is disruptive of the dominant hegemonic methodology, which is studying down.

3 For an account of some features of the gift-exchange framework, see Snyder (1990) and Hyde (1979).

4 Rogers (1997).

5 See Andrews (1998).

6 Among other things, to give all equal weight would be to ignore particularistic claims and responsibilities, as well as obliterating the great variety of context dependent considerations that might need to go into decisions. See Marilyn Friedman (1993).

7 For a very helpful discussion of ranking, generalism and context see Brian Luke (1995; on contextual ethics see Warren (1990).

8 Quoted in Curthoys (1997: 13). However Curthoys, strongly committed to a form of human essentialism, mistakenly attributes this feature to an essential and invariant moral characteristic of humans themselves, instead of attributing it where it belongs, to the logical difference in the way ranking is involved.

9 See Luke (1995) and Smith (1997).

10 On attentiveness and attention as a virtue see Weston (1998), Walker (1995), Ruddick (1989) and Birch (1993).

11 Scientific arguments supporting this stance can be found in Rogers (1997). Beston (1928) provides a famous statement of incommensurability: 'they are not brethren... not underlings... they are other nations'.

12 When we take account of particularistic relations and responsibilities to non-humans also, we do not necessarily wind up with a universal ranking in which all humans always outweigh all non-humans.

13 For example the disposition to make a highly intellectualised concept of belief central to all other intentional functors.

14 Perhaps one of the best sources of examples here is the role of 'external observation' in the history of racist and sexist science. See Harding (1993a,b) and Birke and Hubbard (1995).

15 I do not claim that it is incompatible with any and all possibility of ranking. I doubt if any schema could satisfy this last claim: there is no way to stop compulsive rankers ranking – even when doing so has very little justification or meaning. For example, Andrews has even found a way to rank humans and oak trees as choice-makers, although it seems to depend on the usual closure to non-human potential and grossly underestimates the diversity and intricacy of ways in which a tree's choices can be expressed in its mode of development and self-elaboration.

16 Walls (1995: 86) quoting from von Humboldt's journals.

17 The de-intentionalisation of the more-than-human sphere has been an important element in the ancient western war between poetry and philosophy, and has contributed greatly to the disempowerment and irrelevance of the former.

18 The fact that all these locutions are in appropriate contexts quite 'natural' shows I think that at some level we already half-recognise nature as a sphere of intentional others, and must do so minimally to lead 'normal' lives. But we have been conned into denial and mistrust of these attributions by a superimposed pseudo-scientific theory that claims they are irrational.

19 I am not claiming here that intentional recognition is sufficient for agency, as Andrews asserts (with no textual foundation) on p. 15, but that it is necessary if the other is to be grasped in active terms that give purchase to critical, political, ethical and anti-hegemonic discourses, for example as an originator of projects that demand our respect – the sense in which agency is commonly used in political philosophy, (see for example Cohen (1995: 239). Andrews' sense of agency (p. 18) as the capacity for 'imposing one's desires and choices' on the world is so strong it would eliminate both most human and political agency, as well as being composed in the logical terms of mastery. See also Dennett's (1996: 22–28) discussion of agency and Emily Martin's in Birke and Hubbard (1995).

20 See Birch (1993 and Weston (1996, 1998).

21 Andrews seemingly has not noticed that I have chosen my terminology with care to avoid the polarised on/off picture of mind I want to reject as part of rejecting the dualistic picture. Thus, contra Andrews, I would not be happy to say of such items as mountains that they 'have minds', or 'have mental states', the 'on' terminology Andrews has me using (p. 14), although I am willing to say that mountains express or exhibit elements of mind, or have mind-like qualities, the graduated claim. I think that the kind of intentionality we can justly attribute to mountains is too diffused into processes and aspects to sit comfortably with the highly polarised and individualised on/off terminology of 'having a mind'.

22 These include of course Johnson (1987).

23 Included here is Dennett's project of discovering 'the wisdom in the wing' (Dennett 1996).

24 These count as intentional to the extent that they are sensitivities to something, involving a content.

25 Griffin (1992), Rogers (1997). Now my thesis does not require the strong claim there are no differences in degree and complexity also available for discovery in this framework – of course there are.

26 Such a misunderstanding appears in Andrews (1998).

27 See Andrews (1998).

28 I think many of these may be better understood as quotation, multi-lingual or cross-cultural behaviours than as mechanical 'imitation' or 'reproduction', in the fashion of the tape-recorder.

29 Dennett (1996: 27).

30 Dennett (1996: 6–7).

31 Dennett (1996: 7).

32 Cheney and Weston (1999).

33 For an attempted justification of this assumption, see Dennett (1996: 7). Rogers (1997) is one scientist who has noted the Catch 22 set up this onus of proof demand produces in the typical experimental context.

34 As it is not, see Dennett (1996: 7).

35 In fact the 'as if' approach and the attempt to confine 'real' intentionality to the human have much of the methodological aspect of the ad hoc hypothesis, devised in the face of counter-indications to 'save' a strongly entrenched theory.

36 Our suspicions about the extent to which the 'as if' position does just this should initially be raised to the extent that the 'as if' account provides no independent grounds for deciding when 'as if' rather than real intentionality is present other than whether or not the subject is human. Other indications of hegemonic construction of non-human otherness in the 'as if' interpretation appear in Dennett's conclusion that dogs emerge highest on the scale of mind because they have been 'civilised' by their long association with humans – a clear parallel to the colonising mindset and its hegemonic moral extensionism which values the other just to the extent that they resemble or reflect the self. Surely we have sufficient evidence of the high levels of sensitivity of many species of non-humans towards one another to understand the attempt to make the recognition of mind revolve around the relationship to the human for the exercise in colonial thinking it is. If it is to avoid these kinds of distortions and their irrational monological outcomes, philosophy of mind needs to make better connections with critical environmental thought and adopt a systematic counter-hegemonic program and posture on non-human intentionality.

37 This is a very common conflict situation where a familiar such as the family pet comes into conflict with free-living individual animals or communities of free-living animals. See Plumwood (2000).

38 Held (1995).

39 Gilligan (1987, 141).

40 Walker (1995).

41 Murdoch (1970)

42 Walker (p. 140).

43 Ibid.
44 See Gare (1998), Benhabib (1992) and Warren (1990).
45 Dryzek (1990a, 1996a) has argued for a communicative ethic.
46 A low redefinition eases criteria for class membership so that too many items fall under it, whereas a high redefinition tightens them so that too few items qualify.
47 Habermas' view that only those beings who can will their communication to be universal can communicate is often made the basis of a highly intellectualist and exclusionary account that places conditions of the concept of communication that are impossible for non-humans and very hard even for many humans to meet. If, on the other hand, we take the extension of any ethical 'universal' to include earth others, as I have argued we should, we could turn the argument around, contraposing to draw the conclusion that we humans ourselves are not (or not fully) communicative beings, given our typical stance of closure to non-human communicative potentials and our failure to will it to be universal.
48 Young (1995).
49 Birke (1997).
50 Stamp Dawkins, M. (1998: 15–16)
51 Cheney and Weston (1999).
52 Weston (2001: 98).
53 Mathews (1997).
54 Weston (1996).

9 Unity, solidarity and deep ecology

1 Reed (1989: 67).
2 Benjamin (1990: 46).
3 Benjamin (1990: 48)
4 See Plumwood (1996).
5 See Plumwood (1993a).
6 hooks (1989: 42).
7 Zimmerman (1994), Spretnak (1997b).
8 On some of the problems of ideals of unity and community in politics, see especially Young (1990).
9 The stress deep ecology has placed on the concept of unity is highly functional for some positions such as transpersonalism, and associated concepts of impartiality, devaluation of particular attachments and transcendence of self/relationships are functional for masculinist agendas. Some feminists have detected similar problems in Buddhist frameworks of unity, and stress on these concepts is often the site of an internal struggle between men and women in Buddhism. See Gross (1993).

10   For a discussion of some of these techniques for constructing a double perspective from above and below in the work of Gary Larson, see Minahen (1997).

11   This attitude trades on reason/emotion dualism, and also benefits the status quo of dominance. Such 'irrational' emotions are not 'capricious' but can be taught and developed, or alternatively blocked, in certain social contexts.

12   See Harding (1991: 288).

13   On these points see Harding (1991: 283).

14   See Harding (1993b).

15   Cohen (1995: 239).

16   Weston 1995).

17   Plumwood (1993a).

18   Zimmerman (1994).

19   Ferry (1992)

20   Zimmerman (1994, 1995).

21   Young (1997a).

22   Others include Zimmerman (1995), Singer (1997).

23   Not only is no such trade-off necessary, but there are numerous respects in which consideration for non-humans and consideration for humans augment one another. See Midgley (1983) and Plumwood (1993a).

24   Spretnak (1997a).

25   Baumann (1989), Proctor (1993).

26   On the parallels and contradictions of the relationship between the Nazi treatment of animals and that of people, see Arluke and Boria (1995). Critics of the blurring of the human/animal boundary like Ferry have failed to note that there are importantly different directions from which this boundary breakdown can come: we can extend the consideration reserved for humans to non-humans (which need carry no implication of diminishing the former) or extend the lack of consideration, control and technical manipulation characteristically applied to animals to humans. The Nazis seem to have done both, but it is the second form which is implicated in their atrocities, and the first which is characteristic of animal and ecology movements today.

27   Proctor (1993).

28   Takaki (1979).

29   diZerega (1995).

30   diZerega (1996). Although just how private property would be made more accountable is not explained.

31   For a discussion of an alternative democratic approach to funding community groups more like the erstwhile Australian system of public funding, see Dryzek (1996b).

32 Although as Takaki (1979) notes, Jefferson had errant slaves flogged and engaged in other abuses.

33 Takaki (1979).

34 Gomez-Pompa and Kaus (1992).

35 Cohen (1996: 239)

36 See Vandana Shiva (1994).

37 These have often been asserted historically. See Plumwood (1995b).

10 Towards a materialist spirituality of place

1 Cook (1998).

2 See Ruether (1975), Spretnak (1989), Griffin (1978).

3 Passmore (1974).

4 Warren (2000: 198).

5 As Karen Warren (2000) recognises, the term 'life-affirming' is not sufficient to cover the full range of relevant ethical and political considerations.

6 Even some Gaian spiritualities can take this form. I discuss some examples in Plumwood (1992a, 1993a).

7 Plumwood (1993a). There is another sense in which 'materialism' can mean insisting on the primacy of material as opposed to ideational causality. This can be dualistic and reductionist, and in mainstream Marxist hands often was. In the hands of feminists and ecofeminists the term has signalled a critique of the denial and devaluation not only of the physical sphere as in rationalism but also of the denial of the sphere of women's labour, reproduction and renewal in capitalist patriarchy (Merchant 1980; Mellor 1997, Salleh 1998).

8 We are often urged to bypass such non-western examples and stick to cases drawn from 'our own culture'. Stated reasons for this prohibition vary, and include the idea that any such consideration of other cultures must amount to 'appropriation'. However, this is to stereotype and over-generalise drastically about the knowledge context, which includes cases where the indigenous knower adopts the role of teacher in relation to those from the dominant culture. Another objection is that tribal cultures are very different from one another, and that their lands have anyway not been exempt from environmental damage. However, it is not necessary to assume that all indigenous cultures are the same or that all have always been benign in order to find impressive and instructive examples of ecologically aware and dialogical spiritualities among them. The prohibition essentialises and immobilises cultures and denies vital processes of cultural movement through learning and borrowing.

9 Gifford (1992, Arrowsmith version, p. 67). In the better known Perry

version this passage is rendered much more briefly as 'Your dead go to walk among the stars, but our dead return to the earth they loved' (Gifford 1992: 54).

10   Neidjie (1986, 1989).

11   Hyde (1998: 123).

12   Haraway (1991).

13   In specific terms, the performance alluded to here is that of the *Litoria peronii* species of the family Hylidae (previously *Hyla peronii*).

14   See Mathews (1997).

15   See Hayden (1995).

16   On journeying, (see Mathews 1999).

17   See Polanyi (1994).

Bibliography

Adams, C. 1990 *The Sexual Politics of Meat* Continuum, New York.

Adams, C. 1994. *Neither Man nor Beast.* Continuum, New York.

Adams, C. 1993. 'The Feminist Traffic in Animals'. In Gaard, G. (ed) *Ecofeminism* Temple University Press, Philadelphia.

Aditjondro, G.J., 2001 'The Politics of Indonesia's Forest Fires', *Ecopolitics*, 1(1) 2–12.

Anderson, F.H. 1960. ed. Francis Bacon: The New Organon and Related Writings. Bobbs Merrell, Indianapolis, IN.

Andrews, J., 1998. 'Weak Panpsychism and Environmental Ethics', *Environmental Values*, 7(4) 381–396.

Arluke, A., Boria, S. 'The Nazi Treatment of Animals and People' in Birke L., Hubbard, R. (eds.) *Reinventing Biology.* University of Indiana Press, Bloomington, pp. 228–260.

Asante, M.K., 1987. *The Afrocentric Idea.* Temple University Press, Philadelphia, PA.

ASTEC, 1978. 1997–1978 Report of Working Party on Ethics and the Conduct of Research in Protected and other Environmentally Sensitive Areas. ASTEC, Canberra.

Bammer, G. et al., 1986. 'Who Gets Kicks out of Science Policy?', *Search*, 17(1–2) 41–46.

Bartlett, R., 1986. 'Ecological Rationality: Reason and Environmental Policy', *Environmental Ethics*, 8(3) 221–239.

Baumann, Z., 1989. *Modernity and the Holocaust.* Verso, London.

Beck, U., l995. *Ecological Enlightenment.* Humanities Press, Atlantic Highlands, NJ.

—— Giddens, A., Lash, S., 1994. *Reflexive Modernisation.* Polity, Cambridge.

Benhabib, S., 1992. *Situating the Self.* Routledge, New York.

Benjamin, J., 1990. *The Bonds of Love: Psychoanalysis, Feminism and the Problem of Domination.* Virago, London.

Benton, T., 1989. 'Marxism and Natural Limits: an Ecological Critique and Reconstruction', *New Left Review*, 178 51–86.

—— 1993. *Natural Relations.* Verso, London.

Berndt, R.M., Berndt, C.H., 1989. *The Speaking Land: Myth and Story in Aboriginal Australia.* Penguin Books, Ringwood.

Beston, H. 1928. *The Outermost Houses*, Ballantine, New York.

Birch, T., 1993. 'Moral Considerability and Universal Consideration', *Environmental Ethics*, 15 313–332.

Birke, L., 1994. *Feminism, Animals and Science.* Open University Press, Buckingham, UK.

—— 1995. 'Exploring the Boundaries: Feminism, Animals and Science' in Adams, C.J., Donovan, J. (eds.) *Animals and Women.* Duke University Press, pp. 32–54.

—— 1997. 'Science and Animals, Or Why Cyril Won't Win the Nobel Prize', *Animal Issues*, 1 (1) 45–55.

—— Hubbard, R., 1995. *Reinventing Biology*. Indiana University Press, Indianapolis IN.

Bok, G., James, S. (eds.), 1992. *Beyond Equality and Difference: Citizenship, Feminist Politics and Female Subjectivity*. Routledge, London.

Bookchin, M., 1982. *The Ecology of Freedom*. Cheshire Books, Palo Alto, CA.

Bordo, S.R., 1987. *The Flight to Objectivity: Essays on Cartesianism and Culture*. State University of New York Press, Albany, NY.

Braidotti, R., 1991. *Patterns of Dissonance*. Routledge, London.

Brennan, A., 1992. 'Moral Pluralism and the Environment', *Environmental Values*, 1 15–33.

—— 1997. 'Ethics, Conflict and Animal Research', *Animal Issues*, 1(2) 40–56.

Brennan, T., 1993. *History After Lacan*. Routledge, London.

—— 2000. *Exhausting Modernity: Grounds for a New Economy*. Routledge, London.

Bullard, R.D., 1990. *Dumping in Dixie: Race, Class and Environmental Quality*. Westview, Boulder, CO.

Butler J., 1726. 'Upon the Love of Our Neighbour', *Fifteen Sermons upon Human Nature* London 2nd ed. 1729. Reprinted in Milo, R.D. (ed.) *Egoism and Altruism*. Wadsworth Publishing Co, Belmont CA, pp. 26–36.

Callicott, J., 1984. 'Non-anthropocentric Value Theory and Environmental Ethics', *American Philosophical Quarterly*, 21 299–309.

Carter, A., 1999. *A Radical Green Political Theory*, Routledge, London.

Cavarero, A., 1995. *In Spite of Plato*, Routledge, New York.

Chassudovsky, M., 1997. *The Globalisation of Poverty: Impacts of IMF and World Bank Reforms*. Zed Books, London.

Cheney, J., 1989. 'Postmodern Environmental Ethics: Ethics as Bioregional Narrative', *Environmental Ethics*, 11 117–134.

—— Weston, A., 1999. 'Environmental Ethics as Environmental Etiquette: Toward an Ethics-Based Epistemology in Environmental Philosophy', *Environmental Ethics*, 21 115–134.

Chodorow, N., 1985. 'Gender, Relation and Difference in Psychoanalytic Perspective' in Eisenstein, H., Jardine, A. (eds.) *The Future of Difference*. Rutgers, New Brunswick, NJ, pp. 3–19.

Code, L., 2000. 'The Perversion of Autonomy and the Subjection of Women' in Mackenzie, C., Stoljar, N. (eds.) *Relational Autonomy: Feminist Perspectives on Autonomy, Agency and the Social Self*. Oxford University Press, Oxford, pp. 181–212.

Cohen, G.A., 1995. *Self-Ownership, Freedom, and Equality*. Cambridge University Press, Cambridge.

Collins, D., Barkdull, J., l995. 'Capitalism, Environmentalism, and Mediating Structures: From Adam Smith to Stakeholder Panels', *Environmental Ethics*, Fall 227–234.

Cook, J., 1998. 'The Philosophical Colonization of Ecofeminism', *Environmental Ethics*, 20 (3) 227–246.

Cox, S.J.B., 1985. 'No tragedy of the commons', *Environmental Ethics*, 7(1) 49–61.

Crosby, A.W., 1986. *Ecological Imperialism: the Biological Expansion of Europe*. Cambridge University Press, Cambridge.

Cuomo, C.J., 1998. *Feminism and Ecological Communities*. Routledge, London.

Curthoys, J., 1997. *Feminist Amnesia*, Routledge, London.

de Beauvoir, S., 1965. *The Second Sex*. Foursquare Books, London/New York.

Dean, J., 1996. 'Civil Society: Beyond the Public Sphere' in Rasmussen, D.M. (ed.) *Handbook of Critical Theory*. Blackwell, Cambridge, MA, pp. 422–443.

DeGrazia, D., 1996. *Taking Animals Seriously: Mental Life and Moral Status*. Cambridge University Press, Cambridge, MA.

Deloria, V., 1970. *We Talk, You Listen*. MacMillan, New York.

Dennett, D.C., 1989. *The Intentional Stance*. MIT Press, Cambridge, MA.

Dennett, D.C., 1996. *Kinds of Minds*. Weidenfeld and Nicholson, London.

Dewey, J., 1961. *Democracy and Education.* London, Macmillan.

Diamond, J., 1998. *Guns, Germs and Steel.* Vintage, New York.

Dickson, D., 1984. *The New Politics of Science.* Pantheon, New York.

diZerega, G., 1995. 'Individuality, Human and Natural Communities, and the Foundations of Ethics', *Environmental Ethics,*17(2) 23–37.

—— 1996. 'Towards an Ecocentric Political Economy', *The Trumpeter* 13(4) Fall 173–182.

Dobson, A., 1990. *Green Political Thought.* Routledge, London.

Dodson Gray, E., 1979. *Green Paradise Lost.* Roundtable, Wellesley, MA.

Dowie, M., 1995. *Losing Ground.* MIT Press, Cambridge, MA.

Dryzek, J., 1987. *Rational Ecology: Environment and Political Economy.* Blackwell, Oxford.

—— 1990a. 'Green Reason: Communicative Ethics for the Biosphere', *Environmental Ethics,* 12 195–210.

—— 1990b. *Discursive Democracy: Politics, Policy and Political Science.* Cambridge University Press, Cambridge.

—— 1992. 'Ecology and Discursive Democracy; Beyond Liberal Capitalism and the Administrative State', *Capitalism, Nature, Socialism,* 3(2) 18–42.

—— 1996a. 'Political and Ecological Communication' in Mathews, F. (ed.) *Ecology and Democracy.* Frank Cass, Portland, OR, p. 330.

—— 1996b. *Democracy in Capitalist Times.* Oxford University Press, Oxford.

—— 1997. *The Politics of the Earth.* Oxford University Press, Oxford.

During, S., 1987. 'Postmodernism or Postcolonialism Today', *Textual Practice,* 1(1), 32–47.

Eckersley, R., 1992. *Environmentalism and Political Theory: Toward an Ecocentric Approach.* UCL Press, London.

Elliott, R., 1985. 'Meta-ethics and Environmental Ethics', *Metaphilosophy,* 16 103–117.

—— 1989. 'Environmental Degradation, Vandalism and the Aesthetic Object Argument', *Australasian Journal of Philosophy,* 67 191–204.

—— 1992. 'Intrinsic Value', *The Monist,* 75(2) 180–190.

England, P., 1993. 'The Separative Self: Androcentric Bias and Neo-Classical Assumptions' in Ferber, M., Nelson, J. (eds.) *Beyond Economic Man: Feminist Theory and Economics.* University of Chicago Press, Chicago, IL, pp. 37–53.

FAO, 2000. Fisheries Report No 638, FAO, New York. 'Papers Presented at the Expert Consultation on *Economic Incentives and Responsible Fisheries'.* 28th November–1st December 2000. FAO Fisheries Report Supplement No 638, 96 pp., ISBN 92-5-104554-2. FAO Publications.

Ferber, M., Nelson, J., 1993. *Beyond Economic Man: Feminist Theory and Economics.* University of Chicago Press, Chicago, IL.

Ferry, L., 1995. *The New Ecological Order.* University of Chicago Press, Chicago, IL.

Feyerabend, P., 1988. *Against Method.* Verso, London.

Fox, W., 1990. *Toward a Transpersonal Ecology.* Shambala, Boston, MA.

Fox Keller, E., 1985. *Reflections on Gender and Science.* Yale University Press, London.

Frank, T., 2001. *One Market Under God,* Secker and Warburg, London.

Fraser, N., 1989. *Unruly Practices.* Polity Press, Cambridge.

—— 1995. 'From Redistribution to Recognition? Dilemmas of Justice in a PostSocialist Age', *New Left Review,* Sept/Oct 68–95.

—— 1997. *Justus Interruptus.* Routledge, London.

Freire, P., 1972. *Pedagogy of the Oppressed.* Penguin, Harmondsworth.

Friedman, M., 1993. *What Are Friends For?* Cornell University Press, Cornell.

Frye, M., 1983. *The Politics of Reality.* Crossing Press, New York.

Galtung, J. 1986. 'Towards a New Economics.' In Elnins, P. (ed) *The Living Economy.* Routledge & Kegan Paul, London, pp. 99–109.

—— 1979. Development, Environment and Technology. UN/UNCTAD, New York.

Gare, A., 1995. *Postmodernism and the Environmental Crisis*. Routledge, London.

—— 1998. 'MacIntyre, Narratives and Environmental Ethics', *Environmental Ethics*, 20 (2) 3–18.

George, S., 1993. *The Debt Boomerang*. Pluto, London.

Gifford, E., Cook, R.M., 1992. *How Can One Sell the Air? Chief Seattle's Vision*. Native Voices, Summertown, TN.

Gilligan, C., 1987 'Moral Orientation and Moral Development'. Fn: Feder Kitlay, E. and Meyos, D. (eds) *Women and Moral Theory* Rowman and Littlefield, Totowa NJ, pp. 19–36.

Gomez-Pompa, A., Kaus, A., 1992. 'Taming the Wilderness Myth', *BioScience*, 42(4) 271–279.

Goodin, R., 1985. *Protecting the Vulnerable: a Reanalysis of Our Social Responsibilities*. University of Chicago Press, Chicago, IL.

—— 1992. *Green Political Theory*. Polity, Cambridge.

—— Pateman, C., Pateman, R., 1997. 'Simian Sovereignty', *Political Theory*, 25(6) 821–849.

Goodpaster, K., 1979. 'From Egoism to Environmentalism' in Goodpaster, K.E., Sayre, K.M. (eds.) *Ethics and Problems of the 21st Century*. University of Notre Dame Press, Notre Dame, IN.

Gould, S.J., 1981. *The Mismeasure of Man*. Norton, New York.

Grey, W., 1993. 'Anthropocentrism and Deep Ecology', *Australasian Journal of Philosophy*, 71(4) 463–475.

Griffin, S. 1978. *Women and Nature*. Harper & Row, New York.

Grimshaw, J., 1986. *Feminist Philosophers*. Wheatsheaf, Brighton.

Gross, E., 1993. 'Bodies and Knowledges: Feminism and the Crisis of Reason' in Alcoff, L., Potter, E. (eds.), *Feminist Epistemologies*. Routledge, London, pp. 187–216.

Gross, P., Levitt, N., 1994. *Higher Superstition: the Academic Left and its Quarrels with Science*. Johns Hopkins University Press, Baltimore, MD.

Gross, R.M., 1993. *Buddhism After Patriarchy*. State University of New York Press, Albany, NY.

Haack, S., 1996a. *Deviant Logic Fuzzy Logic*. University of Chicago Press, Chicago, IL (second edition; first edition 1974).

—— 1996b. 'Preposterism and its Consequences', *Social Philosophy and Policy* 13 (2) 296–315. [also in Paul, E.F. (ed.) *Philosophy and Public Policy*. Cambridge University Press, Cambridge, 1996].

—— 1997. 'Science, Scientism and Anti-Science in the Age of Preposterism', *The Skeptical Inquirer*, Nov/Dec 37–43.

Haller, S., 2000. 'A Prudential Argument for Precaution under Uncertainty and High Risk', *Ethics and the Environment*, 5(2) 175–189.

Hampton, J., 1993. 'Selflessness and Loss of Self' in Paul, E.F., Miller, F.D., Paul, J. (eds.) *Altruism*. Cambridge University Press, Cambridge, pp. 135–165.

Hanson, P., 1986. 'Morality, Posterity and Nature', *Environmental Ethics: Philosophical and Policy Perspectives*. Simon Fraser University, Burnaby.

Haraway, D., 1989. *Primate Visions*. Routledge, London.

Haraway, D., 1991a. *Simians, Cyborgs and Women: the Reinvention of Nature*. Routledge, New York.

Haraway, D., 1991b. 'Situated Knowledges', *Simians, Cyborgs and Women*. Free Association Books, London, pp. 183–202.

Haraway, D., 1997. *Modest Witness @ Second Millenium: Feminism and Technoscience*. Routledge, London.

Hardin, G., 1968. 'The Tragedy of the Commons', *Science*, 162 1234–1238.

Harding, S., 1986. *The Science Question in Feminism*. Cornell University Press, Ithaca, NY.

Harding, S., 1990. 'Feminism, Science and the anti-Enlightenment Critiques' in Nicholson, L. (ed.) *Feminism/Postmodernism*. Routledge, London.

Harding, S., 1991. *Whose Science? Whose Knowledge?* Cornell University Press, Ithaca, NY.

Harding, S., 1993a. 'Rethinking Standpoint Epistemology: What is Strong Objectivity?' in Alcoff, L., Potter, E. (eds.) *Feminist Epistemologies*. Routledge, London, pp. 49–82.

Harding, S., 1993b. *The Racial Economy of Science: Toward a Democratic Future*. Indiana University Press, Bloomington, IN.

Harris, M., 1998. *Lament for an Ocean: The Collapse of the Atlantic Cod Fishery*. McClelland and Stewart, Toronto.

Hartsock, N., 1990. 'Foucault on power: a theory for women?' in Nicholson, L. (ed.) *Feminism/Postmodernism*. Routledge, New York.

Hayward, T., 1995. *Ecological Thought: an Introduction*. Polity, Cambridge.

—— 1998. *Political Theory and Ecological Values*. Polity Press, Cambridge.

Held, V., 1993. *Feminist Morality*. University of Chicago Press, Chicago, IL.

—— 1995. *Justice and Care: Essential readings in Feminist Ethics*. Westview Press, Boulder, CO.

Hickory, S., 1995. 'Environmental Etiquette /Environmental Practice: American Indian Challenges to Mainstream Environmental Ethics' in Oelschlaeger, M. (ed.) *The Company of Others: Essays in Celebration of Paul Shephard*. Kivaki Press, Durango, CO.

Hooks, B., 1989. *Talking Back*. South End, Boston, MA.

—— 1994. *Outlaw Culture*. Routledge, London.

Hyde, L., 1979. *The Gift*. Vintage, New York.

—— 1998. *Trickster Makes This World: Mischief, Myth and Art*. Farrar, Straus and Giroux, New York.

Jaggar, A. (ed.), 1994. *Living with Contradictions: Controversies in Feminist Social Ethics*. Westview Press, Boulder, CO.

Jennings, A.L., 1993. 'Public or Private?' in Ferber, M.A., Nelson, J.A. (eds.) *Beyond Economic Man*. University of Chicago Press, Chicago, IL, pp. 109–129.

Jennings, C.L., Jennings, B., 1993. 'Green Fields/Brown Skin: Posting as a Sign of Recognition' in Bennett, J., Chaloupka, W. (eds.) *In the Nature of Things*. University of Minnesota Press, London, pp. 173–196.

Johnson, M., 1987. *The Body in the Mind*. Chicago University Press, Chicago.

Jones, R.C., 1994. 'The End of Africanity? The Bi-racial Assault on Blackness', *The Western Journal of Black Studies*, (18)4 201–210.

Kant, I., 1981. *Observations on the Feeling of the Beautiful and Sublime*, trans. University of California Press, Los Angeles, CA.

Kheel, M., 1990. 'Ecofeminism and Deep Ecology' in Diamond, I., Orenstein, G. (eds.) *Reweaving the World*. Sierra Club Books, San Francisco, CA, pp. 128–137.

King, Y., 1989. 'The Ecology of Feminism and the Feminism of Ecology'. In: Plant, J. (ed.) *Healing the Wounds*. New Society Publishers, Philadelphia, PA.

—— 1990. 'Healing the Wounds: Feminism, Ecology, and the Nature/Culture Dualism' in Diamond, I., Orenstein, G. (eds.) *Reweaving the World*. Sierra Club Books, San Francisco, CA, pp. 106–121.

Kuhn, T., 1962. *The Structure of Scientific Revolutions*. University of Chicago Press, Chicago, IL.

Latour, B., 1987. *Science in Action*. Harvard University Press, Cambridge, MA.

Latour, B., Woolgar, S., 1979. *Laboratory Life*. Sage, Beverly Hills, CA.

le Doeuff, M., 1989. *Hipparchia's Choice*. Routledge, London.

Lloyd, G., 1984. *The Man of Reason*. Methuen, London.

Longino, H., 1992. *Science as Social Knowledge*. University of California Press, Berkeley, CA.

Lovins, A., 1976. 'Energy Strategy: the Road Not Taken?' *Foreign Affairs*, October 1976.

—— 1977. *Soft Energy Paths*, Penguin.

—— Lovins, L., Hawken, P., 1999. *Natural Capitalism: the Next Industrial Revolution*. Earthscan, London.

Luke, B., 1995. 'Solidarity Across Diversity: a Pluralistic Rapp.rochement of Environmentalism and Animal Liberation', *Social Theory and Practice,* 21 (2) [also in Gottlieb, R., 1997 (ed.) *The Ecological Community.* Routledge, London, pp. 333–358].

Mackinnon, C., 1987. *Feminism Unmodified.* Harvard University Press, Cambridge, MA.

Mahoney, T., 1997. 'Platonic Ecology: a Response to Plumwood's Critique of Plato', *Ethics and the Environment,* 2 (1) 25–42.

Mannison, D., 1980. 'A Critique of a Proposal for an "Environmental Ethic"' in Mannison, D. et al. (eds.) *Environmental Philosophy.* ANU, Canberra, pp. 52–64.

Mazama, A., 1994. 'The Relevance of Ngugi Wa Thiong'o for the African Quest', *The Western Journal of Black Studies,*18(4) 211–218.

Marglin, S., 1974. 'What Do Bosses Do?', *Review of Radical Political Economy,* 6 60–112.

Marglin, F.A., Marglin, S., 1990. *Dominating Knowledges: Development, Culture and Resistance.* Clarendon Press, Oxford.

Martin, E., 1995. 'Flexible Bodies: Health and Work in an Age of Systems', *The Ecologist,* 25(6) 221–226.

Mathews, F., 1991. 'Fertility Control in Wildlife: an Ethical Overview', *Habitat,* 19(1) 9–12.

—— 1994. 'Cultural Relativism and Environmental Ethics', *EWG Circular Letter,* 5.

—— 1997. 'Living with Animals', *Animal Issues,* 1(1) 4–20.

—— 2000. 'Ceres: Singing up the City', *PAN* 1(1) 5–15.

McKenna, E.,1995. 'Feminism and Vegetarianism: a Critique of Peter Singer', *Philosophy in the Contemporary World,* 1(3) Winter.

Mellor, M., 1997. *Feminism and Ecology.* Polity Press, Cambridge.

Memmi, A., 1965. *The Coloniser and the Colonised.* Orion Press, New York.

Merchant, C., 1980. *The Death of Nature.* Wildwood House, London.

—— 1995. *Earthcare.* Routledge, New York.

Midgley, M., 1983. *Animals and Why They Matter.* University of Georgia Press, Athens, GA.

—— 1996. *Utopias, Dolphins and Computers.* Routledge, London.

Mies, M., 1986. *Patriarchy and Accumulation on a World Scale.* Zed Books, London.

—— Shiva, V., 1993. *Ecofeminism.* Zed Books, London.

Minahen, C.D., 1997. 'Humanimals and Anihumans in Gary Larson's Gallery of the Absurd' in Ham, J., Senior, M. (eds.) *Animal Acts: Configuring the Human in Western History.* Routledge, London, pp. 231–251.

Murdoch, I., 1970. *The Sovereignty of Good.* Routledge and Kegan Paul, London.

Naess, A., 1973. 'The Shallow and the Deep, Long-range Ecology Movement: a Summary', *Inquiry,* 16(1) 95–100.

—— 1990. '"Man Apart" and Deep Ecology: A Reply to Reed', *Environmental Ethics,* 12 185–192.

Neidjie, B., 1986. *Kakadu Man.* Mybrood Publications, Canberra.

—— Taylor, K., 1989. *Story About Feeling.* Magabala Books, Broome, WA.

Newman, S.A., 1995. 'Carnal Boundaries: the Commingling of Flesh in Theory and Practice' in Birke, L., Hubbard, R. (eds.) *Reinventing Biology.* Indiana University Press, IN, pp. 191–227.

Noske, B., 1989. *Humans and Other Animals.* Pluto Press. London. [Reissued 1997 as *Beyond Boundaries: Humans and Animals.* Black Rose Books, Montreal.]

Norton, B., 1983. 'Environmental Ethics and Weak Anthropocentrism', *Environmental Ethics,* 6 211–224.

Norton, B., 1991. *Towards Unity Among Environmentalists.* Oxford University Press, New York.

O'Connor, J., 1998. *Natural Causes: Essays in Ecological Marxism.* The Guildford Press, New York.

Okin, S.M., 1989. *Gender, Justice and the Family.* Basic Books, New York.

Orr, D., 1992. *Ecological Literacy: Education and the Transition to a Postmodern World.* State University of New York Press, Albany, NY.

Orr, D., 1994. *Earth in Mind.* Island Press, Washington, DC.

Passmore, J., 1974. *Man's Responsibility for Nature*. Duckworth, London.

Pateman, C., 1989a. The Civic Culture: A Philosophic Critique. In: *The Disorder of Women*. Polity Press, Cambridge, pp. 141–178.

Patracca, M.P., (ed.) 1992. *The Politics of Interests*. Westview Press, Boulder, CO.

Pepper, D., 1993. *Eco-Socialism: from Deep Ecology to Social Justice*. Routledge, London.

Phillips, A., 1991. *Engendering Democracy*. Polity Press, Cambridge.

Pierce, C., 1979. 'Can Animals be Liberated?' *Philosophical Studies*, 36 69–75.

Plant, J., Plant C., 1992. *Putting Power in its Place*. New Society Publishers, Philadelphia PA.

Plumwood, V., 1982a. 'World Rainforest Destruction: the Social Factors', *The Ecologist*, 12(1) 4–22.

—— 1991a. 'Nature, Self and Gender: Feminism, Environmental Philosophy and the Critique of Rationalism', *Hypatia*, 6 13–27.

—— 1991b. 'Ethics and Instrumentalism: a Response to Janna Thompson', *Environmental Ethics*, 13 139–150.

—— 1992a. 'Conversations with Gaia', Newsletter on Feminism and Philosophy, *The American Philosophical Association*, 91(1) 61–65.

—— 1992b. 'SealsKin', *Meanjin*, 51(1) 45–58.

—— 1993a. *Feminism and the Mastery of Nature*. Routledge, London.

—— 1993b. 'The Politics of Reason: Towards a Feminist Logic', *Australasian Journal of Philosophy*, 71(4) 436–462. [Reprinted in Hass, M., Joffe Falmagne, R., 2002. *Feminist Approaches to Logic*. Rowman and Littlefield, Totowa NJ.]

—— 1995a. 'Feminism, Privacy, and Radical Democracy', *Anarchist Studies*, 3 97–120.

—— 1995b. 'Has Democracy Failed Ecology? an Ecofeminist Perspective', *Environmental Politics* 4 (4), Special Issue '*Ecology and Democracy*', 134–168.

—— 1996. 'Anthrocentrism and Androcentrism: Parallels and Politics', *Ethics and the Environment*, 1(2) 119–152.

—— 1997. 'Prospecting for Ecological Gold Among the Platonic Forms', *Ethics and the Environment*, 2(2) 149–168.

—— 1998a. 'Ecojustice, Inequality and Ecological Rationality'. In: Dryzek, D., Schlosberg, D. (eds.) *Debating the Earth: the Environmental Politics Reader*. Oxford University Press, Oxford, pp. 559–583.

—— 1998b. 'Knowledge in an Ethical Framework of Care', *Australian Journal of Environmental Management*, [Supp.] 5 27–38.

—— 1998c. 'Wilderness Skepticism and Wilderness Dualism'. In: J. B. Callicott and M.P. Nelson (eds.) *The Great New Wilderness Debate*. University of Georgia Press, Athens GA.

—— 2000. 'Integrating Ethical Frameworks for Animals, Humans and Nature', *Ethics and the Environment* 5(2), pp. 285–322.

—— 2001. 'Towards a Progressive Naturalism', *Capitalism, Nature, Socialism*. December (forthcoming).

—— 2002. 'Feminism and the Logic of Alterity' in Hass, M. and Falmagne, R. *Representing Reason*, Rowman and Littlefield, Totowa.

—— Routley, R., 1979. 'Against the Inevitability of Human Chauvinism' in Goodpaster, K.E., Sayre, K.M. (eds.) *Ethics and Problems of the 21st Century*. University of Notre Dame Press, Notre Dame, IN.

——, —— 1980. 'Destructive Forestry in Melanesia and Australia', *The Ecologist*, 10(1/2) 56–67.

Polanyi, K., 1994. *The Great Transformation*. Beacon Press, Boston, MA.

Price, J., 1999. *Flight Maps*. Basic Books, New York.

Proctor, R. 1993. 'Nazi Medicine and the Politics of Knowledge' in Harding, S. (ed.) *The Racial Economy of Science*. Indiana University Press, Indianapolis, pp. 344–358.

Prokhovnik, R., 1999. *Rational Woman*. Routledge, London.

Pusey, M., 1989. *Economic Rationalism in Canberra*. Cambridge University Press, Cambridge.

Quine, W.V.O, 1960. *Word and Object*. Wiley, New York.

Radford Ruether, R., 1975. *New Woman New Earth*. Seabury, Minneapolis, MN.

Ralston Saul, J., 1993. *Voltaire's Bastards: the Dictatorship of Reason in the West*. Penguin, London.

Reed, P., 1989. 'Man Apart: an Alternative to the Self-Realisation Approach', *Environmental Ethics*, 11 53–69.

Rogers, L.J., 1997. *Minds of Their Own: Thinking and Awareness in Animals*. Allen and Unwin, Sydney.

Relph, E., 1976. *Place and Placelessness*. Prion, London.

—— 1981. *Rational Landscapes and Humanistic Geography*. Croom Helm, London.

Rogers, R.A., 1995. *The Oceans Are Emptying: Fish Wars and Sustainability*. Black Rose Books, Montreal.

Rodd, R., 1992. *Biology, Ethics and Animals*. Clarendon, Oxford.

Rose, D.B., 1992. *Dingo Makes Us Human*. Cambridge University Press, Cambridge.

—— 1996. *Nourishing Terrains*. Australian Heritage Commission, Canberra.

Routley, R., 1984. 'Maximizing, Satisficing, Satisizing: Differences in Real and Rational Behaviour under rival paradigms', *Discussion Papers in Environmental Philosophy Series No. 10*, RSSS ANU.

Ruddick, S., 1989. *Maternal Thinking*. Beacon Press, Boston, MA.

Said, E., 1978. *Orientalism*. Vintage, New York.

Sale, K., 1980. *Human Scale*. Secker and Warburg, London.

—— 1992. '"Free and Equal Intercourse": The Decentralist Design' in Plant 1992, pp. 20–27.

Salleh, A., 1998. *Ecofeminism as Politics*. Zed Books, London.

Sanchez, C.L., 1993. 'Animal, Vegetable and Mineral: The Sacred Connection' in Adams, C.J. (ed.) *Ecofeminism and the Sacred*. Continuum, New York, pp. 207–228.

Seager, J., 1993. *Earth Follies: Feminism, Politics and the Environment*. Routledge, New York.

Seidler, V.J., 1994. *Unreasonable Men*. Routledge, London.

Skocpol, T., 1979. *States and Social Revolutions*. Cambridge University Press, Cambridge.

Shiva, V., 1988. *Staying Alive*. Zed Books, London.

—— 1994. 'The Seed and the Earth' in Shiva, V., Mies, M. (eds.) *Close to Home: Women Reconnect Ecology, Health and Development*. Earthscan, London.

—— 1995. 'Democratising Biology: Reinventing Biology from a Feminist, Ecological and Third World Perspective' in Birke, L., Hubbard, R. (eds.) *Reinventing Biology: Respect for Life and the Creation of Knowledge*. Indiana University Press, Bloomington.

Singer, P., 1980. 'Animals and the Value of Life' in Regan, T. (ed.) *Matters of Life and Death*, Random House, New York.

—— 1998. 'Ethics Across the Species Boundary' in Low, N. (ed.) *The Global Ethics of Environmental Justice*. Routledge, London, pp. 146–157.

—— Russell, D., 1997. 'An Interview with Professor Peter Singer', *Animal Issues*, 1(1) 37–44.

Smith, M., 1997. 'Against the Enclosure of the Ethical Commons: Radical Environmentalism as an "Ethics of Place"', *Environmental Ethics*, 18(1) 339–353.

Snow, C.P. *The Two Cultures and the Scientific Revolution*, Cambridge University Press, New York.

Snyder, G., 1990. *The Practice of the Wild*. North Point Press, New York.

Soule, M., Lease, G., 1995. *Reinventing Nature*, Island Press. Washington, DC.

Spretnak, C., 1989. 'Toward an Ecofeminist Spirituality' in Plant J. (ed) *Healing the wounds*. New Society Publishers, Philadelphia PA, pp. 127–132.

—— 1997a. *The Resurgence of the Real: Body, Nature and Place in a Hypermodern World*. Addison-Wesley, New York.

—— 1997b. 'Radical Nonduality in Ecofeminist Philosophy' in Warren, K.J. (ed.) *Ecofeminism: Women, Culture, Nature*. Indiana University Press, Indianapolis, IN, pp. 425–436.

Stamp Dawkins, M., 1998. *Through Our Eyes Only? The Search for Animal Consciousness.* Oxford University Press, Oxford.

Stanner, W.E.H., 1979. *White Man Got No Dreaming.* ANU Press, Canberra.

Steinbrecher, R.A., Mooney, P.R., 1998. 'Terminator Technology: the Threat to World Food Security', *The Ecologist,* 28(5) 276–279.

Stepan, N.L., 1993. 'Race and Gender: the Role of Analogy in Science' in Harding, S. (ed.) *The Racial Economy of Science.* Indiana University Press, Indianapolis, IN, pp. 359–376.

Stilber, J., 1998. *Opening Address,* World Conference of Philosophy, Boston, MA.

Takaki, R.T., 1979. *Iron Cages.* Knopf, New York.

Taylor, A., 1996. 'Animal Rights and Human Needs', *Environmental Ethics,* 18 249–264.

Tierney, P., 2000. *Darkness in El Dorado.* W.W. Norton, New York.

Thompson, J., 1990. 'A refutation of environmental ethics', *Environmental Ethics,* 12 147–160.

—— 1996 'Towards a Green World Order: Environment and World Politics' in Mathews, F. (ed.) *Ecology and Democracy.* Frank Cass, Portland, OR, pp. 31–48.

Tilman, D., Cohen, J.E., 1996. 'Biosphere2 and Biodiversity: the Lessons So Far', *Science,* November 1150–1151.

Tronto, J.C., 1993. *Moral Boundaries: a Political Argument for an Ethic of Care.* Routledge, London.

UNEP 1997, 1999. United Nation's Environment Program. *The Global Environmental Outlook,* New York.

Walker, M.U., 1995. 'Moral Understandings: Alternative 'Epistemology' for a Feminist Ethics' in Held, V. (ed.), *Justice and Care: Essential Readings in Feminist Ethics.* Westview Press, Boulder, CO, pp. 139–152.

—— 1998. *Moral Understandings: a Feminist Study in Ethics.* Routledge, New York.

Walls, L.D., 1995. *Seeing New Worlds: Henry David Thoreau and Nineteenth Century Natural Science.* University of Wisconsin Press, Madison, WI.

Warren, K.J., 1990. 'The power and promise of ecological feminism', *Environmental Ethics,* 12(2) 121–146.

—— 2000. *Ecofeminist Philosophy: a Western Perspective on What it is and Why it Matters.* Rowman and Littlefield, New York.

Waring, M., 1988. *Counting for Nothing.* Allen and Unwin, Sydney.

Walzer, M.L., 1983. *Spheres of Justice.* Basic Books, New York.

Weaver, J. (ed.), 1996. *Defending Mother Earth: Native American Perspectives on Environmental Justice.* Orbis Books, Maryknoll, NY.

Weil, S., 1987. *The Need for Roots.* ARK Paperbacks, London and New York.

Weston, A., 1992. *Towards Better Problems.* Temple University Press, Philadelphia, PA.

—— 1996. 'Self-Validating Reduction: Toward a Theory of Environmental Devaluation', *Environmental Ethics,* 18 115–132.

—— 1997. *A Practical Companion to Ethics.* Oxford University Press, Oxford.

—— 1998. 'Universal Consideration as an Originary Practice', *Environmental Ethics,* 20 279–289.

—— 2001. *A 21st Century Ethical Tool-Box.* Oxford University Press, Oxford.

Williams, B., 1992. 'Must a concern for the environment be centred on human beings?' in Taylor, C. (ed.), *Ethics and the Environment.* Corpus Christi College, Oxford.

Wittgenstein, L. 1953 *Philosophical Investigations.* Macmillan, New York.

Wood, C., 1998. 'Our Dying Oceans', *Macleans Magazine,* October, 5 50–59.

Yencken, D., 2000. 'Sustainable Australia: Refocussing Government', Tela Series, ACF and Nature and Society Forum.

Young, I., 1989. 'Polity and Group Difference: a Critique of the Idea of Universal Citizenship', *Ethics,* 99 250–274.

Young, I.M., 1990. 'The Ideal of Community and the Politics of Difference' in Nicholson, L.J. (ed.) *Feminism/Postmodernism.* Routledge, London, pp. 300–323.

Young, I., 1991. *Justice and the Politics of Difference.* Princeton University Press, Princeton.

——— 1995. 'Communication and the Other: Beyond Deliberative Democracy' in Wilson, M., Yeatman, A. (eds.) *Justice and Identity.* Allen and Unwin, Wellington, pp. 134–152.

——— 1997a. *Intersecting Voices: Dilemmas of Gender, Political Philosophy and Policy.* Princeton University Press, Princeton.

——— 1997b. 'House and Home: Feminist Variations on a Theme' in *Intersecting Voices: Dilemmas of Gender, Political Philosophy and Policy.* Princeton University Press, Princeton.

Young, O., 1999. 'Fairness Matters: the Role of Equity in International Regime Formation' in Low, N. (ed.) *Global Ethics and Environment.* Routledge, London, pp. 247–263.

Zimmerman, M.E., 1994. *Contesting Earth's Future: Radical Ecology and Postmodernity.* University of California Press, Berkeley, CA.

——— 1995. 'Ecofascism: A Threat to American Environmentalism', *Social Theory and Practice,* 21(2) 207–238.

Index

activism 10, 111–14, 123, 126–8, 131, 136, 143, 153–5, 196, 197, 202 (*see also* traitorous identity)
Adams, C. 156, 158, 247, 259, 260
Aditjondro, G. 64, 247
agency, hegemonic construction of 17, 27–37, 99, 104–6, 109–11, 214–17
agency of nature, nonhumans 40, 49, 51, 54, 56, 110–11, 206, 214–17, 227–9, 243, 253, 263
agriculture, 1, 2, 34, 38
    agricultural land 1,2, 15, 38
    rationalist agriculture 2, 15, 27, 34, 38, 116, 117, 119, 144, 153–66, 192 (*see also* factory farming)
Afrocentrism 256
anarchism 66, 78
Andrews, J. 262–4
animals 2, 15, 18, 19, 27–9, 54, 56, 59, 106, 111, 119, 141, 143–66, 186, 189, 190, 197, 199, 204, 223, 243, 254, 255, 257–62, 264
    animal defence 143–66
    animal liberation 126
    animality 42, 56, 100, 106, 111
    contracts with 161–6
androcentrism 30, 32, 99, 100–6, 118, 124, 138, 148, 187, 205, 245, 246, 255, 256
anthropocentrism (human-centredness) 10–12, 26, 32, 43, 45, 48, 51–3, 56–61, 77, 91, 97–100, 106–9, 114, 123–42, 147, 143–52, 167, 168, 175–7, 180, 181, 190, 191, 193, 197, 201, 202, 205, 218, 220, 221, 223–5, 227, 245, 247, 248, 251, 253–6

activism and 111–14, 123, 126–8, 131, 136
cosmic 123–42, 254–6
countering 111–14, 147
defenders of 115, 123–42, 254–6
ecocentrism and 256
egocentric parallel 128–42
inevitability of 124, 127–42
liberation model 97–122, 136–8
locatedness confusion 130–9
logic of 106–10
subtle forms of 115, 143–53
anthropology 54
anthropomorphism 56–61, 193
    weak, 57
appropriation 17, 19, 27–37, 100
    and hyperbolised autonomy 30
    model of anthropocentrism 100, 105, 111
    naturalising 30, 100
Aristotle 20, 30, 67, 97, 104, 151
Arluke, A. and Boria, S. 266
Asante, M.F. 256
assimilation (incorporation) 60, 104–5, 108, 109, 111, 115, 138, 143–52, 167, 201, 203, 204, 259, 261, 264
    and injustice 115
Australian Aboriginal people 101, 104, 105, 203
autarchy 74–80
authoritarianism 62, 63, 70, 71
autonomy, hyperbolised 4, 17, 27–37, 61, 98, 100, 104, 110,111, 226–7

Babe 160–6
backgrounding (*see also* hegemonic constructions of agency, hyperbolised

autonomy, denial) 17, 27, 28, 30–1, 98, 99, 100, 104–10
Bacon F. 55, 244, 245
Bartlett, R. 68, 247
Baumann, Z. 209, 254, 266
Beamish, R. 40
bears 117
Beck, U. 84, 90
Beck, U., Giddens, A. and Lash, S. 65
Benhabib, S. 265
Benjamin, J. 247, 265
Benton, T. 253, 259, 261
Berndt, C. and Berndt, R. 232
Beston, H. 100, 262
bioregionalism 72, 74–80, 88, 207, 248, 249
biosphere 2, 121, 243
Birch, T. 258, 262, 263
Birke, L. 191, 265
Birke, L. and Hubbard, R. 262, 263
blindspots 2, 10, 16, 23, 25–31, 45, 97–100, 117–22
body (embodiment) 5, 15, 17, 19, 20, 24, 34, 42, 46, 93, 97, 110–12, 156–66, 171, 179, 190–2, 198, 201, 219, 220, 222–5, 246 (*see also* dualisms: mind/body)
Bok, G. and James, S. 259
Bookchin, M. 257
Bordo, S. 244
Brennan, Teresa 7, 15, 22, 41, 241, 242
Buber, M. 198
Buddhism 199, 265
Business Man 28, 30
Butler, Bishop 134, 255

capitalism 6, 9, 12, 14–16, 21, 28, 45, 62, 66, 90, 99, 204, 207, 210–12, 214–17 (*see also* property)
    global 9, 15, 16, 62, 64–6, 73
    'natural' 6
    and science 39–41
care perspectives 35, 36, 42, 43, 53, 112, 113, 116, 138–42, 169, 171, 186–8, 258
Carlyle, T. 245
Carter, A. 66, 244, 247
Cartesianism 49, 57, 59, 61, 143–9, 151–3, 157, 159, 161, 163, 164, 176, 178, 179, 184, 185
    neo-Cartesianism 175, 178, 179, 245
    post-Cartesian 176, 179

Cavarero, A. 246
centrism (hegemonic) 4, 10, 11, 14, 28, 29, 71, 74, 76, 79, 80, 97–106, 110–11, 117–22, 138, 139, 167, 168, 170, 252, 255
    counter strategy for 111–14
    economic 110–11
    and egocentrism 134–42
    hegemonic form 252
    illusions of 117–22
    logical structure of 100–6, 139, 197, 201, 202, 252
Chassudovsky, M. 242
Cheney, J. and Weston, A. 264, 265
Chief Seattle 225, 226
Chodorow, N. 256
Christian rationalism 218–22, 252
civic republicanism 92
civilisation 19, 20, 102, 104, 105, 117, 257
    classical 19, 20, 102, 104, 105
    and reason 20
class 2, 20; 84, 85, 93, 94, 96, 110–11, 204, 250, 251
Code, L. 243
Cohen, J. 247
Coleridge, S.T. 245
collectivity 82, 83, 86–91,110, 152 ff, 186
Collins, D. and Barkdull, J. 88, 89
colonisation 20, 21, 28, 29, 49, 59, 60, 76, 102–6, 118, 141, 200, 203–5, 209, 214, 256, 257, 264
    colonising patterns 14, 15, 28, 76, 100–6, 173, 256, 264
commodification 5, 6, 12, 16, 22, 27, 34, 41, 45, 99, 117, 143–66, 190, 192, 211–13, 229–35, 260
common good, politics of 83, 84, 92
communication 19, 51, 56, 61, 63, 71, 73, 87, 89–91, 93–6, 122, 140, 142, 144, 161–9, 174, 175, 178–81, 188–97, 202, 206, 213, 227–32, 254, 264
communitarianism 84, 92
communities 73–8, 207–9
    autarchic 74–6, 78
    defined by shared ecological consequences 75
    interspecies 152 ff, 186–8, 198, 199
    local 74–6, 78
compliance 62, 63, 71
conflict resolution 19, 33, 89, 138–42, 193, 196–201

consciousness (sentience, awareness) (*see also* mind)
consumption, linked with production 16, 71, 74, 77
continuity
    affirmation of 201, 202, 204
    (of planetary life) 17, 101–3, 107, 108, 143–5, 148, 152, 155, 206, 227
Convergence Principle 125, 126
Cook, J. 267
Copernicus 130, 131, 255
correctiveness 1, 9, 16, 24, 40, 41, 45, 64–8, 71–80, 82
cosmic (rationalist) anthropocentrism 123–39, 254–6
counter-hegemonic ethics (stances, virtues) 10, 111, 124, 167, 168, 174, 175, 181, 183, 185–6, 194, 195, 206
counter-hegemonic methodology (*see also* "studying up") 11, 56, 111, 145, 167–70, 173, 174, 183–5, 189, 190, 194, 206, 261, 262, 264
counter-hegemonic spirituality 222–7
coverture 208, 210–12, 260
crocodiles 117
cultural studies 52, 53
    classical 19, 20
    of consumption 87
    difference 58, 59
culture 3–4, 5, 8, 15, 17, 20, 42, 87
    democratic 91
    rationalist 31–7
    reason-emotion dualism in 42
    'two cultures' division 51–6
culture/nature dualism 4, 29, 35, 51–6, 61, 112
Cuomo, C. 258
Curthoys, A. 262

Darwin, C. 55, 56
de Beauvoir, S. 100, 104
Dean, J. 251
decision-making, distortions of 2, 3, 62–5, 71–96
deep ecology 111, 114, 125, 137, 196–217, 255, 265
    and cosmic anthropocentrism 255, 256
    and deep pockets 211–13
    politics of 207–17
    transpersonal 202, 265

deep/shallow contrast 114, 123, 125, 127, 207
Deloria, V. 214, 215
dematerialisation 6, 8
democracy, 2, 3, 7, 8, 65, 70, 72–4, 82, 83, 90–2, 94, 95, 98, 173, 208, 247, 248, 250, 251, 266
    communicative 93–6
    deep/shallow 65, 82, 87, 91
    deliberative 87, 88, 90–2
    discursive 92
    economic 83
    liberal 2, 72, 74, 81–8
    participatory 91–3
    procedural 93–6
    radical 88
denial (of dependency) 4, 5, 15, 17, 19, 24, 27–9, 34, 35, 49, 104–10, 112, 113, 120, 121, 139, 140, 200, 201, 206, 225, 242, 252
    ecological 97–110, 252
Dennett, D. 143, 145, 183–6, 263, 264
Descartes, R. 49, 57, 59, 61, 143, 148, 149, 176 (*see also* Cartesianism, neo-Cartesianism)
Dewey, J. 73, 248
dialogical ethics 11, 33, 169, 170, 175, 178, 188–95
    and conflict resolution, 19, 33, 89, 142, 193
Diamond, J. 117
dichotomy, distinct from dualism 101, 201 (*see also* hyper-separation)
difference, respect for 59, 93–6, 103, 112, 113, 180, 193–5, 203, 204, 251 (*see also* homogenisation, assimilation)
    axis of equality 167, 168, 172
    and deep ecology 196–206
    as incommensurability (heterogeneity) 172, 173, 178–80
    as inferiority 104–6
Dillard, A. 54
discontinuity, human/animal 59 (*see also* hyperseparation, dualism)
disengagement 17, 20, 31–9, 41–5, 53–6, 62, 80, 93, 202, 241, 244, 249, 265 (*see also* impartiality, dualisms: reason/emotion)
    in ethics, as universalist/impersonalist tradition 114, 124, 130, 131, 134–42, 148–51, 187, 188, 190, 241

ideology of 42–5, 53
and power 43
and subject/object dualism 41–5
distribution *see also* redistribution, marginality 82–4, 90
and ecological vulnerability 84–7
diZerega, G. 210, 212, 214, 266
Dobson, A. 126, 254
dogs 13, 160–6, 264
dolphins 163
double gesture (of exclusion) 151, 152, 164
Dowie, M. 250
Dryzek, J. 67, 68, 70, 72, 77, 82, 92, 241, 242, 247–9, 265, 266
dualisms (splitting) 4, 17, 19, 20, 29, 31–7, 101–3, 108, 110, 244, 266, 267
    as distinct from dichotomy 101
        human/nature 4, 10, 19, 43, 51–3, 57, 97–100, 107, 108, 123, 168, 170, 180
        male/female 4, 20
        mind/body 4, 15, 19, 20, 34, 75, 110–11, 178, 179, 190–2
        nature/culture 4, 29, 35, 51–6, 61, 111
        reason/emotion 4, 9, 10, 20, 22, 31–7, 42, 53, 80, 103, 159–66, 266
        reason/nature 4, 5, 17–19, 91, 93
        respect/use 27, 34, 143–66, 212
        subject/object 9, 10, 20, 27, 34, 41, 42, 46–56, 244, 246
    logical structure of 102–6
    person/property 9, 20, 27, 34, 41, 60, 99, 111, 143, 147, 152, 159–66
    prudence/ethics 9, 11, 20, 80, 99, 124, 128, 129
        gender coding 9, 10, 17, 19, 20–2, 32–7, 42, 103
        and knowledge 20, 21
        and rationalism 20
    public/private 32, 159–66
    self/other 66, 196–207
    theory/practice 75, 110
        and spirituality 222–7
ducks 163, 165
During, S. 200

Earth Summit 70
Eckersley, R. 256
ecofeminism 11, 218, 219, 226–7, 267

EcoGuardians 62, 63, 68
ecohumanities 8, 10, 52–6
ecojustice (environmental justice) 72, 73, 82, 84, 89, 90, 250
    and empowerment of the vulnerable 89, 90
ecology 2, 10, 45, 52, 54, 67
    as crisis of reason 15 ff, 97, 98
    ecological communication 65, 71, 77, 86
    ecological crisis 1, 2, 5, 15, 40, 45, 62, 65, 69, 70, 97, 98, 178
    ecological decision-making 62–5, 71–87
    ecological denial (*see also* denial, ecological)
    ecological education 111–14, 142
    ecological embeddedness 3, 16, 24, 25, 29, 45, 67–70, 97–100, 108, 112, 123, 171
    ecological failure/damage 5, 45, 64, 67–71, 73, 76, 83, 111, 117, 119, 121, 140
    ecological oligarchy 62, 63, 64, 71
    ecological priority 69, 82
    ecological rationality 15, 18, 62, 67–89, 91, 92, 99, 100, 178, 185
    ecological reductionism 69
    ecological responsibility 36, 62, 72, 79, 80, 91
    ecological systems 7
    public ecological morality 87
economic centrism 110–11
economic fundamentalism 22
economic liberalism 65
economic rationalism (*see also* neo-liberalism) 17, 21–31, 39, 45, 65, 66, 242
    and gender 31–7
    and historic rationalist imaginary 17, 19, 22, 31
    and modern (economic) rationalist imaginary 21, 22–37
    and nature 28, 30
    and science 39–41, 45
economism 22
ecorationalism 62–4
EcoRepublic 3, 62–5, 68–72, 74, 80, 90
egocentrism (egoism) 23, 66, 80, 81, 116, 117, 124, 129, 134–8, 199, 200, 202 (*see also* dualisms: self/other)
elephants 2, 112
Emerson, R. 245

emotionality 5, 19, 20, 31–7, 42, 46, 53, 62, 103, 107, 112, 135, 140, 155–66, 258
empire, (*see also* centrism)
  British colonial 101–6
  of the farm 161
  of reason 62
  Roman 62
empiricism 46–50, 245
  rationalist–empiricist model 47–50, 52, 245
    empiricist transition 47–50
    and subject/object dualism 45–56
enclosures 24
energy consumption/efficiency 2, 6, 7, 79, 80, 249
England, P. 242, 243
enlightened self-interest 115–17
Enlightenment 43, 47, 48, 50, 150, 208, 221, 258
  empiricist transition in 47–50
environmental ethics 115
  anthropocentrism in 115
environmental (eco) harms 83, 84, 251
  ecological vulnerability
  generalisable 84, 92
  redistributable 84–6
environmental history 54
epistemology
  complex 82
  empiricism 46–50
  equality 17, 20, 64, 65, 79, 80, 82, 90, 93–6, 151
  equality, distributive 65, 83, 87, 89, 90, 93–6
  inequality 17, 20, 64, 65, 74, 81–7, 89, 90, 93–6, 102, 110 (*see also* ecojustice)
  interspecies egalitarianism 169, 172–4, 186 (*see also* non-ranking, counter-hegemonic methodology)
  moral 44, 51–6, 98, 99, 104, 169, 173–6, 178–80, 184, 187
  rationalist 41–5
  rationalist-empiricism 46–50
  rationalist imaginary of 47–50
  transfer across social spheres 74, 82, 89
ethical economy 80, 154, 160–6
ethical minimalism 143–7, 152
ethical stance of openness 11, 45, 56,

142–66, 153–5 168, 169, 173–6, 178–81
  (*see also* moral epistemology)
ethics 9, 11, 20, 31, 35, 52, 73, 167–96
  communicative 168, 169, 188–95
  conflict resolution 19, 33, 89, 138–42, 193
  contextual 154, 168–70, 173, 187–9, 262
  dialogical 11, 33, 169, 170, 175, 178, 188–95
  double disembedment 36
  hyper-separated from prudence 9, 11, 16, 32, 44, 45, 68, 73, 80, 124, 128, 129, 138–42
  partnership 3, 11, 36, 55, 68, 80, 124, 134–42
  rationalist universalist/impersonalist tradition 114, 124, 130, 131, 134–42, 148–51, 187, 188, 190
  and moral epistemology, (*see also* epistemology: moral)
  vegetarian 154–66
  and economic rationalism 31–7
  and private sphere 36, 180–6
  in rationalist imaginary 33–6
  and women/feminism 35, 36, 187–8
eurocentrism 59, 99, 100–6, 118, 124, 178, 191, 214–17, 256, 260
externality 4, 21, 28, 77–80, 110–11, 249
extinction 2, 38, 125

factory farming 2, 15, 27, 34, 38, 117, 119, 144, 153–66, 192, 260 (*see also* rationalism: agriculture)
FAO 242
federation 78, 249
feminism 106, 124, 127, 137, 138, 151, 152, 187, 197, 200, 201, 204, 205, 207, 210, 246, 248, 256, 261, 262, 267
  and philosophy 11, 35, 179, 187, 201, 242–4, 246, 247, 256, 261
Ferry, L. 208, 266
Feyerabend, P. 244
fisheries 1,2, 14, 25, 26, 34, 38–41, 45, 83, 119, 121, 128, 242
flexibility 62, 63, 71, 77, 88, 248
forest fires 64–6, 70, 71, 80, 92
forestry science 38
forests 2, 8, 15, 25, 38, 64–6, 69, 70, 71, 80, 82, 83, 247
  collective action problem 83, 250
Fox, W. 137, 255

Fox Keller, E. 42, 46, 244, 246
Frank, T. 242
Fraser, N. 83, 94, 243, 250, 251
Friedman, M. 114, 115, 241, 253, 262
Frye, M. 100, 104, 253, 256

Galapagos 56
Galtung, J. 75, 79, 249
Gare, A. 265
geese 165
gender 83, 93, 98, 234, 246, 252, 255–7, 261, 262
    and empiricist transition 47–56
    metaphors in rationalist imaginary 34–7
    and reason 17–20, 22–37, 46, 83, 98, 202
    and science 42, 47, 48, 50–6
    and 'two cultures' knowledge division 51–6
genetic engineering 34, 38, 49, 108, 243
Gifford, E. and Cook, R.M. 267
Gilligan, C. 187, 194, 244, 259, 264
global market 7, 14, 21, 62, 63, 71, 80, 81
    global capitalism 9, 15, 21, 62, 63, 66, 80
global warming 2, 6, 7, 10, 15, 38, 64, 69, 128
globalisation 29, 36, 75, 79–81, 249
    as centric system 29, 75, 79, 80, 110–11
Gomez-Pompa, A. and Kaus, A. 267
gorillas 2, 182
Gould, S.J. 245
Greeks 46
Grey, W. 130–5, 137, 138, 254, 255
Griffin, S. 267
Grimshaw. J. 256
Gross, E. 4, 241, 242
Gross, R. 265

Habermas, J. 92, 94, 265
Haller, S. 10
Hampton, S. 141, 256, 257
Haraway, D. 228, 243, 244, 247, 268
Hardin, G. 64
Harding, S. 44, 243–8, 262, 266
Harris, M. 242, 243
Hartsock, N. 100, 252
Hayden, D. 268
Hayward, T. 43, 73, 130, 244, 247, 248, 254, 255
health, human 15, 17, 70, 71, 82, 85, 87, 128

planetary 15, 69, 85, 99, 112, 121
    and vulnerability, marginality 85–7
hegemonic construals of agency 27, 30–1, 35, 61, 78, 99, 104–6, 110–11, 214, 217
    and intellectual property rights 30
hegemony 20, 43, 86, 87, 89, 90, 93, 95, 99, 167, 168, 170, 173, 176, 178, 181, 182, 185, 193, 202, 204, 207, 210, 213, 244
Held, V. 187, 243, 264
hens 165, 191–2
Heraclitus 51
heterocentrism 124
Hickory, S. 260
hierarchy (of species) 20, 1468, 153, 161–6, 169, 262 (*see also* interspecies: egalitarianism, non-ranking)
Hitler 218
homogenisation (substitutability) 25, 26, 29, 107, 108, 112
hooks, b. 241, 265
hubris 1, 2, 25
humans (*see also* human/nature dualism)
    decentring 168, 169, 176, 194–5, 202–6
    identity 4, 8, 9, 98–100, 169, 188ff, 196, 198, 200, 258
    situated ecologically 54, 97–100
human-centredness (*see also* anthropocentrism)
human/nature dualism (*see also* polarisation, hyper-separation) 4, 10, 19, 43, 51–3, 57, 97–100, 107, 108, 123, 132, 143–52, 155, 168–70, 176, 180, 189, 194–202
human self-enclosure 97, 98 (*see also* anthropocentrism)
humanism 147, 148, 150, 151, 197, 207, 208, 258
humanities 52–4 (*see also* ecohumanities)
Humboldt, A. von 55, 56
Hyde, L. 227, 228, 262, 268
hyperbolised autonomy 4, 27, 30, 34, 104–5, 110, 214–17, 225–7
    and intellectual property rights 30
    and reason 30
    and separative self 30
hypercar 6
hyper-separation (*see also* polarisation) 4, 52, 56, 61, 80, 101–3, 110, 178, 179, 196, 198, 201–6
    of cross-species vocabularies 56, 61, 108, 175, 193

idealism 52, 53, 260
identification 17, 22, 102, 196–206
illusions (*see also* blindspots) 2, 3, 16, 17,
    26–31, 34, 40, 45, 51, 95, 97–100,
    117–22, 132, 186, 189, 198, 253
  of disembeddedness, 97–100, 108, 109,
    112, 120, 121, 132
  of hyperbolised autonomy 9, 16–18, 26,
    27, 120
  of invulnerability for privileged groups
    84, 85
  of rationalist imaginary 97–100
impartiality 20, 31, 32
(*see also* disengagement: in ethics, as
    universalist/impersonalist tradition,
    objectivity)
incommensurability (*see also* difference) 172,
    173, 178–80
incorporation *see* assimilation
indigenous people 54, 101, 102, 104–7, 118,
    157, 167, 177, 200, 202, 203,
    214–17, 225–7, 234, 260, 261, 267
individualism (*see also* communities,
    hyperbolised autonomy, privatisation)
    48, 49, 66, 78, 116, 152, 186, 187,
    207–10, 214–17
Indonesia 64, 80
industrial revolution 24
instrumentalism 9, 11, 35, 38, 39, 42, 43, 46,
    48, 49, 55, 95, 105, 106, 109–11, 116,
    117, 123, 124, 129,139, 140–2, 144,
    146–9, 157, 158, 164, 165, 185, 196, 201,
    210, 212, 219–21, 229, 233, 234, 247,
    248, 253, 254
intellectualist (cognitivist) fallacy of
    rationalism 98, 174, 175, 177, 178, 180,
    184, 185, 187, 191–3, 223, 262
Intentional (Recognition) Stance 149, 174,
    176–86, 223, 226
  and performativity 184, 185, 223, 262
intentionality 45, 54, 56, 59, 61, 149, 150, 157,
    175–80, 180–6, 193, 223, 246, 262, 263
interspecies
  conflict cases 125–7, 143, 145, 146,
    196–202
  conflict resolution, 19, 33, 89, 142, 193
  difference, respect for 59, 188–95
  egalitarianism 169, 172–4, 186 (*see also*
    non-ranking, counter-hegemonic
    methodology)

justice 115–17, 169, 186–8, 190
  negotiation (*see also* dialogical ethics)
    169, 170, 175, 178, 188–95
  representation 58–61
intrinsic value 123–31, 146, 180, 181, 186,
    188, 199, 206
Irigaray, Luce 179
Irish famine 24
irrationalism 18, 29–37, 208
irrationality (of rationalism) 16, 18, 29–37,
    41, 61, 66, 69, 72, 80, 97–100, 103
  of altruism 32–3
  of ethics (in rationalist imaginary) 32
  of the Other (in rationalist imaginary)
    101–6

Jefferson, T. 212, 214, 267
Jennings, A. 242, 243
Jennings, C. and Jennings, B. 250
Johnson, M. 244, 263
Jones, R.C. 252
justice 11, 35, 36, 65, 73, 80, 94, 115–17,
    145, 146, 153, 157, 241, 255, 257–9 (*see
    also* ecojustice)
  and care 187, 188, 241, 259
  interspecies distributive 117
  interspecies justice 114–17, 168, 169,
    171, 186–8, 190

kangaroos 163
Kant, I. 115, 129
Kheel, M. 256
knowledge 3, 9, 41–56 (*see also* science,
    scientists)
  ecohumanities 8, 10, 52–6
  imaged as sexual violence, significance
    of 47–51
  sado-dispassionate 2, 22, 31–7, 39,
    41–50, 53, 55, 61
  subject/subject models 46
  two cultures' knowledge division 51–6
Kuhn, T. 244

Larson, G. 266
Latour, B. 244
Latour, B. and Woolgar, S. 244
Leopold, A. 54, 183
Liar Paradox 96

liberalism 2, 3, 60, 65, 74, 78, 81–7, 89–91, 208–17, 252
  classical 88
  and distributive equality 83, 93–6
  failure of ecological rationality 83–7
  failure to register ecological vulnerability 86, 93–6
  interest group interpretation 82, 83, 87, 89
  public sphere 86, 89–96
liberation model of anthropocentrism 106–10, 114, 134–42
liberation movements 11, 100–6, 111, 113, 124, 126, 127, 153, 154, 166, 205, 206, 252
limits 16, 23, 26, 27, 29, 35, 40, 43, 69, 70, 85, 99, 104, 105, 121, 122, 139, 140
  insensitivity to on the part of privilege 85, 103, 105, 106, 108, 109, 112–13, 121–2
literature 54
lizards 165
Lloyd, G. 248
Lockean concept of property 21, 146, 204, 210, 214–17, 229, 253
logic 3, 4, 9, 14, 23, 33, 101–6, 117–22
  of centrism 101–6, 117–22
  of the global market 14, 23
  monological 3, 4, 9, 33
Longino, H. 245
Lovins, A. 7, 111, 241
Luke, B. 170, 174, 258, 262
lyrebirds 192, 230

McClintock, B. 246
McKenna, E. 258
Mackinnon, C. 256
Mahoney, T. 247
Malthus, T. 69
managers, rational 110, 111
Mannison. D. 130, 254
Marcuse, H. 67
marginality 21, 68, 70, 73, 83, 84, 87, 89, 91, 93–6, 99, 110–11, 250 (*see also* privilege)
  and vulnerability 84–7, 250
Marglin, S. and Apfel-Marglin, F. 75, 110, 247, 249, 253
market 210–12, 232, 233

  as disengaged, impartial 22, 23, 31, 32
  dissociation of 71–80
  dualisms and 27
  failure to register ecological vulnerability 86
  free (disembedded) 21–4, 64
  as gendered 31–7
  global 7, 9, 24, 70, 71, 74, 80, 121
  as information system 86
  maximising forms of 26
  and nature 2
  and neo-liberalism 24
  as rational god 23
  as rational mechanism 22, 23
Martin, E. 248, 263
Marxism 3, 39, 66, 67, 253, 267
master subjects 17, 28, 32, 98–100 (*see also* othering (the Other))
  Business Man 32
  Man of Property 32, 207, 211–17
  Rational Economic Man 8, 31
materialist spirituality 222–3, 267
materiality 19, 42, 46, 171, 179–80, 218–33, 245 (*see also* body)
Mathews, F. 246, 247, 261, 265, 268
Mathieson, P. 218
maximisations 30, 33, 34, 66, 67, 81, 118–20, 159
Mazama, A. 253, 256
meat, concept of 155–66, 260
mechanism, 40, 42, 46, 48, 49, 54, 57, 108, 109, 120, 143, 146, 157, 179, 197, 201, 227–9, 243, 246, 262, 264. (*see also* intentionality, Intentional Stance, Descartes, Cartesianism)
Mellor, M. 267
Memmi, A. 100, 252, 253
Merchant, C. 11, 48, 243–5, 254, 267
Midgley, M. 56, 57, 157, 242, 247, 257, 259, 261, 266
Mies, M. 243
Mill, J.S. 73
Minahen, C. 266
mind (*see also* intentionality) 45, 46, 49, 51, 56, 61, 168, 169, 172, 174–80, 192, 218–23, 243, 263, 264
  as consciousness 143–52, 176–86
  incommensurability (heterogeneity) of 172, 173, 178–80

Minimalism (in ethics) 143–7, 152, 258
monological relationships 4, 9, 14–16, 18,
19, 24, 26, 29, 33, 34, 40, 42, 45, 46, 49,
51, 53, 54, 63, 64, 98, 111, 177, 178, 184,
190, 193–5, 229, 233, 234
logic 4, 9, 33
models 11, 18
systems 9, 24
moral dualism 143–46, 152, 155, 164, 168,
196, 206, 210, 259, 260
moral epistemology 44, 50–6, 98, 99, 104,
169, 173–76, 178–180, 184, 187
moral extensionism (*see also* assimilation,
persons) 143–66, 168, 196, 197, 202,
210, 259, 260
mountains 196, 197, 263
Murdoch, I. 187, 264
mutuality 19, 33, 46, 122, 140–2, 175, 193,
194, 197, 202, 206

Naess, A. 137, 196–200, 207, 208, 213
Natural Capitalism 6–7
naturalising 67, 99
appropriation 17, 19, 27–31, 35–7, 101,
103–6, 203, 214–17
oppression 17, 18, 36, 99–106
nature 5, 11, 16, 17, 21, 26, 27, 30, 34, 45,
46, 49, 51, 73, 85, 89, 97, 104, 123–42,
168, 169, 172–4, 245, 250, 252
as agent 214–17, 227–9, 233
denial, profound forgetting of 28, 30,
100–10, 225
as externality (in economic rationalist
imaginary) 28
as lacking agency, autonomy 35, 40, 45–
51, 55, 56, 214–17
as mindful 51, 56, 61, 174–80
as (narrative) subject 45–56, 227–35
as Other 106–11
as resource 110–11
undamaged 85, 87, 250
Nazism 44, 206–10, 266
Neidjie, B. 225–7, 268
neo-Cartesianism 143–53, 159, 164, 175,
178, 179, 202
neo-liberalism 24–31, 80 (*see also* economic
rationalism)
Newman, S.A. 243
Nicholson, L. 243
Nicomachean Ethics 98

non-ranking 147, 148, 150, 151, 168–74,
257, 262
Norton, B. 125–7, 254
Noske, B. 157

objectivity 43–5, (*see also* disengagement)
oceans 2, 7, 15, 25, 69, 242
Ockemism 51, 246
Okin, S.M. 210, 243
Ophuls, W. 64
oppression 36, 44, 97–110, 204, 206, 252,
253
orang-utans 2, 64
Orientalism 100–6
Orr, D. 242
Othering (the Other) 4, 11, 16, 17, 19, 22, 28,
30, 33–7, 44, 87, 100–6, 114–20, 122,
127, 138, 139, 157, 167–9, 202, 205, 206,
252, 253, 258
and justice 114–17
of nature 106–11

palm oil industry 64
Parry, B. 105
parsimony versus generosity 143, 175, 185,
194
participation 74, 76, 91, 92
partnership model (*see also* dialogical ethics)
3, 11, 36, 55, 68, 80, 124,
138–42, 167, 189–95, 214–17
and conflict resolution 11, 33, 138–42,
169, 170, 175, 178, 188–95
dysfunctional partnership 11, 134–42
and property 214–17
Passenger Pigeon 125, 183
Passmore, J. 219, 254, 267
Pateman, C. 86, 89, 94, 96, 210, 250, 251,
261
penguins 13–15, 163
Pepper, D. 248
persons (*see also* moral extensionism, human/
nature dualism) 143–152
pets 144, 160–6, 260, 261, 264
Phillips, A. 251
philosophy 11, 113, 123, 124, 127, 128, 131,
134–7, 143–5, 147, 167–72, 174, 179,
183, 196, 202, 257, 258, 264 (*see also*
counter-hegemonic methodology)
pigs 160–6, 182, 184

place 76, 77, 229–35, 262
  communicative 230–1
  critical sense of 77
  and dualism 231
  place-based spirituality 229–35
  rationalism and 227, 231, 232
Plant, J. 248, 249
plants 149, 155, 189, 196, 259 (*see also* trees)
Plato 20, 24, 42, 46, 50, 96, 103, 244, 245
Plumwood V. 4, 15, 19, 56, 87, 176, 178,
  197, 198, 242–4, 247, 248–53, 256, 257,
  259, 261, 264–7
Plumwood, V. and Routley, R. 247
Polanyi, K. 242, 268
polarisation (*see also* dichotomy, dualism) 17,
  101–3, 107, 108, 178, 259
  complementary 103
positivism 206
possums 192
postmodernism 15
poverty 82, 84, 89 (*see also* marginality, class)
Precautionary Principle 10
predators 125, 177, 259
Price, J. 16, 242, 243
primates 133, 147, 254, 257
Principle of Convergence 125, 126 (*see also*
  Norton, B.)
Principle of Parsimony 12, 51 (*see also*
  parsimony versus generosity)
Principle of Tolerance 207
privatisation 49, 86, 110
privilege (*see also* marginality) 71, 73, 79,
  85–7, 90, 91, 93, 96, 100–6, 144, 146,
  147, 161, 166, 204, 250
  and the distortion of ecological
    rationality 86, 96
  and invulnerability 84–7
privilege (cultural influence of) 20, 21, 42,
  43, 65, 71, 74, 79, 80, 82–7, 90–6
  experience as hegemonic 86, 87
  and vulnerability 85
process/product distinction (in procedural
  democracy) 91, 94, 95
  as reciprocally corrigible 95
Proctor, R. 266
production and consumption, relationship
  30, 71, 74, 77, 79
  linked by meaning 71–3, 79
productivism 21, 39, 40, 113
Prokhovnik, R. 246

property (private), 61, 99, 207, 209,
  211–17
  formation 16, 17, 21, 26, 28, 30, 99, 111,
    143ff, 146, 148, 155–66, 209,
    214–17, 233, 234 (*see also*
    commodification)
  partnership model 214–17
  and public/private distinction 32
prudence 9, 11, 16, 33, 44, 45, 68, 73, 80,
  106, 113–14, 127–34, 138–42, 146, 256
  oppositional to ethics 32
  and rational egoism 32–7, 80, 138–42
public/private division 32–7, 48, 49, 89, 90,
  91, 159–66, 261
  and economy 33–7, 160–6 (*see also* pets)
  in ethics 32, 33
Pusey, M. 242

Quine, W.V.O 247

racism and racial supremacy (*see also*
  eurocentrism) 21, 44, 49, 82, 84–6, 89,
  93, 100–6, 115, 118–19, 137, 141, 167,
  173–5, 178, 191, 200–10, 212, 214–17,
  234, 252, 256, 257, 259
Ralston Saul, J. 242
ratiogenic damage 7, 14, 15, 25, 38, 41, 44,
  49, 55
rational substitutes for nature 25–7, 243
rationalism 4, 8–12, 14, 16–37, 45–7,
  61–4, 68, 69, 73, 75, 80, 83, 91, 93, 94,
  97–106, 108, 110, 111, 114, 117, 124,
  130, 131, 137, 143, 144, 146, 148–51,
  157, 159, 168, 171, 174, 175, 184, 185,
  187, 189–93, 202, 208, 209, 218–22, 225,
  228, 231, 242, 243, 245, 258, 259, 267
  and agriculture 2, 15, 27, 34, 38, 116,
    117, 119, 144, 153–66, 192 (*see
    also* factory farming)
  Cartesian 42, 49, 57, 59, 61, 143–9, 151–
    3, 157, 159, 161, 163, 164, 176,
    178, 179, 184, 185, 258 (*see also*
    neo-Cartesianism)
  classical 20–5, 42, 245
  and cyber-rationalism 97
  distinct from reason 5, 18, 68, 69
  economics (*see also* economic
    rationalism) 17, 21–31, 39, 45,
    65, 66, 242
  ecorationalism 62–5

in ethics as universalist/impersonalist
    tradition 114, 124, 130, 131,
    134–42, 148–51, 187, 188, 190
and intellectualist (cognitivist) fallacy
    98, 174, 175, 177, 178, 180, 184,
    185, 187
and knowledge 42–50
and mastery of nature 5, 19, 99
and objectivity/disengagement 41–5,
    62
Platonic 20, 24, 42–50, 62, 63, 97, 245
resurgence of 97
in science 41–50
rationalist economics (*see also* economic
    rationalism) 17, 21–31, 39, 45, 65, 66,
    110–11, 242
rationalist economy 39–41, 64, 65, 110–11
and capture of science 39–41
and correctiveness 41
rationalist imaginary 18, 20, 21, 31–7, 42,
    101–6
and ecology 16–19
economic rationalism 17, 21–31, 39, 45,
    65, 66, 110–11
and gender 19, 31–7, 46
historic rationalist imaginary 22, 31
and knowledge 20, 21
    blindspots 25–31, 97–100
    and body, materiality 20, 97, 110
    and colonialism 20, 21
    and emotions and senses 20
    and impartiality, disengagement 20,
        31, 41–5
    and male elite 20
    and racial supremacism 21
    of reason and nature 17, 19
    and slavery 20, 105
modern (economic) rationalist imaginary
    22–37, 110–11
and progress 19
and property formation 21
    and global capitalist economy,
        market 22, 97
    and science 41–50
    and theoretical/practical division 110
    and unemployed as externality 21,
        110–11
rationality 1, 2, 7, 8, 10–12, 14, 25, 45, 61,
    64–8, 80, 99, 100, 112, 168, 242
administrative 39, 64, 65, 241

of care 53–5, 138–42
ecological 2, 11, 15, 18, 67–80, 82, 89,
    92, 96, 100, 248
economic 65, 79, 80
as egoism 23, 66, 80, 81, 116, 117,
    123–42, 146, 159
and elite males 19
ethical forms of 36, 55–61
instrumental 67, 253, 254
political 39
scientific 39, 44, 45, 62–4
self-critical 64, 65, 67, 68, 167
spheres of 39, 66
Rawls, J. 94
realism 52, 53
reason 1–3, 8, 9, 16, 21, 46, 105, 251
administrative 8
centredness 251, 252
as dysfunctional 5
economic 1, 2, 16
hegemonic 16
ideals of 21, 99
opposed to emotion and ethics 5, 62, 63,
    98
as plural 5
political 16
and racism 21, 46, 100–6
rationalist forms of 4, 100
sado-dispassionate
scientific, 2, 63, 64
redistribution 82–4, 91, 92–6, 167–8, 175
reductionism (towards non-humans) 3, 27,
    40, 41, 53, 54, 56, 59, 107–9, 113, 157,
    158, 169, 175–8, 181, 183, 184, 190, 194,
    195, 221–3, 228, 245, 246, 260, 267
economic 3, 39, 66
Reed, P. 197–200, 265
Regan, T. 143, 147, 152, 258
relativised 67
relativism 43, 67
Relph, E. 231
remoteness 16, 30, 63, 65, 71–82, 85–8, 90,
    91, 96, 98–100, 112, 213, 231,
    247–50
communicative 72, 80
consequential 72, 75, 78–80, 85, 86, 88,
    247, 249
as ecological invulnerability 85–7
epistemic 72, 75, 78, 98–110
equivalences 79

political conditions for 81–7
spatial 72, 74, 75, 77, 81, 85, 86, 88, 249
spiritual 75, 218–22, 225, 228, 231
technological 72, 73
temporal 72
reproductive labour, of women 29–31
Reuther, R.R. 253, 267
rights 152–9, 259
Rogers, L. 257, 262–4
Rogers, R.A., 26, 40, 243
Rolls, E. 54
Romanticism 207–8, 245
Rousseau, J.J. 92
Routley, R. 247
Ruddick, S. 262

sado-dispassionate mode 2, 22, 31–7, 39,
    41–50, 53, 55, 61
Said, E. 100–3, 252, 253
St. Martin of Tours 218
Sale, K 248
Salleh, A. 267
Sanchez, C. 223–5
satisficing 67, 247
science, scientists 2, 3, 9, 10, 12, 18, 25, 26,
    38–65, 113, 118, 167, 172, 174, 175, 177,
    180, 184–6, 209, 221, 242, 245–7, 257,
    258
    capture by capitalism 38–45
    ethically-integrated 50–6
    and rationalism 45–50
    and reductionism 41, 53, 56–61
    sado-dispassionate mode 2, 22, 31–7, 39,
        41–50, 53, 55, 61
    self-critical 39, 41, 44, 45, 53–6
    and subject/object dualism 41–56
    and technoscience 38–9
    and 'two cultures' division 51–6
scientism 18, 242
Searle, J. 183
security and ecological vulnerability 84–7,
    236
Seidler, V. 252
self 23, 29, 30, 32–4, 67, 78, 112, 116, 139,
    141, 142, 200, 227, 236, 261
    and autarchy 78
    and gender 256, 265
    and mutuality 33, 34, 236
    self-in-relationship 33, 78, 112, 116, 141,
        142, 200

self/other dualism 196–202
self-realisation and unity 196–207, 265
separative 23, 29, 30, 32–4, 67, 78, 139,
    227 (*see also* egocentrism)
self, disembedded and disembodied 23, 29,
    67, 78
self-maximisation (as rational strategy) 30,
    33, 34, 66, 67–70
self-reliance 79, 80
services, of nature 99, 254
Shiva, V. 243, 267
Singer, P. 143, 147–52, 155, 257–9, 266
Skocpol, T. 247
slavery 19, 20, 46, 49, 101–6, 149, 151, 204,
    214, 253, 267
small-scale communities 74–80, 84, 207
Smith, Adam 88
smog 84
snakes 117, 171, 188, 192
Snow, C.P. 246
Snyder, G. 97, 98, 251, 262
solidarity 11, 91, 113, 196–206, 258
Soule, M. and Lease, G. 246
Soviets 21, 88
species hierarchy 168, 169, 172–4, (*see also*
    non-ranking)
speciesism (*see also* anthropocentrism) 148,
    255
spirit/matter dualism 219–26
spirituality 218–29
    and commodified land relationships
        229–35
    consumerist 222
    counter-hegemonic 224, 229–35
    dialogical 224, 227–35, 267
    dualistic 222–6
    human-centred 223–5, 233–5
    materialist 222–3
    and rationalism 218–22, 225, 228, 231,
        232, 234, 235
    remote 75, 218–26, 229, 231
Spretnak, C. 265–7
stakeholder panels 88
Stamp Dawkins, M. 59, 191–2, 247, 265
standpoint 9, 12, 100, 117–22, 177, 206,
    256
State Primacy Thesis 66
Steinbrecher, R. and Mooney, P. 243
Stepan, N. 253
stereotyping 101–3

stochastic ordeal 90
"studying up" 11, 98, 167, 168, 180, 181, 261, 262 (*see also* counter-hegemonic methodology)
subject/object division 9, 10, 20, 27, 34, 41, 42, 45–56, 183, 190, 193, 244, 246
substitutability *see* homogenisation
survival 61–3, 67, 117, 121, 122, 138, 139, 155, 167
sustainability 1, 3, 25–31, 68–70, 73, 112, 113
Suzuki, D. 111

Takaki, R. 266, 267
Taylor, A. 258
technical fix 6–8
technologies 26
techno-optimism 5–8
terra nullius 104, 118
third world 21, 92
Thompson, J. 130, 248, 254
thylacine 125
Tierney, P. 54
Tilman, D. and Cohen, J.E. 243, 254
Titanic 1–3, 237
trade (exchange) 79, 80, 249
traitorous identity 11, 113, 205–6
translation and indeterminacy, problem of in interspecies context 58–61
transparency (of ecological relationships) 81
trees 145, 148–50, 196, 218, 226, 258, 259, 262
Tronto, J. 243
two cultures 50–6

uncertainty, veil of 84, 90
UNEP 1999 242
unity interpretation 196–217
    in ethics 196–206
        oppressive projects of unity 92, 202–6, 212, 214
    in politics 207–17

Utilitarianism 148–51, 186, 258, 259
utopia 62, 63

vegetarianism 154–60, 166, 259
    contextual 154–66, 259
    plant/animal boundary 259

Walker, M. 187, 254, 262, 264
Walls, L. 245–7, 262
Walzer, M. 248, 250, 251
Waring, M. 243
Warren County 82
Warren, K. 253, 262, 265, 267
waste dumping 82, 87, 250
Weber, M. 67
Weil, S. 173
Weston, A. 194, 206, 258, 260, 262, 263, 265, 266
whales 2
wildness/wilderness 165, 186, 198–200, 261
Wittgenstein, L. 158, 260
wolves 161
wombats 165, 181, 182, 199
women 19, 28–30, 32, 35, 42, 44, 47, 49, 101, 104–7, 138, 148, 162, 187, 191, 204, 205, 208–21, 219, 260–2, 267
    and androcentrism of property, economic system 32–7
    and coverture model 210–12
    and empiricist transition 45–50
    and gender blindness 138
    as Other 35, 101–6
    and property 32
    reproductive agency 30, 33, 104–6, 107
    reproductive labour 29–31, 33, 104, 105, 111, 267
Wood, C. 242, 243

Yanomami people 54
Yencken, D. 241
Young, I. 92, 93, 95, 251, 255, 256, 265, 266
Young, O. 251

Zimmerman, M. 265, 266